Praise for *A Privilege to Die*

"Where some writers talk about the Arab streets, Cambanis has walked them. Along the way he encountered warriors and hospital workers, polished intellectuals and women who sell nuts by the curb, ideologues and theologians, those who engage in small acts of resistance and those who prosecute total war of the most brutal sort. What becomes clear is that the key to Hezbollah is its ability to spread virtue along with the violence."

—*The Boston Globe*

"Cambanis' intimate account of recent history, enhanced by stories of a handful of Hezbollah's true believers and sympathizers, paints a gripping portrait of this radical religio-political movement."

—*Foreign Affairs*

"Brilliant and revealing. It positively frightened me. Interviews in which you can touch the people, coupled with a scholar's command of Islam's history, allow Cambanis to explain what Islamic moderates and the rest of the world are up against. A serious story with emotional power."
    —Leslie H. Gelb, President Emeritus of the Council on Foreign Relations

"Cambanis provides crucial insights to those who might hope to counter Hezbollah's increasing power and influence in the region, as well as an important reminder that in any war, one's enemies are human."

—*Publishers Weekly*

"Hezbollah is a formidable presence that cannot be ignored, and Cambanis's book, a well-balanced blend of journalism, history and geopolitical primer, is a significant aid to understanding it."

—*Kirkus Reviews*

"No global flashpoint today is more important than the Hezbollah-Israel conflict, and no book I know does a better job than *A Privilege to Die* in getting inside the thought-world of Hezbollah's followers. Nuanced, textured, and brutally honest, the book should be required reading for anyone who cares about war and peace in the Middle East."

—Noah Feldman, author of *Scorpions: The Battles and Triumphs of FDR's Great Supreme Court Justices* and *The Fall and Rise of the Islamic State*

"A revelation. Cambanis, one of the most talented foreign correspondents of his generation, has traveled far into the heart of Hezbollah, and what he has found there needs to be read about and studied by general readers and policymakers alike. His reporting is not only fearless but sophisticated and penetrating, providing us with a vibrant image and unprecedented understanding of this powerful and secretive Islamist force."

—Matthew McAllester, Pulitzer Prize–winning author of *Bittersweet: Lessons from my Mother's Kitchen* and *Blinded by the Sunlight: Surviving Abu Ghraib and Saddam's Iraq*

"A gripping, street-level view of Hezbollah. Cambanis brings Hezbollah out of the shadows to show how it has become the world's most sophisticated resistance group."

—Richard Engel, Chief Foreign Correspondent, NBC News, author of *War Journal*

"Illuminating and terrifying. Thanassis Cambanis journeyed to the heartland of the most important, least understood armed actor in the Middle East. The souls he met along the way are rendered with compassion but not spared the same unflinching lens that Cambanis turns on his own biases."

—Quil Lawrence, Kabul Bureau Chief, National Public Radio, author of *Invisible Nation: How the Kurds' Quest for Statehood Is Shaping Iraq and the Middle East*

"Cambanis combines extraordinary reportage with sharp analysis and a clear voice to explore the many sides of Hezbollah. A series of highly evocative portraits of the people who make up the core supporters of Hezbollah makes *A Privilege to Die* a must read for anyone who seeks a better understanding of the region and its people."

—Farnaz Fassihi, *The Wall Street Journal,* author of *Waiting for an Ordinary Day: The Unraveling of Life in Iraq*

A PRIVILEGE TO DIE

INSIDE HEZBOLLAH'S LEGIONS
AND THEIR ENDLESS WAR AGAINST ISRAEL

THANASSIS CAMBANIS

FREE PRESS
New York   London   Toronto   Sydney

Free Press
A Division of Simon & Schuster, Inc.
1230 Avenue of the Americas
New York, NY 10020

First Free Press trade paperback edition July 2011

FREE PRESS and colophon are trademarks of Simon & Schuster, Inc.

For information about special discounts for bulk purchases, please contact Simon & Schuster Special Sales at 1-866-506-1949 or business@simonandschuster.com

The Simon & Schuster Speakers Bureau can bring authors to your live event. For more information or to book an event contact the Simon & Schuster Speakers Bureau at 1-866-248-3049 or visit our website at www.simonspeakers.com.

Designed by Carla Jayne Jones
Map by Paul J. Pugliese

Manufactured in the United States of America

10 9 8 7 6 5 4 3 2

Library of Congress Cataloging-in-Publication Data

Cambanis, Thanassis.
    A privilege to die : inside Hezbollah's legions and their endless war against Israel / Thanassis Cambanis.
        p. cm.
1. Israel—Military relations—Lebanon. 2. Lebanon—Military relations—Israel. 3. Hizballah (Lebanon). 4. Lebanon War, 2006. I. Title.
    DS119.8.L4C36 2010
    956.05'4—dc22
            2010001528

ISBN 978-1-4391-4360-5
ISBN 978-1-4391-4361-2 (pbk)
ISBN 978-1-4391-5006-1 (ebook)

For my father, Stamatis, who made me a good detective;
Anne, who gave me wings;
and Odysseas, who made everything new.

CONTENTS

PROLOGUE   XI

PART I: THE BATTLE
  1. THE PARTY OF GOD   3
  2. RANI BAZZI'S HOLY STRUGGLE   21
  3. THE DISPOSSESSED   41

PART II: WAR WITHOUT END
  4. DIVINE VICTORY   137
  5. THE ISLAMIC VANGUARD   203
  6. HEZBOLLAH RISING   245
  7. ETERNAL RESISTANCE   274

ACKNOWLEDGMENTS   291
NOTES   293
INDEX   309
ABOUT THE AUTHOR   320

It would be a privilege to die for Sayyed Hassan [Nasrallah].
We are happy to sacrifice our homes if he asks us to.

ASSEM HARB, Sunday, July 16, 2006, after driving his family to safety in
Beirut from his heavily bombed border village in South Lebanon

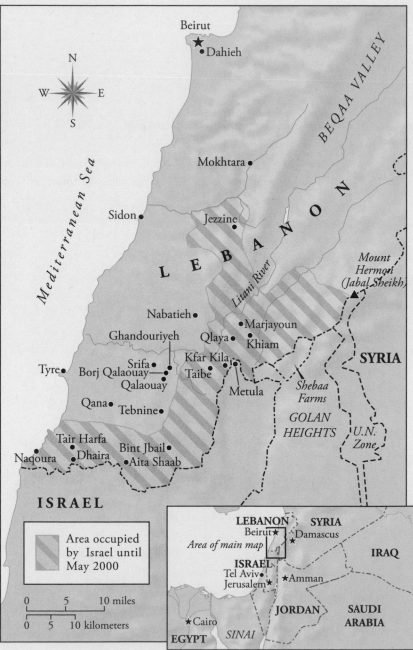

Prologue

In the waning days of Israel's 2006 war with Lebanon, I was reporting from the front lines trying to understand the motives of Hezbollah's fighters and loyalists. At the beginning of August, Israel warned that it would consider any car south of the Litani River a military target. I abandoned the free-fire zone of South Lebanon for the relative safety of Beirut. At a slight remove from the rocket whistles and bomb thuds—Israeli bombardment still shook the Lebanese capital several times a day—the big questions raised by the conflagration came into focus. Israel and Hezbollah had fought many times before. But Hezbollah had now advanced a new idea whose destabilizing implications would persist long after this current conflict. Hezbollah had put back into popular currency a notion that had lain in tatters since 1967: that Arab forces could do more than terrorize or harass Israel—they could defeat and destroy it. In August 2006, even as much of Lebanon lay in ruins, no one could stop talking about Hezbollah's ascendance: refugees and their hosts, politicians and their constituents, government officials, party activists, and Western diplomats.

Hezbollah's conviction terrified some and galvanized others, but it had transformed the debate in the Middle East. Now, in 2006, the Party of God thought it could prove its position on the battlefield, provoking a war with Israel and promising to weather the storm. The war unleashed a torrent of street-level support for Hezbollah across the region that surprised Arab moderates and extremists alike. In Beirut in August 2006, even as the battle unfolded another struggle already was taking shape over the meaning of the war, a narrative with high stakes: who had won and why, who was a traitor and who honorable, and would the Arabs ever give up fighting Israel? Who knew the route to victory? The Axis of Accommodation, the compromise-seeking governments and movements that wished to avoid war? Or the Axis of Islamic Resistance, which believed the only principled stance was a fight for total victory? Much pivoted on the outcome of the 2006 war. The front of bellicose Islamism finally had a test for its confrontational approach. Its failure would strengthen forces of pragmatic realism across the Middle East; its success would embolden religious maximalists.

Late one afternoon after a long day of political interviews during the war's last weekend, I went to one of the few restaurants still open in Hamra, the normally hopping commercial drag in West Beirut. It was at the very end of the street, a fast-food joint that offered a decent *narghileh*, or water pipe. I sat facing the road, halfheartedly scribbling in a notebook, trying to make sense of everything I'd seen and heard. When my water pipe came, I put my writing tools away and pulled on the hose with long thirsty breaths, until my head was enveloped in sweet apple and honey scented smoke, and soothing nicotine surged into my blood. A chunky man at the next table started talking to me in American-accented English. He was Lebanese, a religious Shiite who had taken refuge in this secular Sunni neighborhood. He was twenty-eight, and his name was Ayman. He had two young daughters, and was a great admirer of Hezbollah. "I'm sick of all these other assholes," he said. He ticked off the rest of the country's political movements and dismissed them one by one; they had no respect for the common people, no courage to fight Israel, and no sense of responsibility toward the country's finances. The current prime minister was an embarrassment, a weakling who wept in public. Other than Hezbollah, whose probity and competence Ayman admired, he bemoaned the remaining parties as corrupt or incompetent.

"The government doesn't give a shit about the people," he said with genuine amazement, as if Lebanon's ruling class had it in for him personally. "They're crying because of the money they lost. They're probably already planning how much they're going to steal when the rebuilding starts after the war."

Ayman wanted to know what I'd seen in the South. "Did you ever have the chance to talk to a Hezbollah fighter?" he said. I told him about my encounters along the front, including a day in the frontier village of Bint Jbail with two fighters. "You're really lucky," he said. "Most of us Lebanese never get to meet a real fighter, at least that we know of." He had grown up in the United States, he said, but was happy that fortune had allowed him to raise his children in an environment of Islamic Resistance. He spoke elliptically and withheld details like his family name or where in the South he lived. I assumed he was either wary since I was a foreigner or cautious because he had links to Hezbollah. We were both exhausted, and eventually lapsed into silence, drawing at our narghilehs and watching the evening light bounce through the thick smoke. "Good luck," he said when I left. "Make sure to tell the truth."

PART I

THE BATTLE

Crying brings sadness to a country, blood brings strength. God willing, our operation for Shebaa will continue. We will keep fighting to liberate our land. The day will come for the Israelis, you must have faith. Their day will come.

SAMIRA SHARAFEDEEN, after burying her three cousins who were
Hezbollah fighters, in Taibe, Lebanon, August 21, 2006

As far as I'm concerned, the war ends when there's nothing left of Israel. After we all die, that's when Hezbollah is gone. When you kill the Shia, that is when Hezbollah is gone.

ALI SIRHAN, a volunteer fighter for the Islamic Resistance,
standing a few hundred feet from Israel in the Lebanese border village
of Kfar Kila, August 21, 2006

The Party of God

Hezbollah has captivated the Arab world with a radical new belief, decisively changing an entire region's dynamics and paving the path to a long series of wars. Put simply, Hezbollah has convinced legions of common men and women that Israel can be defeated and destroyed—and not just in the distant future, but soon. With more success than any other Islamist group, Hezbollah has harnessed modern politics and warfare to mobilize millions of dedicated supporters and soft sympathizers under its banner of resistance against Israel. Theirs is not a quixotic quest for dignity, a symbolic but doomed fight for the sake of empowerment; Hezbollah's militancy has had concrete consequences for Israel and has unleashed a new Islamist wave. Hezbollah has achieved military success in nearly three decades of guerilla war against Israel, first expelling the Israel Defense Forces from the "security zone" it occupied in South Lebanon for nearly two decades, and then frustrating Israel's objectives in the war it fought against Hezbollah in 2006. Now Hezbollah, the Party of God, has the Islamic world's ear, and is spreading a gospel of perpetual war. Hezbollah is persuading a growing swath of Arab society to follow its example: militarize fully and confront the enemy at every opportunity. An even greater number has added its moral approval. In 2006, Hezbollah captured two Israeli soldiers and provoked a war that left Lebanon physically in shambles. But Hezbollah emerged elated. It had held out against Israel longer than any Arab army ever had. Its militia had thwarted Israel's land advance, and the Jewish state failed to reach any of its declared war aims—the release of its captured soldiers, stopping Hezbollah from firing rockets, and dismantling Hezbollah's militia along the border. Hezbollah moved from the backbenches to the center of power within the Lebanese government. And Hezbollah's rise thwarted the United States' carefully laid plans for a friendly, secular, liberal Lebanon securely at peace with Israel. Today Hezbollah preaches humility to its followers while acting anything but humble to expand its power and influence across the Islamic world.

Sayyed Hassan Nasrallah, the secretary-general and charismatic supreme leader of Hezbollah, commands more popularity in the Middle East than any other leader.[1] Unusual among the region's militants, he has frequently shown restraint and political savvy, but Nasrallah has encountered his greatest political success through confrontation. Speaking in November 2009 on the annual holiday that commemorates the "martyrs" of the Islamic Resistance, Nasrallah sounded like he was spoiling for another war with Israel:

> I say we are ready. Here I vow again before the souls of the martyrs, which are alive and present, saying: O Barak, Ashkenazi, Netanyahu and Obama![2] Let the whole world listen. Send as many squads as you want: five, seven or the whole Israeli army. We will destroy them in our hills, valleys and mountains.

Well into another millennium, Nasrallah and Hezbollah have woven a new reality for their followers, built on ideology, identity, faith, and practice. Hezbollah has delivered tangible social gains for its followers, like the $400 million reconstruction of southern Beirut to be completed in 2010, replacing refugee slums with gleaming glass residential towers that resemble luxury hotels. It has won tactical military victories against Israel, unlike the other Middle Eastern regimes that ineffectually rail against the Jewish state. As a growing movement with transnational appeal, Hezbollah has broken the crusty traditions of Arab politics to craft a big-tent party platform that speaks to people's mundane aspirations: economic reform, affordable health care, round-the-clock electricity, efficient courts, and community policing. Most important of all, however, Hezbollah has shifted the norms of Middle Eastern politics with its fast-spreading ideology of perpetual war.

The Party of God's new world is most vividly on display in the living rooms of its rank-and-file partisans, where Hezbollah's bourgeoisie explain their devotion to a movement that organizes their daily lives and ideology, and which every decade or so leads them into a catastrophic war. The first time I visited the village of Aita Shaab, at the close of the war in 2006, virtually every structure bore the marks of Israeli mortars. It was from this heavily militarized border village that Hezbollah had launched its raid into Israel in July of that year, initiating the most recent war. It was here that Hezbollah guerillas had laid a second ambush, destroying the first Israeli tank that crossed the border into Lebanon. House-to-house fighting had reduced much of the village to rubble.

At the edge of the village closest to the frontier, I met a pair of local Hezbollah officials, surveying the wreckage of the war from a hilltop that looked like a rock quarry but which had recently been a crowded neighborhood. One of them, a man named Faris Jamil, told me how the local villagers had instantly mustered when war broke out and compared them to the National Guard. The doomsday destruction, he said, wouldn't deter committed Hezbollah supporters; they felt they had won, and the loss of their homes would amount to no more than a temporary inconvenience. I found it hard to imagine that Aita Shaab would ever function like a normal town again; I thought of other war zones where even decades after the last clashes fallen buildings still marred the landscape and makeshift roads wound like goat paths around the detritus of uncleared bombing grounds.

In January 2009 I returned to Aita Shaab to find out how the villagers— still in the process of rebuilding—felt about future conflict. War was raging not far away in Gaza, between Hamas and Israel, and many Hezbollah activists were urging the Lebanese Party of God to attack in support of their Islamist allies in Gaza. To my surprise, the drive was an hour shorter than it had been before the war, because of a network of gently graded and freshly paved roads paid for by the government of Iran. The village was unrecognizable, bustling with construction crews, packed stores, and new villas. The ruined bluff where I first had met

Faris Jamil was once again a crammed neighborhood, with two houses on lots meant for one.

Now 52, Faris was still living in the unfinished basement of his almost fully rebuilt family home. He was well off, and before the war had lived in a pleasant two story house on a hill. He had rebuilt it one notch better, as a mansion, three stories tall, with marble columns and hand-carved floral accents above the windows. This too he saw as a form of resistance. Israel wanted Hezbollah to leave the border villages, so it was the duty of patriots of the Islamic Resistance to stay—if possible, in style. Aita Shaab's full-time population had expanded since 2006; Faris Jamil implied that Hezbollah had subsidized the boom with payments to families willing to relocate from Beirut. "We want peace. We don't want to suffer another war," he said. "But we must have our plans in place. Last time there was a war, only a few hundred people stayed here. Next time, we want thousands to stay. We will send the children to Beirut, since they can do nothing. All the men must stay, along with some women to cook and support them."

Faris had lived in Manhattan for years and for a time had worked for a Jewish man who dealt wholesale in fabric. He remembered his boss fondly. He was unusual in that during his long complaints against Israel he didn't slip into ranting about Jews. He wasn't itching for war, but he was planning for it. As a businessman he had trained himself to anticipate the future, and in his opinion two things were guaranteed: Hezbollah would run his world, and Hezbollah and Israel would keep fighting wars. Neither eventuality upset him. "Our life is hard, and that is mainly because Israel refuses to let us live like a normal country," Faris said. "There are some people who want peace at any cost in their life, but we feel that in life you have to have respect. Without respect, it's not a life."

His main preoccupations were his house and the businesses he had established for his sons, including a restaurant and an internet café. His quotidian struggles were material, and yet to Faris they did not contradict his complete submission to the higher aim of the Islamic Resistance. He was not a violent man, nor was he an impulsive hothead. But he willingly and calmly served a movement whose commitment to armed struggle guaranteed that his world and livelihood would be blasted apart every few years. Like Ayman, the young man I had met smoking the water pipe in Beirut, Faris Jamil had voluntarily relocated from a prosperous merchant's life in America to the borderlands of South Lebanon, choosing near-certain war over prosperity. New York, in his view, was a dangerous place to raise kids, riddled with gangs, drugs, and other temptations. Better to relocate his young family to the cradle of Islamic Resistance, a place where their spirits could thrive, and any violence they encountered would be part of a meaningful, epochal battle. He was not rare in choosing the battleground of south Lebanon over a career in the United States; I met a half-dozen families that followed the same trajectory. They always explained their decision to return as a result of contemplating what would become of their children in America's public schools. In Aita Shaab, Faris pursued daily dreams quite similar to those that animated him when he worked at 37th Street and Broadway in Manhattan. Yet he was happy to let his commercial livelihood go up in smoke, literally, when Hezbollah deemed it time for another war with Israel. "Life is for more than to make money," Faris said. "We will continue, and if we make peace, it will be through power."

Hezbollah has inculcated millions—including many beyond Lebanon's borders—into its ideology of Islamic Resistance, which is coupled to an unusually effective operational program. That recipe has put Hezbollah in the pilot's seat in the Middle East, steering the region into a thicket of wars to come. And it has made Hezbollah dangerous not only in the short term, as a military threat to Israel and to the pragmatic, compromise-seeking Arabs in its neighborhood, but over the long term as the progenitor of an infectious ideology of violent confrontation against Israel and the United States, vilified in the region as the ultimate backer of the Jewish State.

During six years of reporting in the Middle East I encountered no popular movement that rivaled Hezbollah as a militia or an ideological force. In Lebanon I met men and women prepared to die, or sacrifice their children, for Hezbollah's program, but they defied the mold of dreary desperation that characterized other would-be martyrs. Educated middle-class types populated Hezbollah's legions, professionals with alternatives and aspirations, who lived multidimensional lives not much different from those of my friends in America. They were engineers, teachers, merchants, landlords, drivers, construction workers; they had jobs and children. They weren't broken, miserable people, turning to Hezbollah out of hopelessness; they were willing actors who had come to embrace Hezbollah's view of the world, a heady mix of religion, self-improvement, and self-defense that translated into a sustained surge of toxic and powerful militancy. I met mothers who grieved their dead children but encouraged their surviving brood to join Hezbollah's militia; they projected the confidence of patriots, rather than the fanaticism of a death-cult. They radiated a victor's confidence I rarely encountered among Palestinian militants. These Hezbollah mothers sounded proud and sad, but never unhinged or cornered. Hezbollah's followers were as notable for their discipline and restraint as for their willingness to die.

Hezbollah coalesced in the crucible of Israeli occupation. Israel occupied about one-tenth of Lebanon's territory from 1982 to 2000, a strip of south Lebanon that Israel euphemistically termed "the security zone." The first generation of Hezbollah fighters came of age during two decades of guerilla war against Israel. When Israel quit the occupied area under fire from Hezbollah in May 2000, it left behind thousands of collaborators, including men who had beaten and tortured Hezbollah fighters on behalf of the Israelis. Hezbollah's rivals expected a raft of vigilante executions, but Nasrallah ordered his followers to keep their hands off all collaborators, leaving their judgment to Lebanese courts. This decision shocked everyone. I met Hezbollah fighters who recalled years later how they had wanted to take revenge, but instead had cordoned off the collaborator villages and protected their erstwhile tormentors from harm— an act less of mercy than of political calculation, which eased the fears of some opponents and ultimately gained Hezbollah more power than it ever before had possessed.

Nasrallah's personal charisma has played a major role in Hezbollah's rise. He has run the party since 1992, steadily consolidating the fidelity of its inner ranks while expanding Hezbollah's reach among soft supporters. A pudgy man with a handsome mouth, a mellifluous voice, and the black turban that signals direct descent from the Prophet Mohammed, Nasrallah has matured along with the Islamist Party that he took over almost two decades ago when he was only thirty-one years old. His speeches alternate between humor and invective; between steady exposition of Arab politics and appeals to gut anger; between systematic analyses of Israeli policy, and racist hatred of Jews.

Under Nasrallah's leadership, Hezbollah steadily has expanded its number of followers and its share of political power, in large part because the Party of God is just as happy to use the tools of coercion as of persuasion. Within its primary target constituency of Lebanese Shia, Hezbollah ruthlessly quashes any serious threat to its monopoly on force and power. Hezbollah has thwarted any attempt to organize alternative Shia parties, either religious or secular. It has crushed individuals who publicly question Hezbollah's militant approach. The party tolerates free speech and political dissent only from weak actors, to forge the impression of openness. Hezbollah accepts only one other Shia political party, the Amal Movement, which has long been subsumed into Hezbollah's ambit as a junior partner. Those who dare challenge Hezbollah's policies or bona fides face the withering power of the party to ostracize and economically marginalize them. Those suspected of plotting against Hezbollah might disappear or end up imprisoned and charged with treason or espionage on behalf of the Israelis. Hezbollah's constituency and its skeptical neighbors know that the hand extended in invitation easily turns into a fist. But Hezbollah has convinced many audiences to overlook its brutal side as an unavoidable consequence of war, highlighting instead the party's humanitarian wing and ideas-based agenda. So long as Hezbollah is perceived to be defending the Arab world against Israel, it can put its Arab critics on the defensive.

Hezbollah's ideology might seem incoherent were it not so successful; but the Party of God has been able to market its ideas effectively because success sells. Perpetual war has perpetuated the movement; Islamic Resistance has brought power to its adherents; and Hezbollah's web of embedded institutions, including courts, schools, militias, and hospitals, has dramatically raised its community's standard of living. Faris Jamil truly believes in the war against Israel, but Hezbollah buttresses that abiding belief with the formidable material resources it spends to rebuild its communities after each war. So long as it continues to deliver, Hezbollah's number of followers continues to grow.

Roughly put, Hezbollah teaches a sort of Islamist prosperity agenda, a doctrine of militant empowerment. People must live with dignity, and that means taking the offensive on every level: against Israel, the regional military bugbear; against poverty; against immorality; and against ignorance. Power is the antidote to powerlessness, Hezbollah counsels. It's a compelling gospel of self-improvement, and it easily translates into specific prescriptions for demoralized Middle Easterners, especially members of the long-downtrodden Shia sect of Islam. Hezbollah lectures about everything from safe sex and hygiene to family responsibilities and financial planning. Individual power, in the party's ideology, stems from the *ummah*, or community. The more powerful the ummah, the stronger its members. Hundreds of thousands have joined Hezbollah's community, freely volunteering their time or donating their money to the Party of God, adopting its militia and bureaucracy as an extension of their own families. Millions more extend their sympathy and political support to the Islamic Resistance.

The holy struggle against Israel weaves together these manifold ideological strands. Anger toward Israel unifies Hezbollah's followers in the face of internal contradictions that might otherwise unravel the movement. An almost primal and simple dictum informs and at times dwarfs all else for Hezbollah's community: Resistance. It is difficult to contain a militant movement that includes not only fully indoctrinated Shia Islamists but soft sympathizers lured by identity politics and held in place by Hezbollah's impressive network of social services. When it proves too daunting to hold this coalition together with Islamist teachings, Hezbollah can always invoke its trump card—the War Against Israel. Many people across the region dislike Hezbollah but loathe Israel's policies even more. And for many of Hezbollah's followers, Israel's very existence amounts to a casus belli.

Nasrallah regularly reminds his millions of listeners across the Arab world that Hezbollah and its allies—the "Axis of Resistance"—have wrung more concessions from Israel by force than the pro-Western "Axis of Accommodation" has won through decades of negotiation. As Nasrallah said in his November 2009 Martyrs Day speech:

> Eighteen years of [Palestinian] negotiations resulted in failure, frustration, forfeiture, humiliation and the persistence of occupation. On the other hand, eighteen years of resistance in Lebanon [from 1982 to 2000] led to the liberation of Beirut, the Southern Suburbs, Mount Lebanon, Beqaa

and the South from the Zionist occupation and the restoration of our dignity and esteem without anyone in the world begrudging us that. . . . God willing with our resistance, unity, cooperation and firmness and the moral blessings of the blood of martyrs, we will turn any threat into an opportunity.

Hezbollah's followers have embraced the notion that it's better to fight and die with dignity than live comfortably without it. They scorn the pacific Arab governments that support coexistence with Israel.

In taking the leadership of the region's militant renaissance, Hezbollah has capitalized on diffuse anger about Israel's policies toward Gaza and in the West Bank, including the growth of settlements. The failure of the Palestinian Authority to reach a settlement with Israel nearly twenty years after signing the Oslo Accords has weakened advocates of compromise while strengthening Hezbollah's "resistance camp." But Hezbollah also draws on a deep well of hatred of Jews, knowingly and cleverly intertwining it with the bubbling vein of anger at Israeli policy. Still sensitive to international opinion, Hezbollah leaders speak pointedly about Israeli, rather than "Jewish," policies in their speeches. Ever since an infamous speech in May 1998, Nasrallah has avoided anti-Semitic invective. On that occasion, he mourned the "historic catastrophe and tragic event" of the founding of "the state of the Zionist Jews, the descendants of apes and pigs." Since then, Nasrallah's rhetoric has been more measured; he has carefully observed that Hezbollah's complaint is against "Zionist policy," and not Jews in general or the Jewish religion. Whether sincerely or not, the party has excised hatred of Jews from its official doctrine. In November 2009, Nasrallah unveiled Hezbollah's new official manifesto, its first update since the "Open Letter" released in 1985. "Our problem with them is not that they are Jews," Nasrallah said, reading from a document that had been debated for months by the party's leaders. "Our problem with them is that they are occupiers who have usurped our land and sacred places." The Hezbollah leader went out of his way to call the Jewish State by its name, Israel, in addition to making the usual references to "the Zionist entity."

Throughout the Arab world, many people use the words "Israeli" and

"Jew" interchangeably when discussing the Middle East conflict. In the modern Middle East, racist attitudes thrive even among populations that coexist peacefully, including Arabs and Jews living within Israel's pre-1967 borders and between the region's sometimes violently opposed sects and ethnicities (Kurds, Turkomen, Armenians, and Arabs; Shia and Sunni; Christians and Muslims). Many Hezbollah supporters I met professed to harbor no malice toward Jews, only toward the specific Israelis who had wronged them. But when they grew comfortable, some of them would lapse into racist generalities or even virulent anti-Semitism, a disturbing ambiguity that tainted Hezbollah.

Although Hezbollah's undercurrent of anti-Semitism prompts much distrust in Israel and the West, the Party of God if anything is less vitriolic in its expressions of anti-Semitism than other Middle Eastern movements. In fact, many of the most stalwart advocates of peace with Israel, like some Lebanese Christians, paradoxically hold the most racist attitudes. Hassan Nasrallah's party has attracted supporters and swelled into an unmistakable strategic threat because of its uncompromising and violent opposition to any peaceful negotiating process. Anti-Semitism doesn't distinguish Hezbollah. Hezbollah is committed in deed, not just in word, to destroying the Jewish state of Israel—a position that is far more cause for alarm than the racist beliefs held by some party loyalists. Hezbollah's updated manifesto declares Israel "an unnatural creation that is not viable and cannot continue to survive." Hezbollah deems it every Muslim's duty to fight to "liberate the entire usurped land however long it takes and however great the sacrifices." Well into the twenty-first century, more than six decades after Israel joined the fold of nation-states, Hezbollah remains determined to deny "the legitimacy of [Israel's] existence" and oppose any negotiated settlement. "This stand is firm, permanent, and final, and it does not tolerate any retreat or compromise even if the entire world recognizes Israel," Nasrallah said. Hezbollah seems determined to disestablish Israel, and after nearly three decades of trying to do so believes its goal is in reach. It's the Party of God's ability to do something tangible about this notion that makes it unique among militant movements in the Middle East.

If parts of its ideology have remained rigid, Hezbollah has taken a far more flexible approach to matters of commerce and lifestyle. I would come to learn that Ayman, the young father I met at the café during the 2006 war, made good money as an international merchant, buying diamonds wholesale in Africa and selling them in Antwerp or New York, and financing the mining ventures of other Lebanese. His life seemed profoundly modern and international: a bilingual dual national who had lived in the United States and enjoyed driving his new Mercedes sedan. None of that stopped him from fully embracing Hezbollah. Like many Lebanese, Ayman was convinced there would be violence along the Israeli border whether Hezbollah fought or not, because of scarce water resources, renegade Palestinian factions sheltering in Lebanon, disputed border territory, and Israel's ambitious strategic designs. In his view, Hezbollah merely improved the odds against Israel, the regional power. He found meaning in Hezbollah's frontal war, which gave the Arab world the initiative and, Ayman believed, had a significant chance of success. Israel had dominated and demoralized Arabs for decades without effective opposition. Hezbollah now was holding Israel to account for its worst excesses of expansionism and occupation. Hezbollah's ideological teachings also shaped Ayman's personal life, guiding him as a new father and enabling him to find equanimity when his own father died and the family faced financial strain.

During the 2006 war I set forth on a three-year quest to understand Hezbollah's juggernaut, through the individual men and women who had joined the Party of God's movement. They ran the gamut from fully committed ideologues and activists to occasional volunteers, sympathizers, and, on the fringe, fellow travelers who made few sacrifices for it but wouldn't stand in the party's way. Through them, I learned that three things distinguish Hezbollah from other Islamist movements in the region: its clearly articulated ideology; the fervor of its followers; and its success at expanding membership and inflicting military harm on its enemies. I met supporters who liked it that Hezbollah picks up the garbage, and activists who wanted to expel every last Jew from the Middle East. Only a few people, perhaps tens of thousands, actually join Hezbollah as fighters or paid party members. To a degree unparalleled among other Islamist movements in the region, Hezbollah has leveraged that driven inner core to appeal to hundreds of thousands more, sympathizers who never rise to the level of official membership, but provide Hezbollah much of its political, cultural, social, and military clout.

Islamism has been on the rise for a century, spreading the idea that political life is a subsidiary of one particular interpretation of Islamic faith. Islamist groups have experimented with approaches ranging from peaceful incrementalism to maximalist violence. If any group today can claim the mantle of revolutionary Islam in the Middle East, it is Hezbollah. Iran's Islamic Revolution has calcified into a rigid and orthodox theocracy. Hamas wages a quixotic war against Israel from its isolated, crumbling enclave of Gaza. Al Qaeda recruits from the limited ranks of Salafi fanatics. By contrast, Hezbollah, in an unlikely journey, has emerged as a quasi-state of its own in the ruins of the failed state of Lebanon. The Party of God has eased itself into comfortably wielding power, governing its own constituents without losing its revolutionary pedigree.

In the 1980s, Hezbollah literally exploded into the world's consciousness with a series of shocking acts of violence: the bombing of the U.S. Marine barracks in Beirut in 1983, which killed 241 Americans; kidnappings of prominent Americans in Lebanon; and a sustained frontal assault in southern Lebanon against the occupying Israeli army, waged first by suicide bombers and then by increasingly effective guerillas. At almost every turn, then and since, the movement has defied expectations with its military as well as its political success. At its founding in 1982, the group was so secret its members claimed Hezbollah didn't even exist. Gradually the Party of God emerged from the shadows, winning the loyalty of Lebanon's Shia community and claiming the lead role in the anti-Israeli resistance in occupied Lebanon. In the two decades that followed Hezbollah's founding, the Party of God methodically refined a messianic theology and political philosophy that appealed to frustrated people all across a roiled and confused Middle East. Diplomatically, Hezbollah forged deep and enduring relationships with the governments of Iran and Syria that were responsible for its creation. In turn, Hezbollah exported its own revolution, sharing knowledge and materiel with radical movements of every sectarian and political stripe, including secular Palestinians, Hamas, the Shia Mahdi Army in Iraq, the Sunni Muslim Brotherhood in Egypt and Jordan, and even, allegedly, with Latin American communist guerillas. Militarily, Hezbollah has evolved into a classic guerilla warfare organization, discarding the early tactics that branded it a terrorist organization in the eyes of America and Israel. Even though it cultivates a vibrant culture of martyrdom among its supporters, the party hasn't launched a suicide bomber since December 30, 1999, when a Hezbollah fighter drove a car bomb into an Israeli military convoy. In the 1990s, its suicide bombers attacked only military targets. American intelligence warns that Hezbollah sleeper cells could strike in the West, but Hezbollah hasn't been compellingly linked to an international attack since 1994. Hezbollah disputes the West's definition of terrorism and yet has tried to keep its military tactics within the West's norms.

At each stage of Hezbollah's growth, rival politicians in Lebanon and intelligence experts in the United States and Israel have predicted its imminent demise. Instead the group has consolidated its strength with shrewd political maneuvering and military flair. Radical and patient at the same time, Hezbollah has brick by brick laid the foundation of a limited Islamic state within its Lebanese constituency, perhaps the first experiment in Islamist governance that is both militant and pragmatic. The Party of God accommodates both fanatics and moderates, and it has historically refused to coerce followers or non-Shia who live under Hezbollah control into following religious rules (though it does demand piety from its inner core of supporters). Impressively, it has appealed across sectarian and cultural divides. Its most significant ally in Lebanon is the largest Christian party, the Free Patriotic Movement. Under the banner of Hezbollah's Islamic Resistance, normally fractious groups set aside their differences: Persians and Arabs, Sunnis and Shia, religious and secular, Islamist and Communist.

Unlike the Salafi extremists who feed groups like Al Qaeda, Hezbollah's leaders quite comfortably navigate modernity. They espouse a form of Islamic living in conjunction with contemporary mores; Hezbollah's leaders tend to lead Spartan lifestyles but they're happy to see the party's supporters engage in commerce, grow rich, and live well. A thriving and prosperous constituency makes for a healthy Islamist militant party, Hezbollah's leadership believes. Lebanese rivals, including Christian militias and the Shia Amal Party, have in the past built impressive but unsustainable networks to provide social services, jobs, and graft without approaching Hezbollah's level of success.[4] Hezbollah has had the luxury of unabated funding from Iran since its inception, by some estimates receiving a minimum of $200 million a year from Tehran and much more than that in times of crisis. But that funding alone cannot account for Hezbollah's continuous growth over the decades; Hezbollah's primal appeal and sustained popularity stem from the group's deliberate, patient cultivation of ideological loyalty. Party activists are God's shock troops; they can choose to wage war not only by wiring bombs but also by designing buildings, teaching school, babysitting children, and clearing roads. The majority of Hezbollah's loyalists are engaged in social projects, to which they apply the same militant fervor as a guerilla fighter. Hezbollah does much more than simply fight, but without fighting it loses its holy identity.

This is Hezbollah's secret: its followers believe. Ideas matter to them. Hezbollah has steeped them in a consuming way of thinking about God, their neighborhoods, their habits, and the omnipresent enemy. The party's followers have redefined their personal goals and habits in line with the party's ideology—a melding of the political idea of resistance with the religious idea of fully committing oneself to God. The most religiously devoted members of Hezbollah's community are passionately devoted to a messianic Shia mission of bringing the Mahdi, the last Shia *imam,* or spiritual leader, out from hiding to rule the earth with perfect justice. A far greater number have embraced the ideology of Islamic Resistance, which resonates with notions of restoring pride, dignity, and self-determination to the dispossessed. And the greatest number of all of the party's supporters, the million or more in the outer ring, have found in Hezbollah an avenue to a restored sense of communal strength or a stricter Islamic faith, without wholly subscribing to Hezbollah's political project. Faith and ideas lure people into Hezbollah's fold; prosperity and services keep them there. The material benefits of Hezbollah's community grease the engine, but they don't make it run. At Hezbollah's heart lie constructive elements, like a view of Islamism as self-empowerment, requiring volunteerism and discipline from every member of Hezbollah's community. Alarmingly, they are balanced by destructive elements, like perpetual war, authoritarianism, a conviction that strength comes only from military superiority, and a brisk current of political rage.

After "Operation Truthful Promise," Hezbollah's July 2006 raid into

Israeli territory and the thirty-four days of war that ensued, Hezbollah perfected a strategy that has spread to other militants in the region: the notion of winning by simply surviving. Israel, with American backing, made its war aim nothing less ambitious than the destruction of Hezbollah. Nasrallah's war aims were equally grandiose: he vowed to end the American dream of a "New Middle East," to keep Israel out of Lebanon, and force the release of prisoners in Israeli jails, top among them Samir Quntar. A Lebanese Druze, Quntar was convicted of murdering an Israeli man and his four-year-old daughter in a bungled 1979 raid that left a two-year-old smothered to death as well. He was sentenced to spend the rest of his life in jail. In Israel, Quntar symbolized the worst brutality of the Jewish state's enemies; in Lebanon, Quntar became a national hero. Israel vowed never to release him from prison, and Hezbollah made his freedom a central demand. In 2006, Israel defeated Hezbollah by conventional military measures; but in the estimation of the Arab world, and of many Israelis, Hezbollah prevailed by fighting longer than any previous Arab army, withstanding the most fearsome punishment the Israel Defense Forces could rain on its guerillas, and emerging strong enough to rearm and fight again.

Its influence is growing. Hamas has remodeled itself on Hezbollah's example. In the 1990s, Hezbollah taught Hamas how to conduct suicide bombings; now Hezbollah openly advises the Palestinians on tactics and broad strategy. Hezbollah's political and military teachings were evident in the January 2009 war in Gaza between Israel and Hamas. Somehow Hezbollah, an organization that is neither Sunni nor Palestinian, has assumed a position of leadership among Palestinian militants. Nasrallah's party has tapped into a deep unslaked thirst among Arabs for revenge and redemption. And unlike other Islamist movements, Hezbollah has convinced the well-heeled as well as the downtrodden to make major, repeated sacrifices for the party's militant messianic ideology.

Hezbollah's people aren't meek and demoralized; they're contradictory individuals, poor but empowered, jubilant activists aglow with religious fervor. They love martyrdom, but they also love life. Their parents lived on the margins, their sect was oppressed, and now, in what seems like a flash, they've inherited the future. Hezbollah's success stems not from any single great figure, but from the legions of everyday men, women, and children who have flocked to the movement, giving their lives but also their weekend afternoons, their fervor and frenzy but also their workaday devotion. To understand Hezbollah, its threat and its potential, is to understand the fighters and engineers, the women who raise the martyrs and the scouts who plant trees, the clerics and politburo members and school headmasters, the nine-year-old girls who take the veil over the objections of their less-devout fathers, the holy struggle against Israel and the Holy Struggle for Building Reconstruction. It is individuals who have endowed Hezbollah with its power. Their devotion and humanity appear poised to give it a long lease on life, into the next generation and beyond. Their stories, in the battlefields of southern Lebanon and the ghettoes of south Beirut, answer the question of why Hezbollah has grown so quickly and exerted such influence over the Shia, Islamic, and Arab worlds. They help explain why Hezbollah has managed to persist as a threat to Israel; why the United States considers it a major terrorist threat event though it has avoided direct attacks on American targets for decades; and why it has made Arab regimes so uncomfortable. They explain why Hezbollah appeals to militants worldwide who at first blush would be expected to eschew a group built on the idea of an Islamic state; Hezbollah has become every radical's model. And these common men and women also help us understand the ideological and religious roots of today's conflict in the Middle East.

It's comforting for some to think that Hezbollah and similar groups cultivate loyalty only by providing services: a job and a stipend in exchange for hanging a banner and parroting party slogans. If that were the entire story, then another group, perhaps one less interested in armed struggle and religious indoctrination, could woo Hezbollah's followers away with a package deal that promised even better services and more prosperity. But the uncomfortable truth that I learned from the individuals in Hezbollah's orbit is that the people of the Middle East, like people everywhere, value their beliefs at least as much as their pocketbooks—if not more. Hezbollah's members hew to its line not only because the party enhances their livelihoods but because they share its ideology. Its wider constituency, the millions who support Hezbollah without officially joining, are moved more by the party's credo and its psychological appeal than by handouts that buy temporary sympathy. If we listen to the followers of Hezbollah, they reveal what motivates the groundswell of loyalty that has endowed this Party of God with such power, and they can describe to us the new Middle East that they hope to create.

2

RANI BAZZI'S HOLY STRUGGLE

On July 31, 2006, Rani Ahmed Bazzi strode out of the apocalyptic rubble of downtown Bint Jbail into a clearing that had once been the main street. His uneven beard, dirty cargo pants, and heavy walkie-talkie marked him as a Hezbollah field officer. He was fighting in one of the deadliest parts of the southern Lebanese front in that year's war. The Israeli military had obliterated the entire central market district of Bint Jbail, mortaring each house until it was reduced to a small hillock of pulverized concrete. Only the fallen electricity poles marked the path of the city's streets. A brief truce between Israel and Hezbollah had opened the border town to rescue workers. Working in tandem with fighters, they had coaxed shocked families from the basement shelters where they had cowered during the previous weeks' bombardment. Journalists entered the town for the first time since the war began. Many of my colleagues spent the morning helping the Red Crescent volunteers. As the day wore on, several colleagues and I sought in vain the fighters supposedly lodged in the town. Now it was late afternoon; the civilians had been evacuated, and the last Red Crescent workers were packing up their stretchers. The glare of the midday sun had slackened, along with its raw, dry heat.

Almost everyone who could walk and wasn't a guerilla fighter had left Bint Jbail after the first week of fighting. Both Hezbollah and the Israelis had mythologized Bint Jbail to the point that the Israelis were obsessed with leveling the town and Hezbollah supporters almost delighted in the number of times that it had risen again "like a Phoenix," as Rani put it that day. Hezbollah prized the town's status as the "Capital of the Resistance," and had made it one of the most fortified garrisons along the Israeli border. For the Israelis, Bint Jbail was an almost irresistible military target, an epicenter of "terrorism" where almost everyone in the community openly supported Hezbollah. For the Lebanese Shia, Bint Jbail represented more than just Hezbollah's prowess: it embodied their will to rebuild, to prosper, and to fight any challenger. Because of the town's emotional and tactical importance, it had quickly become a focal point of the fighting. Hezbollah fighters ambushed Israelis and destroyed several armored vehicles, killing five Israelis in nearby Maroun al-Ras and eight more in Bint Jbail. Israel's military leaders, inflamed, vowed to seize the town. Before sending more soldiers, however, they first pummeled Bint Jbail with ordnance. Wave after wave of mortar shells crashed down on the city. The gunners fired mortars until the roofs collapsed, the walls buckled, and finally, the foundations lay exposed to the sky. Perhaps the Israelis meant to clear the battlefield, or perhaps they simply wanted to show Hezbollah how intent they were on vengeance.[5]

Either way, the town had become even more unlivable than the other southern Lebanese villages under the Israeli bombardment, although throughout the South it was much the same. Mortars fell almost constantly, causing a shudder in the eardrums and the gut. Drones buzzed overhead, and occasionally a rocket would zip into range, making an incongruously whimsical sound like a balloon releasing its air before crashing into its target. More rarely, the Israeli Air Force would drop a large bomb. Those caused the ground to buckle, sending a sonic jolt up the knees and into the belly, a physical sensation indistinguishable from dread and nausea. By the end of the fighting two weeks later, only one in every ten buildings in Bint Jbail would stand unscathed.

Most of the residents who could had fled on foot through the mountains to safer towns, further north and away from the border. A handful had stayed out of solidarity with Hezbollah. Some were taking part in the fight. The rest were too old or infirm to move. Up the hill behind the stadium one family emerged from their shelter when they heard a Red Crescent volunteer calling. They had huddled in a basement during two weeks of nerve-frazzling explosions. The head of the family, a man who wore glasses and a greasy dress shirt, carried a suitcase with all the family's belongings, so heavy that he could only drag it down the front steps onto the street. The Red Crescent volunteers kept up a patter of comforting words to stave off shock: "We just have to make it up that hill, the ambulance is parked in the center, everything's going to be fine now." The wife was mute, and the children scampered in circles around the knot of adults. Daylight revealed a panoramic vista of their hometown's ruins. "God curse Israel!" shrieked an elderly woman, maybe the grandmother.

Back at the town center, the elderly shuffled uncomprehendingly toward ambulances, leaning on the arms of Red Crescent volunteers or news photographers who had set down their cameras to aid them. Several of them were blind, and others clearly in the grips of some form of senile dementia. Issam Moussa, a retired soccer player who was working as my translator, carried one lady in her seventies on his back. She had no teeth; she seemed to be trying to say something, gumming the air and emitting nonsense syllables. Issam brought her to rest in the shade outside a half-bombed minimart in the town center, near the ambulances. We looted juice and soda from the store's defunct refrigerator and gave the old lady a drink. When we tried to speak with her, we realized she had no idea what year it was and which war—she seemed confused about whether the Israelis had just invaded southern Lebanon, or had just left, or whether she was simply recalling traumatic memories from the past. She clung to one fact, that she had been left alone and without food. All the destruction made the onlookers volatile. Issam wept after he set down the old lady. As we roamed the town, he muttered and cried at each small outrage. He chastised reporters for not showing enough respect as they examined the photos and keepsakes left behind in one abandoned house. Angrily, at another point, he accused his colleagues of being enemy collaborators—a baseless accusation, but in the paranoid climes of southern Lebanon, also a very dangerous one. Still taut with emotion, Issam noticed a shoe store, the stockroom still intact after an explosion had sheared off its front. Voicing apologies to the absent owner and asking God pro forma for forgiveness, Issam ransacked the shelves, choosing a pair of new work boots after trying on several styles. "Whoever owns this shop, I will find him after this war and pay him," he announced to everyone in earshot.

After hours of noise and scrambling the rescue crews and their earth-movers ceased, and quiet fell over the dazed town. It was the time of day that Lebanese—in keeping with a Mediterranean tradition—usually take a siesta, to while away the last hours of heat before the cooler evening sets in. A pair of burnt bodies embraced in the rubble of a home near the town reservoir. Unspent shells littered the street. It was there on the road from the reservoir, snaking uphill to the town center, that Rani Bazzi materialized.

In their rhetoric, Hezbollah and Israel had painted each other as fanatical, self-deluded, and addicted to the catastrophic logic of total warfare. Normal life appeared to have halted entirely in Beirut's southern suburbs; across the pastoral hills of southern Lebanon, abandoned at the peak of the tobacco season; and all over northern Israel, where villages in range of Hezbollah rockets had been evacuated and those who remained in the cities stayed in underground bunkers. Hezbollah and the Israelis seemed locked like sadomasochistic lovers, engorged with desire to destroy one another. The civilians on either side had suffered the war's endless volleys of rockets, bombs, and missiles showered indiscriminately upon them. Millions were displaced in Israel and Lebanon, and levels of violence and bombardment that had beggared comprehension in mid-July, during the first week of the war, now felt commonplace two weeks later. There had been a massacre at Qana, dozens of women and children killed as they slept when Israel dropped a bunker buster on an apartment block. Outrage over that bombing had prompted Israel to declare a day's pause in the air barrage, so civilians still trapped in southern Lebanon could leave. After weeks of endless explosions, on this July afternoon in 2006, suddenly, oddly, it was quiet.

Rani Bazzi loomed almost cartoon-like, a hallucination in the shimmering quiet of late afternoon. Where the reservoir road curved uphill to the town center, a small mosque remained partially intact. Its front door faced the street, and its minaret, punctured by mortar shells, was still standing. The rear room had been hit, its back wall entirely gone. Rani bounded into the street from the mosque door. The top of his large, round head was bald, and the black hair along the sides was cropped short. His beard was scraggly and uneven. He smiled at us, a small, mischievous grin with his lips packed tightly together, but his ruddy cheeks bulged enthusiastically.

He looked like he wanted to laugh but was restraining his face. We bore the unmistakable evidence that we were reporters—a camera slung over a shoulder, notepads in hand, tape recorders and cell phones spilling from the pockets of our cargo pants. We were ready to quit Bint Jbail and return to the coast, away from the front lines. "Are you happy? Did you get your story? Can you go home now?" the fighter asked, in perfect English. He seemed to be aiming for a sarcastic delivery, but instead, his tone came across as genuinely interested. "There's no point in you being here. It's been the same story for two thousand years. You don't make any difference. If you have the power, you can change things. If you don't, you can't. We have the power. I will be buried here."

I sensed an invitation, but I was afraid to spook him by betraying my curiosity too openly. The soldiers of Hezbollah are supposed to flit like phantoms from the shadows. Those outside the Party of God are not supposed to know who is a mere supporter, who is a member, or who is a trained commando; that uncertainty is part of Hezbollah's mystique. Any man you pass on the street could have a secret life as an Islamist fighter, and in the villages of southern Lebanon, many of the men in the marketplace and the teashops are, in fact, Hezbollah operatives. Fighters like this man are under orders not to talk about their work for Hezbollah even within their community, and especially not to outsiders.

Only later would I learn Rani's real name. At the time he told us without fanfare that he couldn't reveal his true identity, so he asked us to refer to him by a generic *nom de guerre*. We preferred not to use any name at all, rather than a fake one. "Did you see all this?" Rani said. He waved his hand in a general motion, taking in the town and the mountains on either side, capped with smaller villages. "Look at this, my friend. Look at this. There was a mosque here." Rani spoke with a comical nasal twang that made me think of Elmer Fudd. "I've been here the whole time," he said. "I could tell you so many stories." He invited us to join him inside the mosque where he'd been napping. Shattered glass and concrete dotted the floor, and the rear wall had collapsed, affording a view across the valley to the west and the ridge he called Tel Masoud. It was great luck to come across a fighter willing to talk at all, but we had no reason to expect anything other than the rote platitudes and slogans with which party activists usually spoke.

A man called from the street. Rani started, and then ran outside. By the time we followed him, we found him wildly hugging and kissing another fighter. They grabbed each other's shoulders, shook one another. Rani kissed the other man's forehead and cheeks, and hugged him again. They kissed each other's shoulders, a gesture of respect. All the while they spoke rapid-fire sentences to one other, almost whispering. Finally Rani turned to us: "This is Hamid. I haven't seen him in three weeks. I thought he was dead." Encountering his friend had clearly shaken him out of his initial mood. Now he was delighted to hear his friend's news, and because of our accidental presence, he was willing to share with us that happiness and the unguarded loquaciousness that came with it.

They turned back into the mosque, motioning us to follow. The two men were giddy, euphoric. Their state of mind reminded me of the American soldiers from the Third Infantry Division whom I encountered beneath a highway overpass outside Baghdad in April 2003, in between firefights. Still surrounded by the bloated corpses of men they had killed the previous day, they voraciously devoured their precooked meals beside their tanks, while recounting in almost pornographic detail their last battle against Saddam's troops. They eagerly anticipated more shooting before the show ended. The adrenaline of the combat high still coursed through them during the day-long break, and in their downtime they plied each other with gruesome stories of the heroics and mechanics of killing, as if to maintain their edge for the next clash. Like those soldiers, Rani and Hamid weren't off duty; they simply had a pause. They had already finished their work for the day, restocking food caches and rendezvousing with their command. Now they had a chance before the killing resumed in a day or two to kick back and revel in their military success from the past two weeks of war. Besides, they had an audience. A constellation of events conspired to put Rani in a revelatory mood, from the exhaustion so clearly etched on his face to his ardent conviction that he would be martyred before this war's end.

More than any speech by Nasrallah or any analysis of the Shia Islamist group's huge body of doctrine and propaganda, the behavior of these two men revealed to me the foundation of the vast power and popularity of the Lebanese Party of God. These were family men, men of faith, well-trained but passionate soldiers. When they talked about their motivation and their hopes, it was clear how deeply they identified not only with Hezbollah and Nasrallah but also with a transnational Shia family, a single righteous tribe in God's extended family. They brought into battle a potent blend of nationalism and Shia partisanship. They were galvanized by indignation at their foreign target, the Israelis, their domestic rivals inside Lebanon, and finally, their sense that they were engaged as Shia Muslims in the end-of-days battle for humanity's salvation. They were paving the way for the return of the Mahdi, the last imam who will return on judgment day to redeem the faithful. The psyches of these two men revealed the power and appeal of the messianic faith and the potent, simple message of resistance that had made Hezbollah a model for radical activists of all sects across the Middle East. I sensed from them what I came to understand better over time, that ideology and Armageddon theology bound them to Hezbollah as much as the famous social service network that so many outsiders give sole credit for the party's popularity. True, they were movement activists, the most fully indoctrinated and dedicated of Hezbollah's members. They represented the party's elite, not its mass of casual supporters. But theirs was the ethos of Hezbollah that inspired others to join full-time, and an even greater number to admire the party and become fellow travelers.

Sitting cross-legged on the mosque floor, the two men spoke joyfully about how they drove the Israelis back from Bint Jbail. They were proud despite the biblical cost—the city center crushed, nearly every house shelled in retribution by Israel. They spoke in the patter of all religious zealots, explaining how their faith in God made them superior in battle to their opponents. But they didn't rely on faith alone to protect themselves. They were guerillas who loved war in all its technical minutiae. Rani and Hamid exchanged tips about their redundant radio systems, their cellular command and control network that left standing orders for units whose commanders were killed or out of contact. They talked with passion about the Kalashnikov. "No one has done more for the world's dispossessed than Mr. Kalashnikov. His gun plays like a piano," Rani said. "There's a special corner of *jana*"—paradise—"reserved for him."

Rani warmed to the conversation as we sat in a circle on the mosque floor surrounded by shards of glass. He started to drop hints about his personal history. He told us he was a teacher, and that he had lots of relatives in America. "I could go to Dearborn, Michigan, but I don't want to. I hate America. I will never go." As in most of rural Lebanon, emigration had decimated the population of Bint Jbail. More of its people lived in Canada and Michigan now than in Lebanon. Rani said he had convinced some of his cousins to return to southern Lebanon to rebuild after the Israeli occupation ended in 2000, leaving behind their businesses in Michigan for an uncertain—but, Rani believed, much more meaningful—future. "In America, they take their dogs to the hospital or to the swimming pool. We are treated worse than they treat their pets," he said. "No, I will not go there."

Because Rani spoke English, he did most of the talking. At first, he spoke with bravado. "We buried the Israelis. They ran like rats," he said. "The Israelis can never beat us. They can't even fight us. We turned them back here in downtown Bint Jbail, there on that hill, and on that ridge." Although the Israeli military outnumbered Hezbollah and in a direct confrontation was almost guaranteed to smash its fighters, Rani—like many in the Party of God—truly seemed to believe that the Shia could and would eventually win a divinely ordained victory. "At the moment we are winning. We have many cards we have not yet played. The Israelis are suffering and the resistance has not yet started," he said. "By the grace of God, we will eat them on the battlefield." He was repeating an often-voiced Hezbollah talking point, the threat of a secret, game-changing weapon. In a literal sense such a weapon never materialized during the summer war with Israel. But perhaps Hezbollah did have a secret weapon in its followers' cultural resiliency and sectarian loyalty. The Lebanese Shia overwhelmingly believed in Hezbollah because of their religious faith, and followed the party regardless of whether it best served their economic interests or promised any pragmatic political dividends. Rani explained the advantage of the Hezbollah guerillas against the better-armed and more numerous Israelis: "There is a secret between man and God. This is the strategy of Hezbollah. It is that we are not afraid of death. This is the center of the training of the fighter, to make him unafraid of death, so you prefer to die rather than live humiliated."

When we first encountered him, Rani Ahmed Bazzi gave as his fake name: Hussein, the grandson of the Prophet Mohammed whose martyrdom in

680 C.E. is the signal event in the founding of Shia Islam. The Shia are so named because they are the Followers of Ali (or partisans, *Shi'atu 'Ali* in Arabic). Ali, the prophet's son-in-law, was the fourth caliph until his murder in 661. His followers—the first Shia—challenged what they saw as the usurpation of the caliphate by Ali's main rival. Their quest was doomed, collapsing after the murder of Ali. His son Hussein led a quixotic military expedition to the city of Kufa in southern Iraq, where he and his partisans were massacred by cavalrymen loyal to the caliphate. With their deaths began a Shia narrative of dispossession and victimhood. The sect always formed a minority within Islam, and only provisionally recognized the temporal leaders of the Islamic world. According to mainstream Shia theology, the ultimate just ruler was the Twelfth Imam, the Mahdi, who disappeared in Samarra, Iraq, after his father's death in 874. Only the return of the "occulted" Mahdi would bring justice to earth.

Over the course of that long afternoon in Bint Jbail, Rani told us why the struggle of the Party of God was even more important to him than the wife and two sons he treasured, the students he taught at the technical school, and even the Hezbollah militia recruits under his command. A man in his thirties who presented his arguments deliberately, Rani was no hormone-driven teenage foot soldier. He sought martyrdom in the war with Israel, but his motivation was neither rash nor impulsive. He had deeply considered his life's goals, and had invested years of work in building his community. The climax of that effort, in his studied opinion, could take only one form—glorious death in the Shia tradition of martyrdom that has defined the sect since its inception, when the sect's original leaders were massacred on the plains of Karbala. Rani saw his mission as political, cultural, and military. He was fighting as a sworn enemy of Israel, and as a soldier of Islam; but it was as a Shia that he planned to enter paradise, and as a Shia that he had matured from an adolescent hothead into a Hezbollah community pillar. Shia theology endowed his quest with a sense of justice and victimhood that buttressed his courage and his mission. Technically, we were Rani's enemies. He had been indoctrinated to see us as part of an evil complex of Americans, atheists, Jews, and Sunni Muslims that for centuries had poisoned life for the Shia. He considered many types of people his foes: secular Beirutis who opposed Hezbollah's struggle, collaborators, nonbelievers, Sunni Muslims and Christians who cantonized Lebanon and marginalized the Shia, Jews across the border, the faceless Americans across the sea—all arrayed as one against the true Islam. But by his nature, Rani viewed everyone he met as a possible convert to his worldview. He was convinced that anyone who really listened might join him on his path.

Senior Hezbollah cadres are unfailingly polite, but the party's culture promotes a stern asceticism and a pathological paranoia about outsiders. Rani stood out among Hezbollah veterans for his infectious enthusiasm and effusive friendliness. The non-Shia, foreigners, academics, and journalists rarely gain any access to the organization, and when they do they meet with guarded, highly politicized officials conscious of how their every statement might be construed abroad. These spokesmen and women tend to talk in generalities, or to quote documents, or to enumerate well-trodden history, rather than discuss their own work or role in the party, or anything personal about their own background and how they came to join Hezbollah. The result is usually less illuminating than reading Nasrallah's speeches, which at least reveal the organization's doctrine and policies. Although Rani hovered close to the party's stern principles in the way he led his life, on a personal level he was incapable of smothering his love of conversation and his proselytizing instinct. The long Shia history of persecution has imbued the sect with sympathy for the underdog and a mistrust of power. Shia parties in the modern era have co-opted those strains, often attracting workers, peasants, Communists, and Socialists who find in the Shia rhetoric an echo of their belief in egalitarianism and empowering the dispossessed. The Karbala passion play tells a story about betrayal, martyrdom, repentance, and redemption that exhorts the faithful to fearlessly fight the powerful; and on the odd chance that they win, they can avoid moral corruption so long as they wield their power only on behalf of the dispossessed. It's a vision at once fanatical and ecumenical, exclusive and big-tent.

Capitalizing on his engineering background, Rani was trained to kill on a large scale, with antitank mines that can rip through the undercarriage of any vehicle that passes over the road. Hezbollah had anticipated an Israeli ground advance into the South. Rani told us that Hezbollah had built underground bunkers and a network of tunnels so that fighters could mount surprise ambushes and retreat unscathed. They had stockpiles of food and ammunition scattered across the South so that guerilla fighters could resupply themselves if the militia's logistics capacity was compromised. Rocket launching teams fired short-range Katyushas and longer-range rockets from the valleys. In Bint Jbail, he said, they fired from the narrow strip of grape arbors just downhill from the mosque.

It was unusual, and certainly against orders, for Rani to divulge so much information about his work as a fighter. Nothing he said could have compromised Hezbollah's military operations, but his revelations would have earned him a reprimand from his commanders. He was making clear that he trusted us and wanted to share his most personal side, which for him meant confiding the details of his work for Hezbollah. Rani said he played a "battlefield support" role across several sectors. He would drive from town to town in his small white Renault Rapid truck, delivering special mines or other supplies. At times, he said, he would fire mortars in support of front-line combat units. Fighters operated in small units, keeping in touch with commanders through long-distance two-way radios. In case they lost touch with their commanders, they had standing orders to fight the Israelis to the death. Even as we spoke, Rani's radio was clipped to his cargo pants, the volume just loud enough to hear the chatter of the Hezbollah command-and-control, which on this day mostly consisted of reports about which roads in the South were still passable.

"The only order was, when you see the Israelis, attack them," Rani said. "We were waiting for combat like a man awaits his bride." Rani and Hamid described the battle of Tel Masoud, just across the valley. An Israeli advance team had landed by helicopter at a palatial house, two stories tall, which sat on several acres at a commanding height atop the ridge east of Bint Jbail. It's locally known as "The Castle." A tomato patch and a low wall surround it. A Hezbollah squad immediately attacked the house. At such close range, the Israelis' superior weapons gave them less of an advantage; the two sides traded machine gun and grenade fire. Hezbollah soldiers had rocket-propelled grenades and a few antitank missiles, Rani said. We asked Rani and Hamid to take us to the site of the battle so we could better understand their story, although it made us nervous, even on a truce day, to put a pair of Hezbollah combatants in our vehicle and drive around the war zone in plain sight of the Israeli surveillance drones buzzing overhead. We parked at the bottom of the hill and walked up toward the location of the battle. Rani pointed out the first spot from which Hezbollah had opened fire. Hundreds of AK-47 bullet casings littered the ground. Further up the hill, at the point where Israeli soldiers had returned fire, lay a pile of stouter M-4 or M-16 casings. As we rounded the bend toward the house, we saw it had been flattened by a bomb. After a night and day of nearly constant fighting, Rani said, the Israelis had evacuated the house. Immediately afterward they had bombed it, to destroy any equipment they might have left behind and, presumably, to deny Hezbollah the chance to use the structure as a position from which to shoot at Israelis if they made another ground advance into the town below.

Issam, my translator, was giddy with excitement. Most of his neighbors were active supporters of Hezbollah or Amal, the smaller, less militant Shia party, but he'd never been privy to a real fighter's conversations. Issam himself was something of a celebrity, briefly starring on the Lebanese national soccer team in the 1990s before his sports career precipitously unraveled and he moved to Tyre. He had worked for the sappers clearing Israeli minefields in southern Lebanon, left behind from the occupation that lasted from 1982 to 2000. Even though Issam was a bit of a peacock, in the presence of these two Hezbollah officers he acted like a schoolkid in the thrall of a pop icon. Fighters endow their entire communities with the sense that they possess supernatural powers, yet like fluoride in the water, are never seen.

As we walked through the rubble, Rani spotted something. After a minute on his knees, he fished out a working pair of Israeli night vision binoculars. "These are precious!" he declared. "We don't have much night vision. You can't buy these on the market." The two fighters clucked disapprovingly. "They say to the fighters of Hezbollah that your equipment is like your woman, so if you run away, you take your woman," Rani said. "Apparently it's not the same for the Israelis." His friend Hamid said the loot would be shown on Al-Manar, the Hezbollah satellite television station. "When we show these on television, all the people will be happy," he said. "This is our prize, the people's happiness."

In the garden outside the shattered "castle," Rani grew quiet. He prayed alone, a little ways down the hill, and then told us about his family, his wife and two sons, and his cousins and neighbors. Now the human contradictions in his personality came more clearly into focus. Since the war began, Rani said, he tried to send text messages every day to buck up the spirits of his relatives who had sought safety north of the war zone. As he spoke, he absentmindedly squatted to straighten a pine sapling that had bent into a shell crater. Every few days, if it was quiet, he would call. Families collectively supported the fight against Israel and were eager to sacrifice their loved ones to the struggle. Two of Hamid's younger brothers had been killed that week, in part, Rani said, because they were inexperienced fighters. "They are experienced now, the beginners," he said grimly. "Experienced or dead." Hamid wore a smile on his face, but his eyes looked glassy and disconnected, perhaps from fatigue or grief, or perhaps from a deep sense of purpose. "Look at him," Rani said. "Two of his brothers are under the rubble, but he is happy."

Rani was thirty-nine years old, and had spent his entire adult life fighting Israel. When he graduated from university he moved to Israeli-occupied Bint Jbail at a time when most inhabitants of South Lebanon were moving to Beirut. He had been imprisoned twice for his guerilla activities, and the second time had spent nearly a year in Khiam Prison, a colonial-era fort on the border where Israel detained those it suspected of fighting for the Islamic Resistance. Interrogators there routinely applied electrodes to the inmates and chained them to a flagpole in the courtyard to scorch in the sun and wind. Lebanese collaborators ran the prison under Israeli direction.[6] Rani, like most of the prisoners in Khiam, was held without charge or trial, and was only released when Israel ended its occupation of South Lebanon in May 2000. In prison Rani had come to some of his more doctrinaire beliefs, such as his vision of healthy eating as "the holy struggle for good digestion," or the digestive jihad. He emerged from Khiam Prison more determined than before to steer his young sons onto the path of armed holy struggle against Israel.

In loyal Hezbollah communities, Rani said, children are trained for combat from a young age even if they aren't selected as Hezbollah fighters. "How do you think our children are raised?" he said. "To fight the Israelis. My son is thirteen years old and knows how to fire a mortar." Candidates for Hezbollah's fighting force must be deeply devoted, "to get the secret." "He must want it. It is not too easy to become a fighter. He must be an honest guy. He must not be following girls, he must not drink alcohol."

He leaned down and picked three ripe red tomatoes from a spot in the in the dry clay soil where I'd not noticed anything growing. He wiped them clean on his shirt and offered one to each of us. "This is how we eat," he said. The tomato was small but packed tight with sweet juice, hot from the sun, which erupted against the back of my throat at the first bite. "Truly, when you fight, you are a friend of the forest. You eat onions, you eat tomatoes. You eat what you find. You gather water from the rain. It's the story of our lives. Our life is a rough life, not an easy life."

As he talked about how it felt to fight, he teared up a little. "You think a lot about life when you fight. How fragile it is," he said. During one particularly rough day, he recalled, he had been trapped in a position by Israeli mortar fire. He was down to his last can of tuna, when he saw a starving dog. "I gave him the can of tuna. His tongue was hanging so far out. If I showed mercy on the dog, maybe God would show mercy on me." If he saw any inconsistency between his generosity to the dog and the disdain he had previously voiced for Americans' care for their pets, he did not say.

An urgent voice cracked over the radio. "A helicopter is coming our way," Rani said. "Let us go from here. We will come back later to look for more." We packed into our SUV and drove back toward Bint Jbail.

We reentered the zone of wreckage. Up close and amid the unique geography of destruction, it's hard to remember the rationale that justifies the annihilation of a city (be it Knin, Fallujah, Dresden, Nagasaki). To Rani, though, the logic of the Israelis appeared impeccable, a mirror image of his own: it is imperative to destroy the enemy. Not merely defeat, but destroy. He disagreed about which side was right, but not about the tactics.

As we parked in front of the hospital filled with wounded soldiers, Rani, sitting in the front passenger seat, put his head in his hands. At first it seemed a gesture of fatigue, from a man who'd been on the run in a battlefield for two weeks. His shoulders were shaking, though, and then we heard the high pitch of his sobs. We sat silently with him. After a long moment, he sat up, and wiped his face. "There is so much I have seen. I'm not crying for the fighters. The fighters can handle it. I'm crying for the ordinary people. I cry for the whole world that thinks we are less than the animals, less than the bugs. Nobody cares."

He went on: in the first weeks of the 2006 war, Israel dropped bomb after bomb on Lebanon and as many as a million people, or one fourth of the population, left their homes. But only when Hezbollah's rockets began killing Israelis in Haifa, and other long-range rockets struck deep into the Jewish state, did powerful international actors like the United States start talking about a ceasefire. (The United States and its allies had encouraged Israel to quickly finish off Hezbollah, and had only begun encouraging ceasefire talks once it became clear that Israel wouldn't achieve a speedy victory.) "I'm sorry the world doesn't understand anything but power," he said, still sniffling. "I cry every day."

His eyes gleamed whenever he talked of death; he saw angels on the battlefield and he said he envied the brothers of his friend Hamid who already had been chosen to enter paradise. Maybe God had further plans for Rani, or maybe God had found him wanting. He was afraid sometimes, he said, that he had some unknown imperfection that he had to cleanse before God would accept his martyrdom. "I have been everywhere," he said. "I have been in Khiam. Even in Palestine. I have seen much." It was clear that he was crying for much more than just the politics of the current war.

He warmly embraced us in turn, kissing our cheeks. "I want you to visit my family after the war and share a meal," he said, with genuine welcome in his voice—unaware of or uninterested in the paradox of his personal friendliness and his general hatred of the West. His face wiped clean, he got in his Renault and sped off.

Hezbollah has exerted a charismatic pull over its members. The party has shifted the political spectrum acquiring the power to start wars and re-orient the regional agenda. Across the globe groups whose approach mirrors Hezbollah's are upending old norms and shaping new taxonomies of power, in defiance of our traditional understanding of politics and religion. These militants have grown powerful and popular in many vastly different contexts. In the Middle East, Hezbollah has positioned itself as the exemplar, exporting its model to other radical movements eager to learn its techniques for recruitment, mobilization, and warfare. How should we comprehend Hezbollah? I believe the key lies with individuals like Rani, who rarely lay bare their personal loyalties and the Gordian knot of their psychological motivations. When they do, however, they unveil the social history of the movements to which they have pledged allegiance, a history that begins and unfolds in villages, bunkers, boy scout meetings, and small mosques. Rani helped me understand the kernel at the heart of Hezbollah's message: a Shia worldview that implanted confidence and power in place of the pervasive sense of humiliation and fear in Israeli-occupied southern Lebanon. His everyday work suddenly imbued with a greater purpose, Rani could carry his head high, stave off any private doubts, and draw on an international Shia network for spiritual solidarity and material support. Hezbollah secured his love not only because of what it could *do* for him, but for what it made him *believe*.

Of course, the history of the contemporary Middle East would make no sense without a reckoning of Khomeini and Sadr, Nasrallah and the Sauds, Blair and the Bushes, and so many other instrumental leaders. But I found my understanding hollow without the story of the common men and women whose will created those leaders. They found inspiration in the figureheads who reflected their own desires. Rani lived in a symbiotic relationship with his leaders. Sure, those with power could mold their followers, but just as surely, those followers could withdraw their trust and leave the leaders illegitimate shells. In Lebanon, I came to see that the grassroots individuals who gave their loyalty—and often their lives—to Hezbollah offered the most revealing insight into its nature as a dynamic sectarian group, a fortune-teller's glimpse of the future. Most of the Shia that I met didn't sound like extremists when they talked about their faith and their personal goals; they considered their piety a work in progress, refrained from judging others, and accepted their own sins as faults to be repaired. Yet, these same laid-back Shia were willing to wholeheartedly back Hezbollah in war and politics, even if they didn't want to commit fully to the party's austere and all-encompassing code of personal behavior. They didn't want to live exactly like the full-time members and fighters, but they wanted to try to emulate them. Men like Rani Bazzi were the soldiers and proselytizers, the teachers and after-school volunteers whose humble labor taken collectively created the grand threat posed by Hezbollah. Their wives formed the foundation that made the culture of martyrdom possible. They raised their sons to see glory in an honorable death, taught their daughters to love men who brooked no fear, and venerated the example set by the original Shia martyrs. The leaders at rallies and on television embodied the movement, but at root it was fueled and maintained by the masses of common folk and their everyday contribution to the party's ideological leviathan. Nasrallah was important, but so were the anonymous musicians who churned out new propaganda songs every week, which blared from the speakers of minibuses and corner sandwich shops. How could Rani Bazzi be so likable and thoughtful, and at the same time so violent and absolute? Why did so many of his friends and neighbors choose to risk death during the Israeli bombing, staying in their homes in south Lebanon or south Beirut rather than fleeing to safety, even though they weren't active members of Hezbollah? This man, and the circle of friends, family, and institutions that made his life choices viable, could explain Hezbollah.

A sweeping change in religious identity politics over the last century made possible movements like Hezbollah and men like Rani Bazzi. Their actions only make sense in the context of the renaissance that began taking shape in the early twentieth century and gathered momentum in the 1970s and 1980s. Rani came of age at the zenith of a Shia renaissance midwifed by Ayatollah Ruhollah Khomeini and his 1979 Islamic Revolution in Iran. Khomeini convinced millions that religious faith had supplanted nationalism, communism, and other secular ideologies. In the nineteenth and twentieth centuries, religious and secular politics had vied for dominion in the Middle East. The odd and tenuous order that emerged from World War I, with artificial borders drawn by colonial powers, gave rise—for a brief historical moment—to a generation of secular states in the Islamic heartland. Arab republics governed Egypt, Syria, and Iraq. A secular dictator ruled Iran, and Maronite Christians—a single sect amidst a panoply of competing groups—dominated Lebanon. In the 1950s, for a time secular political movements appeared to eclipse religious groups. Arab nationalism had carried the day in much of the region, and fascist-style organizations like the Ba'ath Parties in Iraq and Syria promised modernization, wealth, prosperity, and a strong military that could stand up to Israel and the Western colonial powers. But Israel's humiliating defeat of the secular Arab regimes in 1967 strengthened the Islamists.

Rani Bazzi's Lebanon had devolved into an almost absurd test lab of religious fracturing. The state today recognizes eighteen official religious confessions, each of which is given a specific share of government power

under a series of agreements negotiated since Lebanon was granted independence from France in 1943. The power-sharing formula was revised
most recently in the Taif Accords of 1989, which ended the country's civil
war. For sixty years, however, Lebanon has nurtured a bureaucracy where
the path to power has always climbed through semi-tribal religious leaders.
Want a marriage license? A job at a post office? A building permit, a church
to preach in, a license to open a religious nonprofit? Go to the warlords
who represent your sect. During Lebanon's tortuous civil war, from 1975
to 1990, factions from almost every sect, along with Palestinian militants,
fought in a fluid, constantly morphing front—Christians fighting Muslims
and then later turning on each other, some Shia helping Palestinians, others opposing them, the coalitions shifting so frequently as to seem mean-
ingless. In this environment, however, with sectarian loyalty dominating
everyone's identity, Hezbollah's comparatively simple and ecumenical message propelled its dizzying rise. Certainly Hezbollah was a Shia movement,
but the fact that it rhetorically welcomed members of any faith to join the
Islamic Resistance made it unique in its native country. Political parties lost
their moral authority during the civil war; even those that shared common
ideas were wary of each other. The well of trust had run dry. It was in this
Lebanon that Hezbollah took shape and gave Rani Bazzi a template for his
hopes.

In 2006, voices across Lebanon demanded that Hezbollah disarm. Israel
had left six years earlier. Lebanon was prospering and had its own national
army in the event of a foreign invasion. Even some Shia wondered aloud
whether their community's efforts should be invested in economic growth
rather than in the underground militia that was forever drilling for the
next war with Israel. Internally, Hezbollah leaders debated whether their
enduring commitment to militancy was costing them Shia support after a
protracted period of quiet. Should they increase their emphasis on politics,
and move away from their fundamental identity as a Shia Islamist militia?
Would normal politics reduce Hezbollah to yet another sleazy Lebanese
political machine, trading patronage for influence?

Hezbollah found itself under siege, its *raison d'être* questioned even by
some of its most devoted constituents in the South, the Dahieh, and the

Beqaa. If Israel wasn't attacking anymore, they asked, why do we need to live in a constant state of alert? Can't we get on with our lives, and can't the Party of God act more like a party and less like God's special forces battalion? In the Islamic world writ large, Hezbollah's allure had also been called into question. America occupied Iraq and Afghanistan; Israel occupied the West Bank and Gaza; dictators who did business with Jerusalem and Washington held sway in Saudi Arabia, Egypt, and Jordan. What good had come of Hezbollah's model of armed resistance? In Lebanon as well, Hezbollah's rivals and supporters alike questioned whether Hezbollah's tactics worked any more. Had Hezbollah made Israel any weaker since 2000? Had Hezbollah acquired for itself any tangible power in the years when Lebanon was tentatively reacquiring a measure of its sovereignty? Syrian troops had pulled out in 2005. Maybe Lebanon was on a path toward some normal political life, in which Hezbollah's hypermilitant culture would have no place.

For so long the Middle East's nastiest practices had taken shape first in the petri dish of Lebanon, tested there and then replicated with greater fury elsewhere. Lebanon's Euroglam culture had blazed the trail for elite Iranians and Arabs in the 1950s and 1960s to whore it up with petrodollars. Lebanon had pioneered money laundering and international smuggling. The country invented institutionalized sectarianism, designing the lethal and unstable political model that Iraq unwisely copied in the prelude to the sectarian civil war that killed hundreds of thousands of Shia and Sunni Muslims from 2004 to 2007. A constellation of groups (some of which came together to form Hezbollah) refined the hard ideology of Islamic militancy, and developed a mode of warfare built on suicide attacks, hostage taking, and roadside bombs. Now, with the civil war and the Israeli occupation in the South behind them, some Lebanese hoped their country could be a pioneer once again, but this time for something hopeful: the transformation of an armed Islamist militia into a peaceful political party in a pluralistic polity.

All these once-taboo questions had been broached in the summer of 2006. Nasrallah had promised Lebanon's government that his fighters would avoid provoking Israel until after the tourist season. Then Hezbollah seized the two Israeli soldiers, sparking an instantaneous and cataclysmic Israeli response. Hezbollah and its rivals immediately defined the war that broke out as one about the future of Hezbollah as much as a war with Israel. If Hezbollah emerged defeated, organizationally broken, the Shia Party of God would join the ranks of humiliated parties in Lebanon and around the Arab heartland. If Hezbollah emerged victorious or more popular, on the other hand, it could dictate a new set of norms, reshaping Lebanon as a platform for its unending war with Israel and its eternal quest to intensify Shia worship. In that first week of the war Hezbollah veered close to a precipice. Previously, the party could argue that its military missions were shrewd and balanced, doing far more harm to Israel than to the Arabs swept up in the retaliatory attacks. But the foray into Israel in July 2006 seemed suicidal. It had brought war to every single community in Lebanon, not just to the special forces of Hezbollah or the people of the borderlands. Within days, the party was hit with a barrage of derision. Hezbollah now looked like an uncontrollable, reckless confederacy of doom-seekers. Even governments of those Middle Eastern and European nations whose citizens reflexively side with Israel's enemies found themselves rooting for Israel. Only in Syria and Iran did demonstrators take to the streets in favor of Hezbollah from the start, but some Iranians complained to reporters that the Islamic Republic should spend its money on the needy at home rather than in Lebanon. Lebanese leaders who used to complain about Hezbollah in private or off the record stood behind microphone banks and denounced Nasrallah. Hezbollah's critics preferred some kind of flawed peace to perpetual war, and argued that a Muslim could love God and his ummah, or nation, without embarking on an endless battle.

3

THE DISPOSSESSED

Assem Harb didn't believe in Lebanon. It was the first Sunday of the 2006 war, and he had just made it safely to Beirut in a car that didn't look fit to cross town, much less traverse the bomb-pocked dirt roads of the South and the Chouf Mountains. He believed that divine providence had saved his family, and for that he thanked God and Hassan Nasrallah. On the first day that the bombing slackened, he borrowed a car and took to the road, part of a human stream of hundreds of thousands, all heading north. Overnight, they remade Lebanon's human geography, and Hezbollah's firm guiding hand was clearly behind the awesome logistical feat of their speedy migration. In a lawless state at war, displaced families typically can expect to contend with chaos, squabbling over cars, fuel, food, and cell phones as they flee the kill zone. Not so for the Shiites like Assem Harb seeking refuge from Israeli bombs. There was still a law in Lebanon, and that law was Hezbollah. Party of God operatives advised their followers when it was less risky to traverse the bombed roads. Men with walkie-talkies patrolled the towns and guarded the schools where women and children sheltered in basements. Hezbollah couriers, boys on motorcycles, brought fresh bread and canned tuna to civilians who stayed in remote mountain hamlets.

Without losing any time, Hezbollah set up a kind of underground railroad. One-tenth of Lebanon lived south of the Litani River, and another quarter of the population in the Dahieh, the Shia suburb in south Beirut. For the million Shia living in the targeted part of Beirut, safety lay a ten-minute bus ride across town, but most of them had nowhere to take refuge beyond their neighborhood. For the southerners, escaping north felt impossible. There were only two major routes out of southern Lebanon with bridges across the Litani, one from Tyre to Sidon and one from Marjayoun through Nabatieh to the coast. Both already had been bombed. The main highway from the South to Beirut ran along the coast, and was exposed to withering fire from Israeli gunships offshore. The ships were invisible, over the horizon, but their gunners had clear sight of the highway.

Undaunted, Hezbollah dispatched engineers and earthmovers to the Litani River. Overnight, they created a series of earthen dams to bridge the water, in the middle of a banana plantation and resort called Abou Deeb. They rerouted the highway to Tyre, the major city in the part of the South most heavily under attack. Engineers hand-scrawled signs on cardboard and pinned them to trees, oil drums, old car axles, to point the way north. The new route narrowed to one lane and snaked through a cemetery, the banana grove, and along a cliff's edge over which some refugees plunged. Their cars were now planted vertically in the soil, poking skyward among the crowns of the banana trees like eggs in an Easter basket. Hezbollah men directed traffic over the Litani, changing dams every hour. From there, the new route snaked through Sidon and then east, up into the mountains through Druze territory, before descending westward again to Beirut. Each time another bridge was bombed, the route was instantly adjusted. Foot soldiers would radio the latest route updates to motorists at major crossroads. In normal times, you could drive from Tyre to Beirut in an hour and a half. Now the trip could take six hours or more.

It didn't take long for Assem Harb to decide he wanted to take his family far from their farm in Arab Saleem. His village was situated on the border of the zone in southern Lebanon that had been occupied by Israel until 2000. That meant he lived on the front line of the decades-long fight between Hezbollah and Israel. Four decades of fighting had pitted the Shia and their allies against the Israelis, and most of the unfortunate villagers who remained among the tobacco rows, grape arbors, and mine fields ended up choosing sides. You had to collaborate with the resistance (that is, Hezbollah) or the occupier (Israel), whether you did so out of sympathy or necessity. Otherwise you could move north. No one was allowed to stay above the fray, especially not with intelligence officers from both sides regularly peppering residents with threats and bribes for information.

Assem's family—like many Shia in South Lebanon—had stayed put during the previous wars between Hezbollah and Israel in 1993 and 1996. The 1996 operation dubbed "Grapes of Wrath" by the Israelis had featured a lot of cross-border fighting, including the infamous shelling of the UN compound in Qana, where more than a hundred Lebanese civilians were killed (the Lebanese government put the death toll at 106). This time around, it felt more like a total war to the peasant farmers accustomed to guerilla fighting and military occupation. This time, it felt to Assem Harb less like the Israeli military versus Hezbollah than Jews versus Shia (Israeli gunners and bombers largely steered clear of the smattering of Christian, Druze, and Sunni villages south of the Litani). "This is the first time we've left. I've gotten older, now I have kids, responsibilities," he said. He was used to artillery shells, he explained somewhat apologetically, but not to the large bombs Israeli planes were now dropping. "We used to get bombed all the time. We're used to it, not just today," he said. This time around, he suspected, Israel was more determined and more dangerous. "The Israelis put out a warning this morning. We started to worry about free-for-all bombing. We were also afraid of getting cut off."

So Assem Harb turned to the local authorities—Hezbollah. He was fifty-four years old, with five children and a pregnant daughter-in-law. A neighbor lent him his car, a beat-up Toyota sedan. They had to trace their way to Nabatieh, an inland city that was southern Lebanon's economic capital and had been subject to massive bombing. Two of his sons were of fighting age, and although he wouldn't say outright that they were fighters, he said they had to return the borrowed car in which Assem had driven to safety and they would stay in the South afterward. "I'm expecting a Hezbollah victory, with the strength of our mujahideen," he said. "I hope it will be over quickly."

Rhetorically, Lebanese were uniting in the face of the Israeli assault. Individually, however, most Lebanese reacted along sectarian lines. Because Israel focused its initial bombardment on Hezbollah areas, the 25,000

Lebanese who fled their homes in the first five days were almost exclusively Shiite, and they looked to Hezbollah and Amal to resettle them—not to the government, or international aid groups, or nonsectarian Lebanese charities. Hezbollah's help only started with arranging the transportation and pointing the way north. Where does a poor farmer with no connections stay in the big city? Hezbollah had set up a massive intake center in an underground garage, where families could stay for a few days until they, or the party, found them more suitable lodging for the duration of the war.

Beirut Mall hulked above a roundabout in the neighborhood of Chiah, in the middle of the city, right on the border between the "safe" zone of Christian and Sunni Beirut and the Dahieh dead zone. It was an almost-finished mall, with a four-level underground garage, a grocery store already operating at street level and two floors of shops above it that were still under construction. Hezbollah had commandeered the whole complex, including the grocery store. Families with nowhere else to go camped in the empty parking spaces in the third and fourth garage levels underground—safe from the bombs, and insulated even from the alarming thuds and echoes. An outer ring of Hezbollah operatives guarded the complex. The guards with guns stayed out of sight, behind columns and inside nearby buildings. One of the men in charge, a thirty-six-year-old former cop from Baalbek named Jihad Lakkis, said he normally worked as a security guard at the mall. Hezbollah drafted him to manage the refugee intake center with a blue Motorola walkie-talkie, a cell phone, and a troupe of aides in cargo pants. Headquarters radioed clearance to let foreign reporters into the garage, and Jihad led three of us past the cordon. Outside and in the stairwell a handful of men loitered, smoking. The mall had an air of abandonment, and the refugee men looked like squatters in their soiled, untucked dress shirts. Down three levels, however, the garage door opened onto a humming subterranean world. More than two thousand people were camping there, and Jihad said he was prepared to house as many as four thousand at any one time. Meanwhile, families were assigned numbered parking spaces as their temporary home, and had set to work making each area as homey as possible. Clotheslines were strung across some of the concrete support pillars, and some families had hung blankets for privacy. Hezbollah had distributed foam sleeping mats to half the refugees before supplies ran out. Some families had brought butane stoves.

The air was dank and the small bathrooms stank of urine, which steadily overflowed the toilets and seeped into the garage, where a volunteer dutifully mopped it up. Five generators throbbed, running the pumps and air conditioning that kept the air breathable and the fluorescent lights on. Hezbollah sent bottled water, fresh bread, processed cheese, and crates of canned tuna. "We call it fast food here," Jihad joked. I was struck by the discipline of Jihad and the other operatives as well as the calmness of the arriving refugees. None of them seemed as terrified or hysterical as I would have expected, especially after I had seen the fear and stress etched on the faces of the much safer Christians and Sunnis in Beirut. None of them claimed full membership in Hezbollah—they described themselves as reserves, volunteers who supported the party and helped when asked. Without being asked each and every one of them delivered a sort of ode to Nasrallah and conviction in the coming divine victory against Israel. Such displays of groupthink are always unnerving, but this one was particularly impressive, because Jihad, Assem Harb, a gaggle of unrelated kids, the guy mopping piss off the floor—all of them wanted to confide to us their abiding love for Hezbollah and Nasrallah even when none of their peers was watching or listening. It wasn't an act for their fellows, or even for us. They didn't care if we wrote it down; they felt compelled to tell the story of their love affair with Hezbollah, and if it was for show, the audience was themselves. The Hezbollah men with the beards and radios who roamed throughout the complex weren't minders, making sure the refugees toed the party line when they spoke to reporters; everyone was working in concert in the first place. When it came time, for example, to talk about the hostilities that had just broken out, everyone in the garage simply echoed what Nasrallah himself had told the nation on television the night before. In the garage, the only complaint I heard was from refugees who wanted a television so they could watch Al-Manar, the Hezbollah satellite television station that to Israel's annoyance continued broadcasting despite the Israeli Air Force's persistent attempts to bomb it off the air.

Of course Hezbollah assiduously monitored the progress of its propaganda. If any of the volunteers with radios had given Assem Harb a look, he would have refused to talk to us. And just because no one was forcing them to talk to us didn't mean they all told the truth. As reporters for American news outlets we structurally were in league with the enemy, even if we happened to be seen as decent people. Therefore any partisan of the party would mindfully tell us the story that best served the party's propaganda aims. It's quite likely that Jihad Lakkis really was a trustworthy member of Hezbollah's auxiliaries rather than a full-time operator. But if he were a full member, or a reserve fighter, or a Hezbollah intelligence asset, he certainly wouldn't tell us; he would still describe himself as a Good Samaritan in the neighborhood just doing what he could to help the people of the Party of God. Hezbollah's party line held that the party and the people were indistinguishable, a position that encouraged some members of the inner circle and militia to keep their official duties secret. Most of the party's activists were civilians who supported Hezbollah by giving money, volunteering their weekends, serving on community boards for various party organs. Many civilian men partook in occasional military training so that in a time of crisis they could backfill the militia ranks. Even soft supporters paid close attention to Nasrallah's speeches and listened carefully to full party members. Without instruction, Hezbollah constituents intuitively grasped the propaganda points they were supposed to make; they learned the scripts and arguments from Nasrallah's speeches, Al-Manar programs, their prayer leaders, and their Hezbollah neighborhood wardens. When Nasrallah proclaimed that only civilians had remained in the South and that Israel targeted these innocents, the refugees understood without direct orders that they were to claim—entirely falsely—that they had seen no Hezbollah militants, that no Hezbollah fighters were firing rockets from village centers, and in fact, that no one who had been killed or wounded was a fighter at all.

Assem Harb embroidered the apparently true story of his family's flight with an extra layer of this bombast. In his village, he said, there were no fighters, just civilians. Same on the roads. To hear him talk, there wasn't a single Hezbollah fighter to be found in the whole country, just millions of innocent civilians, mostly women and children, haplessly falling to their deaths in a hail of unprovoked Israeli fire. For good measure, Assem hastened to tell us just how much he loved Hassan Nasrallah: "It would be a privilege to die for Sayyed Hassan. We are happy to sacrifice our homes if he asks us to." He meant it, but his zeal stemmed from his trust in the leader's judgment. He said he was willing to die for his leader, and he knew his leader didn't take that commitment lightly—in fact, Sayyed Hassan preferred to keep his followers alive when possible. Nasrallah really did care about the Shiites, Assem Harb believed, and the leader wanted to make them strong. Nasrallah didn't want his people to die needlessly, which is why Hezbollah encouraged men like Assem Harb to flee with their families.

You can beat cream with a whisk for a long time without seeing any change. Then, it abruptly goes thick, fluffs and turns to butter. Lebanon's sectarian essence had been churning for a long time; once the war started, it was a matter of days before it was whipped enough to take solid form. Feckless optimists hoped that Christians, Druze, Sunnis, and Shiites would rally to welcome each other into their homes and neighborhoods—which they did—and that somehow these natural and individual acts of kindness would plaster over the fissure between the "community of resistance" and the "community of accommodation." Several government officials mistook sectarianism for the great danger. They were afraid Lebanon would split between the Shiites on one side and all the other confessions on the other. In many ways, however, they were stuck mentally fighting the last war. Those sectarian divisions could strain but no longer dissolve Lebanese society, and in fact, they provided Hezbollah a magnificent opening. Alone among the country's political movements, Hezbollah understood how to claim the dividends of sectarianism while simultaneously transcending it. The Party of God galvanized its base through a shared Shiite experience, and then inspired that base along with a wider public by calling on them all to shed the old parochial shackles of sect and rally around the universal identity of Resistance. The Arabs in control of the government, comfortably bound to the axis of accommodation that ran through Amman, Cairo, and Riyadh and had a direct line to Washington, D.C., failed to notice that the bulging ranks of Hezbollah included plenty of Christians, Sunnis, and Druze. Hezbollah was a Shia Party of God but it was also a captain in the axis of resistance, a pan-Arab and pan-Islamic phenomenon that appealed across sect, race, and nationality.

As the early echoes of the bombs sounded over Beirut, the Sunnis and Christians in their safe areas were the most frightened. They were scared not of the Israelis but of the confident Shia swarming into their neighbor-hoods. On the busy shopping street of Mar Elias, across from the Class cell phone emporium, passersby scuttled away when I asked them if they were concerned that the conflict could reignite civil war. The panicked look on their faces suggested that they were very afraid, and that the wounds of the civil war had never healed or even fully scarred over. In a bakery, I started a conversation with a pair of local customers, urbane Sunni men in well-tailored dress shirts. They were polite but skittish and nervous, avoiding questions about the war and refusing to tell me their names. As we spoke a pair of lower-class Shiite refugees staying in a nearby school entered to buy bread, their headscarves tightly tucked under their chins. They happily identified themselves and bragged about the resiliency of the South and the vitality of Nasrallah—clearly identifying themselves with the Islamic Resis-tance. The bakery owner cut them off: "No conversations about politics in the shop, please." A Lebanese journalist was with me, a trilingual, wealthy Beiruti who considered herself open-minded but was decidedly scornful of the lower classes. At the bakery owner's words, she paled and said, "Let's go." For this colleague the displaced Shiites—poor, less educated, somehow foreign to the capital's Francophone elite—ignited class terror. It was simi-lar to the anxiety that crowds of homeless men camped in the tulip planters might arouse in the patricians of Park Avenue. The Lebanese journalist ran from the store, disappearing down the block without looking to see if I was following. I wasn't, instead loitering outside the shop to talk further with the Shiite ladies. A moment later the bakery owner sought me out. "Sorry I interfered with your work," he said to me in French. "People are so ner-vous now, so afraid. At least inside my store I want to keep things peaceful. It's all we can think about though. This war will be good for Hezbollah, good for the Shia, but I don't think it will be good for the rest of us, or for Lebanon."

At the Beirut port, a Greek Cypriot passenger ferry had been contracted to evacuate those who held foreign passports and were too frightened to drive over the mountains into Syria. American college students, their sum-mer abroad truncated, mingled on the dock with Lebanese expatriates who lived in France, the United States, or Africa, and were cutting short their family vacations. Already the richer Sunni and Christian districts were still as Pompeii; the upper classes had sought refuge in their summer homes.

All who remained in the city were Shiites, or poor Sunnis, Christians, and Druze, and a handful of true believers in a nonsectarian Lebanon, who insisted on staying in the capital in a vain effort to prove that decency prevailed over politics.

The Druze, a once-powerful sect now confined to a small patch of territory in the mountains, were as sanguine as Hezbollah about what was really taking shape under cover of the war with Israel: a rematch of the power struggle between those who prefer to fight and those who prefer to settle, which had played out again and again in Lebanon and throughout the Middle East. While many Druze lived and worked in Beirut, there weren't any distinctly Druze areas in the city. The Druze controlled the Chouf mountains, a contiguous piece of territory inland and south of Beirut. There were two rival Druze leaders, but the main one, Walid Jumblatt, held almost complete sway over the Chouf. His authority over the Druze paralleled Nasrallah's over the Shia, and the two groups were similarly overt about their sectarian identity and their internationalist pretensions. But the two men's styles couldn't have differed more. The Druze are an offshoot of Shia Islam, and the sect keeps its dogma and rituals a closely guarded secret. Druze communities are traditional, but religion is kept out of sight and conversation. As an outsider, it's almost impossible to distinguish a Druze from a completely secular person; Druze tenets seem to require complete pragmatism (which might explain why the Druze in Israel loyally serve the Jewish state while their cousins in Syria are equally loyal to the Ba'ath regime). Jumblatt was a charming patrician, comfortable speaking Arabic, French, or English, always ready to pour visitors a drink and discursively discuss a poet he had just discovered or the latest books about international affairs he had ordered from Amazon. He was also a warlord, in total command of a phalanx of tribal fighters who had secreted stashes of weaponry and ammunition throughout the mountains. Jumblatt received visitors deep in the Chouf in his family's fairy-tale palace in Mokhtara, an ancient-looking stone edifice with a fountain shaded by cedars, Ottoman-style wooden lattice work, a museum-quality collection of antiquities, and a small park full of deer. There on Fridays Druze men in traditional baggy pantaloons and turbans would petition Walid Bek, as their leader was known, to intercede in matters large and small—building permits, property disputes with neighbors, family blood feuds, electricity bills, a child in need of a job. In

Beirut, Jumblatt held court in a lovingly renovated neoclassical apartment building in Clemenceau, with a tiled courtyard shaded by an arched roof, and an interior paneled in light wood with cases to display a collection of hand-carved silver artifacts and mementos.

Unlike the bombastic Christian leaders, with their wooden turns of phrase and almost instinctive propensity for bullshit, Jumblatt spoke bluntly—even if he was equally famous for shameless about-faces when he saw the balance of power shifting. In the past he had allied with Syrians and with Hezbollah, but in recent years he had turned away from his leftist political roots and had grown suspicious of Hezbollah and Syria. Now, for the time being, Jumblatt was allied with the Sunni and Christian warlords in the government, and he was convinced that Hezbollah intended to use its militia to take over the country by force. "The overreaction of Israel is giving him [Nasrallah] an alibi. If you are faced with a leader who is on a divine mission, you can't argue with him. You can see what is happening on the ground." Most politicians were afraid to openly criticize Hezbollah, but not Jumblatt. He had already denounced Nasrallah for refusing to integrate his militia into the Lebanese military. There was no need, Jumblatt said, for a guerilla resistance under Hezbollah's control, armed, financed, and trained with the help of Iran and Syria. No need, Jumblatt cautioned, unless Hezbollah's real goal was to intimidate the parties in the government—all of which in 1991 had dismantled their militias in good faith to mark the close of the civil war. In the first week of the 2006 war, Jumblatt spoke to me and a colleague in the deserted reception room at Mokhtara. He wore jeans and his eyes were baggy from lack of sleep. He sat on a bench with his long legs extended, resting his hand on the head of a panting, lanky Shar-Pei dogs. He felt vindicated in his dire warnings about Hezbollah's recklessness but none too happy about it; Hezbollah had just led the entire country into a war in which everyone would suffer, Jumblatt said. But the war would weaken the government more than Hezbollah, he believed, and at the end of the fight with Israel Hezbollah would emerge as the darling of Lebanon's hard-liners—not only of the Shiites, but members of other sects who opposed American influence in the Arab world, loathed Israel, and yearned for the day when Muslims would fully eclipse Christians in Lebanon.

Hezbollah would impose its political will over the rest of Lebanon after the war, Jumblatt warned. His forecast sounded alarmist: the Shiites wanted a Shiite state, they were buying up land from Druze and Christians, they sought to do the bidding of their state sponsors in Tehran and Damascus, and they had no respect for minority rights and consensual, pluralistic decision making—a precondition for peace in a country with as many different distinct groups as Lebanon. Many in Lebanon dismissed Jumblatt as a hothead, and further discounted his views because just a few years earlier he'd taken a vituperative anti-American line, which he'd now completely reversed. But perhaps it took an opportunist to know an opportunist, and time bore out much of Jumblatt's analysis. Among Lebanon's warlords and political chiefs he could best understand Hezbollah because he was the only unreconstructed and unabashedly sectarian leader, who commanded the unwavering support of his base. He could face the outside world however he liked because he knew he had stitched up his own constituents. Hezbollah's community of true believers might have united around a more complex ideology than Jumblatt's followers, but they were similar in having the agency to plot a more autonomous path than their rivals. Lebanon's other warlords pretended that their movements were broad-based political factions. Jumblatt, however, was free from such a charade. He was a Druze leader, his followers were all Druze, and his only competition came from within the Druze community. Whether he ruled by the gun or by the dollar, in war or in patronage, he knew he had only as much power as he had followers willing to fight and die on his command. A decade and a half of peace had only begun the process of building institutions that could counter Lebanon's old warlords. It was slow work, and Jumblatt thought that in the face of a militant Hezbollah, most of Lebanese civil society would look to the old civil war parties for protection, even though none of them possessed any substantial street power any more. When I asked him whether he really believed that Hezbollah could force its resistance agenda on an unwilling Lebanese polity that cared little for perpetual war and religious mysticism, he replied with a sardonic question of his own. "How many guns do they have? How many guns does Hezbollah have?" A dry and mirthless laugh racked his rib cage. Hezbollah had what no other group had: dedicated legions of followers and a generous outside sponsor, Iran, willing to bankroll its militia. In his youth Jumblatt could drive to Damascus and drive a bargain for tanks and howitzers with Syria's President Hafez al-Assad. Now, like the rest of Lebanon's geriatric warlords, he had to content himself to fight over parliament seats and ministerial fiefs. Jumblatt was the loudest to sound the alarm about Hezbollah changing the rules of the power game, but he would also be the first to explore cutting a deal with Hezbollah if they were to be the new sheriffs in town.

As Jumblatt prophesied, thousands of displaced Shia were speaking the vernacular of insecurity, anger, and sectarianism. Refugees had blanketed Beirut. Literally. In Sanayeh Square, a park across from the Interior Ministry, hundreds of families had made camp. During the day, they hung their laundry and bed linens to air on the park's wrought iron fence. Lebanon's shape shifted. Every day tens of thousands of people, mostly Shiites, moved north. Within a few days, Nasrallah in a speech televised on Al-Manar had rallied the faithful for an unlimited war against Israel. "We are in our full strength and power," Nasrallah said.[7] "Hezbollah is not fighting a battle for Hezbollah or even for Lebanon. We are now fighting a battle for the Islamic nation."

In peacetime, Nasrallah's talk of the Islamic nation often referred to Shia empowerment, social mobilization, and the quest to win more political power for Hezbollah and its international allies. In wartime, his supporters defined the Islamic nation largely by what it stood against: Israel, Western-style atheists, and the extremists waging a Sunni-Shiite war in Iraq that distracted Muslims from their true enemies. An indignant sense of entitlement flowed through the lips of newly homeless people like Jumana Yassin, a young lawyer who had taken refuge with her extended family in a classroom in the mixed neighborhood around Mar Elias. Jumana, twenty-seven, taught at a private college in Beirut. She and her brothers lived on the third floor of an apartment building in the Dahieh about 200 meters from Hezbollah's administrative headquarters. Bunker busters had obliterated several Hezbollah buildings in the neighborhood, shattering the Yassins' windows. The family worried their apartment block might get hit. They hired two minivans, picked up some groceries, and drove from school to school looking for space. They settled in a classroom at the Ibn Rashid School. Someone had written on the chalkboard "Operation Truthful Promise. Victory is coming. We follow you, Nasrallah."

One of the brothers, Fouad Yassin, thirty-five, held his newborn baby daughter Hawra in his arms. She was six days old, delivered on July 9 at 1:25 a.m., the Sunday before Hezbollah abducted the Israeli soldiers and set off the war. She had thick and spiky black hair. "Her hair stands on end because of the bombing!" said her uncle, Bassam Yassin, thirty-nine. Both men laughed. Fouad's wife lay on a mat on the floor, silent. Fouad and Bassam and Jumana remembered the civil war well. They had spent countless days and nights in the basement when fighting strayed into their neighborhood. They could count as yuppies: Fouad was a book dealer, Bassam an engineer, and Jumana earned a good living teaching and practicing law. Their place was in the concrete towers of the Dahieh, however, and not amongst the glass offices and boutiques of West Beirut. The siblings were upset at the possible destruction of their family apartment, but they also took the current war as a shared responsibility, a kind of personal sacrament bestowed on all the Shia by Nasrallah. Fouad sounded like he was apologizing to us for seeking safety. "We did not want to leave," he said. His three-and-a-half-year-old son Mohammed couldn't sleep because of the sounds and vibrations from the bombs. He said the boy vomited all night.

"We didn't go to the underground shelter because it has rats and was dirty," Fouad said. "We were planning to stay. We did not want to leave. We were steadfast in our home. But our kids couldn't stand it anymore."

It was Jumana, though, who put into words the Shia exceptionalism fostered by Nasrallah's talk of the inevitable, divine victory. "Even if there might be political differences among us Lebanese, these differences should not be a factor when there's a real threat against the country," she said. "We're the ones being oppressed, we're the ones suffering. These differences will be put aside and people will unite. Since we're in the right, and as long as we're fighting for what's right, I think all the Lebanese people will fight with us." Jumana in a polite way was making a threat, the same threat Nasrallah had made to Lebanon at large: *We're the ones being oppressed.* That is, we the Shia. We are the ones suffering at Israel's hand. If we alone fight back and Israel strikes us all, we dare you to desert us. Join our fight, join us, or perhaps we might destroy you. *These differences will be put aside and people will unite.* Or else.

White collar or blue, turbaned or hatless, Hezbollah had united the Shiites with a call to arms for the dispossessed. Their enemies, they said, were those who hated justice and loved material comfort. Anyone who signed on with the Resistance Project was welcome. Anyone who joined ranks with the enemy by commission or omission had made their choice and must face the consequences. The ranks of the abhorrent included Sunni Muslim extremists who had declared the Shia apostates and were busily blowing up Shia by the dozens in Iraq; states like Saudi Arabia that funded Sunni fundamentalists and terror groups; Israel and the United States; and the Arab detractors of Iran and Syria. All these enemies gave the centurions of the Islamic Resistance a burning sense of purpose. "Our life is always suffering, but we are always smiling," Jumana said. "If Sayyed Hassan Nasrallah wants of us to live like this for a long, long, long, long time, we will do it, smiling in spite of all the suffering. The way of our life is to follow the line of Sayyed Nasrallah. That is my life. Maybe you suffer in your life, but always you must sacrifice for your goals."

Lebanon was in for thirty-four days of suffering, provoked by Hezbollah and meted out almost indiscriminately by the Israeli military. Like a forge, war changed the composition of the country that passed through it, and at the end burned away many of civil society's constructive fictions and left the hardened blade of power politics for Lebanon to fall upon. Versed in suffering after decades of war in their country, and eager to stage anew the Shiite passion play, Jumana and her family were well prepared for what was to come.

In 1991, by the end of the long civil war, it was clear that virtually no one had fought for principles. They had fought for the power of gangs, fascist-inspired militias that rallied around their religious sect or a feudal boss. Lebanon's warlords gathered in 1989 to negotiate a peace treaty at Taif, a town in Saudi Arabia not far from Mecca. In their hearts, they didn't seem any more interested in coexistence or building sectarian bridges than they had been in 1975. They had, however, fought to a stalemate. No one could win a substantial military victory, and eventually, they had found that war profiteering didn't bring in as much cash as a functioning economy with tourists and banks. So at the invitation of the rich Saudi royal family— whose princes promised sizable investment if Lebanon could get its act together, stop the civil war, and reopen the casinos, whorehouses, and beach resorts that made it so attractive to the rest of the Middle East—the lords of Lebanon called a ceasefire and assembled to craft a peace. In lieu of a real settlement, they opted for a round-robin of face saving: slight shifts gave the Muslims and the Christians an even amount of power, and everyone could go home and claim things could have turned out much worse.

And so the absurd system persisted. The balance of power had shifted in reality, but on paper each group kept the offices it had originally won. The Shiites, now clearly the most militarized and dynamic sect—and clearly destined by demographics to be the largest group by the turn of the century—could only name the speaker of parliament. The Taif Accords left in place the destructive sectarianism of the original constitution, and spelled out the exact sectarian spoils system whereby the seats in parliament and the senior jobs in the bureaucracy would be distributed. The agreement required the president and chief of the army to be a Christian but never outlined a durable democratic or legal framework for their selection. Taif was a recipe for persistent warlordism. Christians got to pick the president—but which Christians? And for that matter, who would represent the Shiites when it came time to pick the speaker of parliament? It was clear that in such a system, mass democratic appeal counted for far less than a core group of motivated supporters. The old *zaims* merrily whistled the familiar polka tune, convinced that the confessional system would preserve their domains forever. Meanwhile, Hezbollah was building a malleable Resistance identity on the cornerstone of Shia communalism, maneuvering through the sectarian spoils system while philosophically condemning it.

Some Lebanese dismissively referred to the main warlords of that period as the "seven dwarfs," a moniker that reflected some amount of self-disgust— why couldn't the cosmopolitan and resourceful people of Lebanon elevate more appealing leaders? Hezbollah remained above the fray, deputizing Nabih Berri's Amal Party to negotiate on behalf of all Shia—a brilliant move that allowed Hezbollah equal influence at the negotiations (Berri consulted them constantly) while keeping Hezbollah's hands clean in the eyes of the people.

The Sunnis made their own devil's bargain, successfully jockeying to serve as kingmakers, provisional rulers who could administer Lebanon until the more belligerent Christians and Shiites sorted out their business. Rafik Hariri, a billionaire businessman with close ties to Saudi Arabia, took over as prime minister. He cut a deal with the Syrians, the most important outside power in Lebanon; Syria had some tens of thousands of troops in Lebanon's highlands, and complete control over the country's intelligence services. (At the end of the civil war in 1990, Syria had 40,000 peacekeepers in Lebanon; by the time they pulled out in 2005, they still kept 14,000 fighting men in Lebanon.)

A temporary peace, like a fog, rolled over this fraying sectarian landscape during the 1990s. It was uneasy at best, people trying in public not to talk about the grievances of the civil war or to openly chart their sect's performance in the power sweepstakes. Rafik Hariri grew richer than ever while rebuilding downtown Beirut. Hariri's company built boutiques, cafés, a new parliament (the chamber of deputies was rarely as busy as the Starbucks or the swanky narghileh lounge next door) along the once forlorn Green Line that marked the boundary between Christian and Muslim militias. For decades, the historically enterprising Lebanese had trained their industrious sights on killing one another, with mind-boggling imagination. Now, they deployed the same energy to making money.

From 1991 to 2005, the Christians controlled a presidency and army that were only as relevant as Syria asked them to be; Damascus dictated Lebanon's security. With the civil war over, though, tourism was back, and Christians had the tourism ministry. A leader from the Lebanese Forces— once the most powerful of the Christian militias—ran the ministry, and made sure that regulations kept rental car businesses profitable, since he owned a major chain. The 14 million people in the Lebanese diaspora resumed summering in the motherland.[8] Dollars (and later euros) in hand, they took condos and cottages on the beach and in the mountains. They rented SUVs, shopped at the Virgin Megastore and the new Mac shop at the ABC Mall. All-night dance clubs with thudding bass lines proliferated.

There were plenty of cosmopolitan, good-natured Lebanese, especially in the younger generations, who wanted to set aside the rancor of the civil war and the Israeli invasion. Especially once the Israeli occupation of South Lebanon ended in May 2000, they looked to the future and imagined a nationalist, secular Lebanon, modern and prosperous and heterogeneous. Rancorous reality drowned out their voices: millions in Lebanon, allied with millions more across the Middle East, were still at war with Israel and had not moved on from the questions of violated sovereignty, disputed borders, occupied land, and Palestinian refugees displaced since 1948 (about 400,000 Palestinian refugees live in Lebanon). The old militias cast a shadow over the universities of Lebanon, the best-educated country in the Arab world. The parties of the seven dwarfs ran vicious campaigns for student council, a proxy to measure popular support since the rigged parliamentary elections revealed more about backroom gerrymandering than public sentiment. Informal sectarian quotas governed all public sector jobs. An applicant for a low-level position at the state-owned television network, for example, couldn't apply simply as a Lebanese. She needed sponsorship from one of the recognized sectarian parties, so that if hired she would count toward a quota. This system of sectarian patronage marginalized the multitudes of children of mixed marriages and all those who chafed at sectarian identity. A university lecturer I met was a typical case: a man in his twenties with an advanced degree in literature, a speaker of three languages, who was raised as an atheist socialist by a Sunni father and a Christian mother. Where in the sectarian maze did he fit? In that particular case, the ambitious young man in question followed the course of many similarly minded Lebanese: he went abroad to pursue a doctorate. His leftist parents had named him Jihad, after the Islamic term for the holy struggle to improve one's self and the world, a notion that appealed as much to secular idealists as to the religious. Hezbollah attracted many from this new generation, who could not match themselves to a sectarian palette. Many modern Lebanese, on the leading edge of Middle Eastern thought, invoked a transnational identity—for some flowing from Islam, for others from ideological confrontation with the West, a militant anti-imperialism that fit with sensibilities from the left and right—and found a plausible home for themselves in Hezbollah's axis of resistance.

Materialistic Beirutis, in thrall to their nightclubs and the growing scene of boutique bars and ostentatious restaurants, like the sushi restaurant that served raw fish in made-to-order ice sculptures, forgot that much of the country was not living their life and did not think like them. From 1991 onward they feasted on a peace dividend that never extended in equal measure to the Shia areas of the country. Numerically, the jet set was a tiny fraction of the country's population, but they made its image. The Lebanese on the whole are a pleasant, joyous people, but there's a great variety in degree. For every cocaine-snorting convertible-driving dandy in Beirut, many more Lebanese lived on the periphery, partaking in simpler pleasures: a swim in the sea, a fresh fish dinner, a water pipe, a game of backgammon, a night watching TV on the porch by generator power. In the 1990s, while contractors built condominiums and resort hotels in Beirut and high-flying tourists gambled at the casino in Jounieh and sampled the whores at the "super night clubs," the Israeli military still occupied southern Lebanon. One-tenth of the country's population lived in "the zone," under an arbitrary and violent military rule enforced mostly by the collaborationist South Lebanon Army. Hezbollah led a popular guerilla war against the Israelis that kept casualties high until Israel withdrew in 2000.

The Shia in southern Lebanon were historically small farmers, peasants, and laborers. The Amal Party and then Hezbollah won their loyalty, in part by not dictating an ultra-religious lifestyle. The Southerners were known as an easygoing and hospitable lot, who liked their food and coffee, their cards and dominoes and backgammon, their tobacco, their liquor, and not infrequently, their marijuana. Once in the 1980s Hezbollah tried to preach austerity, in the manner of the Iranian ayatollahs, and popular support plummeted. They retreated quickly, and never again tried to enforce any moral code on the general public. After all, Hezbollah's strength flowed from its following, not its religious pedigree.

Despite their laissez-faire lifestyles and fabulous beaches, the Shia in the South never forgot that much of the rest of Lebanon—that is, unoccupied Lebanon—ignored their struggle against Israel. Why they did so is immaterial; some Lebanese wanted to get on with their lives after the long civil war, others believed the Shiites invited a rough life on themselves by resisting the Israelis rather than collaborating, still more felt a cultural disdain for the Southerners and their distant suffering. Either way, most of the Christians and the Druze and Sunnis cared not a whit for the suffering of occupied South Lebanon, erecting a huge cultural barrier between the Shia and all the other sects. Hezbollah's innovation was to frame this divide not in sectarian terms but as a matter of resistance. In this formulation, the occupied South fought the Israelis so that the rest of Lebanon might enjoy its freedom. The fight wasn't a Shia fight (even if most of the fighters were Shia); it was a sanctified struggle of the Resistance community, open to all. Those who ignored the plight of the South for the most part came to feel ashamed, and allowed Hezbollah to assume a position as the nation's moral conscience. Fun lovers could go about their hedonistic ways and let the Islamic Resistance do the fighting for them—but under this compact, in which Hezbollah became custodian of the nation's honor, the pacifists and moderates and accommodationists slowly lost their authority. When the Israelis finally left in 2000, the people who had turned away while Hezbollah defined a new community found that the Islamic Resistance had gathered such momentum and built such an operation that it had broken conclusively out of the state's reach. In fact, it seemed poised to eclipse the state entirely, or subsume it.

The rebranding of the "new Lebanon" fooled only outsiders. The Lebanese themselves remained well aware of their bitter divisions and the pathologically violent reflexes of their men. The civil war was over but their country was still at war, and would be until the Great Game resolved between Resistance and Accommodation, Saudi Arabia and Iran, Israel and Palestine, the United States and the rest. Who could you trust? Former Prime Minister Rafik Hariri threw the country into turmoil when he quit the establishment and broke the deal he had made with the Syrians. Rich enough, proud enough, perhaps even nationalistic and independent-minded at a critical point, Hariri chose to confront the Syrians, and ask them to end their direct control over Lebanon's internal security. The gambit appealed to independent-minded Lebanese of many stripes, who believed that Syria and Hezbollah were making Lebanon an international pariah. Hariri wasn't a maverick; he was a billionaire whose every political move was made in consultation with his backers in the Saudi Arabian royal family. Syria ran its own Lebanese network of informants and secret police, surveillance and border control, torture chambers, prisons, military bases, and arms supply networks. Hariri gambled that he and his backers and his allies were powerful enough to force a Syrian drawdown, at worst reducing Syria's direct control and at best propelling the country onto a more independent trajectory. He resigned as prime minister and campaigned against Syrian influence. In his personal game of brinksmanship, Hariri lost. In February 2005 a bomb tore through his motorcade, leaving only scraps of his flesh including a severed ring finger. The explosion sheared off the front of the Hotel St. Georges and blew a hole in the Corniche deep enough to swallow a tank. The assassination was a work of bravado; it was assumed that such a complex attack required some cooperation from the ubiquitous Syrian intelligence. It was too brutal and obvious an act to stand. Lebanese who had been content to swallow their pride and seethe (or collaborate) under Syrian tutelage blew their fuses.[9] They took to the streets and asked Syria to leave.

Much was made of the competing street protests that followed. On March 8, 2005, Nasrallah summoned hundreds of thousands to a rally thanking Syria for its largesse. On March 14, a much larger demonstration brought as many as a million into downtown Beirut, calling for the Syrians to leave. The outpouring was too great; Syria had to relent to the international community and the will of the Lebanese, and announced it would withdraw its troops in a rush, just as Israel had five years earlier. The demonstration dates led to the names for the two camps that spent the next years vying for domination: March 8 referred to Hezbollah's coalition, and March 14 to Hariri's, inherited by Rafik's inarticulate son Saad. Both movements took on the name of those dates to evoke the people power at their core.[10] Crowds swamped Solidere, the rebuilt downtown, gathering in front of the mosque where Hariri would be buried. Everyone showed up, from every sect and class, women in designer heels and women in velour sweat suits, men from West Beirut with nose jobs and men from the Dahieh with no jobs. Some linked arms in fraternity, pledging to put Lebanon first. Others merely shared in street theater and chanted irreconcilable slogans. Pro-independence Lebanese in the crowd wanted Syria out, but even the widely shared endorsement of an independent Lebanon foundered when it came to foreign intervention. Depending on where your interests lay, you might consider Syria and Iran to be destructive manipulators waging their own wars in Lebanon but you might welcome the involvement of the Saudis and the French. One man's help was another's outside interference. If the foreign overlords ever got out of the way the Lebanese would have to duke it out for control themselves.

The resistance bloc had no desire to expel Syria, but if the Syrians were leaving anyway, they would need the new political order to guard their interests. The euphoria of the March 14 crowd was less strategic: they wanted Syria out, they wanted freedom, but they hadn't thought too much about how to secure it. People had different names for the uprising that sealed Syria's fate. At first, most people called it "Independence Intifada" or "Intifada 2005," but some people worried how the name would sell in Washington. They started to call it "The Cedar Revolution." As Syria left, a string of mysterious assassinations ensued, which decimated the ranks of independent Lebanese intellectuals who might have staked a claim to the middle ground between the axes of Resistance and Accommodation. Most Lebanese assumed that Syria and the network of local agents it built during decades of occupation had a hand in the killings. President Bush declared the uprising a victory for democracy in the Middle East, and Arab reformers trumpeted the apparent victory of a popular uprising against a despotic Arab dictatorship. The free Lebanese people had triumphed over the venal Syrian Ba'athists, the narrative went.

In fact, for the Lebanese a deferred day of reckoning would come. Without a foreign master in the house, two ideologies would have to compete for primacy. The forces of March 14 had an appealing mien. They opposed dictatorship, they stood for the comparatively free pursuit of wealth and happiness, values and aspirations that sat well with Westerners from liberal democracies. Like secular liberal reformists throughout the Middle East, however, they suffered from a fuzzy lack of definition. They wanted freedom for people to live their lives, but they didn't have an answer for the questions that animated the angriest passions in the region: What to do about Israel? What to do about the Palestinians? How to make room for the aspirations of Islam? What about the lack of economic development and the apalling levels of government corruption? Hezbollah had the advantage of clarity and an active agenda: rapture, resistance, revolution. Lebanon had long been a trailblazer for the Middle East, to which it already had bequeathed a pair of sordid legacies: confessionalism and endless, total civil war. Both Lebanese hallmarks, in fact, were helping to shape a murderous new disorder in Iraq. Now Hezbollah would wrestle with the pragmatists to promote another trope, the winners of history. No more fetishization of Arab defeat; the Islamic Resistance had come to believe it was shaping a new historical reality, in which dedicated Muslims and their supporters, playing a very long game, could equalize the military and political imbalance in the war against the United States, Israel, and their allies.

By the time it was warm enough to swim in the Mediterranean in 2006, Lebanese politics had melted down. In the context of a "national dialogue," the March 14 warlords who dominated the government had held talks with Hezbollah, Amal, and the Aounists who formed the opposition. They had demanded that Hezbollah disband its militia, like all the rest had done at the end of the civil war. Hezbollah had kept its arms then because of the Israeli occupation, but the defanged warlords said that with Israel gone since 2000, it was time for Hezbollah to become a "normal political party." Hezbollah refused, offering various pretexts like Israel's continued occupation of the Shebaa Farms, the southwest side of the mountain known to Arabs as Jabal Sheikh and to Jews as Mount Hermon. On the day the Lebanese state had an army capable of repelling an Israeli assault, Nasrallah said, he would begin to consider cashiering his militia. The talks broke down, but they had never been real. Their entire vocabulary was delusional. Hezbollah never practiced "normal" politics. Hezbollah's organization was decidedly modern, but the enthusiasm of its followers was mystical—grounded in faith, identity politics, testosterone, youthful idealism, and the urge to fight. Hezbollah wasn't a family property, its leadership handed from father to son like most of Lebanon's movements. As the custodian of the Islamic Resistance it offered its members a rallying point, a way of life, rather than just a mundane slice of patronage. The supposedly "normal" political parties were hangovers from the civil war, cults of personality built around warlords who bequeathed the leadership to their children or relatives. Those that had surrendered their weapons only did so because they had been destroyed militarily. Some still operated with fascist trappings like ancient insignia, choreographed rallies, a slavish devotion to the leader, and in many cases a cult devoted to the leader's family. All of the parties fanned hysteria amongst their followers, riling them into a state of fear (the other sects are plotting to shut us out of power entirely!) and indoctrinating the young into Lebanon's sectarian ethos in militaristic summer camps. They liked wearing camouflage but they didn't seem really eager to fight again.

They were like children playing war but still afraid of thunder. Tourists were tentatively starting to return, some investment had taken root, and businesses small and large were counting on a banner summer travel season to flood cash into the economy. At the end of June, despite the political problems, Lebanon looked rosy. Cargo ships were unloading hundreds of new Mercedes, BMWs, and Ford Explorers for the rental market. Several new nightclubs had opened in downtown Beirut. Middle East Airlines, the local flag-carrier, was expanding its routes.

War came unexpectedly to Hezbollah in 2006, a stumble for an organization that took such pride in its planning. Since Israel's withdrawal in 2000, Hezbollah and Israel had clashed sporadically. An occasional rocket fired from southern Lebanon, a few shells fired back from Israel in retaliation. A few Hezbollah commandos would cross into Israel and sometimes would get caught or killed. Hezbollah rebuilt a line of bunkers along the border. Nasrallah had said again and again that Hezbollah's primary military goal was to secure the release of Lebanese prisoners held in Israel and the return of Lebanese dead. The way forward, he said, was to seize Israeli captives and trade them. Dozens of Hezbollah fighters in civilian clothes swarmed the divided town of Ghajar, which straddles the border, half in Israel and half in Lebanon. They attacked an Israeli military post in an attempt to capture soldiers. The Israelis fended them off, and not much came of the incident.

In July 2006, Israel was engaged in a small war in Gaza. Palestinian militants had taken an Israeli soldier, Gilad Shalit, and Israel was dithering on Gaza's edges, maneuvering tanks, making minor incursions—not quite a war, but something like the beginning of one. On Wednesday, July 12, Hezbollah struck Israel's northern border. Commandos had tried similar raids in the past. This time, they succeeded. A Hezbollah team snuck over the border into Israel, hid in the bushes, and ambushed an Israeli military convoy. It took nearly an hour for the Israeli command to learn of the attack; by then, two Israeli soldiers had disappeared over the border into Lebanon, along with all the Hezbollah fighters.[11]

Nasrallah had authorized the raid. He had consulted with his patrons in Tehran and Damascus on Hezbollah's general strategy, to seize Israeli soldiers to trade for prisoners. There was no need to clear every single specific operation once their allies were on board. Hezbollah didn't expect Israel to respond with total war. The party hadn't placed villages on high alert, or warned civilians to steer clear of border zones. Military leaders had not mobilized Hezbollah's full-time fighters or part-time guardsmen. In southern Beirut, party cadres went to work in the concrete office blocks that were always among Israel's first targets during the frequent wars with Lebanon.

As soon as they discovered that soldiers were missing, Israeli commanders sent a tank in hot pursuit across the border toward Aita Shaab, and it immediately ran over a mammoth antitank mine that destroyed it. Within hours, eight Israeli soldiers were dead, two were missing, and a Merkava tank was in shreds. The Israeli response was potent but disorganized, a harbinger of things to come. By noon, Israel had bombed the bridges connecting southern Lebanon to Beirut, in a vain effort to stop Hezbollah from spiriting its Israeli captives out of reach. Hezbollah fired Katyusha rockets into Israel. On television, it looked like a full-fledged war by Thursday morning. The runway of the Beirut airport was in flames. The Israeli navy had blockaded the coast. Civilians burned to death in their cars driving in search of a safe place. Highway overpasses were instantaneously reduced to piles of rubble. Cameras panned over a motley assortment of different-sized rubble piles, that staple of war footage that could come from anywhere, depicting the ruins that could have once been a house, a bridge, a bunker, a goat shed. Hezbollah and Israel Defense Forces spokesmen blustered about their demands. And there on television was Nasrallah, leisurely speaking at the end of every day as if the war were an ancient Greek tragedy and he the chorus. On Friday night, in a piece of emblematic showmanship, Nasrallah instructed his viewers to turn to the sea. On cue—out in the real world, on the high seas—a C-802 missile struck an Israeli navy destroyer, killing a sailor and shocking Israeli intelligence. Until that instant no one knew Hezbollah had such sophisticated weaponry. Nasrallah knew that Hezbollah could no more cripple the Israeli navy and break the blockade than it could challenge Israel's bombers. But one Cornet antiship missile, deployed with fanfare, could strike fear into Israel and inspire the Arab world: an emblematic and brilliant propaganda strike. Hezbollah had pierced the bow of a supposedly impregnable Israeli destroyer. The all-powerful Israeli conquerors had tripped. Defeat was unnecessary. It would suffice for Hezbollah to draw a bit of blood and humiliate the enemy. Just one missile, its symbolic value worth the same as a hundred.

There, on Saturday, was Lebanese Prime Minister Fouad Siniora, a man with a bitter distaste for Hezbollah, weeping in his address to the nation. *Please stop,* he seemed to be saying. *Why are you doing this to us, Hezbollah and Israel?* And what he said in fact sounded a futile cry, like a chained dog baying in the night at some phantom quarry: "Lebanon will remain, will remain, will remain." It would remain, but not as the country Siniora inherited when his friend and mentor Rafik Hariri was blown to bits. For Lebanon, everything was uncertain. For the Middle East, too; occupied Iraq was sinking into sectarian carnage and America's democracy project was on the march, no one was sure in which direction, claiming a balance sheet of Arab regimes and regular people as collateral damage. Israel had moved rightward, building walls around Palestinian cities and giving up on the Oslo Accords. Lebanese reformers played their own part in undermining any momentum for genuinely secular liberal democracy; they had resorted to sectarianism and demagoguery, demonizing their rivals and riling up hatred rather than articulating a coherent program. Iran's feckless reformists had lost to another hard-liner in the 2005 presidential elections. Change was no less in the air for militant Islam, which nihilistic Al Qaeda had threatened to hijack from the broader mass of angry and politicized Muslims. The resistance axis shared some of Al Qaeda's tactics but none of its fanatical Wahhabi puritanism, which just as soon justified killing deviant Muslims as it did foreign infidels. Siniora might as well have been crying for the whole experiment of secular moderation.

All sides played theater. Israel bombed an overpass that had soared across a valley in Mount Lebanon, a gracious span, an engineering marvel, admired as the tallest bridge in the Middle East. The Israeli Air Force with precision rocketed the lamp in the Beirut lighthouse, a romantic hundred-year-old stone landmark. Hezbollah sent rockets as far south as Tiberias, on the Sea of Galilee, to show their range. Israel stood ready to fight symbols with symbols; the Israeli military's chief of staff had just adopted a new doctrine that played right into Hezbollah's hands. The new approach, called "effects-based warfare," pivoted on a novel idea: make your enemy feel like a loser, and he will have lost. Why storm a hill with real live men if you can achieve the same military objective by filming a flag and showing it on TV? It doesn't matter how many people you kill or how much land you seize; your enemy is only defeated when he *thinks* he's defeated.[12] Israel hoped for a speedy victory, and meant to show Hezbollah—and all Israel's enemies, in the Arab world, in Iran, in the West, who thought the Jewish state was going soft—that its war muscles still were primed. Among their most coveted targets was Al-Manar satellite television.

Al-Manar, The Beacon, is the nervous system of the Hezbollah community. Many nations, including Germany and the United States, consider Al-Manar so important that they've listed the network as a terrorist organization in its own right independent of Hezbollah. The United States government pursues Al-Manar as assiduously as it does Hezbollah's trigger pullers. In April 2009 a Pakistani businessman on Staten Island was sentenced to more than five years in prison for selling satellite television packages that included Hezbollah's television station to customers in the United States.[13] Hezbollah's opponents sometimes overstate the raw power of Al-Manar, as if to suggest that without satellite television the militia would lose its legions of supporters or military strike capacity. But on the whole they're right; once Hezbollah chose to become a mass movement, it needed the public sphere, and no network of clerics and underground cells can replicate the reach of television. Without exaggeration, Hezbollah has built its culture on the foundation of Al-Manar, and to the extent that the party cares to make a broader case to outsiders, it largely does so on the small screen. Hezbollah's military planning takes place under a cone of silence, but its ideology flourishes in the sunlight; the Party of God wants to shape a world movement. Like evangelists anywhere the party wants to spread its good news far and wide, which it does through the long arm of television. Hezbollah's myths, its didactic poetry, its political thought, and its platform air around the clock on Al-Manar, and hundreds of thousands watch it. Beyond the Party of God's followers, the wider world also watches Al-Manar whenever Hezbollah breaks into the broader consciousness, as it did in May 2000 and during the 2006 war, when Nasrallah made Al-Manar his own *diwan,* or salon. Almost every night he held forth from a carpeted and cozy studio in an undisclosed location, comforting his angry family of millions with confident, confiding hour-long talks, fireside chats for the whole Islamic world.

Nasrallah took to the airwaves to explain everything in his singsong lisp, his voice occasionally climbing, breaking into a theatrical rasp for emphasis. He would talk about Israel's military tactics and strategy, about the internal struggles among Israeli politicians, and how the rifts would affect the campaign against Lebanon. He would outline Hezbollah's goals, reveal successes on the battlefield, and explain away the failures. Where Hezbollah had repulsed Israelis, Nasrallah would praise the overwhelming power of the resistance; where Israel had displayed superior force, Nasrallah would confide how—given America's limitless backing of the Jewish state—the fact that Hezbollah had made any stand at all proved that the resistance could rattle the world's superpowers. Once the leader finished, Al-Manar would romp onward with its twenty-four-hour programming. Long shots of destroyed homes and bomb craters. Interviews with survivors and the wounded. Political reportage. Talk shows about the resistance. All of it bookended with inspirational videoclips, meant to steel the people and buck up the fighters. Great swelling bagpipes would introduce the segments, updated every couple of hours with fresh images from the war. A typical example might show the rolling hills of South Lebanon; cut to the smoking rubble of a bombed building in south Beirut; quickly cut again to three Hezbollah fighters forging through the brush with Katyusha rockets on their backs; cut to footage of a weeping Israeli; and then finally to an animated cartoon rose bursting forth from the soil. On the soundtrack, Hezbollah's house band would belt out zippy refrains, in a musical style part Klezmer and part marching band:

> *Who's going to save you? Hezbollah, Hezbollah.*
> *Who's going to protect you? Hezbollah, Hezbollah.*
> *You're a gun, you're a flower, you're a rose, you're a martyr.*
> *You're the prince of men, you're Hezbollah!*

Israel vowed to take Al-Manar, which it called "Terror TV," off the air. Hezbollah disputed the terrorist label, but otherwise agreed that Al-Manar was as central to the Islamic Resistance as the officers managing the Katyusha batteries at the border. The Party of God refused any distinction between its civil and military functions. Everything was integrated in a seamless web: warfighting, newscasting, intelligence, political strategy, community organizing, health care, on and on. On the second day of the war, Israel strafed Al-Manar. The staff had practiced, and quickly evacuated the building. The station went into emergency mode, leaving only fifteen employees at the headquarters building in Haret Hreik, the security quarter of the Dahieh that housed Hezbollah's most important facilities. The rest dispersed to other secret locations. The network kicked into overdrive, recalibrating all its programming to gird its audience for war. Well versed in the business end of Israeli airpower, all Hezbollah institutions had contingency plans for bombardment. Al-Manar sent home about half its four hundred employees. There was no need for everyone at the station to risk life and limb, general manager Abdallah Kassir explained, and it would be prudent to keep experienced employees rested and in reserve for the aftermath of any crisis.[14]

The next strike on the station was meant to be fatal. On Sunday, July 16, only a few staffers were on hand to hear the muffled thud with which Al-Manar's high-rise came down on their heads. A roar rang out over Beirut, bouncing off the mountains that created a sort of acoustic drum around the city. Miles from the blast site in a seaside café in West Beirut, the sheer force of the Israeli bunker buster's blast tickled my stomach, sparking a jolt of dread before the lagging sound reached my ears. I heard a low roar, abruptly truncated as if a wave had hit a breakwater. A slight tremor followed, and a second nervous pitch in the belly. It was all over in a second or two.

Instantly, most everyone knew Al-Manar had been hit. Across Lebanon and the whole Arab world, war spectators and stakeholders alike had tuned into the station (it was reportedly playing in the Kirya, the Israeli military headquarters in Tel Aviv, as well as in virtually every home and public space in Lebanon). The image on the screen dissolved into static. Al-Manar was off the air. In the Dahieh, Kassir had been working in an office nearby. He felt the blast, and saw his broadcast go to snow. Within seconds, his cell phone in hand, he rushed up the street toward the site of the building. An acrid smell filled the air: silt, building debris, explosive, a vile potpourri of charred and burning detritus. Kassir knew the death toll couldn't be too high since he'd ordered most of his employees elsewhere.

He ran toward the crater, cell phone to his ear while another Hezbollah official briefed him on the damage. At the edge of the smoking hole, he dialed more Hezbollah officials, summoning rescue teams to search for the trapped employees. "We had wounded and injured," he said. "There were fifteen people inside! It was during that time that I was making phone calls and giving instructions about our wounded employees inside the building that we went off the air." Hezbollah security had already dispatched men to the site, while Al-Manar's staff was scrambling to resume broadcasts from a secondary location. Kassir was so confident that the redundant systems would automatically kick in that he neglected to call his engineers until several minutes had elapsed. It was an uncharacteristic lapse of discipline. "Those were the two minutes that Al-Manar went dark," he said. "When I finally called my engineer, I learned that our uninterrupted power supply had failed. I had to give an order to get another power system running." Even years later he was a trifle embarrassed to recall the instant: he meant to deliver perfection, and he fell short.

Still out of breath from his run, Kassir finally sorted out the technical issues. Al-Manar's broadcast resumed, the unflappable announcers going about their business as if nothing had happened. Kassir, though, saw a marketing opportunity in the attack. "The voice of the resistance cannot be silenced!" he declared, with the penchant for sloganeering that contaminates acres of Hezbollah rhetoric. That was the tagline for the melodramatic video Al-Manar immediately produced. It depicts an Arab family watching Al-Manar on a couch in a cavernous living room the size of a temple. The smiling family is meant to represent the archetypical Muslim hearth. The man wears a white gown. Israeli jets swoop through the sky toward their target, Al-Manar. Then, a huge explosion. In an animated sequence, a pulsing white beam connecting the earth to a satellite—drawn in dark brown comic-book hues—goes dead. In the great living room, a blank screen confronts the suddenly anxious Arab family. *Will the voice of the resistance be silenced?* Of course not! Men scramble in the concrete wreckage. The animated transmission tower shudders with light. A white beam shoots upward and connects with the satellite. The family smiles once again as an Al-Manar announcer reassures them: *The resistance can never be silenced.*

"In the war, when Manar stopped, CNN television and Israeli television almost directly aired that Manar had been taken off the air—as if they knew it was about to happen," Kassir said, and laughed. "But their happiness was short-lived. We were only off the air for two minutes. They wanted to silence Al-Manar, but they failed."

All told, Hezbollah says, Al-Manar was bombed fifteen times, but its transmission never faltered after the first hiccup. It would have been a real disaster for Hezbollah if they'd lost Al-Manar during the war. Their propagandizing depended on it. That's how Nasrallah succeeded at framing the war. Israel spoke in many voices but Hezbollah spoke in one, a single voice that talked at length for an hour or more almost every night. Through Al-Manar, Hezbollah could tell a bedtime story about the gladiatorial faceoff between the Islamic Resistance and the Godless forces that wanted to cram the "New Middle East" down their throats.

On the first day of the 2006 war Inaya Haidar was fighting the crowds, improbably pushing her way south toward the bombs through a tide of friends and neighbors fleeing in the opposite direction. A twenty-two-year-old Shia nurse and self-professed daughter of the South, Inaya had spent the morning at a conference at the American University of Beirut Medical Center. When she heard that war had broken out, Inaya rushed to the bus station in her narrow-cut dress skirt and high heels. Although she was young for the post, Inaya worked as the nursing supervisor at the Najem Hospital in Tyre, the coastal city that sat at the junction of all the tiny roads to the hamlets of South Lebanon. Most refugees, and more important, most casualties, would pass through Tyre on their way to safer and more developed cities further north, closer to Beirut. "If I didn't show up at the hospital, how could I expect the other nurses to work?" Inaya said.[15]

Her worried father called her cell phone; over and over Inaya ignored his calls. She knew he would tell her to stay in Beirut, and she didn't want to disobey him. She would phone him once she had made it to Tyre. The Litani crossing already had been bombed. Inaya and two male passengers waded through the shallow muck at the spot in Abou Deeb's banana plantation where Hezbollah would later build a temporary earthen berm so vehicles could ford the river. On the far bank she found another taxi, and by late afternoon was at her post in the Najem Hospital, where she would remain on duty nonstop for thirty-four days.

That's where I met her a week later. She had two pairs of scrubs, one to wear while the other was in the wash. Her hospital emergency room had become a gruesome triage station. Families driving to safety would often career into the Najem Hospital parking lot—it was on the southern edge of the city and was one of the first buildings a driver encountered on the approach to Tyre—with a bloody or staggering relative who'd been shot or shrapneled. On the day I met her, she and her colleagues were treating the Srour family, civilians all, dual German-Lebanese citizens. The Srours' car was rocketed a few meters from the hospital entrance; from the air their Renault might have looked like the kind of SUV or truck that Hezbollah fighters use. Outside, the car was still in flames. Inside, Inaya was introducing journalists to the surviving members of the Srour family, including a small boy whose face had been gouged by shrapnel. His lips were ripped back, exposing his jaw, and his burnt eye sockets had swollen and completely shut his eyes.

Inaya kept her good cheer, bent on maintaining morale among her patients and colleagues. She wore her waist-length hair uncovered, and when she wasn't working she liked to leave it loose. She had exceptionally large and round brown eyes, and long eyelashes. When she spoke, she held eye contact for the whole conversation, with a slightly unnerving but warm intensity. When she listened, she often tilted her head, smiling faintly, her lips shut; and whenever anyone made a joke she was quick to laugh. Inaya was devoutly religious. Her father, a math teacher and high school administrator, had raised his four daughters and one son in the glow of Islam, science, and education. All his girls were proud, independent, resourceful, with none of the provincial suspicion that deadened the curiosity of many Hezbollah hard-liners. Inaya loved asking foreigners questions, and she looked forward to our daily visits to the hospital, where we'd check for casualties from any newsworthy airstrikes or battles. She spoke fluent English and French, and—unusual for a Hezbollah supporter—intuitively sympathized with the efforts of foreign correspondents. She believed that most reporters tried to tell the truth, and that our reports from Lebanon would help the dispossessed. She could afford to be more open than her colleagues at the Jabal Amel Hospital on the other end of town, which treated the Hezbollah fighters. Najem only admitted civilians.

Inaya wasn't working for Hezbollah, and spent the war on call at her hospital of her own accord, and not because the party asked her to. At the same time, her motives weren't far from Hezbollah's either. Her father wasn't a member, but was an early supporter. Her younger sisters had taken the veil and were active in the Mahdi Scouts, Hezbollah's youth wing. Her older sister had married a Hezbollah fighter. Their village in the hills above Tyre had been a front-line staging ground for the resistance during Israel's occupation from 1982 to 2000, and many of her relatives had fought, some in Hezbollah's militia, some in Amal's militia, and some for the Communists. Inaya's father encouraged his children to study useful trades like engineering or medicine. He also encouraged them to pray and study the Koran; in his living room he kept a small library of tomes about Islamic jurisprudence. They lived on the outskirts of Srifa on a hill known as a Hezbollah neighborhood. Inaya and her father didn't consider themselves members of Hezbollah because they hadn't officially joined the party and weren't employed by any of its manifold institutions. But they considered themselves far more than supporters; they claimed Hassan Nasrallah as their sole political leader, and saw Hezbollah for the time being as the only legitimate representative of Lebanese nationalism, of Islamism, and of Shia aspirations for political enfranchisement.

Like many Southerners who still smarted from the years of Israeli occupation, Inaya believed the freedom she'd known since 2000 could easily be ripped from her hands. Hezbollah's aggressive moves unnerved outsiders, but party loyalists like Inaya assessed their fortunes with an exaggerated sense of communal insecurity; no matter how much weight Hezbollah could throw around, they always saw it as one step away from extinction at the hands of imperial enemy forces. Inaya supported Hezbollah for two reasons above all else: it never wavered in its war against Israel, and it never compromised its Islamic credentials. The party gave her external security, by deterring the Israeli military, and personal security by setting an example of Islamic morality.

Tyre, the coastal city where Inaya worked, was a sailor's town. Its modern precincts huddled on a bulbous peninsula connected to the mainland by a narrow isthmus, giving it the effect of a city marooned offshore. A vast ancient Phoenician metropolis separated the city from the mainland. On either side sprawled the unceasingly ugly and unplanned concrete of modern Lebanon; but on the alluvial spit of land sprouted an Edenic vision of pre-modern Tyre. The Phoenicians launched their empire from Tyre, which was one of the prize cities of the Levant for a millennium before the beginning of the Common Era. The antiquities were only haphazardly excavated. Wildflowers and grass grew in tufts along the main avenue. Uncatalogued marble statuary littered a graveyard and an agora. Through a temple the walkway led to a vast hippodrome. No signs or guides explained the ancient ruins; they'd been dug up, fenced, and opened to the public with no narrative or presentation, like an art installation. Christians give present-day Tyre much of its salty-dog flavor. Their neighborhood, the Phanar, hugged the northwest shore of the city, from its eponymous lighthouse to the harbor. The fishermen set out every night from the jetties beneath a collapsing nineteenth century mansion. At dawn they returned, and once they sold their catch and mended their nets they retired just a few steps away to the cafés where they drank beer and arak. A meandering walk past the Archbishopric led to the old prison, a local Shia militia intelligence post and a few bars decorated in a tacky wooden-yacht-Key-West style. Amal ruled the city, as a sort of regent for Hezbollah. Rowdy drinkers and small-time crooks tended to get along better with the more flexible Islamists of Amal than with the true believers in Hezbollah. But everyone knew that behind Amal's comparatively soft hand lurked the rigid power of the *Hezb*—the Party.

In the summertime, fifty wooden shacks were erected on Tyre's wide and undulating public beach, one of the sweetest strips of sand along the entire eastern Mediterranean coast. Nearly naked men and women preened in the shallows, and then repaired to the shacks for beer and grilled fish. Before Nasrallah took over Hezbollah in 1992, his more uncompromising and less wise predecessors attempted to force a harsh vision of Islamism on the South—and not just in homogeneous Shia villages but also in the seats of relatively cosmopolitan hedonism like Tyre. For a few years in the late 1980s and early 1990s, restaurants served alcohol surreptitiously in opaque mugs, and women swam fully clothed on Tyre's public beach. Smoking and dominoes were frowned on. The people of Tyre choked on this moral policing; Lebanon isn't Iran, they said, and they turned away from Hezbollah even if they recognized its power over their city. Nasrallah saw the mistake in this approach; Hezbollah already had the allegiance of the faithful, and it needed good will from people on the margins to expand its power. After 1992, when Nasrallah was elected secretary-general of Hezbollah, the booze flowed freely in Tyre, the beach robes came off, and people could smoke their waterpipes and play backgammon without trouble. Nasrallah's decision was pragmatic; he certainly didn't endorse immoral, un-Islamic behavior. But he chose Hezbollah's battles deliberately, and in the great game, he wanted first to beat Israel and then to win Lebanon. Afterward the party could worry about perfecting Islamic rule and spreading it over all society.

Typical of Tyre's denizens was Issam Moussa, the sometime United Nations employee I convinced to translate for me during the 2006 war. Issam Moussa grew up in Freetown, Sierra Leone, and spoke English with theatrical flair and a lilting West African enunciation. Issam's family came from Tyre, but like most of the Shia from the South of Lebanon, they had sought a livelihood as merchants, eventually establishing a successful shop in Freetown. Shia tended to flourish in tough lines of business in rough-and-tumble parts of the world: diamonds, shipping, import-export, harbor management, grocery stores, commodities, food staples. Southern Lebanese clans had found fortune in the far-flung reaches of Africa, the Caribbean, and South America. Issam was born in Ghana and summered in Tyre. He showed early promise playing soccer as a striker, and his parents sent him back to Lebanon to pursue a sports career. A teen star in the junior leagues, Issam was drafted onto the national soccer team at eighteen, but his natural talent wasn't enough to keep him on the team. Back in Tyre, he did odd jobs, and ended up making rent as a mine spotter for BACTEC, a British explosive ordnance disposal and land mine clearance company that was hired as a subcontractor by the UN-coordinated demining effort after Israel pulled out in 2000. The Israeli military never turned over mine maps, and left behind thousands of buried bombs. Minimally trained workers like Issam would wander through fields, throwing down red rags to mark suspected mines. Sappers would follow behind and clear the bombs.

Issam was alarmingly skinny, his skin pulled taut over his handsome high cheekbones, his wide smile revealing tall yellowed teeth embedded in receding gums like corn on a desiccated cob. He laughed constantly, nervously. "Hey my mon," he would greet me, with a sort of warm, complicated handshake that changed every time he proffered his hand. He was tall, about six feet, and shifted nervously. He never held eye contact long, and simpered with his whole body: his shoulders always a little hunched, his smile half-cocked, laughing too hard at a joke you might be making before it was halfway out of your mouth.

During the war there was no work. On my first day in Tyre I went to interview the mayor. Locals thronged the waiting room, looking to the municipality for food, medicine, and supplies for the refugees that mustered in Tyre as they fled battleground towns. Issam struck up a conversation with me, and translated a few interviews. I asked him to come around to the Fanar Guesthouse in the evening, around the corner from the house where I was staying. In conflict zones, a few television networks with limitless budgets would hire up the best local journalists and fixers by paying orders of magnitude more than the rest could afford. The practice inflated the marketplace and left the rest of us, who had far less to spend, stuck explaining to a skeptical recruit why we could not pay $1,000 a day for a bilingual driver. When I offered Issam a job, greed took hold of him. "Two hundred dollars a day is not enough," he said. "Other people are paying five hundred." I was discouraged. "I wouldn't want to stop you from getting rich. If you can find someone who will pay you that much, by all means do it," I said. "Two hundred a day is all I can afford to pay. I just don't have more money."

"Two hundred fifty?" he said, smiling and looking away.

He kept trying to negotiate until he realized I wasn't being coy.

"Okay, my mon, as a favor to you, because I can tell you're an honest guy, I'll take the job," he said.

No matter how risky, Issam would go anywhere. He couldn't always get the translations right, and his overwhelming fear made it sometimes feel more risky to have him along than to drive around the war zone alone. He flinched at every explosion, and repeated third-hand rumors as fact. He was afraid to offend any of the Islamists or fighters we met by translating questions that struck him as nosy, rude, or impolitic. He enunciated beautifully and spoke with fluid confidence, but he possessed the English vocabulary of a fourteen-year-old, roughly the age that he left school in Sierra Leone.

Before the war broke out, Issam liked to spend his evenings at a beach stand frequented by lots of deminers, on the far end of the strip of shacks. He had worked the register sometimes for the owner, but they'd had a falling out. Now, with everyone living in terror of an Israeli invasion, and his children sleepless from nightmares (shells and aerial bombing do special damage to the sensitive nervous systems of the young), Issam had hit the jackpot: two hundred dollars a day! One worry dogged him: would the local intelligence officers suspect him of disloyalty if he worked for foreign journalists? I learned months after the war that, better to be safe than sorry, he reported to the local *mukhabarat*, or intelligence, office immediately after agreeing to translate for me. He promised to keep an eye on the journalists and report any suspicious activity. Surely some of the journalists were really spies, and Issam wanted Hezbollah and its allies to know that he was on the right side—their side. "Don't worry," he told me after the war, in the fall. "I never said anything bad about you."

When possible, Hezbollah preferred to catch its flies with honey. The party loved to be loved. Inaya, the nurse, didn't need to join; she helped the party by doing what she already was doing—and burnished the legend of Hezbollah's incorruptibility and moral stature. But Hezbollah was agnostic about methodology, and wouldn't hesitate to turn in a flash to vinegar or worse to achieve its aims. Issam informed to the party because he feared its power. He didn't want to be branded a collaborator. He was easily cowed, and Hezbollah had given him reason to fear. During the occupation, men had disappeared without a trace, their bodies found weeks later. Hezbollah had a long reach and didn't take threats against it lightly, perceived or real.

As a movement, Hezbollah wanted to contain multitudes: bearded village men who would cane a son with alcohol on his breath and clean-shaven beach bums from Tyre who washed down their lunch with beer and their dinner with whiskey. Hezbollah could operate with ease in the freewheeling debauchery of Tyre, sorting through tips from half-drunk informants. But party members were most at home among their own, in the suburbs of Beirut and the interior wadis of the South, where those who supported Hezbollah did so with blood and spit, where the rhetoric of politics and daily life revolved around resistance and honor, the idea of earning life by willingly courting death, and where the struggle never ended.

One of those battleground towns was Qana, on the edge of the former Israeli occupation zone. A small, unremarkable place with a single main street and a few residential lanes branching off into the fields, the Lebanese claimed without any evidence that this village, and not the Cana in Galilee, present-day Israel, was where Jesus Christ turned water into wine. Its was best known for the massacre of 1996, during the war Israel called "Operation Grapes of Wrath," an extensive bombing campaign intended to stop Hezbollah firing rockets into Israel. On April 18, 1996, about eight hundred civilians had taken refuge in a UN peacekeeper compound in Qana. Hezbollah's guerillas have always operated among the local populace, affording them great tactical flexibility and stealth. The Party of God made no distinction between its political and military wings, since all its members are dedicated to the same struggle and tactics; similarly, they made little distinction between their front-line fighters and their supporters in the rear, in their long-running guerilla war that blurred the distinction between civilians and fighters. Hezbollah fired a salvo of rockets from a position a few hundred meters away, according to a UN report.[16] Within minutes Israel responded with shells, some of which struck the civilians sheltering in the open-air UN compound. The strikes killed 106 and prompted a chorus of condemnation. The massacre became a touchstone for Lebanese. Hezbollah built a stark modernist memorial at the site, a sloping minimalist sculpture in white marble, naked to the sun, engraved with the names of all the dead. In Israel, "Qana" became shorthand in the peace crowd for wanton bombing, but in the security establishment the shelling ultimately was viewed as a success. Israel and Hezbollah agreed after Qana to an informal set of rules that required each side to avoid firing at civilians, and it established a successful but short-lived standing committee through which Israel and Hezbollah could communicate to discuss breaches in the understanding.

Ten years later the old Qana agreement had long ago broken down and a much more violent replay of Grapes of Wrath was underway in southern Lebanon. Israeli bombs already had killed several hundred Lebanese, mostly civilians. Hezbollah rockets had driven almost a million Israelis from their homes in northern Israel. Neither side seemed to be paying the least heed to traditional laws of war that require combatants to exercise proportionality and make a concerted effort to avoid killing civilians— although Israel's superior weaponry made its conduct an order of magnitude more lethal and destructive. Many of the people who could already had fled the South, but about half of the area's 400,000 residents remained in the war zone, according to United Nations officials. Not all of them were

Hezbollah supporters—many Christians and Sunnis remained trapped in their villages and dared not venture onto the roads, where several fleeing families had burnt to death. By and large, however, Hezbollah fought from villages whose inhabitants supported the party, or from deserted areas.[17] All along the border and in the hills of the South, Hezbollah rocket launch teams would quickly set up in olive groves or other areas shaded from the Israeli drones overhead, fire Katyushas, and then quickly disperse. Qana was no different. And as in many of the southern villages that supported the resistance, hundreds of civilians had chosen to stay. Hezbollah had ordered nonessential personnel out of the war zone, but "essential" personnel included a core of civilians, including women and children. Their presence was intended to fulfill logistical roles like cooking and medical care; to provide morale and support to the guerillas; to raise the cost of widespread Israeli bombardment; and finally to make a symbolic statement that no matter how great the danger, Hezbollah's people would not bend in the gale of Israeli force. During the Israeli occupation many Shiite villages had gradually emptied; Hezbollah wanted to avoid depopulation in future conflicts. Israel considered many of these civilians "human shields," kept in the war zone by Hezbollah to make it harder for Israel to pinpoint enemy combatants.

A few days before the 2006 bombing I had passed through Qana. Rockets and shells had struck the town, and Hezbollah fighters were active throughout the area. A woman named Amina Aydibi was tending a small grocery on the main street, mainly selling nuts and junk food. In her arms she held her son Mohammed, twenty-one months old. She winced every time we heard a distant explosion.[18] "All the time, the planes fly over. Every moment, they are striking, over and over," she said, looking equally frightened and determined. Her family had fled for a single day to Baqleen, in the Chouf Mountains, but felt cowardly and returned to Qana: "We preferred to die in our homes." An Israeli jet buzzed the village, and she hurried off down the street to a shelter, leaving her store open and unattended.

Sometime before the sun rose on Sunday, July 30, Israeli jets dropped a bomb on a small apartment building in Qana. Dozens of civilians had taken shelter in the basement. By 10 a.m. television crews were broadcasting live footage of rescue workers—most of them swarthy bearded men in T-shirts and cargo pants, indistinguishable from Hezbollah irregulars—

carrying dead bodies from the ruins of the building. Most of the twenty-eight dead came from two clans, the Hashem and Shalhoub families.[19] Their loss was tangible but symbolic as well. Already many innocents had died. Eight transit workers in Haifa, killed in a train station by a Hezbollah missile. Maybe a dozen civilians in Srifa, buried alive in the rubble when Israeli shells hit their homes. The Qana strike, however, was different. The number was higher, and the history of the town too evocative. And then, there was the footage. It's an unfortunate truth of our mediated world that a televised tragedy almost always has more impact than one described with words. On live TV casualties still capture the public imagination, and Hezbollah spoke the universal language of television fluently. The Party of God always sent cameramen along on military missions. Al-Manar broadcast edited telecasts of suicide bombings, commando missions, firefights, rocket launchings, training exercises—a wide sample of all its military activities. The Qana bombing provided a mother lode of heart-wrenching images of limp dead children, clearly noncombatants. In vain Israel and its supporters cried foul as the footage was replayed across the world, prompting criticism of Israel and new demands for a ceasefire.

The site itself was unbearably somber. Men from Amal and Hezbollah pulled bodies from the wreckage with little fanfare. A backhoe tore at the twisted rebar and concrete to unearth the last dead. A local civil defense chief sat on a cinderblock and cross-checked casualty lists on two crumpled scraps of paper. He had repaired to the checkered shade of a rooftop next to the crater, and absentmindedly munched the grapes growing from a trellis overhead. An hour away in Tyre at the Jabal Amel Hospital, the survivors spoke in the numbed cadences of grief. One of them, Hala Ahmed Shalhoub, was twenty-four years old and had lost two daughters. Her sister Zaynab lay on the next bed. We encountered Hala at that precise junction between personal pain and public politics. Her story had fast become everyone's. To hear someone talk of the death of her two children, her only two children, just hours after the fact, beggars comprehension. But how else to really grasp what happened at Qana other than through a single story in the interstice between politics and violence, the story Hala told when she spoke of her babies and not of her love for Hassan Nasrallah?

She spoke for just a few seconds, in an uninterrupted stream of words, mouthed in a hoarse, raspy monotone.

We were sleeping. Before we went to bed we heard lots of bombs around the building. We didn't care. We had to sleep. Some families stayed awake in the night. In the night we heard a big blast. The dust came over us. We thought it was a distant blast. I tried to move myself but I couldn't move. My face was buried in the dust. I heard my baby on my back making noises and also my older child. They were all covered with the dust, and they died. I couldn't scream. I was face down in the dust. I screamed for somebody to take my child. I was about to breathe my last breath. I heard my baby girl moaning in my ears. When I raised my head, I thought my children were alive. My baby was still hot, I could feel her. My children are going to heaven. They are going to join the Prophet. Whoever did this massacre is going to hell.

She had named her daughters for the members of the Prophet's house, the *ahl al-bayt* so venerated by the Shia, and now she said, her children dwelled with them. Fatima was four, named for the daughter of the Prophet Mohammed who married Imam Ali. Rokaya was one and a half years old, named for another of the Prophet's daughters by his first wife, Khadija. Her eyes blank, her face bruised black, Hala intoned her words as if she were reading them from a script. Blood seeped through a bandage and a fresh headscarf onto her pillow. She wasn't angry. She was shocked and destroyed. Her sister Zaynab was a few years younger. She didn't have children of her own, and she had pulled Rokaya's toddler body from the pulverized house. Honest grief engulfed Hala, but her younger sister already had sought comfort in the seductive artifice of movement politics, potent enough to absorb the tiny overpowering infinity of one person's grief.

"I am happy my family all died martyrs," Zaynab said, near tears but in control. "Our martyrs are in heaven. The Israeli dead are in hell." When the Hezbollah volunteers brought fresh clothes to the hospital for the sisters, Zaynab allowed them to wash her robe, but she wouldn't let them touch her headscarf, which she kept wrapped close. "I did not allow them to wash my veil because the blood of my relatives is on it. I want to smell their blood."

Hala Ahmed Shalhoub had a truth to tell, but just as surely as it belonged to her, her story belonged also to Hezbollah, and the party's nimble propaganda organs already had subsumed it into their master narrative of martyrology, Israeli aggression, and the glory of death for the resistance. At the bomb site in Qana, the rescue workers knew they were being filmed, and performed accordingly; grim-faced, they volunteered the grand lesson to any reporter they saw. "Let Israel and America know that from this moment on we will teach every child to be a fighter from their first year of life," rescue worker Mohammed Ismail told me. I hadn't even asked him a question, nor did I point out that Hezbollah already had been teaching children to fight from birth, regardless of the tragedy of the dead children at Qana.

By nightfall Qana was a Hezbollah talking point, and a highly effective one. In the Arab and Islamic world, lots of blame had earlier fallen on Hezbollah. The Party of God had sparked this war, and powerful constituencies hoped it would bring Hezbollah's ruin. Saudi Arabia and Egypt quietly supported Israel's campaign. Many secular Arabs, Sunni Muslims, Christians—forces for moderation who had suffered at the strengthening arms of the Iran-Syria-Hezbollah-Hamas "Resistance Axis"—yearned for a death blow to Nasrallah's movement. Maybe half of Lebanon hated Hezbollah for drawing the wrath of Israel. But as the arc of Israel's punishment expanded, the outrage toward Hezbollah subsided to a chirp. After Qana it fell silent completely. The blame shifted to Israel, and even those who despaired at Hezbollah found themselves far angrier at the Jewish state than at the Party of God. In front of an endless broadcast loop from Qana, resentment of Hezbollah dissolved into rage at Israel. Once again, for the moment, Hezbollah's sins were forgotten.

Each year contained a story. So did every place name. It sufficed to invoke a single name or numeral without going into the details: 1967 for Arab defeat, 1982 for Israeli invasion, Qana for atrocities against civilians, Bint Jbail for Arab rebound. The Qana massacre of 2006 fell directly in line with an existing script. Hezbollah had come of age in a time of cyclical destruction, and had mastered the craft of instant mythmaking. Even as the earthmovers tore the last contorted chunks of rebar and concrete from the ruined pit, Qana already was history, a ready-made icon of martyrdom and victimhood. Israel's doctrine of "effects-based warfare" perfectly explained why Qana was a loser for Israel: it inspired the victimized Lebanese and demoralized the Israelis who felt spurned in the court of world opinion. Dr. Strangelove would have loved the idea of effects-based war, and so did military theorists with a better grasp of game theory than human nature. At any rate, it was a prime example of a state adopting the psychology of its enemy, perhaps unwittingly; from its birth Hezbollah was nothing if not an effects-based war-fighting organization, even if they didn't use that stilted term. Hezbollah videotaped every operation, and generously used the footage for recruitment. Its leaders understood the marketing value of a spectacular attack as well, which is why they could never bring themselves to decry the bombings and hostage takings of the 1980s; those acts had reaped a membership bonanza.

Hezbollah decided from its inception that it could always present a victorious face to its public so long as it carefully defined victory and adroitly redefined it when circumstances changed. The theorists behind Israel's effects-based doctrine might have grasped the concept, but were neither disciplined nor cynical enough to exploit it as Hezbollah did. Sayyed Nasrallah in a single speech could frame any confrontation to Hezbollah's advantage, spotlighting success where he could find a trace and resiliency where he could not. Most crucially, he could rewrite history at a moment's notice, managing expectations downward in order to fuel the resistance flame. By this way of thinking, Israel's strike at Qana wasn't a sign of its military superiority, or even of its dastardly readiness to do whatever it took to win. Rather, it proved Israel's desperation: that the Jewish state wasn't as strong and moral as it purported to be. Even if Israel ultimately took over all of Lebanon, by this logic, Hezbollah would have won, first by frustrating Israel's original military plan, and second, by exposing the evil nature of Israel. It was a brilliant strategy because in almost every conceivable case it gave Nasrallah license to define any real-world outcome—no matter how disastrous—as a victory for Hezbollah and its people, and thus to entrench his political power. Hezbollah propagandists spliced together pictures of Israeli children scribbling messages on missiles with pictures of the Qana dead. "A message from the children of Israel to the children of Lebanon," the legend read. Israel released footage (which it later admitted wasn't from Qana) of a man firing a rocket next to a building, purporting to show that Hezbollah militants used sleeping children as human shields, indifferent to the danger. As Israeli children were schooled to hate neighboring "Arab terrorists," so in Lebanon the children in the sphere of the Islamic Resistance learned from childhood to detest demonized "Jewish terrorist aggressors.". On this score at least both sides had comparable ideological machines.

For Israel, Qana paid some dividends too, regardless of whether the bombing itself was an accident, a mistake, or deliberate. On Monday, July 31, Israel held most of its fire, a cessation of bombing to encourage civilian holdouts to get out of southern Lebanon. At that point the United Nations estimated that only 120,000 Lebanese remained south of the Litani River. On the day after Qana, it looked like most of them were taking the opportunity to get the hell out. Entire villages convoyed north, on tractors, in minibuses, crammed into taxis charging extortionate rates to ferry the poor. An Israeli foreign ministry official told a colleague of mine at *The Boston Globe* that Qana might even be good for Israel. After the 1996 Qana massacre, Hezbollah and Israel entered into an agreement to avoid targeting civilians that lasted a decade, until the present war; maybe another galvanizing image of destruction could yield another period of quiet. "The Americans, this administration, is interested in ending the Hezbollah presence in southern Lebanon," the official said. "They want the bad guys to get what they deserve." Such was the cynical truck of this war, equally a contest of how skillfully each side could manipulate its public as of how lethally they could deploy infiltrating commandos, artillery, and spies.

The logic of total warfare rarely works as intended. The human brain, with its pride and emotional wiring, gets in the way of the simple intended goal of mass submission. The strategic bombing planner, like the theoretical economist, assumes far too much. The bomb will hit the bridge, the shells will scare the villagers, the message will be delivered, and the people will withdraw their support from the militants in Hezbollah. In reality the bomb falls on the nation like a powerful slap in the face. You don't blame the socioeconomic forces that drove your neighbor to lose his job and turn to drink; you blame your neighbor for beating you. Lebanese stopped blaming Hezbollah for provoking Israel, and began to blame Israel.

The little two-lane road connecting the border to Tyre turned into an almost comically crowded escape hatch, bursting with every kind of vehicle, like a children's book about things on wheels. Almost the entire population of the farming hamlet Jibbain had piled onto open flatbed wheat trailers, towed by a single tractor for a two-hour ride to Tyre. Thirty-three cars overloaded with the residents of Tair Harfa made significantly better time. Limbs poked out of the convoy like weeds. Women and children rode upright in open car trunks. I watched this jumbled parade of frightened humanity at the roundabout where the coastal road entered Tyre. No one wanted to stop—this was still dangerous territory—but some of the tractors crawled so slowly that we could walk alongside and conduct shouted interviews with the refugees. "Qana was a warning for us all," shouted one man named Adnan Shabi, towing his extended family in a small utility trailer affixed to his tractor. "Israel ordered us to evacuate the South because it's going to bomb everything near the border. They won't leave a single house standing."

In the parking lot of the Rest House resort hotel, some of the displaced took a break before continuing their journey. An English teacher named Amin Srour sat on a grass median in the parking lot. He was from Aita Shaab, the village from which Hezbollah launched the raid that started the war. The Israelis had responded with a rain of hellfire. Amin was thirty-two years old, with two children and his wife six months pregnant. A few days earlier, he said, on Monday, his aunt, uncle, and a cousin had perished in the bombing. He had fled to the nearby Christian village of Rmeish, a collaborator town full of churches, therefore spared the Israeli onslaught. When Amin walked, his hip traced a stiff and pronounced circle, the exaggerated gait of an amputee. He had a clubfoot, and his other leg had been amputated in childhood. The Christians sheltered Amin's family for the better part of a week. In a manner they also sheltered his dead relatives; it was impossible to safely reach the Muslim burial ground very near the Israeli border, so Amin's family stashed the bodies in the Christian graveyard at Rmeish for temporary safekeeping, with plans to rebury them after the war. "In Rmeish, we started to drink from the same pool as the cattle," Amin said. Finally the Red Cross drove them to Tyre. Taxi drivers willing to rip off refugees the same way they did foreign journalists came to Rmeish asking $100 a head to drive people to safety. Amin said he punched one of them in the face.

Whatever message Israel intended to send the Shia populace had been largely lost in the explosive translation. Issam offered Amin a hand to help him up from the grass. With a flash of fury he refused and rolled himself upright. "Look," he said, and flipped over onto his hands. He walked upside down on his palms across the parking lot, stopping and balancing on one hand for a second to adjust his prosthetic leg. He returned to us and executed an expert handspring onto his feet. He had the short stocky build of an acrobat. The proud show of defiance had the melancholy air of a rural freakshow.

"We suffered a big violence because of Israel," he said with diction precise even if the English grammar was patchy. "Israel must be cancelled from all the human institutions. We hate it because of its actions. All the people of Lebanon experience the suffering. European countries don't feel our pain or suffering. I want to cry but I can't because I am a man. My wife is cry."

Israel wants to destroy Hezbollah, and Hezbollah wants to destroy Israel. A collective urge ripened in the hothouses of a million individual hearts. The party organs distinguish in theory between Jews on the one hand (okay) and Zionists and Israelis on the other (unacceptable). Amin Srour had no time for such fine points.

"They call Hezbollah a terrorist party, but it defends our country. Hezbollah is not terrorists. It protects us from Israel. I like the people of America. But I hate the government, especially George Bush." He drew out the word hate, lingering on the "a" to make it "aaaaaaaaaay," rolling out his tongue.

He started to pull on the ratty blue T-shirt he was given to wear in the few days since he'd been reduced from middle-class teacher to lame, penniless refugee.

"We suffer. Look at my appearance. Look at these clothes," he said, and started to cry, even though he was a man. "I hope you feel our suffering. I love Sayyed Hassan Nasrallah very well. He is the savior of the nation. I think America hates him. But he is the man who protects us. Islam requires us to treat everyone in the right way. We cannot be rude. We hate the government"—here he paused, and reached out to me; he was sitting on the grass on the median, his legs splayed out, and I was cross-legged beside him. He reached out with his strong arm and forced me to him, kissing me on the cheek without any tenderness, locking me in his grip—"but we do not hate the people."

His rage flowed from a deep reservoir, filled long before this war and replenished by every round of destruction. Nothing he said suggested he had actively supported Hezbollah. But in this time of accelerated entropy, with the roofs literally caving in overhead and his entire town shrouded in a fury of organized murder, Amin Srour needed a narrative that would make sense of his family's privations. He needed an explanation that would not rob them of their dignity and would value their sacrifice. Hezbollah's epic tale of resistance and Israeli perfidy was exactly such a story, and it wasn't much of stretch for him to make it his own.

On the second day of the intermission that we called a ceasefire, a small and foolish group of four journalists, in two cars, decided to visit Khiam. We hadn't yet seen the infamous prison and imagined that setting foot on that symbolic and evil spot at the height of the conflict would reveal something important about this war and about Hezbollah. The ride was long and afforded us a desolate tour. Most of the towns and cities we passed had been abandoned by all but the fighters and the small core of civilians who stayed behind to provide logistical support. We drove to the inland city of Nabatieh and just beside the Crusader castle of Beaufort, which accented a commanding ridgeline like a death mask facing the sky. We gunned our engines and drove through the Litani River at a point where it was only three feet deep, between the bombed bridge and a trout restaurant that would usually be doing brisk business by this point in the summer. Several passenger cars were marooned in the shallow river like New Orleans houses, their engines flooded before they could make it across.

Compared to the bereft crescent we traversed to reach it, Khiam was a hive of activity, crawling with Hezbollah fighters. Their spirits were high. They had expected an Israeli onslaught much earlier, a ground invasion by the infantry; if that happened, the Hezbollah regulars knew they could only hold their territory for a limited period of time. To Hezbollah's surprise, the Israelis had played to their enemy's hand: bombing from the air, making only limited forays into Lebanon which were easily ambushed, and massing Israeli soldiers south of the border where they sat in large static concentrations within range of Hezbollah's Katyusha rockets. Hezbollah fighters in Khiam expected to be among the first overrun by an Israeli invasion. Instead, here they were more than two weeks into the war shelling Israel from relatively comfortable bunkers. As we talked to one fighter in a street a few blocks away from the village edge, we watched a boy run mortar shells in plastic shopping bags to a teenager on a motor bike, who ferried them up toward the highest point in Khiam. "Don't go to the prison," the commander warned. "Our fighters are protected from the shells because they're in a bunker. You won't be."

We went anyway. There wasn't much to see. The fighters carried on their work unseen somewhere below us. Aboveground, the café and gift shop lay in ruins, charred postcard sets and memorabilia fluttering among piles of exploded walls. It seemed odd but appropriate in a war fought with as much attention to symbols as to strategy that Israel had dropped bombs on the outer courtyard of their former prison in Khiam, destroying the ramparts most visible to Lebanese tourists, but not the bunkers below. They had destroyed an underground shelter on the prison's perimeter, killing four United Nations observers, but they hadn't destroyed the places from where Hezbollah fought. All they had leveled were the shabby concrete barracks that had imprisoned the once and future Hezbollah foot soldiers of the South, unaware that they had only made future propaganda tours of Khiam Prison more macabre and exciting: another recruiting tool. Other than that single fact, a haiku in high explosive, there wasn't much of a story in Khiam that day, just a hodgepodge of disjointed images. But I shouldn't say "just images," because in the "effects-based" contest between the Party of God and the Jewish State images had as much currency as body counts. As we drove past the 1996 Qana memorial a week before the 2006 strike, Issam had joked that "the Israelis might try to kill the dead."

The few people we came across that day were frenetically busy, fighting, preparing to fight, or salvaging personal property, like the two butchers who were loading all their saws and slicers into a pickup truck to store in the Beqaa until the war ended. The move was prescient, because their shop was obliterated a few weeks later. Leaflets fluttered from Israeli planes like ragweed, announcing that Israel would hereafter consider everyone in the South a combatant. I found leaflets at the Tyre corniche, the orchards of

Khiam, the shoulders of the road in Nabatieh. They were printed on rough heavy construction paper, and looked like they came from another era; they were campy, like something out of a Quentin Tarantino movie. Some, with cartoon caricatures of Nasrallah, mocked the Hezbollah leader for hypocritically endangering his followers. In florid Arabic, they warned the people of South Lebanon to flee:

> *He who says he is protecting you, is really robbing you.*
> To all citizens south of the Litani River
> Due to the terror activities being carried out against the State of Israel from within your villages and homes, the IDF is forced to respond immediately against these activities, even within your villages.
> For your safety!!!
> We call upon you to evacuate your villages and move north of the Litani River.
> The State of Israel

Later leaflets were blunter and more frightening:

> The IDF will escalate its operations, and will strike with great force the terrorist groups which are exploiting you as human shields, and which fire rockets from your homes at the State of Israel. Any vehicle of any kind traveling south of the Litani River will be bombarded, on suspicion of transporting rockets, military equipment and terrorists. Anyone who travels in any vehicle is placing his life in danger.

No one doubted the explicit message. From now on, it would be a free-for-all: every car on the road a legitimate target, every human figure in a field to be presumed a rocket launcher.[20] Faced with that choice—you're either with us or against us—people made a quick and conclusive decision to run away or commit to the resistance.

Al-Manar ceaselessly aired video of civilian war victims. Places like Khiam, Bint Jbail, and Aita Shaab had been deserted by all but the most essential fighters. But a few miles further away from the border, line after line of Shia

villages had shifted to a well-organized and gruesomely calculated war footing. Most civilians were evacuated because they got in the way of the fight.
But a nucleus of families of unquestionable loyalty, usually numbering
several hundred people including women, children, and elderly, stayed in
makeshift shelters or in their own homes. A small handful performed support tasks like baking bread, preparing meals, and nursing the wounded.
The rest served no direct military purpose but played an important ideological role. They fueled the morale of the fighters and of the populace
who had fled; by their presence and willingness to die, they maintained
the narrative of Shia martyrdom and victimhood, and proved Hezbollah's
claim that under the Party of God the Shia would never capitulate again
before Israelis, preferring to die in their homes rather than live in refugee
slums safe in the "belt of misery" in the Dahieh. If they perished, the civilian families achieved instant glorious martyrdom, and created another
public relations debacle for Israel. Granted, these civilians volunteered to
garrison themselves, but it was Hezbollah that encouraged them to stay.
The families uncomplainingly spent their hours underground in the dark,
emerging for the children to play in the fresh air whenever the fighters gave
them the okay.

The other civilians who stayed in the war zone had specific functions,
and formed the backbone of Hezbollah's civil administration. As in many
Arab societies, officials known as *mokhtars* administer every hundred or so
families in a village or urban neighborhood. This position has no counter-
part in modern Western societies, but it is vital to running a tight police
state or community in constant agitation like the state of Hezbollah. The
mokhtar's power lies in his responsibility to know the community and cer-
tify every individual's identity: a rubber stamp without whom they don't
exist. By law, the mokhtar has to sign any application for an electricity
hookup, a phone line, school enrollment, voter registration, any public service. For a small fee the mokhtar confirms that the applicant is in fact who
he claims to be, a function fulfilled in other societies by an identity card or
birth certificate. He is a personal manifestation of the state right there on
your block. The mokhtar embodies the Orwellian compact of communi-
tarian society: the power structure takes care of the neediest, but it never
lowers its invasive gaze from the citizenry.

Normally Hezbollah jealously guarded its organizational methods.[21] It broadcasts reams of material about their ideology, religion, and resistance. But its quotidian methods of mobilization and organization were considered state secrets, only for the membership. Hezbollah's community could be categorized in three decreasing levels of commitment: members, supporters, and sympathizers, terms often used by party loyalists to describe their own roles. Actual party members were comparatively few and far between; these were the cadres fully trained and employed by the party. Most of them underwent a multiyear probationary period after being cleared for membership, during which they received religious and military training. Those in the second tier, the supporters, were by no means a casual constituency. They could better be understood as reservists or members of a national guard. The supporters had been trained and vetted by Hezbollah's security organs. They were trusted as much as full members, but they weren't under Hezbollah's control full time. They had their own jobs, but volunteered a fixed amount of time to train or work with party institutions. A certain subset of these supporters was committed to work full time for the party in the event of a crisis. Finally, the outer ring of sympathizers included the largest portion of the millions who considered themselves Hezbollah loyalists. Many of them subsisted or thrived off Hezbollah's largesse. They followed party orders and turned to it for religious instruction, cultural guidance, economic help, and dispute resolution. Hezbollah to them was mosque, court, tribe, and police. Often it was integral to their livelihood too. The relationship with the sympathizers was more fluid than the rigid hierarchy governing the official members and supporters. Hezbollah didn't directly control the sympathizers; it had to persuade, cajole, or intimidate them. In times of peace, several layers of security and intelligence patrolled Hezbollah communities. They would quickly intervene in local disputes, settling vendettas before they turned violent. They would quickly corral a foreigner or reporter who visited without an official escort. Hezbollah's network of security agents, informants, mokhtars, and intelligence agents had close ties to the national army and police. Most Lebanese I knew assumed that Hezbollah could monitor everything it wanted, including phone calls, mail, border crossings, and airport arrivals.

During the war with Israel, however, these webs of control temporarily frayed, pulling back the curtain on Hezbollah's panopticon. The fighters and villagers were hyperstimulated and proud. They were willing to talk to me, even if many of them were trying to project a manufactured image of the resistance. Most of the villages I visited in my travels around the war zone fell into one of three categories. First were the border battlegrounds, desolate, partially or completely destroyed, and inhabited only by fighters. Second were the places locals called "line-of-fire villages." These suffered extensive bombing, but nothing like the border towns. In Bint Jbail and Aita Shaab, according to the Lebanese government and the United Nations, 90 percent of the buildings in the town were destroyed or so damaged as to be uninhabitable. By comparison, most of the line-of-fire villages sustained damage and destruction rates closer to 30 or 50 percent. Hezbollah fighters regrouped in these towns, and fired rockets from orchards and nearby seasonal riverbeds, or wadis. Mokhtars kept order and a watchful eye. Hezbollah intelligence operatives searched for spies who might be giving targeting data to Israel. Party members and reserve supporters acted as a civil defense corps and logistics chain, organizing the delivery of food and medicine to those who remained, cooking for the fighters, ferrying the wounded combatants and civilians to field hospitals. Civilians slept in the monitored shelters. Everyone in the town was fully under Hezbollah's control, even if they were only sympathizers and not actual members of the party. Those suspected of sympathizing with the enemy were made to leave. Finally in the third ring were rear areas like the cities of Tyre and Nabatieh, which suffered some major air strikes but never the kind of constant fire as the first two rings. Tyre in particular, with its mixed population, was never fully in Hezbollah's grasp and hence was spared Israel's full wrath. Refugees and foreigners streamed through the city, many of them suspicious to Hezbollah, which was convinced that a formidable phalanx of Israeli and American spies hid among the refugees, the hard-drinking locals (even the Shia Muslims), the international aid workers, and the press corps. While still within the war zone, these places operated like open cities. Goods flowed freely from Beirut to Tyre, and everything from whiskey to antibiotics was available on the black market. Throughout the war I could buy increasingly expensive gas for my car from the smugglers at the traffic circle near the Palestinian refugee camp, Bass. Here Hezbollah's political and social affairs echelon brushed against the vestiges of the state, and against competing political parties that wanted to be seen helping refugees or planning for postwar reconstruction and lucrative contracts.

The Christians and the Sunni Muslims mistrusted Hezbollah, but for the most part they endorsed resistance against Israel—either out of conviction or because they feared doing otherwise. Weak men like Issam feared crossing the resistance. Others, like the proprietor of a local Tyre café popular with both Hezbollah fighters and partying teens, considered themselves removed from politics but couldn't help resent Israel's military, which had periodically made their lives hell for decades even though they personally had done nothing to abet Hezbollah. This last group emerged as a sort of swing demographic for Hezbollah, potential sympathizers whom it could marshal as soft supporters. Many of these initially skeptical Shia found themselves first accepting Hezbollah as a necessary evil, a counterweight to Israel, then grudgingly admiring the party's efficacy, and finally, over time, adopting its faith and political dogma. Hezbollah helped create and then became indispensable to a peculiar state of mind, characterized by nervous alertness and sustained political arousal, in tone part campaign rally, part tent revival, and part self-empowerment seminar. The take-home message: March toward the Mahdi and resist Israel.

Those who didn't subscribe voluntarily to the party's agenda could always be coerced. Intelligence officers questioned the translators who worked with foreigners; none to my knowledge refused to serve as informants to Hezbollah's police state (and opting out was not much of a choice given the amount of power in the party's hands). People who wandered astray would be detained and questioned. Some Palestinians were ordered to stay in their camps. A few Christians were informed they might better wait out the war in Beirut and left promptly. International reporters who spoke Arabic fell under especially virulent suspicion; in Hezbollah's mind-set, a non-Arab who knew Arabic most likely was a spy. At least one correspondent for an American news outlet was summoned by Hezbollah and advised to leave. The correspondent bristled at the absurdity of Hezbollah's suspicion and was outraged at being ordered away from a huge story by a totalitarian Islamist party. Still, wise to the risk, the reporter decamped to Beirut until the final stage of the fighting.

In Tyre, the dead piled up from across the South. Until someone figured out where to bury them, they rotted in a pair of container trucks parked across from the UN Hospital in the Bass Refugee Camp. Some were loosely tied shut in clear plastic garbage bags, others wrapped in blankets. We smelled them every time we drove past. The day the bombing resumed in earnest, Wednesday, August 2, Hezbollah organized a mass funeral. Carpenters clapped together rough plywood boxes for coffins. Men and women who came to look for identifiable relatives among the casualties vomited as the bags were opened. Maggots writhed inside the plastic sacks, glinting in the sun. Civil defense workers piled the bodies in the parking lot. A thick sludge had collected in the trucks from the decomposing bodies, a black liquid with a smell rank like rotten egg, charred like burning meat, and sweet like shit festering in the sun. It trickled onto the asphalt as workers rinsed the truck beds with a high-pressure hose. I heaved as I backed away. The Qana dead got special treatment. A civil defense worker named Abu Hadi kept them in a refrigerated truck parked in the alley in front of the hospital. He wore waist-high gaiters and a filthy shirt. Jets roared overhead—the war was in full swing again—and Abu Hadi smoked and chatted. As a civil defense official in Tyre he had a lot of information from ambulance crews and militia sources about far-flung villages that we had not yet visited. Each time a new television crew would approach, Abu Hadi would cast aside his cigarette, affect a mournful expression, and invite the journalists to film the Qana victims, as if he could hardly bear his duty to show such a horror.

He unlatched the doors and hoisted himself into the truck, turning his back on the camera crew for a second. Cold smoke billowed out, like in the macabre music videos on Al-Manar. A gust of cool and mulchy air wafted over us. Abu Hadi emerged with impeccable timing from the cloud, the curled body of a four or five-year-old boy in his hands. The boy was still clothed and had the unmistakably sweet face of a child. Photos of Abu Hadi brandishing this boy had already made their away around the world. He hoisted the little body over his head, all the while maintaining a vacant expression but never turning away from the cameras. He looked as numb as I actually felt. Slowly he pivoted and returned the corpse to the rear of the truck. As he clambered down and swung the doors shut his face reverted to its normal friendly contours, and he casually asked the crew: "Did you get the shots you need? I can show you again." A few minutes later he performed the same routine for another network. Many other bodies had been processed and packed into the makeshift coffins. But Hezbollah fired so many volleys of rockets from the nearby orchards that it feared reprisal bombings against the crowd that would gather to bury the dead in the open field by the ancient hippodrome. The mass funeral was called off. The dead would have to wait another day.

August set in, days that dawned with a salty cool breeze that broke the nighttime clouds and gave way to kiln mornings and sweaty sauna afternoons. I succumbed to the local state of mind: fortitude and resignation, milled by the wheel of war and buffed by some spiritual sense summoned by all the keening and death. I wanted to tour the entire border zone, see towns I'd not yet seen, learn whether the fighting had engulfed as wide an arc as Israeli military briefers and Hezbollah demagogues claimed over their embedded television networks. I set off behind the wheel of my rental sedan, a dark blue Renault Mégane. Anthony Shadid of *The Washington Post* sat in the passenger seat, and Issam cowered in the back. I think Anthony and I both buckled our seat belts (most war zone deaths, after all, are traffic fatalities). I had marked the roof and hood of the car with tape, spelling out the letters "TV," the international sign for journalists at work in a war zone. The letters served more as a talisman than as actual protection; we had seen carloads of bearded Hezbollah operatives crisscrossing the South in beat-up Volvos similarly marked "TV." Surely the Israelis had noticed the same thing from the drones and surveillance blimps. We hugged the coast all the way to the Israeli border, the glistening sea on our right and banana plantations on our left, the trees staggering under the weight of unharvested bananas. At Naqoura we turned east, driving parallel to the border that was less than a mile away. We could see Israeli radar installations, bases, and occasional towns, but not a single person moving on either side. Issam begged us to turn back: "We're the only thing moving on this road. They'll hit us for sure," he said. Anthony and I agreed to stop as soon as either of us felt uncomfortable—a game of chicken, essentially, since we already were both frightened beyond logic. We passed through town after town that had already been taken by the Israelis, according to Israeli news reports; but we saw no people, no military equipment, no vehicles. Finally we came to a small farming town called Dhaira. It seemed foolish to drive any further, so we pulled over by a house where a boy was playing. An extended family emerged from the unfinished second story of a concrete housing block. They were poor tobacco farmers, Sunnis who described themselves as gypsies although they had no apparent connection to the Roma.

"You just missed the firefight!" the mother said brightly. For several hours, they said, Hezbollah fighters north of the border road had been exchanging rocket and mortar fire with the Israelis, and the Israeli army had dispatched armored vehicles toward Tair Harfa, crossing the highway we had just traversed. According to these people, it wasn't a vacant no-man's land we'd just driven through; we had unwittingly, and quite luckily, benefitted from a brief lull in the fighting. We sat on the concrete stoop facing the road. "This is where we watch the battles," the mother explained. "The Israelis know there is no resistance in our village, so they leave us alone." One of the children brought out a tray of tea. Suddenly we heard the zip of a rocket firing, and then another. It came from very close, so close that it felt like someone ripping a sheaf of paper in my ear while tickling the inside of my gut with a feather. Shells shook the ground. Issam collapsed onto the concrete, and Anthony flinched. The family laughed. The shells were actually landing miles away, around Tair Harfa. The rockets were coming from the Israeli side of the border, at least a mile away and probably more. We thought we were in the middle of a firefight, but we were actually quite safely under the volleys. When the shooting subsided we took our chance to drive back to the coast. An older woman in a baseball cap and a grimy T-shirt with a paint company logo picked us three roses. As she presented them to us she said, "These aren't for your funeral, but a wish for your safety." I couldn't tell to what extent her words were a blessing or a macabre joke, the kind of humor necessary for people who can't afford to let their tobacco rot on the stalk and so spend the war watching explosives sail overhead instead of television. This cheerful morbid aplomb is one cornerstone of the Southern State of Mind.

We encountered the other later that same day in Qalaouay. We had attempted to reach the front line from another direction, driving through the mountains toward the village of Taibe where Israeli tanks reportedly had met stiff opposition from Hezbollah. We found ourselves alone in a village and heard mortars striking at two- or three-second intervals, each one sounding closer. We realized that some Israeli gunner was walking the mortars toward us, and we sped away. We stopped in the center of Qalaouay, in the shade of a plane tree. The town was centered on a hilltop, capped by a serene mosque shrouded in foliage. Several young fighters loitered beneath the plane tree. They smiled at us and chatted guardedly. "Hezbollah has made it impossible for Israel to occupy Lebanon again," said one of the men, Mustafa Ayan. A relative, Abdullah Ayan, added, "Hezbollah are still the winners. They are intact." They were writing a narrative of victory even as Israeli tanks relentlessly smashed the homes one valley away. "We've made it impossible for the Israelis to reach the Litani River," Mustafa explained. "In the past they could occupy the whole South in five or six days. Now it's been twenty-three days and they haven't taken a single village."

Just then an authority figure sped into the square on a silver motor scooter and the young men fell silent. He was Hussein Rumeiti, a mokhtar from the next village over, Borj Qalaouay, and clearly a man in charge. He was handsome, tall and skinny, maybe in his forties, with movie-star smoky gray eyes. After a few minutes of conversation he judged us innocuous and signaled that the fighters could relax. He explained that he was taking care of all the civilians in the area, and was on his way to a pharmacy to fill a lady's heart prescription. This close to the front lines—a few miles from where we'd been mortared a few minutes earlier—it seemed bizarre to find an entire society intact under the shade of the grape leaves and olive branches, keeping the guerillas company. Hussein Rumeiti and his young companions were more than intact; they were thriving.

"With all those fancy weapons that America gave them, Israel said it would destroy Hezbollah," Hussein Rumeiti said, leaning against the saddle of his motor scooter. "But all they've done is destroy some houses, some bridges. They said they have destroyed Hezbollah, but Hezbollah remains where it was." He looked meaningfully around us. "This is the proof." The logic was clear and unassailable, so long as people believed it as these men certainly did: Hezbollah had held off the Israelis longer than any prior Lebanese force, or for that matter, any Arab army.

"The victory is clear," the mokhtar explained. "They could get rid of us all. We have nothing to lose. We don't have an army, we are a guerilla movement. The Israelis can't stay in a single one of the Lebanese villages they claim to have taken. That is victory."

Two men we hadn't seen before ran through the main street and dis-appeared out of sight. The young men around us tensed, and a few of them drifted away. Then a great zipping noise momentarily drowned out Hussein's voice. He broke into a huge smile. "That's Khaibar one!" he shouted. The Khaibar was a rocket named for a decisive battle between the Prophet Mohammed and a community of Jews in the infancy of the Islamic ummah. Another ripping noise, close enough to touch: "Khaibar two!" Rumeiti intoned. In rhythm came the final rocket: "Khaibar three!" The fire team had set up barely 100 yards away, in the valley just to the side of the main square. Through the canopy of the tree, we could see rocket trails arcing gracefully into the blue sky. Rumeiti already had straddled his scooter and hit the ignition button. "I think you should get out of here before Israel retaliates," he said and zipped away. We jumped in the Renault and followed his example.

These men weren't out of control, but they were high, inebriated with the act of resistance. They believed they were winning, and that belief wove its own reality. They had stood up to the Israelis, in a way that no one else had done before. They were Hezbollah, and they felt Hezbollah was something that could never be destroyed. Houses could fall, lives could end, land could come under the occupation of Zionists. These life-sized tragedies were but bit measures of temporary earthly power. Resistance, in their worldview, came from another world: It was an act of God. If people welcomed it, resistance could wash away the stain of those setbacks.

That was the other pillar of the Southern State of Mind, erected over the years by Hezbollah's Islamic Resistance. The only way to lose was not to fight. So long as the people of Hezbollah were always under attack—which they would be so long as there was a Jewish state on their bor-der—they must always fight back, and their only legitimate defender was the Party of God. Hezbollah preferred an honorable military defeat to a tarnished peace. Hezbollah maintained its credibility as long as it could muster fighters and fire rockets. Hezbollah's heart, its center of gravity, was the South: a mythic place, a state of mind. Roughly, the South represented a sense of perpetual threat, a thirst to fight, and a belief that death could be a sort of victory. The majority of Lebanon's Shia originally hailed from Al Janoub, the South, mouthed as if it were a specific place and not a sprawl-ing region. The South was a sacred space and a mindset, the Karbala of

Lebanon's Shia. Historically it was their homeland and a source of greatness for global Shiism.[22] After centuries of servitude to feudal bosses,
Imam Musa Sadr empowered the Shia with a galvanized sense of community, identity, and political entitlement, beginning in the 1960s.[23] By the
1970s, the once-submissive Shia were ready to fight for their rights, and by
the 1980s, Hezbollah completed their transformation into a formidable,
militant sectarian community whose power could never again be ignored.
Israel burned and occupied the South. Israel's allies inside Lebanon ter-
rorized Shia communities elsewhere. All told a million or more fled their
homes, most of them relocating to the belt of misery in Beirut's southern
suburbs—Al Dahieh Al Janoubieh, or the Dahieh, the suburb, for short.
The name "Dahieh" recalled that history of displacement and the enduring connection to the South, the magisterial homeland of Lebanon's Shia
still imperiled by its propinquity to Israel. Hezbollah controlled the Dahieh, a leviathan contiguous and inseparable from the rest of Beirut, in
reality no more a suburb of Beirut than Queens is of New York City. Hassan Nasrallah's headquarters were there, as were most of Hezbollah's institutions. The party smuggled armaments over the Syrian border into the
Beqaa Valley, Hezbollah's birthplace, where it housed key secret military
training camps. The South remained largely poor and agrarian, always the
first battleground in a clash with Israel. Many Shia in the Dahieh were still
listed on the registries of their ancestral villages in the South because of
Lebanon's antediluvian voter registration system. If the Shia had arrived,
so to speak, and if their connection to the South was more emotional than
practical, for Hezbollah it remained of paramount importance to connect
all Shiites to a holy battleground, key to preserving the psychology of a
people at war. The Beqaa was Hezbollah's business end, where the party
founded its first seminary and trained its first fighters. The Dahieh bustled
with commerce, selling everything from lingerie to DVDs to SUVs. Yet its
cramped, narrow one-way lanes reminded its inhabitants that the southern suburb sprang up overnight as a refugee camp. The South was the
sacrament of this powerful new Shia generation. It ruled half of Lebanon
and possessed wealth and military might unimaginable to its parents. Unlike other Islamist movements, however, Hezbollah knew how to improve
the lot of its constituents from generation to generation, reaping for them
some benefits of power and development. But Hezbollah, as the prime

architect of this reversal, sensed that a fat and happy populace in short order would lose the willingness to fight and die that made Shia militancy so formidable. The Party of God wanted to strike a balance, between a modern program of economic development and a culture of privation. So it kept the candle of austerity and martyrdom always burning, to remind its people that all success was temporary, of this world and not the next. In a flash the material fruits of the Shia ascension could vanish, but so long as the culture of Islamic resistance flourishes, the Shiites would never lose their position. One quarter of a pious Shia's heart never stopped grieving for Karbala, and a steward of Lebanon's Islamic Resistance always kept one foot in the South.

The self-image persisted even when its people had long shed rural poverty for urban middle class prosperity. (The agrarian South, with its caves, rolling hills, bananas, and tobacco plants, was the ethos of Hezbollah; the Beqaa was its power grid; and the southern suburb of Beirut was its reality, a crowded, saturation-policed honeycomb.) Expatriate Hezbollah supporters rich from the African diamond trade built ostentatious mansions often on hilltops in direct range of Israeli cannons. These compounds, with mirrored windows, swimming pools, and obscenely lush palm gardens, paid homage to the imagined community of the South; these millionaire merchants didn't necessarily spend much time there, but they wouldn't dream of building their palaces anywhere else. Anyone who shared the values of the oppressed could be a "Southerner," and hence a Hezbollah supporter, in this construct. Hezbollah harkened to this Southern community, once occupied by Israel and still always at war, as the idealized homeland of all those who love the dispossessed and the resistance. The South filled the role for Hezbollah that the American Wild West did for rugged libertarian mythmakers in the United States.

Like all identity myths, the Southern Lebanese frontier myth bent history and overlooked some gaps. Multiple forces, some economic and political, others social, contributed to the Shia awakening; it was by no means solely the product of Musa Sadr and Hezbollah. Nor were the dispossessed Shia of the South the only protagonists. In fact, Iran in tandem with upwardly mobile wealthy Shia, including powerful Beirut families and Beqaa clans, underwrote the Shia revolution of the 1970s and provided much of its financial capital, political know-how, and brain trust.

Amal was built on a platform of civil rights, equality for the Shia. Hezbollah, on the other hand, was conceived as part and parcel of a state of constant war, and so it cultivated a culture of endless threat and endless readiness, inspired by the idea of the South, under constant attack by the Jews and their American patrons. Ever ready and ever threatened, Hezbollah's regime invoked the mind-set of the South to justify its selectively totalitarian rule over the Shiite community. Hezbollah kept a tighter watch over its areas than any other militia or sectarian group in Lebanon and perhaps, more ubiquitously than other police states in the Middle East, citing an endless cycle of threats from spies, political conspirators, and the Israeli military.

In 2008 and 2009 Lebanese security rolled up a vast network of people spying for Israel, some of them from the inner echelons of Hezbollah's community. But Hezbollah opportunistically stoked paranoia, even when it did not face verifiable threats: Hezbollah always kept its alarm level at the maximum, and it bombarded its audience with stories of foreign agents, saboteurs, secret plots, and nefarious war plans, most of which it presented with little or no evidence. The party's Shia constituents believed the narrative and bought into the idea that Hezbollah must resort to extreme measures to protect the community. Any outsider appearing in the Dahieh or in a Hezbollah-controlled town in the Beqaa or the South was immediately reported. Young men, often on motorbikes, would accost the visitor and prevent any interaction with locals until a party official arrived. That official determined whether the outsider could go about his business or be detained for further questioning.

But unlike typical totalitarian police states, Hezbollah's domain operated with the enthusiastic buy-in of most of its inhabitants. Hussein Rumeiti appeared to be a nice and friendly man, but he was no stranger to force, deception, and manipulation. He ran his part of Borj Qalaouay shrewdly, in keeping with the interests first of the Islamic resistance and then of his extended family. In the chain of authority he clearly outranked the young fighters in the town square, who all deferred to him and sought his instructions. But he presented himself as a kindly bystander, in the war zone simply to deliver medicine and bread to the housebound elderly. He no doubt saw the conversation with us as an opportunity to register a propaganda point for Hezbollah. Looking at those smoky eyes that betrayed no emotion when the rest of his face smiled, I was frightened to think what he might do if he found us not to his liking.

Men like Hussein Rumeiti looked older than their years—something in the way they would stare off to infinity during lulls in the conversation, or the way they weighed even their blandest pronouncements carefully, or the way their shoulders went limp when they relaxed as if they'd just set down a sack of cement. Part of their exhaustion, and perpetual sense of wonder, might have stemmed from the incredible reversal of the Shia trajectory that they had witnessed in just a few decades. Hassan Nasrallah's generation had reached its majority in an era when the Shia were still the downtrodden of Lebanon and second-class citizens of the Muslim world. The men and women in their thirties and forties who formed the bulk of Hezbollah's constituency were born in an era of bewildering change, the twilight of domination by feudal landlords and the first blush of the society of Islamic Resistance. The Shia had been lambs, not lions. The men and women at the center of Hezbollah's social network, people like Rani Bazzi, Hussein Haidar, Hussein Rumeiti, Issam Moussa, and others I came to know, their wives and cousins and extended families, had experienced a social revolution in a single generation. That whiplash helped explain the swell of energy that Hezbollah shaped into a self-sustaining wave.

At thirty-five, Hussein Rumeiti wasn't an old man, but in his lifetime the Shia of Lebanon had transformed from field hands to Lords of the Resistance. These once-meek splinter Muslims had reinvented themselves to such an unrecognizable extent that foes in Israel and the United States (not to mention Sunni monarchs in Jordan and Saudi Arabia) still struggled to make sense of Hezbollah and the rising "Shia Crescent." The Sunnis could hardly believe that the sons of former porters at Beirut harbor were giving orders to the sons of former landowners. Even the Shia themselves occasionally expressed a sense of astonishment that they had not only arrived but kept right on going: the weak minority now the biggest sect, militants who strived for humility.

From where had this Shia surge sprung? For a millennium or more—really, since the Twelfth Imam went into occultation in the ninth century—Shia Muslims had struggled, with a few rare historical exceptions, on the margins of politics and wars. Their *marjas*, or senior jurists, espoused the dogma of quietism, arguing that until the Hidden Imam returned at the end of time all worldly leadership was helplessly corrupt. The faithful should tolerate governments patiently, avoiding contact with earthly power until the time of true heavenly justice on earth. When necessary, the clerics allowed the practice of *taqiyya*, dissembling about one's religion for the purpose of avoiding persecution or conflict.

By the turn of the twentieth century, Shia thinkers had begun to question quietism. An intellectual revolution swept through the great seminaries of Najaf and Qom. Young jurists reinterpreted Shiite history, viewing the founding of their sect as a parable about justice rather than patience. The occulted imam, they argued, wanted his flock to aspire to a more just and holy world to prepare for his return; he didn't want them to resign themselves to injustice. Students like Ruhollah Khomeini, Mohammed Baqir Al-Sadr, Muhammed Hussein Fadlallah, and Musa Sadr embraced an empowering interpretation of Hussein's martyrdom on the plains of Karbala in the seventh century. The slaughter of the partisans of Ali at the dawn of Islamic history wasn't a failure; it was a liberating object lesson. Hussein led by example. He hadn't avoided earthly politics at all; he had taken a principled stand to resist empire and attack the caliphate, knowing unassailable odds ran against him.

True faith, Hussein's example suggested, manifested itself in the struggle, not the final score. The faithful could draw strength and inspiration from Hussein's brave last stand. The Shia could, and should, always fight for justice, armed with the greatest weapon of all: no fear of death. This radical reinterpretation led a new generation of clerical activists away from the apologetic demeanor prescribed by quietism, and toward a bold reclamation of Shia communal identity. These students rose through the clerical ranks and became the grand ayatollahs and imams of a radical Shia generation. They disagreed among themselves about details, like whether the clerics should rule directly (Khomeini's model) or indirectly, by telling subservient elected officials what to do (the model Grand Ayatollah Ali Sistani advanced in Iraq after the U.S. invasion in 2003). Gone, however, was the assumption that the Shia would wait and pray while others made history.[24]

A fluid international network linked the Shia world, an interconnected community of clerics, merchants, landlords, and laborers who toiled and traveled with little regard for the borders of empires and, later, nation-states. This Shia web promoted flexibility and a very modern identity. Such a dynamic environment later proved very conducive to Hezbollah's operations and ideology. As Lebanon lurched toward civil war in the 1970s, the Shia community had just barely emerged as a player. The traditionally powerful communities—the Christians, the Sunnis, and the Druze, along with the Palestinians—had lined up international patrons to fund and arm their militias. Shiites served as foot soldiers in other people's movements, learning the mechanics of warfare, most notably from Palestinian militant factions. But Imam Musa Sadr, an Iranian transplant with Lebanese ancestry, had irrevocably transformed the Shia sense of self and place. Politically, he assuaged potential rivals with sustained outreach and massaging of egos. Christians were mollified by his endless energy for interfaith dialogue. Nonetheless, he organized the Shia, created out of a vacuum a power structure (under the Shia Higher Council, which Musa Sadr founded), and won a share of Lebanon's sectarian spoils system for the Shia, who had hitherto been shut out. As Lebanon careered toward the law of the jungle, he founded the first Shia militia, Amal. Faith could bring power and spread justice, Musa Sadr taught. He built schools and clinics, agitated for water, sewers, and roads for the Shia areas estranged from modernity, and reminded his people that they weren't alone in the world. Wealthy and educated Shia leaders around the world cared about the Shia of Lebanon, and once awakened, they too would care about the struggles of their coreligionists in Iran, Iraq, Pakistan, Afghanistan, the Gulf, and around the global diaspora.

Young men and women who later were to lead the Shia recalled the electric thrill of Musa Sadr's ministry. Future founders of the Shia parties used to fight their fellow students for a seat whenever Musa Sadr would address their high school assemblies.[25] Musa Sadr disappeared during a trip to Libya in 1978, the same year that Israel first invaded South Lebanon. By then, the dam had burst and Shia empowerment had flowed into the Islamic current. The following year a popular uprising overturned the Shah's dictatorship in Iran, and Ayatollah Khomeini quickly took control of the revolution, purging its secular elements and creating the first Shia Islamic revolutionary republic of the modern age. He promised to spread his radical vision across the Shia world, and nowhere did he find a more ready cadre of messengers than among the Shia activists in Lebanon.

By the 1970s, a small coterie of passionate, competent, and intellectually formidable men already had begun a new movement among Lebanon's Shia. Most of them had studied at the seminary in Najaf, Iraq, and many of them had trained with the underground militant Dawa Party, a secretive Iraqi Shia organization that dared to defy Saddam Hussein, organizing bombings, assassination attempts, and ambushes. Lebanon's most senior Shia cleric, Ayatollah Muhammed Hussein Fadlallah, was one of the theological architects of the new idea of Shia resistance. He endorsed the use of any and all tactics by the weak and dispossessed against the powerful, including "martyrdom attacks," or suicide bombings.[26] Honorable Shia fighting Israel and the United States could resort to any techniques, Fadlallah counseled, including suicide attacks that would kill other Muslims as collateral damage, so long as the number of infidel dead were greater.

The elite militant clerics, an Ivy League of Islamism, had gathered under the banner of Khomeini's revolutionary theology and the imperative to fight Israel and the West. Their ideology was explicitly anti-Zionist, opposing the establishment of a Jewish state in the Middle East. Theologically and culturally, however, many of the movement's leaders, not least Khomeini and later Nasrallah, also preached a hatred of all Jews, citing early Islamic history to justify a demonized view of Judaism and Jews. These Islamist activists in the 1970s already were preaching to bands of followers and searching for the right organization to join and lead. Hussein Musawi had already defected from the increasingly secular and pragmatic Amal Movement to found Islamic Amal. Sheikh Sobhi Tufayli stayed close to Iranian hard-liners and amassed a passionate following in the Beqaa. Abbas Musawi, Hassan Nasrallah, and Ragheb Harb also shared an affinity for armed resistance, Iran, and Islamic Revolution; they worked with Amal but searched for a more godly and militant organization. Iran was looking for a foothold in Lebanon, joining the parade of foreign governments sponsoring militias and political parties in the civil war. Iran and Syria reached an agreement to coordinate sponsorship of a new Shia Islamist militia. The two states shared common foreign policy goals and forged an axis in the region to counter the Washington-allied Arab governments. In 1982, Iran sent a contingent of about 1,500 Revolutionary Guards to Baalbek, in the

Beqaa Valley, where they began to train and indoctrinate the core group that founded Hezbollah. That year the founding members settled on a name, Hezbollah, the Party of God, and a platform of unbending armed struggle against Israel and the West. Responding to the threat of the Israeli invasion, and the initially tepid response of the Shia (many of whom were glad to see someone finally dispatch the Palestinian guerillas who had made their daily lives miserable), the founders of the Party of God wanted to galvanize a "jihadi spirit" to propel "a young movement getting ready to fight a legendary army."[27] In that first year, Nasrallah said, Hezbollah spent all its energies recruiting young men, adding about two thousand to its ranks, and educating the public about the holy struggle. Nasrallah and other founding members recalled in later interviews a time of great camaraderie and ferment in the Baalbek barracks, where they would debate into the night after long days of training under the supervision of the Revolutionary Guard. Hezbollah only revealed its existence with the publication of an "Open Letter" in 1985 that expounded at length on the party's view, at that time rigid, of Islamic Resistance.[28] But its tenets and tactics were set by the autumn of 1982.

At the same time, Iran trained, funded, and armed other operatives, dubbed "special groups" by some observers, who could conduct complicated military strikes and other operations, like kidnappings. These groups intentionally had a murky relationship with Hezbollah, which allowed Iran and Hezbollah when convenient to distance themselves from the spate of hostage takings in Lebanon from 1982 to 1992 and the bombings of the U.S. Embassy, U.S. Marine barracks, and French paratrooper barracks in 1983.[29] A group called the "Islamic Jihad Organization" claimed those attacks, and some observers posit that Imad Mughniyeh (eventually linked to all of Hezbollah's major attacks) and the other architects of the attacks carried them out with the financial and logistical support of Iran and Syria and made up the name to confuse people.[30] Hezbollah's founders certainly used the attacks as a recruiting tool.

Sheikh Sobhi Tufayli was an early Hezbollah hard-liner who went on to win election as the party's first secretary-general in 1989. He was kicked out within two years, breaking with the rest of the party leadership because he thought Hezbollah should boycott the 1992 elections and stay out of the Lebanese government. A formidable intellect and early activist in the Dawa Party in Iraq, Tufayli came from the wild, lawless tribal area around

Baalbek. He was considered one of the central forces behind the hostage-taking campaign and the U.S. Embassy and Marine barracks bombings. As a party spokesman in the 1980s, he frequently appeared in the media praising suicide bombers and hostage takers. In 2008, I met Tufayli and asked him about the deadly suicide strikes against the Americans and the French in 1983, more than a quarter-century earlier. He smiled cryptically and with evident satisfaction. The Islamic Resistance, he said, got credit for those attacks, even if they were technically the "independent" handiwork of Imad Mughniyeh. "Until 1982, people thought they didn't have any power, that the Israelis had all the power, and that the resistance was a fiction. They thought we would fail," Sheikh Tufayli reflected when I talked with him at his mountain redoubt outside Baalbek early one fall morning. His vast marble diwan was colder than the hills outside. The only warmth came from a samovar on a pile of coals in a sand-filled brass table. Guards in argyle sweaters with machine guns patrolled the residence (Tufayli is after all a wanted man, having antagonized at various turns the United States, Israel, the Lebanese Army, Iran, and even Hezbollah). "I knew that people would change their minds if we could prove that we could defeat the enemy. Because of the great success of our operations people became more convinced in Hezbollah, especially after the two operations of the U.S. Embassy and the barracks bombings. We persuaded people that they had the capacity to defend themselves."

In this era—from 1985 onward—virtually every Shiite who stayed in Lebanon entered some kind of relationship with the Shia parties and eventually fell into Hezbollah's orbit, willingly or not. Rani Bazzi was falling under the sway of the Islamic Resistance from a distance—he was growing up in the Lebanese expatriate community in Kuwait, but through friends and occasional visits back home he had come to lionize Hezbollah's fighters and absorb their faith. Hussein Rumeiti, as a secular young teenager in the 1980s, learned to admire the Amal Movement for bringing roads and schools to the South and Hezbollah for fighting Israel when other militants had tired.

Dergham Dergham, a man I hired as a translator in Beirut during the 2006 war, was a teenage hothead living in the Dahieh in the early 1980s, and had no time for faith and discipline. He wanted to ride the bull, so he joined Amal, got an AK-47 and perfunctory training, and took part in firefights that to this day he can't precisely explain, sometimes trading fire with Israelis, sometimes with Palestinians, sometimes with the Lebanese Army. He wasn't sure whom he was shooting at, who ordered him into combat or whether he had something so exact as a commanding officer. "We were too young to know why," he said. "Some politicians made the decision. We were Shia, this was our neighborhood, so we were with Amal." That was Amal's style; the young Shia got a fix of violence, and the party mainlined on their adrenaline. At its peak Amal had tens of thousands of men under arms, but their combat discipline was limited. Dergham was shot and mildly injured. His best friend was killed during the Israeli invasion in 1982. His more devout brothers stayed away from the militias or joined the more restrained and covert Islamic groups. His parents understood the danger that Dergham didn't. Dergham, their second son, was heading for the kind of early pointless death that had become a signature for Lebanese teenagers. They packed him off to an acquaintance in Chicago, with a vague and optimistic admonition to keep out of trouble.

Hussein Haidar, Inaya's father, was another Lebanese man succumbing to Hezbollah's gravitational pull in that era. He refused to leave Srifa even though it lay on the Islamic Resistance's runway. No Israeli occupation would make him raise his children far from their home. His abiding faith lent him backbone along with a resigned fatalism; whatever God had ordained would happen anyway, so why not choose to live life on his own terms instead of the Israelis'? He taught math at the high school and steered his son and daughters toward an education in the sciences. More and more he noticed that the men willing to stand up to the Israelis were Party of God members. The nationalist resistance had withered, and the Amal and Communist fighters still committed to the cause had joined Hezbollah as junior partners. Gradually his steadfastness merged with the party's, and he found himself pulled more and more toward the ascetic passion of Hezbollah.

Hezbollah didn't admit it existed until 1985, when it published its manifesto in the form of an "Open Letter" and belatedly took credit for the November 11, 1982, suicide attack on the Israeli military headquarters in Tyre, even naming the bomber, Ahmed Kassir (a relative of the Al-Manar director). Even then, in the cacophony of militant Lebanon, Hezbollah hadn't conclusively distinguished itself. Religious fanatics of all stripes and confessions had found sponsors to give them explosives, guns, and political cover. Iran paid salaries to Hezbollah fighters, but other powers including Israel, Syria, the CIA, and Saudi Arabia were shipping weapons and cash to their own proxies in Lebanon. At the time it would have been difficult to distinguish the loyalty of Hezbollah's membership (or to predict the longevity of Iran and Syria's commitment) from that of the other sectarian militias that at the time ran mini-states within Lebanon. Other groups also displayed devotion and militancy comparable to Hezbollah's early fighters. Throughout the 1980s, secular groups like the Syrian Social Nationalist Party (SSNP) and Amal had deployed suicide bombers in martyrdom operations, and the secular, pragmatic Amal movement retained its close ties to Syria and contested the leadership of Lebanon's Shia. Amal, the SSNP, and the Communists fought alongside Hezbollah's commandos in the Islamic Resistance against Israel. In its early years Hezbollah vociferously advocated the establishment of an Islamic state in Lebanon, a position anathema to the country's Christians and also to many of its secular Muslims, especially those Sunni and Druze who viewed with contempt the austere and fanatical mores of the Islamist society the ayatollahs had decreed in Iran. An observer of Lebanon and the Middle East at the time could be forgiven for not singling out Hezbollah as a unique movement that would have particularly lasting power.

In hindsight, though, it's clear that Hezbollah was forged in a different fire than the region's other militant Islamist movements. Its founders were clerics and fighters, and they had lived in a space beyond national borders. They felt Lebanese but simultaneously Shia and transnational. They knew how to organize underground. They were trained in sabotage and combat. And they were steeped in a culture of martyrdom that embraced death without seeking death as its own goal. They loved men and women brave enough to risk death. But over and over they told me that they didn't love death itself. A vast Shia awakening was underway across the Islamic world, and Iran's oil-rich government was ready to drench it in money, weapons, and military training. By design and historical accident Hezbollah was appealing to its new followers, building a militia and a network of social institutions, just as many Shia were adopting a distinct and powerful identity. At the same time, Hezbollah took the lead in the military struggle against Israel in the 1980s when the rest of Lebanon's factions had spent their resources fighting each other to a standstill. Some were simply exhausted after years of war; others saw Islamic fundamentalists as a greater threat than Jews; and some, like the leadership of Amal, believed the Shia would be better off if Lebanon stopped quarrelling with Israel, a doomed challenge that would only bring more grief to the Southerners caught in the crossfire. Drawing on Shia momentum and energy other groups had spurned, Hezbollah surged to power, defying expectations for the first of countless times because it did what so few Islamist movements or their rivals ever had: it learned from its mistakes and adapted.

In the final decades of the cold war, during the 1970s and 1980s, political violence was common currency for governments and militant factions alike. State-sponsored murder and terrorist attacks on civilians gripped the global consciousness in a manner that today's Western public might have forgotten, preoccupied by our contemporary post–September 11 struggles with Al Qaeda and other extremist groups. Four decades ago conflict ripped through a Middle East where dictators in Iran and the Arab world treated their citizens with gross contempt and brutality. Israel was fighting a visceral war sometimes village to village, on its own territory as well as on its neighbors'. In a climate of generalized violence, pro-Palestinian militants wielded the weapons of the weak. They hijacked buses, planes, and boats. They massacred civilians. They blew themselves up, and they blew up landmarks. They took hostages, and filmed summary executions. It was a time of raw struggle in which the level of inhumanity often exceeded the actual body count, although the grisly efforts of governments in Syria, Iraq, and Iran kept it close. A million or more died on the battlefields between Iran and Iraq. Thousands more were crippled and blinded in Iraqi chemical weapons attacks condoned by a Machiavellian American administration balancing the two strong regimes in the Persian Gulf. Israel and the Palestine Liberation Organization were locked in a bloody war. Proxy cold war conflicts across the globe featured execution squads, institutionalized torture, mass arrests, and state-orchestrated mass killing, usually by regimes on the payroll of Moscow or Washington. For the insurgents of the world, anything that won attention for the cause was acceptable, be it bombing a Berlin disco or spraying Rome airport passengers with bullets, murdering a man in a wheelchair and tossing him off a hijacked cruise ship or pulling a man out of his car at a checkpoint and shooting him in the head. Lebanon's culture of violence was as deep as any twisted nation's. Hezbollah invoked that heritage of damage for double benefit. First, there was no shortage of young men willing and able to fight, kill, and die. Second, and more important, in a landscape of nihilism Hezbollah understood the intrinsic appeal of spiritual clarity. Lost souls bobbing on a sea of violence, adrenaline, and Hobbesian political competition longed for meaning. Hezbollah taught not mere violence, but violent struggle in the service of a higher power. Hezbollah wouldn't tolerate rampant, thuggish, gang-style violence like many other Islamist and other militant groups that promoted generalized brutality among their members. Hezbollah advocated disciplined, targeted political violence, and would quickly bring to heel members who committed unauthorized attacks. Hezbollah benefited in its early years of growth from a general climate of turmoil among its potential constituents. Faith was at war with disbelief, the Arab world was at war with Israel, but both conflicts in Hezbollah's framework were subsets of a grand struggle, an overarching jihad to make the world a more just, Islamic place. In the eyes of their enemies (and often of their own legal systems) America and Israel were committing aberrant crimes, killing or helping to kill civilians in wars orchestrated for abstract political aims. One such venture was the failed attempt to install a Christian Phalangist government in Lebanon that would make peace with Israel and common cause with Ronald Reagan's administration. Ayatollah Fadlallah propagated an explosive theology that permitted the Muslim to reclaim his political rights by force. The fighter who didn't have access to an F-16 jet fighter or an Apache attack helicopter, under this doctrine, without offending God could deploy himself as a bomb, behind the wheel of a truck full of explosives or wearing a vest laced with ball bearings.

In theory, Fadlallah's theology and Hezbollah's doctrine abjured power in favor of justice. If the jihadists accrued power along the way, it was an incidental gain, to be shed at any point that it became a hindrance. This posture cast a great glow of honor around Hezbollah. Even when entrenched in power, allied with the strongmen of the region and better able to shape events than the Lebanese state, Hezbollah always declared that temporal power was for others, no matter how much power it possessed.

Like Cincinnatus harangued by the senators until he relented to duty and left his farm for Rome, so Hezbollah made great theater of its supposed reluctance for power. If no one would take responsibility for the nation's defense, well then the Islamic Resistance would do the job; if no one would tend to the people's welfare, well then the Party of God would bring them drinking water and education. The mighty Israeli army always threatened to dismantle Hezbollah, while the feeble government of Lebanon failed time and time again to deliver even the most rudimentary services to its Shia citizenry—providing Hezbollah the necessary conditions to construct a network of control. Beginning in those first days, Hezbollah never missed an opportunity to teach its radical theology and political creed. Ideological indoctrination and religious lessons came before, during, and after all its activities: outreach, recruitment, military training, and social services. A generation was reared on Hezbollah's comprehensive teachings about jihad in all aspects of life, from personal hygiene and study habits to the obligation to resist secular Western culture and fight Israeli occupation. These devout and prayerful activists gave their youth to Hezbollah and served the party as it grew, stumbled, retreated, and grew again.

The moment of global turmoil subsided. The cold war drew to a close, and with it many of the proxy conflicts it had stoked. Israel entered negotiations with the PLO. In 1989, Lebanon's factions signed a peace treaty that eventually brought the civil war to a close. Iran ended its war with Iraq, having failed for the moment to export the Islamic Revolution to the second-most-populous Shia nation (arguably it would find success on that front after Saddam was toppled in 2003). Ayatollah Khomeini died and a new group of clerics took hold of Iran's purse strings. Hezbollah clashed with Syria and with the Amal movement, fighting an internecine Shia war that resulted in Hezbollah briefly being pushed out of much of southern Lebanon while Amal was completely driven out of the Dahieh. Hezbollah irritated and alienated scores of Lebanese with its Islamic fundamentalism. The Party of God told women to wear headscarves and threatened restaurants that served alcohol.[31] People in the South and the Dahieh complied resentfully because Hezbollah had guns, but popular support for the Islamist scolds waned. For a moment around 1990, Hezbollah seemed destined to go the way of all Lebanon's fanatical movements; domineering at their apogee, quick to overreach and just as quick to dissipate when their foreign sponsors shifted attention and funds elsewhere. Then Sayyed Abbas Musawi, who had commanded Hezbollah's militia, took over as the party's secretary-general after a period of internal rancor. Sheikh Sobhi Tufayli had been forced out as leader during the internal debate over whether to take part in the 1992 elections, and Hezbollah had reorganized its top bodies: the Shura Council, the executive committee, and the politburo. Musawi began drafting an electoral platform that was a blueprint for good governance and contained little of the invective of the 1985 Open Letter. Israel, still convinced that it could emasculate Hezbollah by killing its leaders, assassinated Musawi on February 16, 1992, killing him along with his wife and child in a targeted missile strike on his convoy. The move backfired.

Sayyed Hassan Nasrallah was immediately elected secretary-general, and he accelerated Hezbollah's turnaround. Nasrallah blended political dexterity, opportunism, and brute force. He preached with genuine religious fervor (some would say fanaticism) and brilliantly sensed how to manipulate and harness the public mood. Like every great charismatic leader he knew when to rile his public and when to follow it. Like a smart CEO determined to regain market share, he scaled back Hezbollah's activities to focus on its most popular product: armed resistance. He increased attacks against the Israeli military and its proxy, the South Lebanon Army, and he cut back on the inflammatory Islamist rhetoric on the domestic front. The core party membership was truly committed to the Islamicization of society, but Nasrallah shrewdly calculated that he could keep them loyal by maintaining internal discipline and a strict Islamic culture *within* the party. For the rest he could open a wider cultural space. Nasrallah issued an invitation to the secular Shia and the rest of the Lebanese: Support our resistance project against Israel and we'll stop talking about an Islamic republic and telling you how to live your lives. Anyone who continued to collaborate with the Israelis or otherwise posed a security threat could be tortured, detained, killed, or ostracized. On the cultural front, though, crusades were suspended. Communities could be persuaded or pressured—to take the veil, study the Koran, fund the resistance—but no longer would Islamic mores be mandated. Nonmembers could drink, visit whorehouses, cavort in bikinis on the beaches of the South. Lebanon was free once again to balance resistance and lifestyle in its own Lebanese way. Nasrallah had concluded that what had worked in Iran wouldn't work in Lebanon, and that Hezbollah would win more power, security, and resources if it comforted its Lebanese rivals rather than antagonized them.

As the new secretary-general, Nasrallah also wasted no angst on Hezbollah's dependence on Iran and Syria. Without Iranian money and Syrian support Hezbollah would hardly have any reach. Nasrallah made no apologies for his party's links to Tehran and Damascus, publicly thanking Hezbollah's patrons in speech after speech. Hezbollah followed the ultimate authority of a Shia Supreme Leader in Tehran, Nasrallah explained, but didn't expect the Lebanese political realm to do the same—a formulation that placated some people's fears of Hezbollah as a fifth column for Iran. Furthermore, Nasrallah ended the squabbling with its sponsors that had cost Hezbollah dearly in the past.[32] In order to grow, Hezbollah would have to seduce a wider public that had hoped to be done with war after the 1989 Taif Accords. The Party of God had to sell Islamic Resistance to a nation accustomed to a loveless marriage of convenience with the mosque. It would have to sell a long war against the Jewish State, the most powerful military force in the region, to a nation intimately acquainted with what Israel's fury could do. And it would have to sell internal accommodation and negotiation to its own members, the fighters it had inspired with a quest to dwell in the unblemished garden of Islamic justice, here or in the hereafter. Such nimble reinvention was a novelty in the Islamic arena; so too was Hezbollah's decision to cross the Rubicon and enter electoral politics without renouncing its Islamist ideology. It published a dry and wonkish electoral platform and stopped calling attention to its founding Open Letter, but only revised its doctrine officially in 2009.[33] Stubborn and anachronistic behavior characterized almost every Arab and Islamist faction in the region. Eager to expand its power base, Hezbollah was taking risks and evolving as an organization, setting off into virgin territory.

For a radical revolutionary group, Hezbollah's decision to stand for parliament marked a dangerous strategic gambit. The Party of God could easily find itself in the same golden handcuffs as the Amal Party, or the opposition Muslim Brotherhood parties in Egypt and Jordan, or even of the Iranian mullahs: once saddled with a share of governance (or co-opted by the tempting booty of official corruption), a rogue's gallery of radical groups had lost their fire and in prompt succession their street credibility and popular following. On the other hand, if Hezbollah could achieve its own version of the golden mean, stoking a radical jihadist hearth at home with its inner constituency while outside playing pragmatic politics with the Lebanese factions and the international community, the Party of God could exponentially increase its military power and political influence—without compromising the religious purity at its heart.

Hezbollah deftly learned to say one thing and do another. The party learned to say new things as well, pacific phrases that initially seemed out of character. Political movements everywhere speak out of all sides of their mouths. Alone among the Islamist movements, though, Hezbollah mastered the art of doing so without appearing to lie or betray its Islamist heart. The Party of God always meant what it said—for example, that it believed in the ideals of an Islamic state—even if it admitted that it couldn't achieve all its wishes and wouldn't *necessarily* try. The party said enough, in other words, to energize its Islamist members while reassuring its un-Islamic neighbors. The scions of Lebanon's old order predicted that Hezbollah would rupture if it tried to be a political party and a resistance movement at the same time. In 1992, a decade after its founding and a mere seven years after it admitted its existence to the world, Hezbollah won one of the largest single blocs in Lebanon's parliament. Its military wing was fighting as effectively as ever. It was the first of many times that the Party of God would defy predictions of its imminent demise. Hezbollah hoped to draw on that recent history, and the strategy it crafted in the early 1990s, to turn the 2006 war into an opportunity rather than a catastrophe.

Hezbollah had declared victory well in advance of the ceasefire that went into effect at 8 a.m. on Monday, August 14, 2006. Huge banners already hung along the airport highway with the war's logo: Nasr Min Allah, literally "Victory From God," translated by the party into English as "The Divine Victory." Crisply designed, in Arabic as well as English, the banners showcased photos of wartime destruction, disheveled Israeli soldiers, and Hezbollah fighters firing weapons or gesticulating in triumph. Clearly, the publicity campaign for the Divine Victory had been designed before anyone knew how long the hostilities would last, and was trotted out with many audiences in mind. Hezbollah was planning for the next phase of the war, a political and psychological marketing campaign aimed at its base at home, its local enemies, and general public opinion in the Middle East, Israel, and the United States. Once again, Hezbollah's growing stable of opponents was joining forces to defang the Islamic Resistance, and once again Hezbollah found itself at a critical point, its fundamental goals called into question and its survival challenged. Sayyed Hassan Nasrallah had issued his nonnegotiable terms for the war (and presumably any subsequent ones). Israel and its backers wanted to destroy Hezbollah and disarm the Islamic Resistance. Since Hezbollah stood still armed at the end of the battle, Israel had failed. Hezbollah, however, had not yet won; its prisoners still languished in Israeli jails, the Shebaa Farms were occupied, and influential Lebanese wanted to shutter the Islamic Resistance's militia.

Hezbollah's agenda was designed to justify its militia for the foreseeable future. Nasrallah had declared three aims: first, to preserve his militia's weapons until the theoretical time when the Lebanese military would take over the war with Israel; second, to secure the release of Samir Quntar and any remaining Lebanese prisoners in Israel; third and finally, to liberate the Shebaa Farms. These major *casi belli*, like nesting dolls, contained other lesser ones. If the major claims were resolved, Hezbollah could trot out other grievances: disputed border villages, water sources, Israeli overflights. Many of the particulars were recognized as legitimate disputes, litigated by Israeli and Lebanese diplomats at the United Nations and other venues; but the manner in which Nasrallah evolved his set of demands made clear that he had no interest in a peace accord with Israel. If one point of contention were resolved, he would add another to the list and give it equal weight as the question it replaced, without granting that any progress had been made. Short of a miracle, it seemed, the very existence of a self-determined Jewish state in the Middle East would always occasion belligerence from the Islamic Resistance, even if it made political sense for Hezbollah to imply otherwise.

Speaking calmly and confidently over the television in his final wartime fireside chat, Nasrallah closed the hot phase of the war with a laundry list of promises.[34] Hezbollah would help everyone displaced return home. The party would rebuild and rearm. The martyrs would be honored and the survivors compensated. Later, Hezbollah would return to the unfinished business of the prisoners and the occupied land. Meanwhile, at least a million were displaced and at least 15,000 homes were destroyed. There was rubble to clear: there were livelihoods to restore. Nasrallah reminded his viewers who had borne most of this price: the Beqaa, the South, and the Dahieh—in short, the Shia. The resistance, Nasrallah said, "was making a new legend." Meanwhile, "some people sitting behind their desks under air conditioners" were plotting to take away Hezbollah's weapons. "They are talking to people whose houses were destroyed and whose children were killed," Nasrallah said. "Do they think that those people and these huge segments of the Lebanese society and those who embrace them, believe in them, and support them have no feelings or emotions?" The followers of the resistance should restrain their anger in the face of this insult, Nasrallah advised. But the message was really a warning to Lebanese politicians who were hoping out of the downdraft of such a destructive war to forge a consensus to disarm Hezbollah.

If a million people left their homes during the war, it seemed at least that many drove into the South on August 14. Some were returning; others were checking on relatives or property; still more were just sightseers, curious to examine the results of the war. Traffic piled up for hours at each bombed bridge or crater where the highway would divert to a single lane through the brush or dirt. Earthmovers were out in force making quick temporary road repairs to speed traffic. The Lebanese army laid pontoon bridges across the rivers. Hezbollah operatives shoved pink leaflets into the car windows. "Congratulations to you for the Divine Victory," the text read, going on to enumerate a detailed list of hazards, including photos of unexploded ordnance, cluster bombs, and unsafe structures that could collapse upon entry. "Be careful!" the flyer concluded.

The trail of twisted infrastructure mapped Hezbollah's next great challenge. Sure, the party had survived the war with Israel with much of its capacity intact. The same could not be said of Lebanon. Power lines hung like entrails at a butcher shop. Shopkeepers' stock littered the roads, and many roads themselves were as impassable as goat paths after a flood. In the South and the Dahieh, those walls that still stood had been punctured to latticework by shrapnel. The rest of the country had paid dues for which it had never subscribed. Beirut, the north, the mountains—areas inimical to Hezbollah—saw their most modern bridges and highway overpasses bombed. Fuel poured from stricken gas depots into the sea, contaminating the entire nation's beaches. These other Lebanese, not in the resistance fold, could blame Hezbollah as much as Israel for the brute force that had sundered their land. Hezbollah's job was to convince sympathizers to blame Israel alone, and to cut off at the knees those who continued to hold the Islamic Resistance responsible for the gyre of war that had once again caught Lebanon in its flow.

In some quarters in Washington and Israel, a debate over who had won the war began, but focused on body counts and infrastructure damage while ignoring the question of political momentum. But Israeli public opinion and the later assessment of the political class didn't depend on the number of dead or the parsing of wartime statements by the prime minister and his cabinet.[35] Most Israelis were beginning to judge the war on whether they thought anything had been accomplished (Was Hezbollah weaker? Had Israel adequately responded to the capture of the two soldiers?) and whether the cost had been worth it (Was the Israeli loss of life and security commensurate to its military gains?). To the consternation of Israel's leaders, most of the public was answering those questions in the negative.[36] So too were most Lebanese applying their own calculus to the post-war balance of power. No one in Lebanon, or in the wider Islamic world, was grading the war's outcome on Hezbollah's high death toll or the formidable cost of fallen bridges. During the thirty-four-day war, most of northern Israel was evacuated. One-hundred and nineteen Israeli soldiers were killed during the fighting and 44 Israeli civilians, including four from heart attacks blamed on rocket fire.[37] That toll didn't include the two captured Israeli soldiers, whose fate remained unknown. The Israeli police tallied 3,970 rocket strikes (most of them Katyushas), which displaced 300,000 people, forced 1 million into shelters, and hit 6,000 homes. Israeli business groups in the north of the country estimated the lost revenue from the war, which wiped out most of the tourist season, at $1.4 billion.[38] In Lebanon, the death toll was much higher and the damage exponentially worse. One-thousand, one-hundred and ninety-one people were killed and 4,405 wounded, according to the Lebanese government's High Relief Council.[39] During the fighting 1 million were displaced; a fifth of them couldn't return after the war because their homes were too damaged. Bombing destroyed at least 7,500 houses and damaged another 117,500. The government estimated the infrastructure would cost $2.8 billion to repair: nearly 700 damaged schools, 97 bridges, 16 hospitals, 65 clinics, and 151 stretches of road.[40] The Ministry of Finance estimated the lost revenue caused by the war at $1.6 billion.[41] Hezbollah never released an official death toll of fighters, although a party official later estimated that about 250 fighters were killed.[42]

On the day after, the people of Lebanon began to tally the power of their national movements and the reputations of their leaders. Many notions hung in tatters like the wind-snapped flags along either side of the border erected to irritate the enemies across the fence. One idea now past its prime was that friendly relations with the United States could insulate an Arab country like Lebanon from a destructive war with Israel. Lebanon's prime minister and his coalition loved Washington. They buttressed much of the neoconservative agenda and they detested Hezbollah, its militia, and Iran. All that, however, gave them almost no capital when it came to pushing for a ceasefire during the war. Another idea increasingly hard to espouse with a straight face was that the Islamic Resistance took to heart the interests of all Lebanese. Hezbollah didn't consult Lebanon's powerful warlords before launching its provocative raid, and few of Lebanon's Christians, Druze, and Sunni Muslims believed that Nasrallah would have altered his plans had he bothered to hear their objections. Other ideas were up for grabs. Did Israel still have deterrent power? Did Hezbollah's performance on the battlefield suggest ways to inflict lasting strategic damage on the Jewish State? Was Hezbollah's strength solely a reflection of Iranian largesse and know-how, and Syrian logistical support? Or was Hezbollah acting and projecting power on its own? Could Hezbollah translate its military success into a lasting political platform?

At a press conference on July 21, American Secretary of State Condoleezza Rice had explained that she wasn't interested in shuttle diplomacy to preserve the status quo and broker some ceasefire with Hezbollah that would only beget future wars. Then, playing right into the hands of the master propagandists at Hezbollah, who monitored every speech by every major Israeli and American official, Rice gave the Party of God the catchline it was waiting for: "What we're seeing here, in a sense, is the birth pangs of a new Middle East. And whatever we do, we have to be certain that we're pushing forward to the new Middle East, not going back to the old one."[43]

Presto! America had another public relations problem and Hezbollah had its slogan. For Americans and Israelis, death and destruction of Arabs and Muslims was less significant even than collateral damage—Arab suffering was something painful but felicitous, "birth pangs." And the hail of explosives was America's idea of how to build a new Middle East, in keeping with the tradition established in Iraq in 2003, where as Arab conventional wisdom had it, America had tried to import democracy on the back of a bomb. Presumably Hezbollah went ahead right then and printed up the sarcastic posters and banners it unveiled at the war's close three weeks later. Some of them read "The New Middle East," in English, and hung over the ruins of bombed apartment blocks. Some posters planted on wooden stakes like front yard campaign placards read "The New Middle Beast," in a clumsy play on words, and featured photos of Rice, or Israeli Prime Minister Ehud Olmert, or President Bush, or some other American or Israeli malefactor.

Across the Arab and Islamic world people on the street began hoisting Hassan Nasrallah's portrait into the air. Here was a leader who resonated like no one had since Ayatollah Khomeini in 1979 or Gamal Abdel Nasser in the 1950s and 1960s. The chants of marching protesters and the essays of impassioned Arab and Persian intellectuals framed the war's broader implications in stark terms: resistance versus accommodation. Much of the Arab world had opted to accommodate the realities of American and Israeli power. Some, like Jordan and Egypt, had made peace, even if they kept Israel at arm's length. The Palestine Liberation Organization settled with Israel and traded its war of liberation for the trappings of statehood. Saudi Arabia funded militant organizations listed as terrorist groups, but had long adopted a pragmatic official policy of working with Washington and inching toward a grudging acceptance of Israel, an unwanted force they could neither dislodge from their region nor comfortably embrace. Not so the Resistance Axis: Iran, Hamas, Hezbollah, the Muslim Brotherhood, the Mahdi Army, and Syria. These regimes and movements claimed they could tailor new strategic realities, using force to empower a Muslim world that eventually would be able to dictate new terms to Israel or even abolish the Jewish State altogether.[44] The idea seemed absurd to many realists, especially those who based their views on Israel's overwhelming strategic advantage in the Middle East. But the audience of the Resistance Axis was made of men smoking waterpipes on plastic chairs in towns like Borj Qalaouay and street corners in the Dahieh, and their counterparts in the souks of Damascus, Tehran, Baghdad, Cairo, and beyond. They weren't interested in a realpolitik political analysis. They wanted to see what the resistance could do to Israel, and then they wanted to see what it could do to Arab political rivals. It was a true test of firepower and political muscle. In 2000, Israel had fled South Lebanon under fire from Hezbollah, even if Israel insisted it was leaving of its own accord. In 2006, Hezbollah had continued firing Katyushas despite Israel's withering high-tech air campaign. Hezbollah had Iran's unconditional backing and vast reserves of cash to draw on. Could it rebuild? Could it keep its battered followers loyal? And could it carve out a permanent slice of political power in Lebanon, to continue its war not from the precarious perch of an outlaw militia but as a pillar of the governing establishment?

People were mad. In the Christian neighborhoods not aligned with Hezbollah, almost everyone I spoke to in August 2006 muttered that Iran had the region by the throat.[45] Many Lebanese Christians believed that a bunch of Shia sectarian fanatics ruled Hezbollah and were willing to burn the entire country in pursuit of their millenarian, power-hungry aims. The dentist who cleaned my teeth feared that Hezbollah would take over the government and force an Iranian-style theocracy on everyone—*hijabs* for all, liquor stores shuttered. Shop clerks fantasized about emigrating. Upper middle class Christians at the cafés raged that Lebanon's nascent liberal democracy, barely sprouting in Syria's shadow, would snap in a storm of Hezbollah-inspired Islamofascism. The Sunni and the Druze too expressed concern. Walid Jumblatt, the Druze warlord, raged in a press conference days after the war. Was the Resistance really Lebanese, he thundered, or was it a tool of Iran and Syria? What of the Lebanese majority never consulted by Hezbollah before it began a military undertaking that engulfed the whole nation? Nasrallah was playing to the back pews in the great arena of Arab and Muslim opinion, the consequences for individuals be damned. "It is easy for these people in remote places to carry your pictures and they have the right to do so, but when we look closely at what happened, we realize that my country has been destroyed and set on fire," Jumblatt said, the cry of a man who believed that it was yet possible to thwart Hezbollah's rise to power.[46] "There is something that has been undermined and this is the trust, the trust the people have that they will not be dragged once again into a new round of the war." Jumblatt sounded passionate but he was calculating as well. He had a personal history of protean political shape-shifting. He had been for the Syrians before he was against them. He had broken ties and reestablished them with all his political allies and enemies. In the final analysis his obligation was to the Druze sect, and he would shift alliances in a flash to advance Druze interests. A theatrical but parochial clan warrior, Jumblatt tried to offer an alternative to Nasrallah as a charismatic leader. It was hardly a fair match.

In the South, the southern suburb, and the Beqaa, people were mad too, but they directed their rage at Israel, and provisionally at the Lebanese government, run by men like Jumblatt and Saad Hariri who seemed to sneer with bourgeois revulsion when confronted by the *basse classe* Islamic Resistance. For the time being, the Shia were prepared to take Nasrallah at his word. He had promised cash payments, a year's rent, and complete reconstruction. They would give him the benefit of the doubt for that year at least. On the other hand, the government, its constituents, and the Arab regimes in Egypt, Jordan, and Saudi Arabia had proved in the early stages of the war that they preferred Israel to Hezbollah, considering the revolutionary Islamist militia a greater threat to their legitimacy than the Jewish State. Arab leaders had given Israel the green light for a quick war with Hezbollah, hoping the Israeli military could finish off the group and remove what they viewed as a canker sore, a violent radical movement that inspired Islamists across the region to rise up not only against Israel but against the ossified Arab regimes that tolerated it.

The Shia forgot none of this either. Hezbollah, they hoped, would erect to their wartime sacrifice a monument of lasting power. All along the border, young men swore to fight again and their mothers and fathers just as resolutely swore they would back them: for the prisoners still in Israeli jails, for the liberation of the Shebaa Farms, for Palestine itself, for Jerusalem, for anything that Sayyed Hassan ordered. Samira Sharafedeen smoothed the dirt at the mass grave in Taibe where she had just buried three of her cousins, Hezbollah fighters. All told seven fighters and eleven civilians had been heaped into a small square pit in the town cemetery. "Crying brings sadness to a country, blood brings strength," she said. "God willing, our operation for Shebaa will continue. We will keep fighting to liberate our land. The day will come for the Israelis, you must have faith. Their day will come."[47]

Ali Sirhan, a twenty-three-year-old I met in Kfar Kila leaning against a concrete pillar a few feet from the fence marking the Israeli border, stared at a neat row of orange trees in Metula, close enough to discern every leaf and branch. His brother, an Amal fighter, had died during the war, he said, and he had fought with him, even though he was a member of the Lebanese government's civil defense corps and not a member of any party militia. Communists, Amal members, Aounist Christians, and independent sympathizers like himself had volunteered under Hezbollah's command, he said, and would do so again. "As far as I'm concerned, the war ends when there's nothing left of Israel," he said. "After we all die, that's when Hezbollah is gone. When you kill the Shia, that is when Hezbollah is gone."[48] Nearby, a sign in English read "Rice, You will not see your new Middle East." A soldier I met in the Dahieh said he would shed his uniform and fight for Hezbollah whenever the party asked, and pointed out (as did dozens of people) that in 1967 Israel had vanquished all the Arab armies in six days, but in 2006 they had fought thirty-four days and failed to take control of a thin sliver of South Lebanon.[49] Virtually everyone I met expected another war with Israel within six years. They spoke to comfort themselves at a moment of loss, and as a form of psychological warfare, against the government of Lebanon, against Israel, against the West. They weren't quaking with fear; they oozed bravado. Like those symbiotic birds that clean the crocodile's mouth, they took nourishment from the party and had come to feel as one with its lethal jaw.

Hezbollah work crews used excavators to pull the rotting dead from houses bombed days or weeks earlier. In Tebnine there wasn't a sapper to be found, so a man used his bulldozer to detonate the cluster bomblets scattered in front of the hospital. The bombed Shia areas had embarked on the grisly business of getting on with life and war. On August 14, 2006, the first day of the full ceasefire, I went to Borj Qalaouay in search of Hussein Rumeiti, the mokhtar I had met a few weeks earlier in the square beside the Hezbollah rocket-launching operation. Graffiti at the town entrance said "I love to die," in English—presumably painted there in case Israeli soldiers made it that far. I found the mokhtar sitting in his yard, in a low flat house at the first fork in the road through Borj Qalaouay. A low wall separated his house from the road, and the front yard was pleasantly shaded by a grape arbor and a eucalyptus tree. A shell appeared to have struck the driveway, destroying the mokhtar's BMW and collapsing the wall of the front sitting room. Through the irregular mortar holes I could see fragments of narghileh bases and crockery. Hussein Rumeiti sat on a cream-colored plastic chair on the gravel beneath the arbor, in a circle of dirt-smeared men. Powdered concrete matted their untrimmed hair, and their pants were filthy. These were the men who had stayed behind. Hussein smoked a waterpipe piled high with raw tobacco, packed into an inverted clay plug and topped with wood coals, planted directly in the moist tobacco. This style of waterpipe was called "Ajami," or Iranian-style. Unlike the sweet fruit- and honey-flavored tobaccos favored by trendy urbanites, Ajami waterpipes delivered a powerful kick of nicotine and tobacco flavor. It smelled delicious to me, like a bonfire of cigarettes. Hussein stood to greet me, kissing me on both cheeks. "I saw you during the war," he exclaimed, as much to his audience as to me. "You are welcome." He motioned us to join the circle of men and ordered a relative to bring us tea. "This is the first narghileh I've smoked in my house since the war," he said.

He had spent much of the day reassuring residents of the village that it was in fact safe to return and that the war really was over. "Come back and we shall all act as one hand to reconstruct our town," he told them. He was tallying the work ahead. The town's water tower had been damaged, as well as lots of individual water tanks on people's roofs. There were mines to clear and roads to repair. Hezbollah had shown what small bands of guerillas could do against the Israeli military. The Islamic Resistance, however, had a far more complex challenge when it came to securing political rights for its Shia clientele.

"The resistance is our army," he said. But, he added, "Everyone distinguishes between Hezbollah's resistance and its political project." Until the next war with Israel, if and when it transpired, Hezbollah's political project would determine the outcome for men like Rumeiti. The Party of God's political fortunes would also set Lebanon's temperature, and perhaps determine whether Hezbollah's resistance fever would spread throughout the Arab and Islamic world.

"Politics will change and life will get better," Rumeiti said hopefully. "We need everything. Everything is destroyed."

I spilled my tea. "It's good luck," he said.

When he spoke of the battles just past, Rumeiti's eyes gleamed with pride. Like Hezbollah as a whole, though, Rumeiti had a lot of responsibility, and he was worried. Incoming Israeli munitions had a way of unifying people. Now the bombs had stopped falling and the Israeli military had withdrawn. Hezbollah was left with the shattered pieces of Lebanon in its hands, and quickly had to show the same prowess in the reconstruction jihad as they had in the jihad against Israel. Rumeiti had helped his region rebuild after Israeli incursions in 1993 and 1996, and had played his part in the great revival of South Lebanon that followed Israel's withdrawal from the occupied zone in 2000. None of those chapters had entailed as much destruction as this one—and never before had Hezbollah faced such overt hostility and resentment from other Lebanese political parties.

"Sayyed Hassan now is being cautious. He knows we have first to care for a million refugees before the resistance can fire its guns at Israel again," he said. Hezbollah's support relied primarily on personal loyalty to Hassan Nasrallah. Even Lebanese who didn't support Hezbollah trusted him. They believed his claims and promises, although now, from within the ruins of Lebanon and possibly the ruins of his own movement, Nasrallah was making a promise that sounded fantastical—to rebuild everything in just a year or two.

During the war, Hussein Rumeiti said, "God protected me." Now, though, he invoked another admonition that he attributed to the Prophet: "God helps those who help themselves." "Now," he said, "I dream things will come back as they were before. We will rebuild the schools and homes. We all are peaceful people here. But war is never far from us. We never will accept Israeli invaders. We want our prisoners released. If they strike us, we strike back. If they strike again, we will strike back again. Even if our losses are greater, we will keep striking back." The determination of these men and women was Hezbollah's main asset.

If Hezbollah could balance a lot of loaded platters at once, it could parlay its Divine Victory into a lasting political gain, a conclusive step by the Shia into the establishment. If the party fumbled just a little, it stood to lose everything it had worked for since 2000. The Shia who objected to Hezbollah, and the more secular political parties, hoped Hezbollah would self-destruct under so many conflicting pressures. They imagined that loyalists impatient to see their homes rebuilt would revolt against Hezbollah's heavy-handed ways as reconstruction inevitably fell behind schedule, and that even militant Islamist Shia would recognize the folly of another aggressive war with Israel. Even those who considered the Islamic Resistance incontrovertibly just surely would acknowledge that Lebanon, like the rest of the Arab world, always lost when it confronted the Jewish State with direct force. Hezbollah too saw these dangers, and proposed to take them head on. The party would have to govern and rebuild with the same fervor that its fighters had brought to the ravines and alleys of the South.

At the end of the summer of 2006, millions of Lebanese girded themselves for the long workaday task of rebuilding their neighborhoods, an ordeal that at best would take several years. Nasrallah and Hezbollah wanted to keep their constituents' eyes on the prize, however. To rile up the desired sentiment the party returned to the symbol on which it had so deftly drawn in past years to mobilize militancy: Samir Quntar, the longest-serving Lebanese detainee in Israel. The issue of the prisoners was dear to many Lebanese, even those who didn't sympathize with Hezbollah, because it summoned a sense of wounded national pride. The prisoners personified the entire regional dispute in a few recognizable faces. Samir Quntar's case might have been only rhetorically central to the 2006 war, but his story illustrated Hezbollah's grand arc: the transformation of secular Arab militancy into a culture of Islamic Resistance.

Samir Quntar was the prisoner Israel had promised never to release. He was considered so evil that a death sentence would have made his crimes too easy to bear. He made an unexpected *cause célèbre* for Hezbollah, and an equally unlikely candidate for Israeli clemency. As a boy in the 1970s he had joined the Palestinian militants waging war against Israel from their base in Lebanon. Back then, the Palestinians had free run of Lebanon, and they used it to harass Israel continuously. Compared to the suicide bombers and rockets that Palestinian factions directed at Israel three decades later, the Palestinian campaign of the 1970s more nearly resembled a full-fledged war. The PLO had organized a ragtag but credible army with artillery and armored vehicles. From the hilltops they shelled Israel. From the valleys and the sea they launched raids to kill or capture Israelis. Militants snuck across the border with the intent to lay bombs, hijack buses, take hostages, destroy military infrastructure, or kill civilians in attention-grabbing raids. Samir Quntar was one of the multitudes of teenagers recruited by the factions. He joined the leftist Palestinian Liberation Front. He was a Druze, and from a family that wasn't especially religious. But the Palestinians cared little about sect when it came to recruiting foot soldiers. They armed and trained any willing Shia, Sunni, Druze, or Christian gunman. Samir fell for the Palestinian cause, which at the time was fresh and beguiled Arab patriots, gun-mad teenagers, and leftist academic theoreticians alike. He acquired confidence with weapons early and won his commanders' endorsement to lead missions almost as soon as he cleared puberty. When he was fifteen, the Jordanians arrested Samir and a guerilla team sneaking across the border, apparently on a mission to seize an Israeli hostage. He spent eleven months in prison.

Shortly after his release, the head of the Palestine Liberation Front, Muhammad Zaydan, better known as Abu Abbas, asked Samir to lead an important raid into Israel. Just a few months shy of his seventeenth birthday, Samir felt strong, just, and ready. He and three comrades were to storm the Israeli coastal town of Nahariya with two goals: to kill a policeman or military officer in his car, in revenge for an Israeli strike against a Palestinian officer, and then to capture hostages and bring them back to Lebanon as bargaining chips. The team sailed out of Lebanon in a rubber dinghy, landing in Nahariya at 2:30 a.m. on Sunday, April 22, 1979. They had trouble finding an officer of the law, so finally, like teenagers, they attracted attention by ringing the intercom of a villa and shouting menacingly in Arabic. Someone called the cops, and when they showed up, Samir and his team fired wildly at their car, killing officer Eliyahu Shachar. Samir alone fired thirty shots.[50]

Then they burst into a three-story apartment block, selected at random. First they broke into an apartment, but the man there had a gun and shot at his attackers. Then they stumbled into the neighboring Haran apartment, where they found a young father and daughter: Danny, thirty-two, and Einat, four. Danny's wife Smadar had hidden in a crawl space with her daughter Yael when they heard the ruckus in their building. Danny and Einat hadn't managed to squeeze into the hiding place in time. Samir Quntar says he lost precious time trying to persuade Danny to leave his daughter. Smadar, listening from the crawl space, didn't recall the men exhibiting any concern at all for Einat. Instead, she said, the men barged through the house searching for additional family members to take hostage. The youngest daughter began to cry, and her mother, terrified that Samir Quntar's team would discover and kill them all, clamped her hand over Yael's mouth. The child suffocated to death. Finally, the fighters gave up on finding more victims and dragged Danny and Einat to the shore only to find that Israeli soldiers had cut off their escape route. Samir Quntar and his three companions traded gunfire for hours with the Israelis at the rocky beach. By 5:30 a.m. Danny and Einat were dead. So were two of the kidnappers. Samir Quntar and the fourth member of his team were wounded and captured.

According to an anonymous eyewitness whose testimony is preserved in Israeli court files, Samir shot Danny Haran point-blank, in front of his daughter, and then smashed her head with his rifle butt. In a few hours the raid was over. Samir Quntar's failure cut a wound into the Israeli psyche. The story, told by the surviving widow and documented during a three-month trial at the end of the year, elevated Samir Quntar to the status of iconic evil: a terrorist without remorse who killed a little girl with his rifle butt. The tale of the surviving mother Smadar and her daughter accidentally smothered to death directly echoed the harrowing experiences of European Jews during the Holocaust. At his trial, Samir denied killing Einat and over the years he never changed his story. He claimed that his hostages fell in the crossfire, killed by Israeli bullets intended for the kidnappers. He believed the Israelis fabricated evidence of the little girl's brain tissue on his rifle butt in order to demonize their enemies and rile their public. The story became a totem in Israel and slowly around the world: Samir Quntar, it was said, showed what happened when militants blind themselves to humanity in barbarous service to their cause. He was convicted and sentenced to five life terms plus forty-seven years.

Israel was only then, in 1979, coming to grips with a new generation of implacable foes. Samir Quntar became the face of the enemy. "A Jewish child's blood will not be spilled with impunity," Prime Minister Menachem Begin said at the funeral of Danny, Einat, and Yael Haran.[51] "Not even the devil has yet invented the proper revenge for the murder of an innocent child." Other prisoners that Israel willingly traded had killed Israeli soldiers—but Samir Quntar was off the table; he had killed civilians, he had "blood on his hands," he was the face of evil. Eventually Smadar Haran remarried and carried on with her life, but she fought hard to thwart any proposal to release Samir Quntar in a prisoner swap. Israel considered trading Quntar for some prisoners of war in 1984. This "terrorist" who had committed "a murder of unimaginable cruelty," Smadar Haran wrote, should never be released; let Israel trade prisoners who were less abominable.[52] Not once did Samir Quntar express a sliver of remorse for the casualties of his raid. "Smadar took me on as her personal project. She could not understand that it wasn't personal. I didn't come [from] Lebanon with a note that said 'Haran family.' I came as part of a conflict in which I was convinced I had to participate," he told an Israeli journalist who interviewed him in prison. "I did what I did for my people, for my country. If I sit in jail for a hundred years, I will never change my opinions. This is what I believe."

Quntar in many ways was an insignificant pawn, an accidental figure of history. There were militants in the 1970s who killed more innocents, or whose acts transgressed morality with equal or greater brutality. Infiltrators, busjackers, and hijackers were already redrawing the calculus of security in Israel and the Western world, writing a new chapter in the history of terror. They targeted civilians to maximize their leverage over the public. The murders for which Samir Quntar was convicted were horrible enough to provoke great outrage and yet personal and narrow enough in scope to be comprehended. In 1979, Samir Quntar was one of many poster children for a particular era in Israel's war with the Palestinians and the West's apprehension of resistance and terror. Other members of that generation died, withdrew from the battle, or mellowed into political animals. Abu Abbas, Samir Quntar's commander in the PLF, was captured by the Americans as they entered Baghdad in 2003, and died in custody within a year. Samir

Quntar evolved, somehow managing against a rotating backdrop of Israeli prisons to reinvent himself—partly by will and again partly by accident—as the face of Israel's future nightmare. In prison Quntar learned Hebrew and studied assiduously, finishing a bachelor's degree by correspondence. He met several generations of Palestinian militants, the intellectuals and the bomb makers, the political strategists and the street organizers. He learned their sophisticated language and he shared in their political discussions. Men from the Palestine Liberation Organization and other factions came through the prisons, Palestinian militants in the mold of the men who had commanded his faction back in Lebanon.

Outside, though, the world was changing; religious movements were taking the lead in the armed struggle as the old leftist nationalists increasingly pursued statehood and accords on the field of politics. Samir Quntar first learned of something called Islamic Resistance from imprisoned members of Hamas and Islamic Jihad. Through them and the information network that reaches into even the most isolated prisons, Samir Quntar heard about Hezbollah as well; it sounded as if this Party of God, which hadn't even existed when he was arrested, had become the sole standard-bearer of the militant creed that Samir had adopted, to fight to the death against Israel with no quarter and no compromise. He took part in twelve hunger strikes, which secured many new rights for Arab prisoners in the Israeli jails, not least among them access to Arab newspapers and television channels. Through the media and through other prisoners he learned the details of Israel's calamitous withdrawal from Southern Lebanon in 2000.

Twenty-four years after his capture, in 2003, he discovered something startling: that Hassan Nasrallah, the leader of Hezbollah, had made the liberty of Quntar and that of the few remaining Lebanese prisoners in Israel a central issue of his Islamic Resistance. Hezbollah, the Party of God, was carrying the torch that had passed through the hands of Samir Quntar and his comrades-at-arms in a long-ago era. This Islamic Resistance was doing right by Quntar and the other prisoners. If he couldn't serve the fighters with a gun any more, let him serve them from captivity as a symbol. The behavior of these unknown Lebanese Islamists nudged him to reexamine his faith. Samir Quntar came to consider Hezbollah his brothers. He found more and more inspiration in the Koran. Islam, he became convinced, had become the language of resistance, and resistance was his entire animating idea. It made sense to him as a maturation of his existing commitment to the struggle. His fight always had been holy to him; now it would be holy to God as well.

With the fighting over in August 2006, Nasrallah resumed his calls for Samir Quntar's release, agitating the faithful and maintaining the sense that the struggle continued even if the guns had quieted. Nasrallah made it clear that Operation Truthful Promise would only end when the last Lebanese prisoners returned to Lebanon. The August 2006 ceasefire agreement had brought only a tentative truce to the Middle East, but nothing so enduring as peace. Nasrallah hoped to reassert Hezbollah's long-term strategic advantage, outlining a tangible achievement—the release of Samir Quntar—that he judged achievable and that if accomplished, he could cite to declare another victory. Hezbollah needed Samir Quntar's plight and potential redemption to help the party recover from the major blunder that the 2006 war itself had been. In this phase, the war returned once again to the plane of symbols and propaganda, narrative and strategic communications—the realm of Al-Manar.

In 2008, two years after the war, I went to visit Abdallah Kassir, Al-Manar's general manager. Hezbollah's foreign press office had banned any more party officials from meeting me, and had even suggested to me I could not use any of the interviews I'd already conducted with Hezbollah leaders since Hezbollah did not endorse my book. "You can't possibly write a book about Hezbollah without the party's permission, right? You'll have to move onto another project?" one party functionary brightly asked me. She was crestfallen when I explained that in fact, Hezbollah didn't get to decide what I would write and whether it would be published. Like many Hezbollah officials, she overestimated the party's ability to control or manipulate a foreigner like me, and she thought the prospect of future access would tempt me to relinquish writing this book. Hezbollah was convinced (not entirely without reason) that an American-published book was unlikely to advance the cause of the Party of God and therefore, the party saw no use in wasting time talking to me. Al-Manar, however, had a different calculus. The campaign in the West to designate Al-Manar a terrorist group had limited the station's range, and in response Hezbollah had taken the logically contorted position that Al-Manar was independent, a private enterprise in which Hezbollah holds a 55 percent stake.[53] The pary's own rhetoric hamstrung it; it couldn't forbid me from calling the station or its director from talking to me, without admitting its political control over Al-Manar. As a result, on an unseasonably sunny and warm December morning in 2008, I drove to Al-Manar's new headquarters in a part of southern Beirut called Ouzai, the tallest building on the small knot of land jutting into the Mediterranean beside the airport runway.

Behind the automatic sliding glass doors, my translator and I encountered a formidable checkpoint, like White House security: metal detectors, X-rays for the bags, quick pat-downs by polite, anonymous security guards. A smiling, burly man kept our passports, and sent us unescorted up the elevator to the fourth floor to the director's office suite. Another labyrinth of halls, rooms, and guards, and then his anteroom. The only way into the director's office was through a metal door with no handle: Abdallah Kassir himself had to buzz in visitors, from a console panel hidden inside his desk. The party promoted him in 2005 to head Al-Manar Television after a successful turn in parliament. Kassir had a direct line to Hezbollah's Shura Council, but he got his job because the leadership also could trust him to improvise. When things went wrong, they believed Kassir would know what the party wanted and would get it done.

Kassir knew English but preferred not to speak it; he didn't want to make a mistake. He was one of the main brains behind Al-Manar, and he wanted his accomplishments to speak for themselves. He wasn't above a little flash, though; by Hezbollah standards he had the ostentatious flair of a Hollywood mogul. He wore a bright pink dress shirt, collar open; stylish wire eyeglass frames; and most unusually, he smoked cigarillos. His office décor was modern and less austere than the usual Hezbollah affair. There were a few plants, real ones, not plastic, and a private bathroom with a gold door handle. On the walls there weren't any posters of Shia martyrs, or Mecca, or Ali's sword, or Hussein on his horse at Karbala: none of the usual religious iconography at all. Instead, one entire wall of his office was lined with maps and tables depicting Al-Manar's satellite transmission pathways, with the range drawn in pink or blue and the coordinates listed in dense charts below. Primary satellites, secondary satellites, backup satellites. Abdallah Kassir's mission was to keep Al-Manar broadcasting under any circumstances: the programming had no value if Hezbollah's public couldn't see it. Kassir oversaw the construction of the new headquarters in a matter of months in late 2006. His corner office was identical to his previous one in every detail, down to the desk and plants.

"Psychologically, the people depend on Al-Manar. None of our other media assets can completely replace it. Al-Manar holds a special symbolic place in the resistance," Kassir said, pulling at a cigarillo and fidgeting with the ash while he spoke. "Al-Manar's message tries to unite the community through religion and culture against the great challenges, especially the challenge posed by the existence of Israel. Our values make it necessary for us to promote the culture of resistance and internal unity."

He was most proud of the station's news department and its portrayal of Israel—two areas that spoke volumes about Hezbollah's distinctive and much imitated approach. In its news bulletins, as opposed to its advocacy and opinion programming, Al-Manar worked hard to cultivate a record of accuracy, which it upheld better than most television networks in the region. Its rhetoric, politics, and talk shows were one thing, the station's director reasoned, calculated to stir sentiment for the resistance; but the newscasts should stick to facts when describing political developments, military attacks, numbers of dead and wounded, movements of refugees, and similar events. This approach reinforced the credibility of Nasrallah and Hezbollah as well as Al-Manar; in contrast to lying government officials, their initial accounts tended to square with reality. When it came to Israel, Hezbollah blazed another trail. Since 1948, Arab governments had railed about Israel and spewed venom about Jews. But Al-Manar broke new ground, adding information to the invective. It broadcast extensive footage from Israeli TV, reported on political developments in Israel, quoted and analyzed reports from Israel's vibrant print media. The hateful and naysaying tone sometimes sounded similar to Arab state television, as when announcers referred to Israel as "the Zionist entity," but Al-Manar paid attention to the detailed reality of Israel. Hezbollah loyalists who spoke Hebrew analyzed Knesset debates about Israel's welfare state and argued about whether Israel's internal political divisions had made it more vulnerable to military strikes by Hezbollah. The real theatrics come in the rest of Al-Manar's programming, the talk shows and game shows, talking head debates and slickly produced series like *Eye on Palestine*. Each week, that particular show featured one Palestinian refugee who hears emotional appeals from relatives in Gaza or the West Bank by telephone, and eventually gets a virtual tour of his lost home. The programming is carefully designed to fan outrage and anger.

Like Hezbollah's political leaders, Al-Manar decided not to waste much energy on dialogue with the West. ("Al-Manar faces a tough cold war with the Zionist lobby," Kassir told me. "We make every effort to talk to the Western communities, but I don't think the Westerners care.") Al-Manar used to broadcast the news every day in English and French, but Kassir determined soon after taking over the station in 2005 that few people watched and he could better spend his resources translating select stories on the website into English, French, Spanish, Hebrew, and Farsi. Now Al-Manar tried to draw readers to its English-language website. The news in the main well was more or less straightforward, with a few pronounced tics like the "Zionist entity" category header and the propensity to splice "so-called" into otherwise anodyne wire stories, as in "the so-called Jewish state." Screeds of pure invective usually lined the sides of the web page, but were occasionally published in the main lineup alongside pieces about the latest in Lebanese politics.

Al-Manar broadcasted Hezbollah's Platonic ideal of itself, and in the process revealed the group's most ambitious agenda. While Hezbollah was resolutely Shia and focused more than anything else on its armed struggle against Israel, Al-Manar strived to fire up Muslims of all sects around a more general "Muslim Pride" agenda: self-reliance, morality, family values, military strength, the possibility of victory against Israeli and American culture and power. "The Western media showcases the weakness of the Arab world. Our mission is to transmit the experience of the resistance to the Arab world, to shed light on our strong points and our unity," Kassir said. "We promote the virtues of the Arabs, our strong families that contrast with the fragmented West."

After the war the station management hung a banner over the rubble of its original headquarters, put a TV set up, and turned the bomb site into a tourist attraction with yet another new tagline: "An Inextinguishable Torch."

Part II

War Without End

Usually people escape from the fighting. Even the believers. Almighty God says: "Fighting is ordained for you, though you dislike it." It is human nature to prefer to turn to politics, economic activity, cultural activity, and commercial activity, but people do not want to hear about fighting, staying up all night, captivity, wounds, sacrifices, hunger, staying in the valleys and plains. What is this thing which we are monopolizing and for which we are envied? Are we envied because our youth are in prisons, and that we are getting them back? Or are we envied because hundreds of our young have lost the flower of their youth to defend this homeland, and we get back their dead bodies? We will ask everyone to contribute to protecting and defending this country, and whoever abandons this duty is the traitor.

HASSAN NASRALLAH, addressing his followers at a rally to
celebrate the release of Lebanese prisoners held by Israel on
July 16, 2008

4

DIVINE VICTORY

The 2006 war had proven once again that Hezbollah could fight. Whoever doubted it had been made wise. But in the aftermath of the war, could the party govern? Could it—would it—win the political game it had played since 1992? Iran's money and weapons would help. So too would Syria's support. But ultimately Hezbollah had to execute a gargantuan logistical task of reconstruction, compensation, and political maneuvering, or otherwise face a surge of disgruntled Lebanese unlike any in its short life. Historically, Hezbollah had benefited from low expectations. Until 2000, in fact, the party could advertise its network of hospitals, social service organizations, and schools as a bonus supplement to its core mission of expelling the Israeli occupation. With the Israelis gone and Hezbollah indisputably in control of the Dahieh, South Lebanon, and most of the Beqaa, the Party of God had taken on greater responsibility, but had studiously remained in opposition in the government—a cynic would say so that they could always blame any failures on the state. Immediately after the war, Hezbollah's enemies smelled weakness in a militant party exhausted by an unexpected war and saddled with huge social burdens. The party's supporters had their own high expectations: They had stood by Hezbollah during the struggle, given their children and their property. Now they expected Hezbollah to build it all back, as good as it was before, even though the scope of destruction surpassed that of any of the previous wars since Hezbollah had declared itself guardian of the Shia.

Hezbollah faced a zero-sum choice. It could fight for the aspirations of its constituents and its own hard-liners, or it could pursue an easier, conciliatory agenda and risk losing its militant momentum. Six years earlier Hezbollah had swept into the liberated South disciplined and flush with confidence. That was easy; the party had had years to plan. At the end of the 2006 war, Hezbollah had no such luxury, its declarations of "Divine Victory" notwithstanding. The Shia militia had lost hundreds of fighters and hundreds of supporters. Thousands were wounded. Its infrastructure lay in ruins. No amount of raw enthusiasm on the Arab street or petrodollars from Iran could make life normal in Lebanon, certainly not overnight. This time around, Hezbollah was cornered. It had squandered the tolerance of the other Lebanese warlords, who felt that Hezbollah had betrayed the nation by unilaterally starting a war that concerned them all.

Within a week it was clear that Hezbollah would aim for a total victory. It had withstood Israel. Instead of moving to a peacetime footing, it would remain mobilized and on high alert, but this time fighting for its political agenda. It would rebuild, and at the same time it would contest the Lebanese political structure. The international community and the Lebanese government were discussing ways to disarm Hezbollah, face-saving solutions that would preserve Hezbollah's political autonomy but mute its force, like incorporating the Islamic Resistance into the Lebanese military. Hezbollah wouldn't even entertain the notion. Instead, the party proclaimed it would disarm the day that Israel ceased to pose a military threat, and demanded that the Lebanese government give Hezbollah veto power over all state decisions. The demands shocked everyone who had expected a Hezbollah chastened by the 2006 conflict.

Shortly after the end of the war I finally met the Hezbollah official most appreciated by foreign journalists, its house policy intellectual Ali Fayyad. I was still new to the milieu, and I expected Hezbollah to behave like a clandestine underground insurgency. My experience during the war hadn't fully dispelled the misimpression I'd gathered from afar and from decades of reading overdramatic reportage. What might have been true in the 1980s had long ceased to be the case. Journalists and diplomats who wanted to meet with Hezbollah didn't have to don a hood, switch cars, and pass through secret underground garages on their way to a safe house. They could call Hezbollah's press office on the phone, make an appointment, and drive themselves to a well-known address in the center of the Dahieh. It might still be a cloak-and-dagger affair to meet Nasrallah, but long ago Hezbollah had outgrown the methodology of the secret cells in its political operations. In so many respects Hezbollah had taken on the functions of the state. When it came to practical affairs, Hezbollah was as accessible and transparent as most governments, and by the authoritarian standards of the Middle East, it was even easier to reach and hold accountable than most regimes.

During the war I had by chance and proximity to the front lines gained more candid access to Hezbollah fighters than the party would ever like to give. At the same time, because I hadn't yet covered Hezbollah under normal circumstances, I had no idea how much of a traditional political apparatus the party had constructed—the Bureaucracy of God. I asked some Lebanese friends where to turn for a better sense of Hezbollah's goals and programs. "Have you visited Hezbollah's think tank yet?" several of them asked. I would have never guessed that this bugbear of the West, the party held responsible for spreading suicide bombing and roadside booby traps across the Middle East, would have a think tank. As far as I knew in the region only the government of Israel funded serious think tanks that influenced policy. The handful of institutes and study centers in the Arab world for the most part provided patronage jobs to academics or churned out papers that echoed official government positions.

Hezbollah in this too broke the pattern. Its think tank studied issues far afield from resistance against Israel, like water rights, electoral reform, and telecommunications regulation for Hezbollah so its parliamentarians and ministers could make a credible attempt at good governance. And, unique among Middle Eastern Islamist movements, its political scientists sought to engage in intellectual dialogue with Westerners and outsiders, inviting hostile journalists and academics to conferences in Beirut and sending delegates to meetings in Europe and England. Its Consultative Center for

Studies and Documentation provided a crucial influx of data and policy ideas into the generally moribund field of Middle Eastern politics. Ali Fayyad, the director, was an avuncular political science professor with a crew cut and a clean-shaven face. He was also a bit of a dandy, favoring tailored shirts with his monogram halfway down the front and French cuffs. His firm belly protruded decisively over his waist. Ali Fayyad met me in a barren new apartment overlooking the new airport highway. The center's old office had been bombed. He was in the process of establishing a new headquarters. The library had been saved, he said.

Much of his work was spent scouring the latest literature in social sciences and policy to find ideas that might help Hezbollah. He read up on subjects like water treatment and public utility management, that might advance Hezbollah's agenda to provide better constituent services. He studied the latest theories on failed states, which Hezbollah might harness in its political campaign to supplant the Lebanese government. He apologized that he was unable to conduct our interview in English; he was taking lessons but was not comfortable enough yet. Hezbollah, Ali Fayyad said, had managed during the war to crack Israel's deterrent power. However, he argued, that alone wouldn't assure a Hezbollah victory in the regional context unless the Party of God could manage to fend off internal threats to its authority. For the time being the government possessed a disproportionate share of power, he said. "No one can have all the power. It is an illusion to think so," he said. "There is an imbalance between the state authority and the popular will. This imbalance cannot continue indefinitely."

Ali Fayyad and his institute represented Hezbollah's mild and inquisitive face. Their contribution to the party's policy manifested itself in the great command for data and detail evident among almost all of its officials. The more rabid politicking and posturing were left to other officials, whose job it was to meet political rivals or appear on talk shows arguing, cajoling, and intimidating. One of the more slick of these operatives was Ibrahim Mousawi, a Hezbollah intellectual and journalist who had served as a party spokesman and international news editor at Al-Manar. When I met him at a West Beirut hotel he compared Israel to the Nazis and laughed at the idea that Hezbollah would temper its demands after the war.[54] The time was ripe for Hezbollah to collect its due in politics, beginning with a third of the cabinet ministries, which would give it the power to block any government decision. The Party of God was ready to break Lebanon's central taboo, and claim more power for Muslims. Mousawi estimated that the population of Lebanon was now 70 percent Muslim, yet the Muslims got only half the positions in government under the outdated gentleman's agreement that privileged the once-strong but now demographically marginal Christians. The region's staid and corrupt power brokers expected Hezbollah to lurk on the fringes of power in part because Islamist movements preferred to criticize rather than to govern. Now, though, at its most precarious moment, Hezbollah decided to seize a potentially transformative opportunity, rather than retrench and regroup.

"Let them make a poll in Lebanon and see how many people want Hezbollah. Hezbollah is exercising a basic right," Mousawi said. The political struggle inside Lebanon was critical. "There are two very different projects for this country. We're lucky that the other side doesn't have guns. They aren't ready to go into a civil war." He went on to list the demands of the Islamic Resistance. It must be allowed to keep its militia and weapons. Israel must release its Lebanese prisoners. Israel must end the occupation of the Shebaa Farms. Then the list grew more fantastical. Israel must withdraw from all occupied lands, implying perhaps all of its territory. Israel must bring home the 400,000 Palestinian refugees currently in Lebanon. The list made clear that Hezbollah didn't plan to forfeit its armed struggle against the Jewish State any time soon. "They are afraid the Arabs will throw them in the sea, while they pick up their nuclear weapons?" Mousawi said. "Who will throw whom into the sea?

"Operation Truthful Promise" would either sanctify Hezbollah or embarrass it. Nasrallah left no doubt about his strategy. Hezbollah founded a new corporation called Al Waad, or the Promise, to manage the major postwar reconstruction. The militia quickly regrouped, reburying its dead in their hometowns and planning memorials for fallen fighters in every locality. Hezbollah announced that its rocket-firing capacity within weeks had surpassed prewar levels. The politburo managed the political campaign.

The party's public opinion machine lurched back on line. Now, as before the war, almost nobody would talk without a minder. Dozens of Hezbollah media officers fanned across Beirut, the Beqaa, and the South. Nasrallah gave speeches about the new political agenda, and members of parliament elaborated in a torrent of private meetings and interviews with the local and regional media. Foreign reporters once again had to submit copies of their passports, credentials, and interview requests to Hezbollah media officials, who would pass on their information for vetting by Hezbollah intelligence. Wafa Hoteit, a stern traditional religious woman, or *muhajaba*, who wore her headscarf primly and tightly fastened around her head, replaced her voluble and flirtatious pedecessor. Wafa spoke English but you would hardly know it since she preferred to pass messages through Lebanese fixers and translators. Almost every request was ignored or outright denied. Not without reason, Hezbollah had decided to shut out the Western press and focus on Arab and Persian correspondents whose governments supported Hezbollah and whose audience loved the Islamic Resistance and Nasrallah. Almost daily, Hezbollah's house band cut new mixes of their best tunes and Nasrallah's latest speeches. The music was catchy—chants, bagpipes, synthesizers, multiple drummers—and in the style of well engineered hip-hop, the most popular songs sampled rousing refrains by Nasrallah, and usually ended with choral chants of fealty to the secretary-general. Tour guides in the Dahieh welcomed Lebanese disaster tourists. General Aoun's Christian followers were invited to the heavily bombed Shia areas. Groups of a dozen or more teenagers in neon orange Free Patriotic Movement T-shirts would stage fellowship visits or cleanups, usually filmed, to show off Hezbollah's cross-sectarian appeal. Hezbollah flung itself headlong into the Sisyphean task of girding popular support and marshaling its own ideological brethren. The Party of God might fail, but it wouldn't be for lack of trying.

Dergham Dergham was exactly the kind of man that Hezbollah would have to woo in order to make the transition from opposition to control. Dergham Dergham lived on the fuzzy margins of Hezbollah's community. Geographically his home lay on the edge of the Dahieh. He was nominally Shia, but in practice an agnostic who veered toward sacrilege in his freewheeling lifestyle. Politically he was labile and unsophisticated, sympathetic to Hezbollah's message of strength and empowerment but irritated by its piety and discipline. Hezbollah's soft support came from inconstant men like Dergham. Their active loyalty would be required to maintain Hezbollah as a mass movement that could muster numbers and brute muscle.

The first time I met Dergham Dergham he was out of his element, in the upholstered lobby of the Sofitel in the Christian quarter of Ashrafieh. He sat nervously on a plush sofa, back straight and muscular shoulders tensed, starting intently ahead as if he were preparing to go on trial. Even as he made small talk about mutual acquaintances, he wouldn't make eye contact. He was tall and sculpted like a body builder. His forehead was broad, his cheekbones round and pronounced, his nose battered like a streetfighter's. But his face was carefully shaven and his T-shirt and jeans fresh and ironed even in the middle of a war. He looked like the monosyllabic goons who often told me to get lost when I worked in Hezbollah areas. The second he opened his mouth, he shattered my impression. He looked like a Hezbollah watchman, but he talked like an Atlanta bouncer, with an accent that was a cross between American Southerner and Latino.

We quickly came to terms: the war was halfway over, Dergham needed a job, and I wanted a translator who wasn't afraid to work in combat areas. As soon as we got out of the stuffy hotel, with its floral print *chaises longues* and heavy damask curtains, Dergham relaxed. He started to talk, and it seemed like he never stopped. I liked him immediately. His story came out in explosive bursts, like thunderstorms. One question—"Where did you learn English?" or "Do you have kids?"—would provoke a flutter of facial twitches, like the onset of an epileptic fit. After a stage pause, he'd harrumph his vocal cords into gear, smile a small tight smirk that looked like embarrassment. "Well, to tell you the truth . . ." he'd begin, and launch yarns that sounded too good to be true.

He was the perfect guide to Hezbollah's postwar street campaign. He lived in the Dahieh and some of his brothers were full-fledged party members. So were most of his neighbors. His family was an old south Beirut dynasty, one of the few Shia families whose presence predated the great refugee influx of the 1970s and 1980s. They had owned property for generations when the Dahieh was mostly farmland, and still kept a sizeable orchard behind their home. He lived just behind Sahel General Hospital on a short street named after his family. He was well known around town and apparently trusted—it took some time to understand exactly why—but he made no secret of his sense of the ridiculous. The "Hezbollah guys," in his opinion, did great things for the country when it came to fighting the Israelis. The rest of the time, though, he thought they took themselves far too seriously. He approached everyone with a smile that overran his whole face, and when he spoke he'd bob his head while babbling warm strings of greetings and flattery, instantly putting all but the stiffest people at ease. We'd pass a Hezbollah tough at a traffic checkpoint and Dergham would slow down, roll down the window, and fire a round of chatter at the fellow, all the while nodding his head and grinning like a madman. As we would pull away he'd switch without interruption into English, still smiling in the thug's direction and bobbing his head: "*Y'atik el 'afieh!* God grant you health! Man, what a stupid fucking asshole. I know that kid. He think he something, but I tell you what, he ain't nothing but a stupid motherfucking asshole!"

Nothing spoiled Dergham's good cheer. To my knowledge he never read a newspaper, and he preferred not to dwell on the epistemological questions raised by his environment. "I'm a dumbass," he would say. He definitely wasn't, but he'd learned to avoid trouble by playing the part of the laughing clown with an unpredictable violent streak. One time, he said, a small crowd came after his brother, for some vague reason that Dergham thought might have been justified. Dergham snuck up behind the ringleader in the dark, shoved the barrel of his AK through the man's hair, and fired into the air. The man fainted, thinking he'd been shot in the head, and his followers dissipated in terror. "People know I'm crazy," he said about his neighbors. "They know if they fuck with me I might just go crazy and get my gun and start shooting people." What he knew about Hezbollah evolved day to day, and he absorbed it directly—from his neighbors and family through a sort of osmosis, and from the television set. He only watched Al-Manar. He was also a man of the moment. If the political situation was tense, he'd get jittery and talk extra fast, as if he were on cocaine or amphetamines. "Everyone's alert. There's something going down. The fighters are ready, they're ready for something. The word's gone out." The next day he'd be languid, slow, like a Southerner on the front porch with a beer in his hand on a Saturday afternoon. "Everything's cool. Nothing's happening. Hezbollah got it all under control." Like Hezbollah was a gang that had just averted a turf battle. He would seem to have forgotten his previous day's alarm. This impressionability made him a poor political historian but a fabulous bellwether of the mood on the street—specifically, of the mood that Hezbollah was trying to cultivate at any given time.

When we first met, Dergham let drop that he'd spent some time in the States and added cryptically, "I can't go back. Not my choice. I'm not allowed." But he hated to let a good story go untold, and within a few days was obviously bursting to tell me. On a long car ride one afternoon, I barely had to prod him. "You want to know the truth?" he asked.

"No," I said, "I want you to make up some bullshit. Of course I want to know the truth."

"Well, the truth is . . ." he inhaled, and this time cracked open a big smile, already excited about the expected effect. "I was a drug dealer." He savored the hammer strike, and turned to me like the Cheshire cat. "Mmmm hmmmmmm. You name it, I sold it. Marijuana, cocaine, heroin. I ran coke up I-95 from Atlanta to New York. You wouldn't believe how much cocaine I moved. I ain't proud of it, but I did it." His protestation notwithstanding, he did sound proud.

What followed was a tale part *Miami Vice,* part *LA Confidential,* part Ramadan soap opera, and part pure Lebanese civil war. The company he had kept in America had reinforced his teenage lifestyle choices and had given him his startling accent.

When Dergham was born in 1964, there was no such thing as the Dahieh. Christian farming hamlets punctuated the fertile expanse south of Beirut. Haret Hreik was just one of them, prosperous for a farm town, and quite close to the city. It was inhabited mostly by Christians with a smattering of established Sunni and Shia families, including Dergham's. A rich Christian family lived in an ornate villa at the end of Dergham's street, close to the airport road. Dergham, the second child, was born on the second story of the family home, which his father expanded as he and his wife went on to have five sons and a daughter. Most of the village kids liked to play soccer, but Dergham preferred bird hunting with his BB gun. Every chance he got, he would hunt with his father or his cousins, often in the forest beside the airport road, and on lucky occasions in the hills of the South or in the Beqaa, his favorite of all. He handled the BB gun and later the shotgun with proficiency and grace. He loved guns; school, he wasn't quite so crazy about. At age thirteen, when he heard that the PLO was giving every new recruit a Kalashnikov, he quit school and joined the Palestinian militia with one of his bird-hunting cousins. "Oooh, I was corrupt!" he said with relish. By then, the civil war had pushed waves of Shia refugees from other parts of Lebanon into the area south of Beirut, where they quickly overran the small farming villages. The Christian landowners fled to Christian-controlled mountains or East Beirut, and the Shia squatted on their property. The shantytown that resulted had exploded by the early 1980s into the Dahieh, a city of its own, a hastily built jumble of apartments off the grid, with no state water and sewer hookups, and no electricity.

Dergham's personal trajectory paralleled the explosive growth of the Dahieh, the rise of Hezbollah, and the emergence of a militant Shia Islamist identity in his community. The unbroken urban behemoth of the Dahieh swallowed the Christian farming towns. Haret Hreik lost its identity as a distinct village and became just another neighborhood of the Dahieh. Dergham Street, named for his family, became a claustrophobic lane crammed with concrete dwellings. The refugees paved every spit of earth and erected sloppy structures on top of and between every existing house. Older houses like Dergham's doubled in size to accommodate the new generation; when Dergham inherited the ground floor of the home where he was born, it had grown to four stories. Since there was no urban planning whatsoever, all but the busiest arteries could handle only a single lane of traffic. Minivans and taxis competed for space on lanes barely adequate to handle the donkey cart traffic for which they were intended. Cars parked against the front doors of homes. It took hours to drive a few miles during the daily tie-ups. The hassles of daily life accentuated the lack of water, sewer, and power. This sprawl became undisputedly Shia territory, ripe recruiting ground first in the 1970s for the Amal Party and later in the 1980s for Hezbollah.

Dergham fought with Palestinian and Shia militants in the early years of the civil war, until he fled to the United States in 1982, at age eighteen. He spent nearly two decades in America, mostly in Atlanta. He experimented with various odd jobs before settling on a career as a drug dealer. He married an American woman named Jackie, had two children, and visited his family in Lebanon when he could. Finally, after one too many brushes with police, he returned to Beirut in 1999 to find that his neighbors had become religious and his old buddies from the early militia days of the civil war had become self-disciplined Hezbollah activists. His daughter

A Hezbollah supporter plants the party flag atop the rubble of his destroyed apartment building in the Dahieh, Beirut's southern suburb, on August 14, 2006, the day the summer 2006 war with Israel ended. *Photo: Bryan Denton*

An enormous banner portraying U.S. Secretary of State Condoleezza Rice as a vampire hangs from a highway overpass in downtown Beirut at the height of the 2006 war. *Photo: Bryan Denton*

An elderly woman moans while evacuating her house in the heavily bombarded border town of Bint Jbail during a one-day ceasefire on July 31, 2006. *Photo: Tanya Habjouqa*

Rani Bazzi, an engineer and Hezbollah fighter, photographed during a clandestine training mission.
Photo: Bazzi family

Rani Bazzi prays at Tel Masoud, a hill outside Bint Jbail, on July 31, 2006, before showing journalists around the site of a recent battle between Hezbollah and Israeli soldiers.
Photo: Tanya Habjouqa

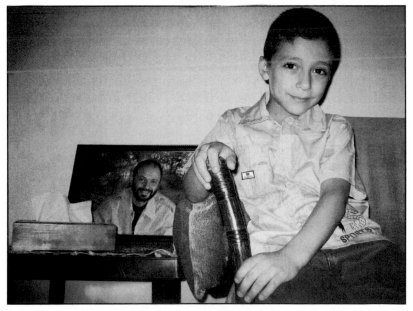

Shaheed Bazzi, six years old, in October 2006 beside a photograph of his father, Rani, less than two months after his death. The boy's name means "martyr." *Author photo*

Tens of thousands of Hezbollah supporters flood downtown Beirut in December 2006 on the tenth day of a massive civil disobedience campaign to bring down the pro-Western government. Pictured here, followers of the Maronite Christian Free Patriotic Movement are joined in a tight alliance with Hezbollah. *Photo: Bryan Denton*

Solidere, the once-bustling commercial center of Beirut, becomes a ghost town during Hezbollah's months-long "sit-in." Here a Hezbollah activist prays in front of a shuttered bank in January 2007. *Photo: Bryan Denton*

As part of its campaign to weaken the government in January 2007, Hezbollah members blockaded major streets with burning roadblocks like this one. *Photo: Bryan Denton*

Supporters cheer a speech by Hezbollah leader Sayyed Hassan Nasrallah broadcast over massive television screens in the Dahich, on the Shia religious festival of Ashoura, in January 2007. *Photo: Bryan Denton*

Graduating members of the Mahdi Scouts march in a ceremony at Scout City in the Beqaa Valley, the central training facility for the scouts. *Photo: Bryan Denton*

Female members of the Mahdi Scouts take part in training in South Lebanon. *Photo: Bryan Denton*

A Party of God supporter photographs his two sons in front of a Hezbollah rocket launcher at a fair organized in Nabatieh, South Lebanon in August 2008 to celebrate the group's military achievements against Israel and its chief strategist, Imad Mughniyeh, who was assassinated in February 2008. Until Mughniyeh's death, Hezbollah had denied any connection to him. *Photo: Bryan Denton*

A young Hezbollah supporter reacts to a skeleton dressed as an Israeli soldier at the Nabatieh fair that memorialized Imad Mughniyeh. The Hezbollah military chief was wanted by the U.S. in connection with a multitude of crimes, including the 1983 Marine barracks bombing in Beirut. *Photo: Bryan Denton*

A boy looks at captured Israeli weaponry and equipment at the August
fair in Nabatieh. Hezbollah regularly organizes month-long public fairs
to promote martyrdom, "the culture of Islamic resistance," and rally
supporters around its militia.
Photo: Bryan Denton

Hezbollah's dispute with the government turned into a full-fledged military battle
in May 2008. Friends restrain an Al-Manar cameraman on the Corniche al-Mazraa
after he was attacked by young men from Hezbollah's rival party, the Sunni Muslim
Future Movement. *Photo: Bryan Denton*

Militiamen from the Shia Amal Movement, a close ally of Hezbollah, clashed with Sunni fighters. An Amal militant runs for cover after firing a rocket-propelled grenade across the Corniche al-Mazraa into a majority-Sunni neighborhood. *Photo: Bryan Denton*

Hezbollah leader Hassan Nasrallah makes his first public appearance in nearly two years on July 16, 2008, at a rally to celebrate the release of Samir Quntar (beside Nasrallah wearing fatigues and a scarf). Quntar spent nearly three decades in prison in Israel, convicted of murder and kidnapping. Two children and their father were killed in Quntar's attempt to take them hostage.
Photo: Bryan Denton

Chloe started wearing a headscarf, and Dergham's brothers gently chided him whenever he drank alcohol. His wife couldn't stand it. She found the Dahieh suffocating, and eventually left with their son, returning for good to Atlanta. Dergham was lonely. He missed his American lifestyle. He brought in a special plumber to install an American-style toilet, where the bowl always has water in it. At first he found Hezbollah's ubiquitous presence stifling. The party controlled everything from small claims court to traffic regulation to security. "They think they own this neighborhood," he fumed. To his surprise, though, he discovered that no one judged him for his drug-dealing past, and they gave him no trouble as long as he sated his thirst for vice—like drinking and visiting strip clubs—out of the Dahieh.

I was fascinated to learn that despite his lifestyle Hezbollah didn't view Dergham as a liability, but as a solid ally and a potential convert. The party believed that Dergham had its best interest at heart and would never do anything that could constitute a security breach. His brothers in Hezbollah never stopped trying to persuade him to give up alcohol. If he was prepared to heed the Islamic call—quit drinking, learn how to pray—he would be invited to undergo the rigorous process of admission to the party, they told him. He considered it a great honor, but was not ready to surrender the tastes of a lifetime. Deep down, I think, he knew his loquaciousness, temper, and volatility were unsuited to the disciplined double life a real Hezbollah cadre had to lead.

By the time I met him during the 2006 war, Dergham had joined the "Society of Resistance," considering himself an outer-ring supporter of Hezbollah with no official ties. With priming from Hezbollah, Al-Manar, and his neighbors, Dergham would wholly adopt the cause of the moment and oil his machine gun. "Man, these people in the government want to make some problems!" he would declare the morning after a series of speeches, news reports, and press conferences about the brewing showdown between Hezbollah and the state. "If they don't give us Shia our rights, they gonna have a revolution on their hands." A few days later he'd have forgotten about the whole affair.

Dergham's neighborhood had livened up since the war. Bulldozers cleared rubble around the clock. The Jihad for Building Reconstruction had begun its ambitious rebuilding campaign, and the new Hezbollah sister corporation "The Promise" was designing a futuristic Dubai-style glass housing development in the center of the Dahieh's Security Square. Nasrallah had given his followers leave to act cocky. On September 22, 2006, Hezbollah organized a massive outdoor victory rally, in part orchestrated to irritate Israel.[55] Hezbollah, however, had multiple audiences in mind. It was a Friday night at the beginning of the month of Ramadan, a time of reflection and regeneration, when Muslims spend lots of time with their families. The throng pulsated in the early evening, waiting for Nasrallah's address. At times like this, when the risk to the secretary-general was considered high, he spoke to rallies from a hidden location, his image projected on enormous jumbotrons. Suddenly, a phalanx of guards spilled in front of the massive screen. Sayyed Hassan Nasrallah had appeared in person to talk to the tens of thousands assembled beneath the open sky and the enemy's satellites. A wave of rapture broke over the crowd.

"Standing before you and amongst you involves risk for you and me," he said. "My heart, mind, and soul did not allow me to address you from afar nor through a screen." Thus ennobled, everyone in the open square on the edge of the Dahieh understood what Hezbollah's leader was telling them: they were still warriors, and they were still fighting. Divine Victory did not signify the end of the war; it simply marked a turning point in a long fight. The resistance, he said, with the love of the proud Lebanese people, had struck a blow against Israel and, more important, its puppet-master, the United States. It did so on behalf not just of the Lebanese but also of oppressed Palestinians, and proud Arabs and Muslims everywhere. Anyone who felt that Hezbollah had lost, Nasrallah suggested, probably had cast their lot with the enemies of faith and rectitude. Hezbollah proved in the war, Nasrallah argued, that Arab armies could reconquer all of Palestine, "from river to sea," if only the Arab armies would exercise their power against the Jews rather than cling to their thrones.

"Today, your resistance broke the image of Israel," he said. "We have done away with the invincible army. We have also done away with the invincible state." He cited an Israeli opinion poll that gave Prime Minister Ehud Olmert a seven percent approval rating. "Once, an old man, who knew his time, place, and era, said: If every one of us carried a bucket of water and threw it on occupied Palestine, Israel would disappear from existence; yes, just a bucket of water. Two or three hundred million people standing up to Israel can defeat it, especially when a few thousand in Lebanon defeated Israel."

Then, turning to his fellow Lebanese, Nasrallah laid out Hezbollah's demands in simple language. The country would have to form a new national unity government that granted Hezbollah veto power. It was the party's "serious project," he said, which it would pursue applying its "utmost strength." Great menace hung over his evenly delivered ultimatum. When Nasrallah spoke of Israel and the Arabs, he built rhetorical palaces, raising his audience with long complex sentences punctuated by clipped call-and-response climaxes. When he spoke of Hezbollah's ultimatum to Lebanon, he was brief and to the point, like a foreclosing banker who meant business. The secretary-general warned in his lilting voice: "No army in the world can make us lay down our arms." Hezbollah's weapons, he swore, would never turn against other Lebanese. Sectarian critics—the pro-Western leaders who were intimating darkly that Hezbollah's militia had taken Lebanon hostage and would turn it inexorably into a miniature Iran—would ruin themselves before they could harm the Party of God: "This is playing with fire," Nasrallah said. "This is sabotaging the country. This is destroying the country." His message sent, both through his words and through his physical presence on the platform, Nasrallah's guards whisked him away. It was to be his last public appearance for a long time.

The March 14 alliance in charge of the government claimed the moral high ground of liberal pluralism on its side. While Hezbollah and its followers were issuing demands, the governing coalition claimed it was fighting to preserve Lebanese independence, sovereignty, and tolerance even though its leaders often made crass sectarian appeals to their own followers and tolerated no democracy in internal party affairs. Hezbollah, they said, advanced the interests of Iran, Syria, and extremist Islamism. The government, on the other hand, was doing the hard but noble work of forging a distinctly Lebanese consensus, finding a way to accommodate a diverse society's homegrown aspirations. A coalition of parties opposed to Syrian hegemony had won a majority at the polls in the 2005 election, and had united under the banner of March 14, the date of the mass street protest that sparked the end of the Syrian occupation of Lebanon. The government always made a point of calling itself the majority because it commanded the largest parliamentary bloc, even though Lebanon's skewed sectarian electoral system meant that a parliamentary majority didn't necessarily reflect a majority in the popular vote. The March 14 forces took courage from the support of the White House. They were convinced by a parade of diplomats and Bush administration officials that the United States valued Lebanese democracy. The "Cedar Revolution" offered a rare success story for the Bush administration's democracy agenda, and American officials convinced March 14 that the U.S. would do everything in its power to support a new polity independent from Syrian machinations and Hezbollah intimidation. Their blustery assurances gave a false security blanket to the politicians in the government. Hezbollah had learned once again in the 2006 war that it truly could count on Iran and Syria. Meanwhile, the March 14 coalition was hurtling headlong into a confrontation with Hezbollah, unsure whether American backing would amount to more than lofty words.

I got a taste of the wishful thinking that America was feeding its allies in the Lebanese government during a background briefing at the embassy a few weeks after Nasrallah's speech. Lebanon had never been safer for an American. I could drive my rental car by myself to the Hezbollah office in Security Square to call on party officials, with no danger. Meanwhile, almost two decades since the last American was kidnapped, America's diplomats operated like it was still 1983, living in splendid isolation in a hilltop compound that looked like a golf resort a half-hour's drive north of Beirut. In the city they traveled with armed guards in conspicuous SUVs with tinted windows. Their perspective suffered accordingly. A trio of diplomats briefed me on aid, military cooperation, and politics. I hoped they were lying to me, because their assessments were so out of kilter with reality. The aid specialist told me that USAID spending would outweigh Hezbollah's, although even if that dubious claim ever proved true (it didn't), no one would know. USAID never put its name on most of its projects since anti-American sentiment ran so high. The military specialist dreamed of outfitting a Lebanese Army that could supplant Hezbollah's militia, but admitted it was tough since America didn't want to give serious hardware to an enemy state officially still at war with Israel since 1948. The political operative talked in sound bites, and clearly found my questions jarring and irritating. He was convinced that most Lebanese hated Hezbollah and were just dying to throw their support behind a U.S.-backed government. It was no wonder that the Lebanese government, getting Pollyanna-ish advice from a global superpower, thought it might be able to beat Hezbollah.

For his part, Ayatollah Fadlallah—the cleric who inspired Hezbollah but maintained an independent line from the party—delivered week after week of scrappy sermons declaring that the Islamic Resistance was making progress resisting the West's Long War Against Islam. According to Fadlallah's broad analysis, the U.S.-Israel axis was stumbling in its military ventures against the Palestinians and Iraq. America wanted Lebanon and all the Arab countries to submit to Western-Zionist hegemony or else face plots orchestrated by the White House. To the militant or militarized Shia listener, Nasrallah provided the brimstone and Fadlallah the political science. Together they offered a web of reasons why the Shia should consider themselves globally encircled and under threat, their August victory precarious and easily rolled back.

Dergham took me to Fadlallah's mosque one Friday, a few minutes' walk from his house. Fadlallah was warning of conspiracies against the resistance by evildoers, perhaps even within the United Nations. The street outside the mosque had a relaxed carnival air. Fadlallah's words carried over loudspeakers, and men prayed on mats laid on the asphalt lane that snaked around the mosque walls. Street vendors peddled DVDs and fresh produce. Men collected money for various Hezbollah projects—orphanages, schools, weapons. "Hey, come meet my nephew," Dergham said, pushing me toward a muscle-bound youth whose eyes were nearly invisible, sunk in his engorged cheeks. The kid was eighteen, and named Salem. He was bulked up like a football player on steroids. He had a sweet smile and was nearly inarticulate. I couldn't tell if he was very shy or very slow, or whether he was so reticent because of his work as a Hezbollah fighter. Salem had no combat experience, and he'd spent the war in Beirut. Immediately after the ceasefire, Hezbollah had dispatched him to a thirty-day combat course. "I'm training for a martyrdom operation," he said with a smile. Behind him a friend named Mustafa was stuffing donations from passersby into a Plexiglas box. He nodded at me and fanned a bunch of hundred dollar bills that he drew from his pocket. "It's to buy rockets and weapons for the resistance," he said. "There's a lot, lot more."

After the sermon, sidewalk speakers cranked out martial hits, the kind that accompanied music videos on Al-Manar and filled the drive time on Al Nour Radio. One song went like this:

> *Your machine gun has thirty-five bullets—*
> *Each bullet sends a devil back to hell.*
> *Each spent shell casing will blossom like wheat or flowers.*
> *Mother, mother don't feel sorry for the dead—*
> *It's a gift from God to defend the weak.*

The music was loud, rhythmic, and percussive, with lots of harmonies and rousing choruses. It reminded me of the marching songs of the Communist partisans during the Greek civil war in the 1940s; I had heard the songs on folk records as a child, and found myself humming along to their catchy tunes. Only when I grew older did I understand the grisly, bloodthirsty propaganda in the lyrics.

On the surface, the Dahieh seemed calm, but lots of angst percolated beneath the surface. Thousands of people in the neighborhood were doubled up in temporary apartments while they waited for Hezbollah to rebuild their homes. The party had deployed extra groups of operatives to keep the Shia city-within-a-city functioning and also under a tight lid. Newly hired (and by their conduct, hastily trained) Hezbollah traffic wardens appeared at every intersection sporting special black uniforms. "These idiots mess things up more than they help," Dergham observed. But they gave Hezbollah yet another layer of visibility, and another set of eyes on the community. Plainclothes officers circulated on mopeds. Whenever I alighted in the Dahieh's security zone, even if I was parked in front of the international media office and headed toward its entrance, a firm but polite man would fix his eyes on me and ask: "May I help you?" Outsiders were suspect, and under close watch. But Hezbollah took care to detect the faintest whiff of loyalty; the Party of God needed all the support it could get.

* * *

"Hey dude, guess what? I have a surprise for you!" It was my old wartime translator Issam Moussa phoning from Tyre.

"What?" I said.

"You'll never guess who I ran into," Issam said. "Guess, guess, c'mon."

I mulled the possibilities. I didn't want to guess the fighter Rani Bazzi, but there wasn't anyone else I was so interested in meeting again.

"The guy from Bint Jbail?" I said, referring to Rani, already feeling a cold dread that whatever Issam had called to tell me wouldn't turn out to be good.

"No, the other guy, his friend. I have bad news." He fell silent.

"What? What?" I said, exasperated.

"The man we met, that great guy, he's dead. He was a fighter, and he was martyred. On the last days of the war. He was a great man."

Rani Bazzi had been killed.

"I'm sorry," I said. "I wanted to see him again."

"He was a special man, that guy," Issam said. "There was something different about him."

On a Saturday afternoon in mid-October, when Issam was off from his job with the International Committee for the Red Cross, my colleague Hwaida Saad and I drove south to join Issam and look for the dead fighter's family. During the war, I'd worked with shady and inexperienced characters, men sketchier than Issam with no journalism background who spoke passable English and were willing to risk their skin for a spurt of cash. Hwaida was among the small corps of highly skilled Lebanese journalists who worked with the international media, and only now months after the war was she available. I knew and trusted her work and professionalism; I was glad to have her along so I wouldn't have to rely only on Issam's mercurial judgment.

The day was sunny and cool. We climbed the hills to the entrance of Bint Jbail, and stopped by the private hospital at the town's edge. A large banner there pictured the town's martyrs, seventeen in all. Our hunt suddenly became much easier. There on the upper left was Rani Bazzi, the man I'd met in August, although if I weren't looking for him I might not have recognized him. When I'd met the fighter, his face was long, oval, and gaunt; his head was shaved; his beard was long and scraggly. In the photo, a well-fed and younger Rani had bulging cheeks and a round face. His hair and beard were trimmed the same short length, like a furry halo around his entire head. "The Martyr Rani Ahmed Bazzi," was spelled out in simple script below his picture; it was the first time I saw his real name. I stared for some moments at the photograph. I had a felt a flicker of kinship with this man, and I had sensed that he held a key to understanding something inscrutable at Hezbollah's core. This death-embracing Party of God, with its cultish trappings and macabre commitment to endless war against Israel, grew harder and harder to understand and humanize the more I learned. But if I were ever to understand it, I'd have to do so on human terms, where life and death decisions always are made. Behind the rigmarole and fanaticism stood a million or more people with sensibilities and personalities. I needed to break through the frozen grimace of the party's external face to understand why these people had chosen Hezbollah. Almost no one whom I'd met in Hezbollah cared if I *liked* them. Rani had. That was his Achilles' heel, an enticing vulnerability that disarmed his more radical patter. He had talked of the things he hated but he didn't act like he hated anything at all. I would never speak to him again, and I feared I never would experience the revelation that felt in reach during that one afternoon with him.

Now that we had a name, it would be easy to find his house. We drove to the town center through an unrecognizable geography. Bulldozers had cleared rubble from the streets, like little brooks carved through landfill. In the town's partially destroyed outlying districts, every structure was slightly askew or damaged, so uniformly as to look like a film set. The real shock came when we reached the commercial center, the hive of streets where we'd met Rani and where Issam had liberated the pair of boots. Two months earlier, that square mile of downtown Bint Jbail had stunned me; what I had failed to appreciate is the way that utter catastrophe leaves fewer traces. The greater the horror, the less the drama. If I hadn't been there before, I would not have believed this landscape to be a former urban area; it looked an open quarry—a vast field of stone, undulating down the hill. From the cleared street, nowhere was any trace of human habitation apparent. Only the mental image of the former and future street grid put the scene into appropriately disconcerting relief.[56] We asked a few loitering men to point us to the house of the Martyr Rani Bazzi, who apparently was well known. Within minutes we were on a hill on the opposite side of the town, south of the reservoir where the terrain began to climb the ridge to Maroun El Ras and the Israeli border. We were directed to a long, narrow apartment building of unfinished concrete, several stories tall. It stretched directly beside the narrow road, its front entrance in the lee of a hairpin turn. The building looked more like an abandoned warehouse than a home. We knocked and waited several long minutes. We knocked again with no response, and were just walking away when a lady ran out, calling after us. Someone had telephoned her to say a foreigner was in town looking for Rani's house. Her name was Mariam, and she was a cousin of Rani's. We offered condolences and tears came to her eyes. "He was doing what he loved to do. This was his destiny," Mariam said. She chatted hesitantly, and didn't invite us in. During the war, she said, Rani had phoned her or sent text messages every day. "He told me about you," she said. "He said you ate a tomato with him." His widow Farah had left Bint Jbail; Mariam gave us her cell phone number. She didn't feel like talking more, but she wanted to help. She directed us to the house of another relative in Bint Jbail, a dentist named Ali who spoke English because he had lived in Sydney, Australia, for the last two decades. After the Israeli withdrawal he had renovated his old family home in lavish style, with green onyx lions at the front gate and a riotous garden. He returned to his ancestral village every Ramadan.

Ali was not "with" Hezbollah, nor was he especially religious. He was a believer who led a secular lifestyle; although he was fasting for Ramadan he served us juice. We sat beneath a pomegranate tree laden with ripe fruit. Every year Ali and Rani would engage in long heated debates about religion. They both were pious Muslims, but Ali had a much more open-minded view about what constituted a religious life. They never discussed politics, and Ali never knew for sure if his relative was in the resistance, although he suspected it. "When he moved here during the occupation, I assumed he was either with the resistance or a collaborator. There was no other reason to live here under the Israelis," Ali said. He thought Rani was a bit of a fanatic, but he admired him. Rani bore the scars of the torture he endured at Khiam Prison, and he had become especially hard and driven after his release in 2000.

"In our religion, the best thing is to be a martyr," Ali said. During the war, Ali spoke with Rani on the phone twice. "He said to me, 'Indeed, we have our victory. We are right, we are strong, we are fighting.' That was the way of his life," Ali said. "I am very proud of him. He chose his way. He wanted that. This time, he was the one who decided how he would die."

Mariam joined us and this time talked more about her cousin. He was a gifted recruiter, she said, and over the years he convinced many of his relatives and neighbors to intensify their commitment to Islam and to Hezbollah's resistance efforts. He taught engineering at a local technical school. Every few weeks when he was summoned for military training, he would tell his family he was going to his "office" in Tyre for an engineering project. Mariam and thousands of other civilians stayed in Bint Jbail at the outset of the war, thinking they could weather the hostilities in the safety of their basements. By the eighth day, Mariam realized this war was different from previous campaigns and fled. Even during the war Rani viewed himself as a sort of den warden for his Bint Jbail family, phoning and sending text messages to friends and relatives almost daily. He sent a captured Israeli helmet to his mother. In one call, he told Mariam that this battle was just like the battle of Karbala. The angels were helping the fighters, he said as he wept. He wasn't afraid of being spotted by the Israeli drones overhead, known familiarly as MKs because of their model name: "Above the MK," he told Mariam, "there is God." Early in the morning on the day I met him, Rani had taken a wounded fighter to the hospital. "Why is this man wounded and I am not even dead?" Rani had lamented. "Maybe God does not want me."

Hezbollah had cleared a new area in the town cemetery for the 2006 martyrs. They were buried in two long rows, with identical marble tombs bearing the Martyrs' Association logo of a dove and a red rose. "The Martyrs with God have the honor and the light" was inscribed on each grave. Rani was identified as a martyr of Operation Truthful Promise, and as a hajj, because he had made the pilgrimage to Mecca in 2004. The graves flanked a barren field, but a crew of men was clearing the area and said that Hezbollah planned to build a memorial for the fighters and turn their graveyard into a park.

Later in the day we visited with yet another cousin, who had spent decades in the United States but had returned to Lebanon and now worked with Hezbollah. She had some official role with the party but didn't want to tell me exactly what it was. She and her husband were hospitable and warm, but skittish. They were American citizens and still traveled to the United States. They were afraid that talking to me, even anonymously, could get them in trouble with American law enforcement. "If we are mentioned in the same article as Hezbollah, you cannot imagine the problems it could cause us," the husband said. The sun was setting and the family had been fasting all day, in observance of Ramadan. Nothing can pass through the mouth—not a cigarette, not a sip of water, and of course, no food. By the end of the day, people often get tired, cranky, and dehydrated. One of the children brought water, instant coffee, and a tray of dates, rich in sugar and calories to break the fast.

The cousin—I'll call her Umm Abbas—was clearly enthralled by Rani. She had written a poem about him, and her cell phone screen saver was his photo. He had been instrumental in recruiting her to Hezbollah, and he had convinced another cousin still living in the United States to move back to Lebanon and support the Islamic Resistance. He had persuaded others by example and through relentless conversation. Umm Abbas was pretty, and looked younger than her forty-four years. She wore an ironed headscarf tight around her head. She and her husband had earned a lot of money in their business ventures in Michigan and New York; they had laid marble floors in their new apartment in a suburb of Tyre and filled it with hand-carved wooden furniture. The family had a new Mercedes sedan. Most of their children had been born in the States, but the family had decided to move back to Lebanon in the 1990s. When Umm Abbas finally met Rani, she said, his spirituality captivated her. Rani had grown up in the prosperous Lebanese diaspora in Kuwait. He was on track for an unremarkable life of bourgeois achievement as a civil engineer in the Gulf. Like his parents and his peers, he would be able to climb through the ranks in the oil or construction industry, work for an Arab conglomerate, educate his children, and vacation in his homeland. During his studies, however, he grew more religious. He stopped wearing brand-name clothing, and grew less vain and more modest. Why, he asked his parents, should he go to work for a Kuwaiti company that paid Americans more than Arabs for the same jobs? He fought with his mother and father when he turned down a job offer that would have given him a solid middle-class start in Kuwait.

"Nothing will make me leave my country anymore," he told his parents. He moved to Bint Jbail in the early 1990s.

In 1995, the Israelis locked Rani up for a year in Khiam Prison. They had caught him storing weapons in his home, which they destroyed after detaining him. When he was released he resumed his militia activity, and was arrested again in July 1999. All the while he grew more spiritual, and more strident in his interactions with friends and relatives, especially those who lived in America and summered in South Lebanon.

"He would ask, 'Why would you want to live in the States when you have something to give your country?' He convinced many people to move here," Umm Abbas said.

His house in Bint Jbail was still under construction at the time of Rani's death. "He said, 'I don't feel that we'll be living here,'" Umm Abbas said.

She told me some stories, but she didn't want me to learn too much. She was a bit too polished, in the typical controlling manner of a party official. I shouldn't bother Rani's widow, she said; Farah was in deep depression and didn't want visitors. She also avoided any story about Rani that made him out to be anything less than a magnetic, sainted leader of men.

Umm Abbas was waiting for one of her sons to get home so they could all go together to an *iftar,* a Ramadan fast-breaking dinner. As we sipped coffee and snacked on dates we heard someone fumbling with his shoes in the doorway.

"That's my son," Umm Abbas said.

He entered and froze on the doorstep of the salon. I recognized the young father of two I had met at the café in Hamra on the eve of the cease-fire, the man who had exhorted me to tell the truth.

"Ayman?" I said.

"You're the reporter!" he exclaimed.

We kissed each other on the cheeks in greeting. He explained to his mother where we'd met before. I explained the story I was working on, and that the fighter I had met in Bint Jbail turned out to be his mother's cousin.

"God works in mysterious ways," Ayman said. "You were meant to meet my uncle and see what a great man he was. And we were meant to see each other again."

*   *   *

Rani's final day already had become a legend among those who knew him. He was stationed with a small group of Hezbollah fighters in Ghandouriye, which had become the last front line in the war. Israel and Hezbollah had agreed to the terms of a ceasefire, but it wouldn't go into effect for several days. On Saturday, August 12, the fighters knew the war would be over by Monday. Evidence suggested, however, that Israel planned to air drop a large contingent of soldiers deep in Lebanese territory on the last weekend of fighting, so that Israeli troops could claim control over Lebanese territory to the Litani River and leverage a more robust international peacekeeping presence. Hezbollah was equally determined to grant Israel no quarter so that at the close of hostilities Israeli troops would be limited to a narrow zone far from the Litani. Both sides promised to keep shooting until the last minute of the war, which they had agreed to halt at eight o'clock on Monday morning. Although Rani's expertise was in explosives and antitank mines, he had plenty of combat experience and at age thirty-nine was among the more seasoned veterans in the field.

That Saturday morning, Israeli paratroopers landed, as expected, on the ridge near Ghandouriye. Tanks approached the town as well. Rani's contingent numbered about twenty, most of them much younger than him. He shaved his head, washed himself, and prayed. "Who is ready for his martyrdom?" he asked his companions. Two of his fellow fighters said they were, and followed his example. He had seen an Israeli sniper position, which he planned to charge head on. "You will certainly die," one of the fighters said. "Don't do it. Come back."

"Zahra calls me this way," he answered, invoking the nickname of the Prophet's daughter Fatima, Lady of Light. "Would you have me go in the other direction?"

"Ya Hussein!" he shouted as he charged, consecrating his final act of defiance to the great Shia Imam. Hussein might have been forsaken by the faithful in the year 680, but now, more than a millennium later, he was getting his due in the hills of Jabal Amel. Rani and the two men who joined him fell in a burst of bullets. It's impossible to know how decisive their act was, whether it terrified the Israelis who thought they had dug in unnoticed, dislodged them from their position, or merely unnerved them. Hezbollah did head off the Israelis, thwarting their eleventh-hour effort to sweep to the Litani.

What Hezbollah understood and Israel did not was the psychology of Lebanese supporters of the resistance, especially of those who had encountered the Israelis up close. Ali, the diaspora dentist, encapsulated it nicely. A quintessentially reasonable, middle-of-the-road man, he had fled the Israeli occupation and encouraged his two children to pursue the relatively frivolous careers of graphic designer and actor. He found Hezbollah's interpretation of Shia Islam slightly distasteful, but he had nothing but sympathy for their military resistance against Israel. "If I had stayed, I would have been like my cousin," Ali said. "I would have done something to help the resistance." Each war made things worse for Israel and better for the resistance, he believed, no matter who technically won. "The Israelis wanted to send a message. They want to pressure Hezbollah. They think they'll make people hate Hezbollah," Ali said. "Every one they kill, his children become resistance. Every house they destroy, the whole family becomes resistance. I cannot forgive Israel. Israel is my enemy."

We called Farah and she invited us to visit her a few days later, on Monday evening before the iftar. She gave us detailed directions to the apartment so we wouldn't have to ask around and call attention to ourselves. Hwaida got the impression that Farah was meeting us over the objections of Hezbollah. We rang her doorbell shortly before sunset. Farah came to the door after we'd rung three times; she appeared to have woken from a deep sleep. She motioned us to follow her into the living room. She welcomed me in English, which she understood well, although she preferred to speak Arabic. The apartment appeared newly furnished; the family had only moved there in September, when Farah decided to relocate the family to Beirut from Bint Jbail. Her sons rode tricycles back and forth on the enclosed porch.

In the living room hung photographs of Rani, Nasrallah, and Khomeini. In anticipation of my visit, she had arranged two special photographs of Rani on the coffee table. In one picture, Nasrallah was handing Rani a commendation. Both men were smiling at the camera and looked young. Rani was skinny, in full battle-dress uniform, a black beret on his head, with a very narrow beard and mustache. The picture appeared to date from the mid-to-late 1990s. The second picture showed an elated Rani pumping his right fist in the air in front of the podium where Nasrallah was speaking in May 2000, the day after Rani and the other detainees were sprung from Khiam Prison. Rani was wearing a heavy plaid shirt, a black vest, and a red headband. A trace of stubble shaded his head and face, and his eyes were closed. He appeared utterly transported.

Farah was passionately devoted to Hezbollah's cause. She was also in love with her husband, and missed him tremendously. I think she wanted to meet me because she wanted to gather extra memories from the final month during which she hadn't laid eyes on him, and because she was curious to learn what impact her beloved had made on a presumably hostile foreign journalist. Rani's friends and family were convinced that Rani's magnetic appeal would have magically opened my eyes to the righteousness of Hezbollah. For me Rani humanized a worldview that until I met him felt robotic, monolithic, inhumane; I wanted to learn more about him, and the popular movement he espoused and embodied. Hezbollah's followers often confused my empathy and curiosity for something else. Many of the Hezbollah adherents I met, like Umm Abbas and her son Ayman, mistook my inquiry into Hezbollah for a fellow-traveling sympathy for the party's ideology and aims. They hoped I had fallen under a benign spell. Farah, I felt, expected less from me. She didn't try to make me profess anything or explain myself. She asked me concrete questions about my encounter with her husband; she wanted details and pictures, and seemed to take comfort in the opportunity to talk at length about their story.

Her sons entered and greeted me dutifully, kissing me on the cheeks. Amir, the nine-year-old, quickly left. Shaheed, only six and still enamored of his mother, stayed with us in the living room, smiling shyly as we conversed.

She and Rani both grew up in Kuwait, Farah told me, and her family lived near his. Her father was Iranian and her mother Lebanese, but they were part of the Shia expatriate community in a Sunni emirate. Although she was five years younger than Rani, they were friendly as children and teenagers. They stayed in contact after Rani left to study in Beirut. When Farah finished high school and enrolled in university in Lebanon, Rani had set down roots in Bint Jbail and began to woo her.

"He put it in his mind that I would be his wife," she said. "I started to love him."

Farah finished her degree in 1996, the same year that Rani was released from Khiam Prison. Both their parents opposed a marriage, but they went ahead and wed in 1997, and had their first son, Amir, the following year. "All I know is that I loved him," she said.

The Israelis arrested Rani and Farah together in July 1999, when Farah was pregnant again. In detention, they told her they had sent her first son to Jerusalem and she would never see him again. It was a cruel joke. She was released after a week, and found Amir safe in the care of some neighbors.

"There was no mercy," she said. "They practiced so many ways of torturing us."

Her second son was born while his father was still in Khiam, with little prospect of being released. Following tradition, she initially called the boy Mohammed, after the Prophet. Many Muslims name their sons Mohammed until they survive into infancy, and then give them another name. She had no way of reaching Rani to tell him the good news. His captors, however, heard about the birth and figured they could use what they knew to pressure Rani in interrogation. They told him that the child had been stillborn; he would never see his second son except, some day, at his grave. By the time Farah was allowed to visit her husband in Khiam a week after the boy's birth, Rani was deep in mourning for his son.

"I know my son has died," he told her.

"No, he's fine," she said.

"Don't lie," he replied.

She couldn't convince him. Only when the Israeli occupation collapsed and Rani was freed from Khiam did he finally believe that his second son was alive. Farah agreed with his decision to rename him Shaheed, or martyr—an unusual name even among the most devout Shia.

"Everyone was against the name," Farah said. "Even Rani's mother. They thought the name made it more likely that he would die. But Rani and I used to think that death exists in life. If you call your son Shaheed and then one day he dies, well, after all, all of us will die."

For the first time she began to cry, without much drama, just quiet, steady tears. Not the wracking sobs of fresh loss but the steady grief of someone who knows they'll have to get used to an unbearable absence.

"He wasn't living as if he were going to die," she said. "He wasn't going around saying, 'I'm Hezbollah.' He had the philosophy that death is not the end of life: above all there is love. I have so many good memories. I'm not scared. We cried so much already that it hurt us. I feel very proud, surely, but it's very hard. I am proud of what he did, but I miss him. Believe me, believe me, no one likes to die. I am holding myself back."

She fell silent for a few minutes until her tears subsided. I asked her to tell me more about Rani in everyday life. He liked to visit relatives and play with his sons, she said, and he loved to discuss religion and martyrdom. Heaven, he speculated, wasn't only open to Muslims but to good people of other faiths as well. The couple often imagined what would become of the family if he or Farah were to die.

"Next month he would have turned forty," she said. "He used to worry that in his forties he would become tired, become sick. He was so worried about aging. He didn't want to die in his bed."

Her phone kept ringing, and she silenced most of the incoming calls. People were expecting her and the kids at an iftar, and it was long after sunset. The bleating cell phone cast a pall over our conversation, a rebuke to her for sitting with this foreign reporter talking about her dead husband instead of breaking fast with her Hezbollah friends. She seemed to enjoy my company; I enjoyed hers, and was eager to learn more about the martyr I'd met and the family he'd left behind, where he'd come from and why he'd chosen the course he followed. Finally she had to leave, but she invited us to return two days later.

We came back at ten o'clock on a Wednesday morning. Again, we woke Farah up. She had risen with the kids at six, packed them off to school, and then gone back to bed. Hezbollah took good care of the families of martyrs, though. Children went to the best schools and widows were quickly employed. Social workers and psychologists visited the families to make sure they were dealing with their grief and not lingering too long in depression. On the following Monday, Farah was starting a new job teaching art at a Hezbollah school. Soon she'd have no more time for naps. I asked her how the kids were handling their father's death. She explained that they took comfort from their father's role in the resistance. "For sure the kids are very much affected," she said. But if they saw their father's death as the inevitable consequence of Israeli aggression, it became more graspable. The kids had grown up in a conflict zone; they were too young to understand death, perhaps, but they understood fear and instability and the culture of faith and armed struggle that had surrounded them since birth. "You must explain it logically," she said. "For sure, my husband is not the first martyr. The kids here see a lot of cases. They have friends whose fathers are martyrs. They have lived all their lives in Bint Jbail, a place that always is a target. We make them understand why this happened. They're living in their own country, and the Israelis attack. And you must defend your homeland."

Already Farah's sense of individual and family identity was beginning to dissolve into her communal role as a member of Hezbollah and as the wife of a martyr. The party's interests had primacy within its community, and the martyrs held a pivotal position. Martyrs served as inspiration and as points of recruitment; their surviving families were to testify both to the nobility of martyrdom and to the undying commitment of the Hezb, the Party. This culture was carefully engineered. Hezbollah's martyrs were not like the caricatured trope of a Palestinian suicide bomber familiar to readers of Western newspapers. The martyrs whose faces adorned the walls in Gaza and the West Bank are typically young men who had rarely accomplished anything else of note. They were recruited and trained solely to detonate a vest full of metal and explosives, often among a crowd of civilians. Hezbollah's martyrs were meant to be something else entirely: well-trained operatives striking important military objectives, the soul and conscience of their entire community. Anyone killed in service to Hezbollah was considered a martyr. Those like Rani who volunteered for risky missions with a high chance of death were accorded special status. Most prestigious of all were that comparatively tiny number deployed to blow themselves up, on what the party called "martyrdom operations."

Only men of exceptional battlefield prowess could apply for martyrdom operations, and only a small subset of that elite was accepted. A martyrdom operation was meant to cap a notable career and represented the sacrifice of a man of talent. Some had wives and children. Some senior party officials pleaded to be sent on missions but were barred because their skills were needed elsewhere.[57] If Hezbollah deployed callow throwaway teenagers on martyrdom operations the party felt it would cheapen rather than ennoble the cult of death. The party's military planners reserved death missions for otherwise unattainable military objectives. Suicide bombers drove car bombs into Israeli bases or convoys; when they died, they were honored and their exploits strategically recounted to boost popular morale. Hezbollah's first suicide bomber, Ahmed Kassir, remained anonymous for three years after his pioneering attack against Israel's headquarters in Tyre on November 11, 1982. He drove a white Peugeot into the seven-story building and killed seventy-five Israelis along with at least fourteen Lebanese prisoners being held inside. His identity was kept secret for three years, after which he was feted for succeeding in the party's first "martyrdom operation." Israel claimed a gas leak destroyed the headquarters, even after Hezbollah released video footage of the attack and several Israeli officials told the Israeli media that the military knew it had suffered a suicide attack at the time and had failed to adjust its security measures.

Ahmed Kassir's name and legend still packed a punch decades later. Twenty-six years after his attack, in 2008, his story was the centerpiece of a popular Hezbollah propaganda fair entitled "Princes of the Martyrs" at a convention center in Tyre. A sound and light show in a cavernous auditorium portrayed Ahmed Kassir's attack as a natural response to Israeli outrages depicted in a fast montage that began with images from 1948. Black and white footage played over a screen in the dark room. Light then flashed on a twenty-foot-tall mockup of a concrete building, and a video showed the white Peugeot squealing toward the actual headquarters. An explosion rumbled in surround sound and smoke filled the auditorium. Lights played over a sculpture of the now-destroyed building. The Hezbollah guide leading me through the display was an eighteen-year-old film student and *muhajaba*, from the same family as the bomber. Ahmed Kassir the bomber was her uncle, and Abdallah Kassir the director of Al-Manar Television was also her uncle. She sighed blissfully. "What a privilege it would be to be a martyr. Some day, I hope the party lifts its ban on women taking part in martyrdom operations." She turned to me. "Doesn't this make you want to be a martyr?" She was jolted from her reverie when I said no.

The propanda around martyrdom extolled bravery and fearlessness; its main purpose was to encourage party recruitment. But Hezbollah hadn't deployed a suicide bomber since the end of the Israeli occupation in 2000, although Israeli officials accused Hezbollah of training Palestinian suicide bombers. Given their disuse of the tactic, for the time being, I was struck by the concerted energy that Hezbollah spent lionizing the suicide bombers, the men who had driven bomb cars into targets and blown themselves up, as opposed to the more easily found instances of martyrs who like Rani charged impregnable defenses, ambushed tanks from holes in the ground, or infiltrated the Israeli border for reconnaissance or raids. Suicide bombers held a central place in the party's mythology; and since it never knew when it might want at a moment's notice to resume "martyrdom operations," the party kept their ranks trained and ready. Hezbollah's religious indoctrination laid the groundwork for the culture of martyrdom; but the Party of God took care to buttress its doctrinal view of death with a very tangible web of incentives. The fighters who died in the service of the Islamic Resistance bequeathed to their families not just enduring status but a coveted benefits package. The party's model of community building required the families of the martyrs to thrive, and their sons to volunteer to fight like their fathers. To that effect, the party deployed a battery of social workers and psychologists to help the surviving family members grieve and treat their depression. The Martyrs' Association organized a steady flow of social activities to keep the widows and their children busy with group trips and banquets. Over time the widows were encouraged to remarry. The children went to the best Hezbollah private schools. Scoutmasters from Hezbollah's Mahdi Scouts paid courtesy calls on martyrs' families and made sure the kids stayed involved in their local troop. Farah knew her role, and she was gearing up for it. This week was her last as a mourning widow; the next would be her first back on duty as a pillar of Hezbollah.

"Everything is hard," she said. "It is very hard, his leaving. When death has meaning, it makes people stronger. After all, I cannot stop missing him. I think of him all the time."

She delivered a canned speech to me about Hezbollah—"I meant to tell you some things about the party last time, but I was not concentrating"— and I felt that some of her more robotic party impulses were reasserting themselves against her uncomplicated desire to communicate with me. She gave me a copy of Rani's videotaped will and a bunch of photographs prepared by the party. I gave her copies of the photographs a colleague had taken of Rani praying on that day at Tel Masoud in Bint Jbail. She told me that Rani's family had hoped when they first married that Farah would dissuade Rani from fighting Israel and convince him to return to Kuwait. They were disappointed to find Farah fully on board with her husband.

Long ago, she said, he had asked her to forgive him in advance for his death, which would leave her alone in charge of the family. "It's not an easy mission at all," she said. In the videotaped will, addressed to his mother, father, brothers, wife, and children, he asked Farah again to forgive him. "Even though he already had told me this face to face, he said this in his will so that his family would see it. He gave me a support this way," Farah said. "I couldn't watch it. It was very hard. I listened only."

We bade each other farewell. I hoped to see her again. She seemed complex and humane, like Rani, even though at times she veered into speech that sounded more like rote propaganda than conversation. She clung strongly to her beliefs and was paying for them. She had loved her husband and she loved her children, but—incomprehensibly to me—she was willing to lose them to a cause that seemed to me hopeless, impersonal, and at times fanatical. She said she hoped her sons would grow up to be like their father, even though that would make them more likely to die. A good Muslim should struggle in every aspect of life, whether in something as mundane as eating healthy food and treating neighbors hospitably or as final as the decision to volunteer for military training in "martyrdom operations." Unlike most Hezbollah partisans I met, I felt I could learn from her. On a human, interpersonal level, she didn't feel like an unknowable stranger, like a fanatic who valued life less than I did and could therefore make nihilistic choices. She embraced her worldview like a lover willing to follow her passion wherever it might lead, committed in life and death. So many Hezbollah fighters and supporters I met spoke in mantras and slogans, pretending that it was easy to lose loved ones or homes in a holy war. This patter I found hard to believe. Anyone who told me they were happy to see their child die for the resistance, I concluded, was either withholding their true feelings or was crazy. Farah was different. She didn't pretend to like every consequence of the life she and Rani had made, nor did she pretend their choices were easy. She was living in struggle, on the most primal and personal level, and for the first time I could see the choice to die in the service of Hezbollah as a human and even fathomable one. I hoped over time to know Farah better and through her to find a guide to the alternate world of Hezbollah's faithful.

My encounter with Farah was intense, brief, and truncated. I hoped that unlike my affecting meeting with Rani, my relationship with his family would have occasion to ripen over time. But I feared its tenor might abruptly change.

Rani's videotaped will had aired on Al-Manar and was also posted on You-Tube and other sites. Wearing fatigues and bareheaded, his receding hairline visible every time he looks down to read first from a Koran and then from notes in his lap, Rani speaks for eight minutes. Bagpipe music plays on a swelling soundrack, and the shrubbery behind him flutters in the wind. He reads from the Koran about paradise and hell before kissing the holy book and addressing his family.

> The unbelievers will suffer, shackled in hell. The martyrs have their own light. One thing I learned is that humiliation, to be demonized at the hands of Jews and their collaborators, is worse than death. To my family, my tongue is failing to thank you because you are the main reason for my existence in this life. You are the main reason for raising me to love Islam and my religion.
>
> My dear wife, for you I give all the respect and love. You have endured much hardship, but this life is not for rest, it is for patience and endurance. We all walk the road of suffering and privation. I will never forget how you suffered while I was in jail. I will leave for you a written will. We have spoken repeatedly about the afterlife. May God give you rewards, and may you forgive me.
>
> My sons, Amir and Shaheed: I named you Amir because the martyrs need a prince. And you, my young son Shaheed, your name is very clear and needs no interpretation. I advise you to fear God and follow the line of the *faqih,* the jurist, and follow the path of Khomeini and Nasrallah and Hezbollah. Get an education and use this education in the service of Hezbollah. Read carefully the story of Hussein and his followers and servants in the Koran. Serve Islam and not yourselves.

Rani's injunction to his sons repeated the sacrament that propelled him and Farah through their life together. They had united in a sustained love affair with each other, with God, and with the Islamic Resistance. The three passions wove together into a single narrative. Farah missed her husband, but his place was now fixed in the firmament and although her fate hadn't been fully written, so was hers. She would give her own life and those of her sons if the struggle called for it. She had consecrated her family to God, and modeled her holy struggle after that of Imam Hussein. There was nothing unique about their dedication. Hezbollah was simply helping believers like her and Rani fulfill their holy pledge.

Farah was what they called committed. She knew what she was getting into, as a member of an all-in Hezbollah family. That inner core, however, numbered maybe only in the tens of thousands at most—the Party of God's full-time fighters, cadres, reserves, and their families. The rest of Hezbollah's community ran a wide gamut. At the other extreme from the Bazzi family were the soft sympathizers like Dergham, and those outside the Shia orbit, like the Christians or secular leftists who supported the Islamic Resistance politically and financially, but who lived nowhere near the border or the Shia areas that would suffer Israeli reprisals in time of conflict. The Shia in the middle of the bell curve, however, gave Hezbollah its political heft, and they always were ready to be wooed (or able to be cowed) to Hezbollah's side. These were the Shia dispossessed on whose behalf Hezbollah fought and toiled, and whose religious identity itself was a Hezbollah initiative. They benefited indirectly from Hezbollah projects, but most of them weren't employed by the party. They supported the Hezb but had no say over its operations at any level: a voiceless constituency without whom Hezbollah would quickly become a militia without a movement. If the party lost its ability to mobilize them onto the street it would lose much of its power.

At the end of the 2006 war, more than 100,000 dwellings were damaged or destroyed. The Shia who wanted to return to those houses and apartments were politically up for grabs, more so than they'd been at any point since Hezbollah's ascent. It wasn't a question of whether they supported armed resistance against Israel, as the overly optimistic American diplomats thought; almost all of the Shia in Lebanon and a plurality of the rest of the country believed violent struggle against the Jewish State was justified. Where they disagreed was over how much they were willing to sacrifice to exercise this right to jihad. The moderate bloc, the realists who weren't drawn to the millenarian Shia call of the Mahdi, argued that Lebanon had moral authority to attack Israel but a rational obligation to refrain from doing so. It achieved nothing in terms of advancing Lebanon's territorial claims, but crippled Lebanon's economic vitality and slim chances for political stability.

Until 2006, Hezbollah's conflicts with Israel had not extended to the areas of Lebanon outside the Shia sphere of influence. In the July War, however, mainstream Lebanon had suffered along with Hezbollah's community; and more threatening to Hezbollah, the Shia masses, the sympathizers and loyalists who loved the party but were not fully under its control or wholly on board with its religious and jihad programs, had suffered widespread and massive loss of property and livelihood. Hezbollah needed to keep these soft supporters happy, and to do so it needed to deliver bricks and mortar along with ideology. Historically, Hezbollah had kept a promise to the communities under its authority that after every clash with Israel the Islamic Resistance would put everything back the way it was. That meant if a house were leveled or a retaining wall felled, Jihad al-Binaa, Hezbollah's Holy Struggle for Reconstruction, would repair the damage and return the structure to its original state. It was a utilitarian policy, calculated to maintain loyalty in a community that might otherwise turn against the Islamic Resistance. It was also an austere moral position—Hezbollah would leave things no worse for the populace that harbored the resistance, which after all, was every Muslim's duty. But the party wouldn't take the opportunity to make fancy improvements either.

In the first days after the ceasefire, Hezbollah distributed bricks of U.S. dollars, $12,000 to each affected household, to buy temporary acquiescence. Iran had furnished the money, procuring piles of fresh cash. I saw women empty their dainty handbags to make room for the block of 120 bills. The money was supposed to pay for rent and basic furniture for displaced families until their original homes could be rebuilt. It was cynically understood to be hush money, a short-term investment in Shia stability. Already some Shia families that looked askance at Hezbollah's militancy and zealotry grumbled that party members got more money than party critics, and predicted that over the long term Hezbollah's adventurism would leave the Shia worse off than before.

That's why it came as a shock when Hezbollah's commander in the South, the brash and indefatigable military strategist Sheikh Nabil Kawook, announced with great panache that Hezbollah would double down. This time, rebuilding to the status quo wasn't good enough. Hezbollah didn't want to break even after this latest war; it had messianic pretensions, and would emerge either crushed or stronger than ever. Kawook swept into a housing project in Abassiya, a suburb of housing towers just north of Tyre. Several of the main development's structures lay in ruins. One building still bore a large splotch of blood where a Hezbollah fighter had slid down the outer wall as he plunged to his death from an upper-story window during a firefight with Israeli commandos. The sheikh, his bodyguards, and a media unit with video cameras sped through the banana groves, alighted by a pile of rubble, and set up an instant press conference. Kawook looked glamorous amidst the rubble: his cloak was spotless, his white turban neatly wrapped, a beige shawl draped over a green jacket and white shirt. He was the man who for more than a decade had managed Hezbollah's border war against Israel, inventively deploying the party's militia on an asymmetric battlefield. "I declare that today we begin erasing every trace of the Israeli aggression in South Lebanon," Kawook said.[58] "We will rebuild it better than it was before. This triumph belongs to all the Lebanese. Everyone supports the resistance."

Not as good as before, but better. That boast amounted to a major turnaround for Hezbollah, a party whose word was its bond. Nasrallah and his top lieutenants summoned loyalty because of the gold standard behind their rhetoric. The promises never were empty, and this was a promise whose failure would be impossible to hide. Hezbollah was beset with enemies, facing internal discontent and ubiquitous infrastructure damage. *Better than before?* The words carried a whiff of arrogance. Accomplishing any public works project at all was an impressive achievement in Lebanon. So what if Hezbollah had unlimited funding from Iran? Rebuilding all those houses would flummox anyone who tried. But the party meant it; it was going to try to build a new and improved Hezbollahstan; if it succeeded, presumably, it would add civil prowess to its military glory. Like the ostentatious flag-flying bunkers erected along the border after the Israeli pullout in 2000, a bright and shiny new infrastructure would serve the additional purpose of hoisting a middle finger to Israel. Hezbollah had created Jihad Al Binaa in the first place because it knew that physical infrastructure was ephemeral, subject at a minute's notice to be pulverized. Hezbollah took an almost perverse delight in speedy reconstruction, viewing it almost as an extension of direct combat.

Israel hoped the strain would wear on Hezbollah's machinery. The Israeli military said it thought it had killed hundreds or even a thousand Hezbollah fighters and that it had decimated the group's military infrastructure. Israel hoped the Lebanese, in particular the Shia, would blame Hezbollah for the raft of inconveniences saddling their lives. It was perhaps fanciful of Israel and its backers in Washington to think that a quick shock-and-awe style military campaign could uproot a populist guerilla movement that had thrived for twenty-four years; but they did calculate, correctly, that a massive bombing campaign would put unprecedented political strain on Hezbollah. The Lebanese blamed Israel, not Hezbollah, for the bombs. But many of them still resented Hezbollah and the way it chose to execute its resistance project, with seemingly little care for the consequences to those who had never directly bought in to Hezbollah's agenda. Walid Jumblatt and the Druze in the mountains warned darkly of a coup or an Iran-funded ethnic-cleansing campaign, whereby fundamentalist Shia were buying Christian and Druze land, geographically unifying the lands under their control. Sunni and Christian leaders in the government gave lip service to Hezbollah's legal right to resist the Israeli occupation of Shebaa Farms, but argued that Lebanon would fare better if it challenged Israel through a long-term legal and political campaign.

Well aware of the swirling resentment, the faithful throughout the Beqaa, the Dahieh, and the South took on "better than before" as a battle cry, as Hezbollah intended. What would be the point of merely weathering the war? If this was a Divine Victory, a gift from God, a triumph for a new Middle East throwing off the yoke of American imperialism and Zionism, then what purpose would timid apologetics serve? The most devoted took Nasrallah's promise as a personal invitation, like a renewal of vows decades into a tumultuous marriage. The less persuaded masses hung back, many of them eager to see Hezbollah succeed, but doubtful that it could.

In Srifa, inside the Haidar family microcosm, Hussein, his wife Samira, and their four grown daughters were grappling with the same anxieties and obligations that Hezbollah was attempting to resolve across its entire political constituency. The Haidar family took stock and weighed the imperative to make things better than before. They took the exhortation seriously in their different ways. Hussein Haidar, the father, had grown up in the town center. His father had died just before the war, and the home he left behind collapsed during the bombing that destroyed a dozen structures in downtown Srifa. Hussein's mother died of natural causes two months later. During the war seventy-five people from the town had perished, many of them related to the Haidar family. Hussein's parents, sister, and cousins had all lost houses in the Srifa center. The school was closed. Srifa was somewhat unique in the flavor of its militancy; most of the villagers were deeply religious, even those like Inaya, the nurse, who hadn't taken the veil or officially joined an Islamist movement. The Communist Party and the Amal Movement still had vibrant followings and fielded formidable fighting contingents, which coordinated with and when necessary submitted to the command of Hezbollah. Some of Inaya's relatives were Amal, some were Communists, but she viewed them as honorable people who were more or less one with Hezbollah.

Hussein had always admired Hezbollah but was also skeptical of authority. He'd never formally joined the party, serving the resistance in his professional role as a schoolteacher and treasurer of Srifa's public high school: the education jihad, the holy struggle to bring better learning to his community. His son Ali had married in the Ukraine, where he had completed his engineering degree. His four daughters, however, were still living in Srifa, in their twenties, with university educations. Hussein—a mathematician by training and high school administrator by career—had raised his daughters in the spirit of Descartes and the Koran. He wanted them to read widely and think for themselves, and made sure they set themselves up for independent, sustainable careers. Islam, he taught his children, obligated the faithful to a life of inquiry and public service. The Prophet taught that learning and teaching formed the central pillar of jihad. The obligation to tithe one-fifth of one's wealth to the poor extended, Hussein believed, to one's very time and energy, a sizeable portion of which should always be deployed in service of others. Hussein's form of liberalism was not all that unusual for his time. Born in 1955, he came of age in that crucible of Lebanese wars and of the Shia revival. He judged his friends and neighbors not so much by their sect or piety but by their actions—did they collaborate or resist, did they help the manifold needy when they could or did they pad their own accounts? Both spiritual and educated, he was a quintessential self-made man. His parents had farmed tobacco for a pittance, and he felt grateful for his faith and his career. He urged his daughters to postpone engagement or marriage as long as possible, in order to establish their own secure identities before making families. He never encouraged any of the women in his family to take the veil, and he still found it awkward now that his daughters, with the exception of Inaya, wore the hijab. His wife had taken the hijab too, after her three daughters, because it made her feel strange to parade uncovered while her daughters comported themselves with such propriety. Hussein said the hijab created a whole new layer of embarrassment, for even in your own house if you stumbled across a *muhajaba* who was bareheaded, perhaps on the way to pray, "it makes you feel like you've barged into a room where they're naked." When his kids were young he and his wife put up a plastic Christmas tree every year; why not share in one of Lebanon's cheerier holidays? So what if it wasn't an Islamic celebration? It wasn't *un*-Islamic either.

His four daughters inherited Hussein's wisdom and evenhandedness in varying measures. Inaya was the most like him, and Aya the least. Samar, the eldest, had married a Hezbollah fighter and gave birth to a child in the fall after the 2006 war. Inaya, the nurse, was working in Tyre at the Najem Hospital and finishing a master's degree in neonatology at the prestigious American University of Beirut. His two youngest daughters, Aya and Muna, were still in university, but they led the family in religious passion. Aya was a party member and polymath. She loved her family but in the manner of a bright adolescent she was always ready to attack them when their convictions fell short of hers.

Inaya, twenty-four years old at the time of the 2006 war, represented the skeptical sympathizer. Her father had raised her to love a benevolent God, not a God that inspired fear. He also taught her that life entails two intertwined destinies, one that God writes for you, and the second one that you make for yourself. She trusted Hezbollah on matters social and religious, but had few expectations of the party politically. "I like to be neutral," she said. "I like the resistance, I respect Sayyed Hassan, but I cannot go completely into it and give up everything else. Perhaps I am not ready. I don't like to mix logic with emotions. I like to think with my head, not my heart." As a teenager she had volunteered as a counselor at a summer camp organized by Save the Children. She and some other activist friends, including a young English teacher she introduced me to named Mohammad Nazzal, wanted to organize a grassroots community action group, but found it nearly impossible to obtain funding and support if they insisted—as they did—on working independently from any political party. Hezbollah (and less powerful parties like Amal) loved activism, but only within the confines of party-sanctioned or party-funded initiatives. Anything independent threatened the party's social monopoly. "If we organize a celebration, too many people are concerned whether we will put the name Hezbollah or the name Amal on it," she complained. Her grandparents' house lay in ruins. So too did the house of an aunt. Hezbollah's grant was inadequate to cover the cost of rebuilding, so instead of fixing her own home the aunt moved across town to the vacant house of a relative. The human toll gave Inaya pause. After all, she had spent the war treating the wounded and comforting the survivors of the dead at Najem Hospital. Martyrdom was not an abstraction to her, and she felt some responsibility as a medical caregiver for the suffering of others.

Her youngest sister, Muna, was twenty-one at the time of the 2006 war. She was perhaps the most devout and religious (she took the veil at age eleven, the youngest age her father would permit), but also the least inflamed about activism, despite her induction into the party's youth wing. Muna was the most beautiful, her high cheekbones and tight smile offset by the tight headscarf that hid her hair and neck. She was studious and bright; she composed a long ballad in metered verse about the 2006 war, preferring poetry to politics as an outlet. It was Aya, twenty-two, the second youngest, who jumped right into the fire. She loved Sayyed Hassan Nasrallah with the enthusiasm of a teenager's celebrity crush, and she had the energy of a popcorn popper at full tilt. She adopted "better than before" as gospel. She taunted her little sister Muna as a chicken because Muna winced at talk of martyrdom and still trembled when she recalled the wartime bombing. When earthquakes struck, Muna feared the ceiling would cave in and slept in a tent on the lot across the street. Aya on the other hand drew taut with excitement, almost arousal, when she spoke of combat, Israel, martyrdom, and Hezbollah. She was the kind of young piston that Hezbollah delighted and invested heavily in.

Aya had joined the party, wasn't merely a supporter. Hezbollah officials were encouraging her to study politics in addition to graphic design, her major, and told her she could be a star at Al-Manar. Aya was brash, articulate, comfortable in English, French, and Arabic, with rudimentary Farsi. She was a self-taught painter and had an admirable collection of watercolors. For the time being, she had spurned the recruitment to television, preferring to teach at a private Shia school. Her fiancé didn't like the idea of Aya's face appearing on television. Aya herself planned to have children soon after marriage, and she didn't want to distract herself with too much focus on her career. "My goal is to raise Islamic children," she said. "Not fanatics, but real Muslims. I want my kids to be able to recite the Koran at age five. I don't think you can do that as a woman who also works."

Of all the modes of jihad, Aya told me, "the most important is to become a martyr." But she threw herself with equal intensity into all the kinds of holy struggle. She tried to improve herself constantly, almost compulsively— through reading, crafts, teaching, and arguing. She engaged me knowledgeably on the religions of the book, Islam, Christianity, and Judaism, and less so on the history of Western imperial politics and the birth of Israel.

After the war, Aya said, Hezbollah acquired a bevy of new converts, whom she mistrusted. These were the people who hoped to win grants from the party to rebuild their homes or businesses, or politically indifferent Shia who suspected that Hezbollah would obtain more domestic power now and therefore wanted to be seen siding with the presumptive winner. Aya believed the Party of God shouldn't spurn those halfhearted followers, but she had contempt for them. She viewed them as a source of vulnerability that the party had to buy off. They might be mollified and go along with the party's ways, but they weren't true believers. Not only did she loathe these people; she also didn't really understand them.

"Everything changed after the war, even people's mentality," Inaya said as we sat tightly packed around the kitchen table, eating dandelion greens, radishes, fried eggs, and a delicious concoction of lentils and onions. "Many people left to a safer place instead of rebuilding."

"They *will* come back," Aya said. "They just haven't come back yet."

"After May 2000, everyone thought they were safe and could come back," Inaya said. "But after 2006, the events made them think again. Israel is always our neighbor. What happened in 2006 was a surprise, and it means, 'Ah! We are not safe yet.' That's why many people are looking to leave this area."

Aya flushed with anger. "There are two types of people," she said. "Those who are ready to sacrifice their children and their houses are even more prepared than before. Then there are the others who lost nothing but they're chicken. They hate war." She said it like it was the least excusable thing in life, to hate war. "If you hear people say they don't support Sayyed Nasrallah, they don't support war."

Inaya felt her sister was too doctrinaire and judgmental. People who supported the resistance and Nasrallah still suffered even when Hezbollah considered itself to have won a victory. "They feel like they've lost this war twice," Inaya said. "If we lose again, to whom will they turn?"

But Aya thought that Hezbollah's "better-than-before" reconstruction program obviated any legitimate cause for anxiety. Her surviving grand-mother lost a two-room house with one bathroom, she said. Hezbollah was rebuilding it on a grander scale, with more rooms and two bathrooms. "Hezbollah practices a very smart policy," she said, triumphantly turning to Inaya, whom she appeared to believe was siding with the chickens. "There's no reason now to be scared of another war."

"You can't forget about people's feelings," Inaya said. "You must re-member that before she lived in a house where she felt safe."

Aya would have none of it.

"This is the equation," Aya said. "Before the war she had a house. After the war, she had a house and she had a victory. With dignity. There is an equality."

"She was upset," Inaya said, wearily. It was obvious they'd had this argu-ment many times.

"I am very faithful in this," Aya said. "If I had a castle, and could rebuild it without taking money from Hezbollah, I would do it. I would share in it. Some people had the money and still take from Hezbollah because they don't think the war is their fault. Their way of thinking about the war hasn't changed. People say war changed the way of thinking. After they got that victory they are proud to say 'Go, go, Hezbollah,' but just for a few months. Those who loved the party before, love it the same."

Hezbollah had regained its prewar military footing and stockpiled new rockets. Its fighting power rebounded independently of its popularity. It was the public mind-set that still vexed Aya.

"There are two kinds of people, and they are not going to change," she said, with a trace of bitterness. "The first kind is ready to go to war every day. Every day. It's not the war that affects this."

"I support the resistance," Inaya reminded her. "But you have to think about the people."

"I am ready to go put a bomb in my clothes and blow myself up," Aya retorted. "I feel this life means nothing. The issue of Palestine is more important than being alive."

Inaya turned to me: "She is talking about dignity," she explained.

"I do ask myself sometimes, why should we always defend them, the people of Palestine?" Aya went on. "But I must feel the pain of others."

The argument between the two sisters subsided, as they turned to extolling the Shia particularity that made Hezbollah's Islamic Resistance so compelling even to the Sunni Palestinians. "Israeli soldiers are scared of death," Aya said. "They catch this life by their teeth. But we, the Shia, long to be martyrs. We go to death on our legs because we believe in the next life. We are so brave and they are so chicken. We are so brave and they are so chicken, you can defeat them even if they have pump action and all we have is a knife."

The girls' father lost some of his scientist's equanimity when he spoke of Nasrallah. "The Sayyed was able to give the people back their pride and honor," he said. "The people of the South had grown accustomed to feeling downtrodden. But Hezbollah was able to give people a sense of pride so strong that people were willing to lose material things, and even to give family members as martyrs, so long as they could keep this sense of honor. Sayyed Hassan Nasrallah taught us to refuse and reject oppression."

Sometime in the fall after the war, Aya wouldn't say exactly when, she was invited to a small meeting with Nasrallah. He invited about two dozen women, all probationary party members in their twenties, to pepper him with questions. It was the kind of gesture that made Hezbollah's politics so compelling and personal to its membership. The purpose of the audience was to heighten the women's fervor. "It was for morale building, not politics," Aya said. "He wanted to prepare us for the crisis, for the antigovernment protests." The party was carefully preparing its membership and wider community for the wave of protests that would come, sometime after Ramadan, if the Washington-backed government refused, as expected, to hand over a third of the ministries, and thus veto power, to Hezbollah. (Once Hezbollah controlled ten ministries, it could block any decision that required the approval of the cabinet, which all but the most minor policy decisions and appointments did.) There were plenty of lower-ranking Hezbollah officials who could explain party doctrine or policy to the young members. A personal meeting with Nasrallah bestowed something else entirely: an adrenaline injection, a surge of emotion, a blessing. Nasrallah wanted his followers to trust him completely, so they would obey if he exhorted them to question their own instincts, as he had when he ordered them not to harm the former Israeli collaborators in 2000.

The leader had managed to extend nearly absolute authority over his community while charming most of the people that he ruled directly. Nasrallah cultivated this impression by giving latitude on the small things—like Dergham's penchant for partying—and remaining unyielding on matters important to the party, like protecting its militia. The party's hard-core devotees felt that their submission to Hezbollah was entirely voluntary. They saw themselves like swing voters who must be courted, not subjects who had been overruled. In their view, Nasrallah tirelessly championed the people's interests. He convinced them that Hezbollah was at their mercy; party supporters had the impression if they withheld that love, then the Party of God would glide to earth and shatter like a jetliner with dead engines. This account, of course, left out the instruments of coercion so deftly employed by Hezbollah. The Party of God had its own intelligence network, its own army, police, court, and prisons, and it seemed to have access to much of the Lebanese state's security apparatus as well. Shia political rivals who contested Hezbollah could be humiliated, slandered, or economically pressured. Social critics could face ostracizing, harassment, or loss of benefits. I had heard of a dissident Shia doctor quietly driven out of business in the Dahieh when Hezbollah ordered a boycott. I had heard of philanderers blackmailed into informing to party intelligence. And dozens of suspected collaborators had disappeared, only some of them resurfacing in military prisons, the rest never seen again.

But in the narrative of itself that Hezbollah successfully sold, such tools of force were only acknowledged to have been used against the most egregious villains, like traitors who spy for Israel. The skeptics saw the brutal dictatorship that flourished alongside Hezbollah's piety and integrity. It saddened Inaya that the party left no room for autonomous civil society to blossom among the Shia. The nuclear activists like her sister Aya acknowledged no such fault. The party attentively nurtured its membership's energy and devotion, an effort in which Nasrallah's gift for oratory and theater proved most valuable. "He is so warm, and funny. He has such wit and sense of humor," Aya said, sounding like a young girl in love, which after all, she was.

His sense of humor, perhaps more than anything else, endeared Nasrallah to his audience. In the great loamy amphitheater of Arab politics, minor cults of personality regularly sprung up like mushrooms after a rain, and quickly withered. Hoarse leaders screamed that they would refuse this tyranny or reject that insult. In two matters Nasrallah differed from all the other leaders, demagogues, and militants, bar none: he took his cause much more seriously than he took himself, and he liked to laugh, making himself the first butt of his jokes. To his adherents, these traits multiplied their ardor; to the wider Arab public, they had the effect of a superb baklava served at a diwan—they persuaded a guest to stay long enough to listen to his host. Nasrallah's face was round, doughy, and well-fed, his cheeks bursting pleasantly with plumpness. A single graying curl usually protruded from his black turban. During long speeches, the curl would soak up sweat and hang drenched over his brow. He had a sweet, shy smile, and fleshy, satisfied lips. Women found him sexy and he projected a kind of libidinal joy. In his own life he made a love match, not an arranged marriage, and had five children. Nasrallah never tried to hide his slight speech impediment, which made his "r" sounds come out as "w." He opened his speeches with the customary blessing, "In the name of God, the most gracious and compassionate," but instead of *bismillah al rahman al rahim* he would say *bismillah al wahman al wahim*, lending a childlike air to his syllables even when his speech thundered with hate or threats.

The jokes, too, disarmed his listeners and humanized Nasrallah. During his hour-long speeches, you could tell when he was going off script.

His eyes would dart from side to side, he'd stop glancing down at his notes, and the corners of his mouth would tug upward in a hint of a smile. If he stumbled over a word with too many "r" sounds, he'd smile and admit it was too much for him. He often repeated a story about his first encounter at a religious seminary in Iraq with Abbas Musawi, the mentor and cleric who brought him into Hezbollah as a founding member. The clueless young Nasrallah was trying so hard to blend in and impress everyone he met that he addressed Musawi in classical Iraqi-accented Arabic, mistaking the cleric for an Iraqi. "Relax!" Musawi responded. "I'm Lebanese, just like you." It was inconceivable to imagine any other major Arab or Iranian leader telling a comparably funny story about themselves. The leaders of Hamas, Islamic Jihad, the Muslim Brotherhood, and the Mahdi Army rarely told jokes in their speeches. They had in many ways developed in a mirror image to the secular totalitarian states they sought to supplant. They had built cults of personality for their leaders and an organizational hierarchy that served only as an apparatus of control, and not so much as a font of inspiration. Insecure megalomaniacs employ personality cults defensively, to silence doubt and thwart challenges to their authority. Hezbollah under Nasrallah had taken a different approach, using Nasrallah's gregarious personality as a honey trap more than a shield. An image of humility benefited Hezbollah more than a pretense of omnipotence and infallibility, the party concluded.

And given the constant prospect of assassination, Hezbollah had always to be ready to maintain support with a new secretary-general at the helm. Abbas Musawi led Hezbollah for only nine months before the Israeli military assassinated him along with his wife and son. The ever-present threat of murder provoked all the usual militancy, secrecy, and violence of Arab resistance movements. But unusually in this milieu, Hezbollah's seven-member Shura Council responded to its pressure-cooker circumstances with a willingness to adapt, led from the top by Nasrallah. Self-criticism and reinvention were oddities in the Middle East, but not in Hezbollah's world. The four years before Nasrallah took over as secretary-general were turbulent for Hezbollah, to say the least; at many turns the group faced extinction. Hezbollah and Amal fought a suicidal war for primacy in the Shia community that embarrassed both groups and tarnished Hezbollah's reputation for independence and piety. "The War of the Camps," as it was called, raised the curtain and revealed the puppet master's strings. Hezbollah and Amal both depended on their outside sponsors, and in 1988 the groups let their own ideas about their strength get to their heads like paint fumes, and delusionally they fought each other as if they alone determined the outcome. But just as the pious knew they lived two simultaneous fates, one handed down from God and the second made by their own hand, so too did the Party of God have to balance the destiny it carved for itself against the destiny mapped for it in Tehran and Damascus. Relations between Hezbollah and Syria were symbiotic, but as the Lebanese civil war wound down, Hezbollah was still in its toddler limit-testing phase. One day in the Dahieh, on February 24, 1987, a Hezbollah commander refused a Syrian officer's order to disband a checkpoint. The Syrian summarily executed twenty-four Hezbollah fighters. Hezbollah resented the show of force, but took heed. Ultimately, Iran and Syria dictated the terms of the settlement between Amal and Hezbollah, sealing the direction in which the lines of authority flowed. Hezbollah, which was stronger on the ground than Amal, resumed its military control of the South.

The Party of God began as an underground group, its membership rolls secret and its leaders mostly anonymous. Its bombings and hostage takings were often more spectacular than militarily effective. Its leadership was dedicated to establishing an Islamic state, alienating Lebanese Muslims and non-Muslims alike as it denounced the secular lifestyle. A great wave of public sympathy followed Musawi's assassination in 1992. Nasrallah didn't waste an iota of that positive energy. He immediately ceased the scolding campaign. Hereafter, Hezbollah would sweet talk as well as scream. Lebanon's political order might be rotten to the core, as Hezbollah long had emphasized, but the Party of God would work inside that rotten system if that best served its constituents' interests. Nasrallah, unlike some of his predecessors, was comfortable with his party's relationship to Iran and Syria. He wasn't completely forthcoming about the details, never revealing the amount of financing, for example. On occasion he obscured Hezbollah's subservience to Tehran in a coy formulation that emphasized Hezbollah's obeisance to Iran's Supreme Leader Ali Khamenei in his role as *faqih,* or supreme Shia jurist; the *faqih* happened to be Iranian but could in theory be of any nationality. But he made no apologies for Hezbollah's relationship to Syria and Iran. Every Lebanese faction received money, weapons, and political cover from foreign powers. Every Lebanese political party (and most families) depended on remittances from the diaspora. Why should Hezbollah be any different? Furthermore—and this final point Nasrallah deployed to devastating effect—Hezbollah announced that it happily would take money from anyone willing to sponsor the fight against Israel. If the majority of Arab governments would rather kowtow to Washington and Tel Aviv and orphan the last credible military resistance to Israel, well then, they were the evil parties in the equation.

These policy adjustments came with another flavor almost completely unheard of in the region: contrition. Hezbollah made mistakes, and would admit it. Most of the region's leaders-for-life preferred a Stalinist MO. If they had to change a policy, they would do so with no public mention, and would probably deny they were doing anything differently if asked. Leaders who fell into disfavor were simply airbrushed from the record. Nasrallah saw the value of a public apology. If the party had made things too hard for its followers, he would say so. The most striking of these apologies came after the 2006 war, when Nasrallah told an interviewer from New Television that had he known the Israeli response would be so catastrophic, he would not have ordered the July 12 raid. "You ask me now: If there was even a one percent chance that the . . . capturing operation would have led to war like the one that happened, would you have done it? I would say no, absolutely not, for humanitarian, moral, social, security, military, and political reasons. I would not agree to it, and neither would Hezbollah, the prisoners in Israeli prisons, nor the families of the prisoners. This is absolute."[59] Imagine Hosni Mubarak of Egypt, or King Abdullah of Jordan, or Bashar al-Assad of Syria, or Mahmoud Ahmadinejad of Iran comfortably explaining on television that he had made a mistake that had colossal and miserable consequences for his people. It was unthinkable. Nasrallah was able to do so because he knew that such an admission made him stronger in the eyes of his followers. He valued the human cost of his party's policies, and he regretted their losses.

Nasrallah, whose family name means "Victory of God," was born in 1960 in the Karantina district of Beirut, a hodgepodge of refugees of all sects.[60] His family was not exceptionally religious, but in the entropy of Lebanon in the 1960s and 1970s he found kindred spirits in the fledgling community of militant Shia Islamists. He traveled to the nearby neighborhood of Nabaa to hear Ayatollah Fadlallah speak, long before Fadlallah was a famous name. He worshipped Imam Musa Sadr, and prayed before a picture of him that hung in his father's vegetable shop. As a child, Nasrallah said, he dreamed of becoming a great cleric, a dream repeatedly deferred by his work as an organizer, recruiter, and political strategist.[61] When civil war broke out in 1975, Nasrallah's family fled to the safety of Bazouriyeh, their ancestral village in South Lebanon. The precocious teenager already was a seasoned preacher by then, and he joined the Amal Movement, which appointed him its local agent in Bazouriyeh. At the time, most militant young men were drawn to secular anti-Israeli movements—the PLO, the PLF and its offshoots, the Communist Party, the Syrian Social Nationalist Party, and various incarnations of the Nasserist movement and the Ba'ath Party. Nasrallah, contrary to the popular fashion, already was a committed Islamist. By joining at the ground up, he was able to quickly attain responsibile positions. Within a year, though, he left for Iraq to pursue his clerical ambitions; at that time he still intended to put in the decades of study necessary to become an influential Islamic scholar. He entered the seminary at Najaf, studying with a group of Lebanese under the wing of Sayyed Abbas Musawi. Saddam Hussein's first crackdown on the Shia ensued, and in 1978 most of Nasrallah's seminary class was expelled from Iraq. They relocated to Baalbek, in Lebanon, where Musawi founded a new school for them. That class became the seed of Hezbollah. After Israel invaded Lebanon in 1982, the Amal Movement's secular leadership exhibited a pragmatic willingness to negotiate with the Israelis if it could make a deal that benefited the Shia by bringing stability and economic growth to the South—a flexibility that appeared to the Islamists as a rank betrayal, swiftly driving them to resign en masse from Amal. By then a member of Amal's politburo, Nasrallah was one of dozens of Amal leaders who quit in 1982 just as Iran was looking to export its Shia revolutionary fervor and establish a proxy in Lebanon. The Islamic Republic sent 1,500 Revolutionary Guards to Baalbek, and the confluence of interests quickly gave rise to Hezbollah. Nasrallah, Musawi, Tufayli, and dozens of other founding members of Hezbollah bunked up in dormitories, training with the Revolutionary Guard during the day and arguing politics, theology, and resistance at night.[62]

The austerity and piety of Hezbollah's leaders sprang organically from their way of life. Lebanon's other warlords were self-made men who adopted lavish lifestyles as soon as they had money, or hailed from rich dynasties, or like Nabih Berri of the Amal Movement they represented a striving bourgeois upward mobility. The young Shia militants, on the other hand, grew up in slums and moved frequently, displaced by wave after wave of fighting in the civil war. Poverty wasn't an affectation; it was simply the condition into which they were born and with which they remained comfortable. Prosperous businessmen of humble origins would think nothing of hosting their extended family in a palatial summer home where everyone, guests and hosts alike, slept on ratty foam pads on the floor. Ayatollah Fadlallah saw his entire community in Nabaa displaced under fire, virtually overnight. Nasrallah moved neighborhoods and then cities to escape the fighting. It was nothing for a Shia family to live in a half-dozen homes during the first decade of the civil war. Nasrallah and his Islamist cohorts were constantly on the move. The constant state of dislocation and upheaval served Nasrallah well when he began working as a national organizer for the Amal Party after his return from Iraq. From his base in Baalbek he roamed across the Beqaa and Lebanon, recruiting young men to join the Islamic Resistance. He courted his future wife in Abassiya, on the outskirts of Tyre. By the time Hezbollah unveiled itself to the outside world with the publication of its "Open Letter" in 1985, Nasrallah was in charge of organizing the party in Beirut. He had close contacts with the Iranian embassy, with affiliated but nominally independent militants like Imad Mughniyeh, with Amal Movement activists, and with Shia fighters across the country. The future secretary-general was only twenty-five years old and already married with children, including his first son, Hadi, who was born in 1979, the same year as the Iranian revolution.[63]

When he took over the organization Nasrallah was one of the more visible leaders of Hezbollah but by no means the best known. He had even left the country for some months in 1989 for a seminary at Qom, Iran; Nasrallah claimed that he was resuming his religious studies, as he'd always wanted, but many people speculated that he had left because of a power struggle with Tufayli. At any rate, he was invited back to Lebanon in less than a year, and resumed his duties as Hezbollah's top executive officer. His friend and mentor Musawi was elected secretary-general in 1991; at least one scholar reported that Nasrallah would have won the party's top office then, but stood aside in favor of his older and more senior friend.[64] After Musawi's assassination, Nasrallah was the Shura Council's unanimous choice. Hezbollah had only one leader and a tiny handful of public spokesmen, who kept their personal stories steadfastly private. This served two purposes: it burnished the legend of Nasrallah by reducing the rest of the leadership to comparatively faceless servants, and it preserved the mystique of the entire top cadre so that in the event that Nasrallah, or even a series of successors, were assassinated, each new leader could unfurl a new personal narrative on a blank slate. Death became them, though. It ennobled the martyrs, sowed public sympathy, and reminded the rank-and-file that the upper echelon bore the same dangers. Israel hoped its assassination of Musawi would incapacitate Hezbollah; instead, it rejuvenated the group.

With a Hezbollah delegation acquitting itself quite well in parliament, concentrating on tangible matters like electricity and health care, Nasrallah amped up the ferocity of Hezbollah's guerilla attacks against Israel. While Hezbollah never disavowed the bombings and kidnappings that had earned it the terrorist label, under Nasrallah it switched definitively to the tactics of guerilla warfare.[65] As a matter of policy, Hezbollah attacked Israeli and South Lebanon Army targets on occupied Lebanese territory. If Israel attacked civilian targets in Lebanon, like power plants, then Hezbollah would fire rockets at civilian areas in northern Israel. These "rules of the game" were well documented and observed, so much so that from 1996 to 2000 they became institutionalized and monitored by a group of international military observers including Israel, Lebanon, France, Syria, and the United States.[66] Hezbollah's success in 1992 and onward kept the Israeli occupation in the South off balance and gutted the morale of the South Lebanon Forces. Hezbollah already had mastered and then abandoned hostage taking. It had pioneered suicide car bombing. In the guerilla phase of the 1990s, Hezbollah's fighters used surveillance to plan startlingly effective ambushes. The party's fighters deployed ingenuous, simple, and deadly roadside bombs like the ones that a decade later proved the greatest source of American casualties in Iraq. Fighters used wire-guided antitank missiles to destroy heavily fortified concrete pillboxes at Israeli and South Lebanon Army positions. During this period, the tactics developed under Nasrallah's command also greatly reduced the ratio of Hezbollah casualties. In the party's early days, almost all of its operations could be classified as suicide missions because the expected number of Hezbollah casualties greatly outnumbered the number of Israeli dead or wounded, by a factor of 5 or more to 1. By the mid-1990s, that ratio had fallen to 2 to 1.[67]

It was one of those Hezbollah deaths that sealed Nasrallah's stature, earning him a level of respect from friends and enemies alike and raising him to the status of a regional titan. Virtually everybody had experienced a death in the family: sometimes an eager combatant, sometimes a bystander. With death so ubiquitous passing decade after passing decade, the language of martyrdom made a perverse sense. If death always sat at the table and could take you at any minute—whether you sought danger or hid from it—what purpose served caution and fear? Caution and fear evolved to protect humans from avoidable death. In an unnatural environment where these reflexes offered no advantage, a familiar affection with death better prepared people to face their own mortality and grieve the frequent deaths in their community. Martyrdom, it should be remembered, was not the unique domain of the Shia or the Muslims. Most Arabs, Christians included, referred to their dead as martyrs and their passing, especially if violent, as a glorious martyrdom. The Shia, however, cherished a special relationship with martyrdom beginning with the great sacrifice of Imam Hussein at Karbala. In their regional context it was only a difference in degree, not kind.

Like the storied American commanders who nurtured the affection of their troops by coming along on the riskiest combat missions, Nasrallah led from the front. He knew the fighters individually and they knew him; the full-time fighters numbered less than two thousand, and the secretary-general viewed them as the pearls in his crown. His eldest son joined their regular ranks, as did the sons of all the leaders. They wouldn't have it any other way, not the leaders and not their children. If they didn't believe in the State of the Resistance, in the Culture of Holy Struggle, how could they ask others to lay down their lives and forswear their property?

On September 12, 1997, Nasrallah was preparing for a typical Hezbollah propaganda event the next day, an anniversary for "The Martyrs of September 13." The day celebrated the deaths of nine Hezbollah supporters who clashed with Lebanese security forces while protesting the signing of the Oslo Accords in 1993. Hezbollah's biggest holidays (other than Ashura, the Shia observance of Imam Hussein's death, which was the apex of the annual religious calendar for Shia everywhere) revolved around the commemoration of party martyrs. Abbas Musawi as it happened was killed driving home after a festival celebrating the martyrdom of a previously assassinated Hezbollah leader, Ragheb Harb, so both their deaths could be celebrated on the same anniversary. Nasrallah kept up the tradition. Hezbollah celebrated its own general Martyrs' Day on November 11, and then staged various events to commemorate other dead partisans. The only major Hezbollah holiday that didn't revolve around martyrs was Jerusalem Day, an invention of Ayatollah Khomein. It was a sort of militant pep rally akin to a Soviet era May Day parade, during which Hezbollah fighters marched with their weapons and swore to retake Jerusalem from the Jews.

As Sayyed Hassan Nasrallah was preparing his remarks for the following day, four fighters lay in wait in the hills around Nabatieh. One of them was the secretary-general's son Hadi. Hezbollah had intercepted Israeli communications and learned of a planned raid; they intended to surprise the Israeli commandos. The Hezbollah fighters attacked but the Israelis quickly overwhelmed them. Nasrallah's first-born son was killed in the shelling along with two other fighters. A fourth escaped. Hadi was eighteen years old. According to his deputy, Nasrallah wept when he learned the news.[68] In Shia culture, it is not a sign of weakness for a man to weep as an act of mourning. Deputy Secretary-General Naim Qassem called his commander with condolences, and offered to speak in his place at the September 13 holiday; naturally, he said, a father who has just lost his son might want to retire from the public eye and grieve. Nasrallah, however, insisted on taking the podium; he so completely identified himself with Hezbollah and the Islamic Resistance that he couldn't imagine surviving the loss of his son without his community. He opened his speech with the tribute to the martyrs of September 13 before getting around to the more immediate death that was on everyone's mind—that of his son.

> Today, we wish to tell this enemy: we are not a resistance movement whose leaders want to enjoy their private lives and fight you through the sons of their loyal followers and their good and true supporters from among the

ordinary citizens. The martyr Hadi's martyrdom is the proof that we in Hezbollah's leadership do not spare our own sons. We take pride in them when they go to the frontlines and hold our heads high when they fall as martyrs.

He would miss his son, he said, but he was proud of the way he had died, fighting on his own soil, without any special rank or privilege, just another resistance fighter sprung from a deep pool of men equally devoted and equally ready to die. He told the rapt crowd on September 13 that he thanked God for the legacy of the martyrs, the memory of so many leaders and friends and teachers who had fallen before him. Without shame he could now console the survivors: "I used to feel embarrassed in front of the martyrs' fathers, mothers, wives, and children when I visited them, and still do," Nasrallah said. "I wish to tell those families: There is now something in common between us."

The loss was no less heartfelt for being so theatrical. Nasrallah had given his first-born son to the struggle. What further evidence could be sought of his commitment? Such blood proof was commonly invoked in the region, although in modern history more so in Israel than in the Arab world. Many of Israel's most compelling leaders had risked their lives on the battlefield and had scars to prove it, and others summoned the inspirational tales of the death of a family member, like Benjamin Netanyahu's brother. In the Arab world, however, such heroics had become rarer. Syria's dictator, Hafez al-Assad, tried to deify his playboy son after he crashed in a car racing to the airport, but that death resounded as another manifestation of the regime's excess, not as a gift to the people. The absence of compelling personal narratives—an Arab leader who risks his own life and makes a great sacrifice for his people—rendered the martyrdom of Hadi Nasrallah all the more poignant and heroic. Many people already followed Hezbollah, and many more admired its leader, whether or not they counted themselves among his legions. But with the death of his son, Nasrallah's reputation assumed mythic proportions, and commanded a level of love and popular respect that translated directly into increased support and maneuver room for Hezbollah. The Israelis had captured Hadi's body, and Nasrallah would make no special deal to regain his son's corpse. In fact, Hadi's body wasn't returned for nearly a year. Eventually the International Committee of the

Red Cross brokered a deal in June 1998. Hezbollah returned the remains of a single Israeli commando in exchange for the remains of forty dead Hezbollah fighters, including Hadi, and the release of sixteen Lebanese prisoners held in Israel and another forty prisoners held in Khiam.

Farah Bazzi, after her husband died, had struggled to articulate a mix of loss and pride, grief and honor. The use of the word martyrdom often confuses the issue, but the sentiment is not unlike that of a soldier mourning a dead platoon mate, or a mother making sense of the death of her child in a war that she considers honorable. Nasrallah had paid the admission price to fully join the society of resistance that he had been so pivotal in constructing. For the Shia already sympathetic to the cause, he became one of the family, another parent who had loved and lost a child to the Israelis.

In the impromptu eulogy to his son, Nasrallah lashed out at the enemy, raging not against Israel but against Jews—a theme that had surfaced before in his speeches, not only at this moment of personal crisis. "If we search the entire globe for a more cowardly, lowly, weak, and frail individual in his spirit, mind, ideology, and religion, we will never find anyone like the Jew—and I am not saying the Israeli: we have to know the enemy we are fighting," Nasrallah said. Here too, perhaps by calculation or perhaps by accident, Nasrallah exposed the sometimes delicate, sometimes crude machinery that drove Hezbollah's ideological zeal. The disciplined, tactically effective resistance depended on a coldly pragmatic membership, willing to fight or swallow an unpalatable political compromise as the leadership decreed. At the same time, the state of resistance depended on a steady stream of devotees willing to die and be displaced—a passion fed by an extreme obscurantist and apocalyptic brand of Shia Islam, and equally too by a hatred of Israel difficult to distinguish from a hatred of Jews stretching back to the days that the Prophet fought the Hebrew tribes in Badr, Yathrib, and Khaibar.

More often than any other reason, the Shia cited Hadi's death when I asked why they so completely trusted Nasrallah. Hussein Haidar in Srifa considered the death of Hadi a threshold, after which he was willing not only to consider but to yield to the judgment of Sayyed Hassan. Like most Arabs, he referred to the Hezbollah leader familiarly, as Sayyed Hassan, and not by his last name or his title. (*Sayyed* designates anyone directly descended from the Prophet Mohammed.) Other warlords demanded honorifics. The Druze leader was Walid *bek;* some Christian warlords in Lebanon expected to be referred to as sheikh or *rais,* which means "leader" or "chief." The Shia felt ownership of Nasrallah, though, and the rest of the Arab world referred to him with an unusual sort of intimacy, perhaps responding to the candor with which Nasrallah addressed them. When the crowds chanted "Labayka, Ya Nasrallah," "Your wish is our command, O Nasrallah," or "With our souls, with our blood, we fight for you, O Nasrallah," I felt they really meant it. This wasn't the kind of rally Saddam Hussein used to stage manage, where rent-a-crowds would shout their fealty but on the inside tremble with fear or contempt for the dictator. Nor was it like the Phalange gatherings in Ashrafiyeh, where sweaty throngs would chant anti-Muslim slogans and swear to fight for Christianity, but then afterwards quietly describe their efforts to emigrate. Nasrallah was no run-of-the-mill Arab tyrant or demagogue. Some of his methods sounded the same, but his followers really followed him. They weren't simply submitting to him.

Hadi's death echoed on into the present. Every new martyr's family hearkened back to the predecessors, all the way back to Imam Ali. When I heard people talk about Nasrallah losing his son, I recalled Farah Bazzi's words about her husband: "I am proud of what he did, but I miss him," she had told me, her tears still fresh. "Believe me, believe me, no one likes to die." I also thought of something that Hussein Rumeiti told me, when I had asked him how it had come to pass that Hezbollah and its culture of martyrdom had trumped the more workaday ethos of the Amal Movement. Amal's emphasis on results rather than faith had initially seemed to me more in keeping with the garrulous and joyous lifestyle of Lebanon's blue collar and rural Shia. "You reach a stage where you see in every house someone wearing black," Rumeiti had said. "Death has touched every house, because of Israel's continuous attacks on the South. In world history, everyone who is the target of attacks fights back. We love life, we don't like death. But we should preserve our dignity." The constant presence of death, the universal acceptance of a bloody lot, had opened the way for Nasrallah's Hezbollah; he had put a gentler face on a movement that promised to heal the wounds of outrage, to help a shattered people fight back not just to regain their honor but ultimately to regain their land; they didn't intend a symbolic stand like Imam Hussein's at Karbala. They meant to win. Hassan Nasrallah made them feel that they could. Violence and destruction never ceased to be part of the movement's arsenal, but Nasrallah reminded his followers that they were the tactics, not the end.

In the Arab world, derision toward leaders is the default. The longer the leaders serve, the less their people seem to like them. Nasrallah took over Hezbollah in 1992, a pudgy prodigy in the bloom of youth. Around the Middle East eighteen years later, many of the same leaders, or their family heirs, dotted the landscape. Ayatollah Khamenei was still the Supreme Leader of Iran. Octogenarian King Abdullah ran Saudi Arabia as a family enterprise; Mubarak ruled Egypt; and in Jordan and Syria sons took over from their fathers. Nasrallah had not inherited his office, and was chosen by a seven-member Shura Council that actually considered competitive alternatives from within its ranks. Unlike any of the other veteran leaders in the region, Nasrallah commanded more public adoration than he did when he took over his party—in fact, his popularity had steadily increased during his decades of leadership.

Hagiographers and detractors alike fed the mythology of the man. Israeli officials often personified the entire movement of Hezbollah in its leader, multiplying the ranks of his admirers. Israeli officials would mock Nasrallah for "hiding in his bunker," while its military tried repeatedly to find and assassinate Nasrallah during the 2006 war. Were Nasrallah to die, Hezbollah would surely unveil a new leader the next day who could roll out his own personal narrative; one candidate was Hisham Safieddine, a cousin of Nasrallah who was on the Shura Council and bore an uncanny physical resemblance to him. Since taking office, Nasrallah had presided over an increasingly complex party, the first in Lebanon to publish a political platform and the only one to consistently put forward concrete proposals for matters like electoral reform or exploitation of water resources. In his regular flow of speeches, however, the Hezbollah leader followed a simple and hypnotic story line of suffering and redemption, holy struggle and divine reward. It resonated well with his audience. Three times he would chant: "We will not forget our martyrs, not forget our martyrs, not forget our martyrs!" He would repeat again and again, "We will never abandon our prisoners!" And ultimately, there was always the land, the land that was "more precious than gold," as one slogan put it. Hezbollah would fight until that land was liberated, driven by an almost pathological belief, inimical to compromise.

Not everyone in Hezbollah's community paid attention to the crucial details that determined whether the party had finite goals or planned to remain at war forever. Would Hezbollah fight until the small patch of mountainous territory known as the Shebaa Farms reverted to Lebanon? Or until the Palestinians reached a settlement with the Israelis? Or until Israel had withdrawn to its 1967 borders? Or until Israel had ceased to be a Jewish state, or until there were no Jews in Palestine? A close examination of Nasrallah's statements suggested that Hezbollah had espoused all those goals during its history, and that it probably still did even if it found it beneficial not to talk about its more inflammatory and extreme views.

Over the years Nasrallah had given interviews about his personal history, his religious evolution, his political tenets, and Hezbollah's policies and tactics. Sometimes he met with Westerners, sometimes with Arabs or Persians only. He had left a huge body of words in the public record though, with hours-long speeches or press conferences at least every month. Nasrallah unveiled only what the party wanted the public to know about its positions and internal deliberations. Nasrallah's record provided the best repository through which to explore what Hezbollah really wanted. Hezbollah kept certain matters intentionally opaque: its military assets, its logistical capacity, its budget, and its doctrinal relationship to certain concepts of Shia Islamic jurisprudence. The party did not revise the Open Letter it released in 1985 for twenty-four years, but explained the letter was not the same as a charter. It published an electoral platform every four years since 1992 that focused on complex but relatively inoffensive policy questions. When it came to the party's major political goals, however, there was less mystery than some people supposed. Nasrallah's rhetoric made clear his belligerent military position vis-à-vis Israel, and his quest for greater political power inside Lebanon, employing all means at his disposal. Confusion, however, worked to Hezbollah's benefit. The party has allowed its most militant followers to assume Hezbollah shares their most extreme tenets, while insisting to its unnerved rivals that it has nothing but the most moderate intentions. It depends on Iran and Syria, yet operates with a wide amount of latitude, although the exact amount of autonomy is unknown. Well into a second decade, Hezbollah has engineered a cult of personality around its secretary-general, yet the group appears quite prepared to thrive after—and perhaps even take a public relations benefit from—his death. Hezbollah fights Israel specifically, yet many of its leaders and members hate Jews and Judaism in general.

When I first requested an interview with Nasrallah in 2006, the Hezbollah press officer laughed. She told me she wouldn't even bother forwarding the request to her superiors; she denied me outright. Over the years I made the request again maybe a half-dozen times, and was told, with good humor, not to expect results. Since the 2006 war, Nasrallah had met with the American journalist Seymour Hersh, but party officials explained it was a "meeting" between two important men—not an "interview." I was given consolation interviews with other senior officials, and Hezbollah regularly granted audiences with the deputy secretary-general, Sheikh Naim Qassem, as a prize for correspondents. I wasn't too heartbroken by the refusal. It would have been fascinating to meet him one-on-one, but I didn't expect I would learn anything new. What concerned me at any rate was the power he wielded with the public, and the almost erotic hold he had over his followers.

Understanding that group-love demystified some elements of Hezbollah and pointed to the answers to some of the more critical questions about the group. To some devotees, Nasrallah personified Hezbollah; to others, he embodied resistance against Israel. I believed that people followed him for three general reasons. First, they believed what he believed. Second, they believed in him as an exemplary man. Third, they believed he meant what he said: that he told the truth and that he kept his promises.

The first point, shared beliefs, meant follower and leader espoused a similar interpretation of apocalyptic Mahdist Shiism, and saw the current holy struggle against Israel in a continuum that connected the time of Prophet Mohammed to the coming battle at the end of time, when the Mahdi would return to redeem the earth. The end of the world could arrive any day, so like apocalyptic believers everywhere they approached every temporal matter as potentially carrying great consequence. The community of believers rallied around Hezbollah's right to wage armed resistance against Israeli occupation, but connected that right to a desire to drive Israel from all occupied land and perhaps, protestations to the contrary notwithstanding, to terminate the Jewish State and maybe even expel most Jews from the Middle East.[69] Most of Hezbollah's followers knew enough to protest that they had nothing against Jews, citing the small

Jewish communities in Syria and Iran, but in conversation they often reverted to slanderous talk about Jewish villainy and blood libel, quoting the forged "Protocols of the Elders of Zion." More than once I was told about the Jewish propensity to ritually sacrifice Christians by Hezbollah supporters who had believed these lies after learning about them from television or pamphlets.

This confluence between party and public was no accident. Hezbollah had worked hard since the early 1980s to create a community of belief. Its preachers, teachers, military officers, doctors, scout leaders, and so on took every opportunity to refine the theological message, in groups and in private. They taught doctrine ceaselessly, hammering home points about Shia Islam, religious history, teachings of the imams, the essence of Judaism, the history of Zionism, and American imperialism. Far more than their peer movements around the Middle East, Hezbollah invested sustained energy in propagating its beliefs among children and adults, building numerous institutions integral to the purpose. The Mahdi Schools and the Martyrs' Foundation, both offshoots of institutions invented in Revolutionary Iran, made the transmission of ideology their central mission. Hezbollah's relation to its public was not one of mastery and convenience; the masses weren't mouthing party rhetoric about God's struggle in exchange for stipends and subsidized medical treatment. No, this belief system flowed both ways. Hezbollah radicalized its base, over decades, and in turn could only shift its policies within the constraints it had created. Nasrallah was able to convince most of his militant followers that entering Lebanon's political life would not fatally compromise Hezbollah. Similarly, he was able to convince the Shia to desist from revenge attacks, or untrammeled power grabs, in mixed areas of the South after the Israeli withdrawal in 2000. Hezbollah, however, would be hard-pressed to convince its followers to give up the armed struggle against Israel after making it so central to the group's essence and daily activities. The party's very identity precluded dual political-military tracks, in contrast to groups like the Irish Republican Army, which fought the British while its political wing Sinn Fein could negotiate. Hezbollah made a point of having no political wing; its politicians and its armed resistance leaders were one and the same, by design, to thwart any structural pressures that could divide the party into hawks and doves. A dove would have to leave Hezbollah entirely.

Second, Nasrallah's character and charisma elevated him in the Arab and Islamic worlds. He entertained audiences with his speeches. He spoke casually and familiarly. He tapped into humor but also into the common person's rage, giving voice to frustration with those well-timed crescendos and thrice-repeated chants. The apparent simplicity of his lifestyle earned him and his party great credit. Not only did he expect his son to fight like any other Hezbollah stalwart, but he and the leadership lived with the same minimal material comforts as the rank-and-file. Nasrallah amassed influence and power without the trappings of wealth. His legend did not need to fully reflect reality once his public fully embraced it. The imputed traits of Nasrallah were tactical brilliance, patience, a cunning intellect, and great humility. Although he only completed the first stage of his religious education, Nasrallah was a cleric, and a direct descendant of the prophet to boot, both of which gave him additional status among the Shia. People swooned about Nasrallah. A Christian journalist once broke into a long soliloquy about the sexiness of Nasrallah's lips, only blushing when I began to laugh at her over-the-top encomium. Older women wanted to cook for him, men wanted to sit with him or fight under his command, young men and women wanted to grow up to be like him. Hussein Rumeiti summed up the popular sentiment: "He never tells a lie. He never paved a road that was just for his party. He let his son fight and die like the others. They like his personality! He is their *zaim*."

The secretary-general capitalized on his unique style and history to win an unusual amount of trust from his followers, but he did not shy from the excesses typical of the region that gave meaning to the word "cult" in cult of personality. To begin with were the banners, photographs, and oil paintings hanging everywhere. Hezbollah souvenir shops sold clocks with Nasrallah on the face, Catholic-style bracelets with Nasrallah's face on every bead in place of the saints, T-shirts, scarves and keychains with the leader's likeness. You could buy collected speeches on CD, cassette, or DVD, or if you preferred more of a beat, rythmic songs featuring Nasrallah's best lines. Oil paintings marked the entrance to towns in the Beqaa and the South and adorned traffic circles and buildings around the Dahieh. The Nasrallah fervor reached its often ridiculous apotheosis in popular culture, like the songs cub scouts sing or the voice-overs on Al-Manar. The most popular poem on one English-language Hezbollah website[70] captured the adoration-turned-mania well. It was addressed to Nasrallah, "our beloved Sayyed," and some choice verses read like the ode of a heartsick teen:

> *You are our sensitivity,*
> *you help us touch and help us feel,*
> *you are our only medicine,*
> *you cure us and help us heal . . .*

> *You are the river,*
> *calm, quiet and deep,*
> *you are our fantasizing dreams,*
> *you calm us to our sleep . . .*

> *Sayyed, you are the reason why we breathe,*
> *you are our moon, our burning sun,*
> *of all the people known by us,*
> *you are our favorite one !*

> *Sayyed, you are the reason why we live,*
> *you are the pumping heart,*
> *do you believe in love at first sight?*
> *Because we loved you from the start!!!*

More cultish still was the near-divinity attributed to the leader, which exceeded any devotion I'd seen elsewhere. The Sayyed, his followers would say, always had a good reason for anything he did even if it was not immediately apparent. If, God forbid, he made a mistake, he would correct it and tell the public himself. This presumed saintliness trickled down to other party leaders and formed the basis for the widespread hesitation ever to criticize or second-guess the party. Hezbollah was both rational and holy, and therefore, was beyond scrutiny.

Finally, and perhaps most importantly, came the leader's credibility. Across the globe, and especially in the Middle East, bombast had fatally devalued political discourse. Exaggerated and passionate speeches usually reflected impotence. Saddam Hussein was still threatening to humiliate America and paint the walls of Baghdad red with its soldiers' blood even as American troops had overrun half his country and his regime teetered days from collapse. Ehud Olmert ridiculed Nasrallah as a loser hiding in a bunker even as his own government's inquest was cataloguing Israel's failure in the 2006 war and Olmert's party was preparing to dump him as prime minister. Syria's dictator would wax for hours about what Damascus might accept from Israel and America as if he led a superpower that could set terms of a regional peace settlement. Palestinian leaders constantly denounced Israel, declaring that they would "refuse" the Israeli policies that were strangling their militias and subjugating their publics. They were free to resist of course, but not to deny the reality that they had almost no power left to do so.

Sayyed Hassan Nasrallah offered a marked, realist contrast. He quite accurately described the capability and numbers of Hezbollah's rocket arsenal, assessed the turns of international diplomacy, and analyzed the regional impact of Israel's politics. He admitted the deaths of his fighters and the reversals in his party's plans. He laid out Hezbollah's short- and long-term goals, and declared victory only when he could say one of those goals discernibly had been reached—like Israel's pullout from the occupied zone in South Lebanon in 2000. In a bald appeal to his base, Nasrallah might rhapsodize about a Jew-free Palestine, but he always outlined an immediate agenda that was achievable, if toxic. This approach served multiple purposes. Over the years, it greatly enhanced Hezbollah's credibility. If the party said it would continue kidnapping Israeli soldiers until all the Lebanese prisoners held by Israel were released, observers could see that the party held to its word. Foe and friend alike noticed other promises kept as well. Hezbollah said it alone would control the resistance in southern Lebanon. When rogue Palestinian factions fired rockets into Israel, the party's response was swift and draconian. It intercepted the rockets, arrested the militants, and turned them over to the Lebanese Army, which reported the infraction to UN peacekeepers. Nasrallah eschewed bombast and gave his followers a tangible sense of accomplishment at every stage. Instead of motivating his militants with a vast, distant, and likely impossible goal, like the end of Israel, Nasrallah instead gave them smaller, more pragmatic steps to glory: a prisoner exchange, a successful ambush, an intercepted Israeli communication, the liberation of a village or region. Finally, this approach lent force to Nasrallah's bolder declarations. He had proved himself a man of his word, and so audiences both hostile and adulatory came to believe he might achieve his more ambitious projects.

He carefully modulated his rhetoric with pragmatism. Hezbollah was not ignorant about Israel. It counted many Hebrew speakers among its members, and almost obsessively monitored Israeli media. Hezbollah studies its enemies with unquenchable curiosity. Nasrallah once told an interviewer that he was reading the memoirs of Ariel Sharon and Benjamin Netanyahu. I never heard an Israeli politician say he was reading Naim Qassem's *Hizbullah: The Story From Within*. When I met with the party's foreign affairs chief in 2007, he wanted to discuss in detail the shifting fortunes of various figures in the Bush administration to measure Washington's most likely moves in the coming year. Nasrallah's authority has endured because he plays to a base preconditioned by Hezbollah to sympathize with its leader's views, and more important because Hezbollah has delivered on so many of its promises. Teenage boys in the Dahieh can pop a few beers before a Nasrallah address and then pack into the thumping and sweaty Princes of the Martyrs Complex to cheer the speech. Nasrallah has accepted the hooligans and the secular fans even if they share only Hezbollah's anti-Israeli views and not its religious ones. If they submit to party control and discipline when the balance of power is at stake, they don't have to adopt all its beliefs.

Less than two months after the end of Ramadan, Nasrallah finally made good on his threat to take his challenge against Lebanon's elected government to the streets. He mobilized all of Hezbollah's constituencies, the pious families and the thuggish youth. It was a rowdy crowd that surged toward downtown Beirut on December 1, 2006. The disciplined and devout marched side by side with pimply teenagers thirsty to bust some heads. Men and women, religious zealots and people of easy virtue, Muslims and Christians, Amal and Hezbollah—these were the forces of the opposition, summoned by Nasrallah to swarm the center of Beirut and demand a new government, one that gave Hezbollah and its allies what they had decided was their fair share. Nasrallah had been backed into a corner. Months after invoking a Divine Victory, a mandate from God, and persistently demanding veto power for Hezbollah's coalition, Nasrallah held only air in his hands. Lebanon's secular leaders made their calculations and they judged that Hezbollah was crippled, fatally weakened by the war. Now, the accommodationist forces in control of the government believed they had sufficient backing from the United States, Saudi Arabia, and their own people to face down Hezbollah's mob. Some pro-Western leaders in the government told me they expected the Bush administration to rise to their defense, pressuring Syria if necessary to guarantee the survival of the March 14 government. That government, after all, had won a majority at the polls in the elections of 2005. Since when did the losing minority get to dictate terms to the victorious majority? Let them wait until the next elections in 2009 to demand a new government. On the streets, too, some sympathizers whispered that Nasrallah might have overreached. Wasn't it enough that Hezbollah could claim it won the war with Israel and that it controlled a few ministries?

Nasrallah, however, read the power map more astutely than the rest. He couldn't be sure that Hezbollah had the strength to force the issue, but he knew that if he couldn't turn the momentum in his party's favor then he would find his most important asset, his militia, under challenge. The situation wasn't static; there wasn't an acceptable equilibrium. A powerful constellation of players wanted to truncate Hezbollah, integrate the resistance militia into the Lebanese Army, and once and for all subordinate the Party of God to a weak and fractured but determined state. A wall of water was cascading down the mountain; it would wash away Hezbollah's state within a state unless Nasrallah could divert it to another channel. Prime Minister Fouad Siniora called Hezbollah's militaristic march on Beirut's center an attempted coup. The party's demand to control one-third of the seats in the cabinet hardly amounted to a desire to overthrow the government. But the hundreds of thousands who marched out of the Dahieh and into the polished commercial center of Beirut certainly looked like an invasion. Swarthy bearded men bubbled up from the neglected suburb's underclass and imposed themselves on the cobbled streets of Solidere, with its stone facades and outdoor cafés radiating from the quaint central clock tower. Here was a downtown rebuilt almost like a Disney model city by the Sunni billionaire, powerbroker, and slain prime minister Rafik Hariri, flanked by the brand-new, still unconsecrated mosque where he was buried. Up the hill from the mosque the prime minister ruled from an echoing, half-empty Ottoman palace, the Serail. Lebanon's elite was accustomed to eating its best meals in Solidere, sipping its priciest cocktails, and conducting the horse-trading of parliament unmolested by the hoi polloi.

The image of Hezbollah's hordes overrunning Solidere and setting up a tent camp was almost Freudian in its stark simplicity. Physically and aesthetically the entire area represented privilege. Arrayed against it were the forces of the opposition, a seething mass of self-made working-class energy, buttressed by the mass of underemployed men who neither drank nor danced and had all the time in the world to organize an indefinite occupation. And so they did: as Nasrallah had asked them to, the opposition began a "sit-in," their euphemism for an occupation of the heart of Beirut. "We have no other choice," Nasrallah said when he went on television to send his followers into elite Beirut, the part of the city that had been rooting for the failure of Hezbollah and of Islamists. The opposition activists erected tents across the main road through downtown, creating a traffic nightmare as eight lanes of roadway at the busiest intersection of the city suddenly had to divert. Activists from Hezbollah, Amal, and Aoun's Christian Free Patriotic Movement hoisted their flags and swore to stay twenty-four hours a day for as long as it took for Siniora to yield to Nasrallah's demand. Conveniently a compound of Western embassies flanked the Serail and British guards held off the protesters who tried on the first day of the protest to overrun the Serail and physically throw Siniora out of office. Once the protesters had installed themselves, pro-government security forces could not simply arrest them and clear the area. First, they feared clashing with Hezbollah militants who might well possess superior firepower, and secondly, such a forceful move, while legal, would violate Lebanon's post-civil war political code of conduct, which required that serious internal disputes be resolved by consensus.

In that first week of December 2007, Walid Jumblatt, dismissed the men who took up residence in what Lebanese already called Tent City. He thought they would get bored and fade away once the television crews left. "They decided to go to the streets," Jumblatt said. "Let them do that, and let them stay there as long as they want." The sit-in began on a Friday. The following Thursday, Nasrallah appeared again on a screen to address the protesters. They must remain calm and disciplined, he ordered. They could not bear arms or respond to police brutality with violence. Nor, however, could they go home until he gave the say-so. "Those betting on our surrender are delusional," he said. Nasrallah wagered that the government would fold and for the first time had led Hezbollah across a red line; the Shia party was using force, albeit of a muted kind for the time being, against a Lebanese rival. The government thought that Hezbollah's followers would run out of steam, and the weakened party would limp back to the nosebleed seats in the political arena. The two sides were set on a collision course.

5

The Islamic Vanguard

In the aftermath of the war with Israel, the forces of liberal reform seemed determined to shimmy their way through the political crisis on hope alone, relying on the moral rectitude of their position. They had won the elections in 2005, after a million people or more had waved Lebanese flags on the street, demanding that Syria pull out its troops. Now, in September 2007, a few years later, they felt the time had come to translate that moment into a new order. Syria out, March 14 in. Meanwhile, Hezbollah handicapped its odds on more hard-headed grounds. March 14 might have had the popular vote and the seats in parliament to control a technical majority, but against it on the other side of the scale Hezbollah weighed in with its militia and the undiminished backing of Iran and Syria. The United States and Saudi Arabia assured the March 14 forces they were in the right, but they did nothing material to buttress their words of comfort: no deal with Syria to protect Lebanon's new government, no serious money, no decisive military assistance. Iran and Syria, meanwhile, had rearmed Hezbollah beyond prewar levels, and sent planeloads of Hezbollah members on commercial flights to Tehran for training. The scores of men occupying downtown suggested to rest of Lebanon that Hezbollah, for all its rhetorical protestations, might well use force against its fellow Lebanese. Hezbollah officials from Nasrallah on down condemned political violence in their speeches. The sense of menace, however, benefited Hezbollah more than anyone else, and shaped the unfolding power dynamic grimly in Hezbollah's favor. After all, the string of assassinations since 2005 had spared Hezbollah and its allies, striking only pillars of March 14, targeting charismatic and unifying intellectuals, rising young politicians, and investigators pursuing Rafik Hariri's murderers.

No one so far had managed to piece together a precise accounting of the network of assassins. But every observer had to begin with the assumption that the attacks could not take place without some complicity, active or passive, from the only three powers that controlled serious intelligence networks inside Lebanon: Syria, Hezbollah, and the Lebanese security services. These three entities overlapped messily. During three decades in Lebanon, Syria had painstakingly built a police state arguably more imaginative and resourceful than the heavy-handed apparatus it employed on its own territory. Syria's network of hitmen, thugs, spies, informants, and agents certainly included members of every political party and official security agency. In a similar and amorphous manner, Hezbollah exercised control not only through its own operatives but also through alliances with sympathetic officers in other services. For example, Lebanese Military Intelligence cooperated closely with Hezbollah, sometimes for benign reasons, such as sharing information on the activities of Palestinian militants in the southern border area, and other times in ways that suggested Hezbollah had fully co-opted some military officers. The Lebanese security services included several different branches, some of them quite effective. Many Lebanese intelligence and security officers (from General Security as well as from military intelligence) considered themselves fully independent, loyal to Lebanon, while others answered to political parties or outside powers. Complicating the picture, many security players shifted alliances and allegiances on a case by case basis, so it was impossible to guess when a unit of Lebanon's intelligence services would act autonomously in its own interests, in concert with Hezbollah or Syria, or on the instructions of Hariri. Still, it stood to reason that any complicated plot, like the assassination of Rafik Hariri, could not have been carried out without attracting the attention of the three big players—Syria, Hezbollah, and Lebanese intelligence. In the unlikely case that none of them were involved at all, they still would have noticed aspects of the plot, meaning that at the very least elements in all three services were complicit by negligence.

Four senior security officials were arrested by the international tribunal investigating the Hariri assassination.[71] The list of murdered public figures steadily grew, each new death increasing the fear and timidity of the poorly defined and flagging March 14 coalition. In 2005, after the Syrians left, assassins killed Samir Kassir, a crusading journalist and intellectual; George Hawi, the former Communist leader; and Gibran Tueni, a member of parliament and newspaper publisher. Two other critics of Syria survived attempts on their lives, defense minister Elias Murr and journalist May Chidiac. In September 2006, one of the officials investigating the Hariri murder survived a bombing that killed four of his bodyguards. In November, industry minister Pierre Gemayel was shot to death. After a long break, a car bomb in June 2007 killed Walid Eido, another member of the March 14 parliamentary delegation. Another bomb killed his colleague Antoine Ghanem in September.[72] A heavy, murderous hand had gripped the nation, and supporters of the government were convinced it was trying to push them to concede to Hezbollah's demands.

The members of the March 14 parliamentary delegation were terrified. As the end of September neared, many of them told me they were sure Syria was behind the killings and was determined to murder members of the government one by one until they no longer had a majority in parliament. Looking at the numbers, their fear didn't seem so ridiculous. Hariri, a billionaire, paid for many of his supporters in parliament to take refuge in the Phoenicia Hotel, a luxury establishment that overlooked the spot on the Corniche where his father had been murdered. It would be easier to protect the core of the government in a single, easily fortified tower than in their apartments scattered throughout greater Beirut. Some MPs also worried that the Syrians and their henchmen—or whoever had been killing the government and its supporters—might simply block the roads on the day that parliament finally convened to elect a new president, allowing only members of Hezbollah's alliance to travel to parliament and elect a new head of state.

September came and went. Names of consensus candidates were bandied about. The frightened members of March 14 bemoaned the tyranny of Hezbollah and Syria, but admitted they didn't want to antagonize their rivals; they wanted to persuade Hezbollah to elect a president who was fully autonomous from Syria. March 14 had the legal right to elect a candidate without a consensus, they said, but if they did so they would provoke a cataclysmic showdown on the streets with Hezbollah that March 14 was too weak to win. The men in the tent city were but a tiny taste of the force Hezbollah could bring to bear on Beirut. There was still no deal, so the Amal leader Nabih Berri refused to convene parliament. I frequently visited members of the government coalition during this period of their voluntary imprisonment. They were afraid to move, and seemed bored and ineffectual, isolated and impotent while waiting for something to happen. President Emile Lahoud had to physically move out of the presidential palace by November 23, and both sides hoped that an agreement would be reached by then.

The stakes for Lebanon, and by extension for the Arab world, were huge. Hezbollah's terms were simple and anathema to both the values of March 14 and the dream of instilling majoritarian democracy in Lebanon. Hezbollah wanted a president who would not discuss disarming the Islamic Resistance, and it wanted that long-demanded veto power in the cabinet. Giving in to those demands would mean abandoning the entire project of March 14: full independence from Syria, an end to the era of militias and perpetual war, and a promise of stability and prosperity that depended on some kind of entente with Israel and the United States. Saad Hariri literally pouted the days away in Qoreitem, his family's enormous palace in West Beirut. I visited him at the height of the crisis to profile him for *The New York Times,* and found it hard to escape the idea that he was a man who didn't stand for anything. I wanted to admire him, if only because I hoped that March 14 could coalesce into a coherent liberal democratic movement that could provide an alternative in the debate over the future of the Middle East. Genuine liberal reformers throughout the Arab world struggled to make their voices heard in the big-tent coalition of the Axis of Accommodation; sadly, their influence was negligible compared to parties like the Saudi royal family, Egypt's rulers, and the wealthy cliques promoted by the relatively moderate but still authoritarian regimes in the region. Lebanon had a comparative wealth of dynamic figures, in letters, commerce, and politics, who sincerely wished to advance a polity based on rights, freedoms, and shared prosperity, but they couldn't quite succeed at taking the helm of the March 14 movement, much less the Axis of Accommodation. Hariri's followers hoped Hariri would counterbalance the

Axis of Resistance, which spoke eloquently and with conviction. Hezbollah, its most successful manifestation by far, had a clear agenda, an easily described ideology, and a string of successes to advertise. I wished someone would speak as clearly for the Axis of Accommodation, someone articulate and charismatic enough to explain that submission and defeat weren't the only alternative to perpetual war against the Jews. An entire society existed that sought a new modus vivendi, one that was indigenous, Arab, Islamic but not hell-bent on confrontation. Their strain of pragmatism had yet to find its political avatar. To be sure, it was weaker than the current flowing toward the Axis of Resistance, but it drew support at all levels of society. Unfortunately, as leaders like Saad Hariri repeatedly demonstrated, the pragmatists found it difficult to make a persuasive case for themselves.

Saad Hariri, who could pass for twenty-five even though he was thirty-seven, had run his family's billion-dollar telecommunications company in Saudi Arabia before inheriting the Future Movement upon his father's death. I couldn't imagine how this shy, bumbling, and inarticulate man had run a profitable multinational conglomerate. In Qoreitem he played the host graciously. During Ramadan he invited hundreds to nightly iftars where he gave short, bland speeches about the need for restraint and national unity, then shook a few hundred hands and retired. He received visitors in a moribund suite of offices that looked like it hadn't seen a vibrant argument since his father's time. Larger-than-life posters of Rafik Hariri were placed on his favorite chairs—behind his desk, which was no longer used, around the conference table, in the salon. Saad meant the ubiquitous photographs as a tribute to his beloved father, but they seemed to undermine the movement he founded, reminding everyone who set foot in Qoreitem of the unflattering comparison between the wily inspirational father and the laconic unimaginative son. The pictures also highlighted the depressing lack of an ideology inside March 14. The movement was against the murder of Rafik Hariri, and was for bringing his killers to justice. Beyond that, it wasn't clear if its leaders agreed on anything else.

Walid Jumblatt seemed ready to explode with frustration in his apartment on Clemenceau Street. Like the other shut-in members of the government, he had endless spare time on his hands. Along with Saad Hariri, he was considered a prime assassination target, in particular because of his bold and entertaining broadsides against Hezbollah and Syria. Jumblatt devoured stacks of reading material in his salon, which was beautifully lit by parallel banks of facing windows. He had time to talk at length about the competing philosophies of governance, and it distressed him that Saad Hariri couldn't force a single inspirational turn of phrase from his mouth. The March 14 movement's leaders were being picked off one by one in an anonymous murder campaign, Jumblatt said, and yet somehow Hezbollah—clearly the villain in the story he was telling—had managed to take the high ground and rile up its supporters. "The whole world recognized our movement in 2005. The whole world supported our getting the Syrians out officially," Jumblatt said. "Now we have to reach our full potential. If we don't act, Hezbollah's state-within-a-state could end up swallowing the official state." Somehow, the March 14 leaders were failing to translate the outrage of their supporters into political momentum, Jumblatt said, and he seemed to blame his political allies. "It's not enough to be in the right," he sighed.

His complaint captured his movement's pervasive impotence. Members of the March 14 coalition who didn't live in palaces grew pale in the Phoenicia Hotel, where they weren't even allowed sunlight through the windows for fear of snipers. Mohammed Kabbani, a mild and reasonable Sunni member of Parliament who normally lived in West Beirut, would give me a running commentary on the negotiations. They seemed always to stall on the unrealistic expectations of the two sides. March 14 still thought it could force Hezbollah to fold; Hezbollah was waiting for March 14 to accept the Party of God's terms so they could discuss the issues that Hezbollah actually was willing to negotiate—like which of the Hezbollah-approved presidential candidates March 14 preferred, and which ministries Hezbollah and its allies would get in a new government. The air in the Phoenicia was stale from recirculated cigarette smoke. It took nearly a quarter of an hour to clear the many levels of security surrounding the hotel, which resembled those of the American Embassy in Iraq's Green Zone. Each time I visited Kabbani at the Phoenicia, he looked more haggard and yellow. By the end of November, he said his anti-Hezbollah coalition seemed destined to lose, in part because "The United States did not back the majority the way they were supposed to." Washington had diplomatic cards it had declined to play. For instance, Kabbani said, the United States could have announced it would recognize a new Lebanese president chosen by a simple majority of parliament, thereby putting Iran and Syria on the defensive. Power politics in the Middle East responded to actual moves on the political chessboard, not on high-flying rhetoric. Kabbani wished Washington would take the plunge and push allies with interests in Lebanon, like the Vatican, to do the same. But Washington hadn't intervened, leaving the playing field tilted in Hezbollah's favor. "A game is being played against us," a resigned Kabbani said. "We are bargaining in a closed room with an armed group backed by a bigger neighboring state, and we are not bargaining from a position of power."

While the government in which Israel, the United States, and the Arab Axis of Accommodation had invested such high hopes stewed and waited, Hezbollah was busy. Nasrallah had a master plan and Iran was playing a patient strategic game. Their opponents were tied up in tactics, short-term hopes, and long-term fears; Hezbollah was building bunkers, barricades, and apartment blocks. They trumpeted all their endeavors except on the military front. Even there, Nasrallah made his blustery announcement about Hezbollah's rocket capacity quickly exceeding its prewar levels, an assessment confirmed by Israeli intelligence. Other elements of Hezbollah's rearmament program trickled into the public sphere. Arms shipments flowed unhindered by air from Iran to Syria and overland into Lebanon. Fighters flew to Iran for training, and others took part in refresher courses in the Beqaa or in camps in the South. Israel and the United Nations leaked the coordinates of a network of sophisticated underground bunkers Hezbollah had used during the war. Their existence and location had been unknown before the 2006 hostilities, and Hezbollah most certainly had more. Government opponents of Hezbollah began to complain about the party's command-and-control system, which they said included a telecommunications and signals intelligence system entirely independent from the government's. Israeli intelligence echoed the claim, and it seemed plausible. Hezbollah appeared to have been able during the war to intercept Israeli cell phone traffic and military communications. Inside of Lebanon, the Party of God was assumed to be able to listen to every phone conversation and even to crack people's email accounts. Dark conspiracy theories flew around Beirut: one claimed that under the cover of the tent city downtown, Hezbollah was installing surveillance equipment and its own fiber-optic cable network. Another series of rumors concerned Hezbollah's secret nefarious plot to consolidate its dominion over the South and the Beqaa with Iran's help. To that end, allegedly, Iran was building a new network of roads to help Hezbollah distribute weapons and move fighters. Hezbollah supposedly was buying up land formerly owned by Christians and Druze, and resettling Shiites there to create an unbroken crescent of Shiite territory from the Mediterranean Sea through the mountains to Baalbek. These paranoid whispers reflected a popular feeling among those who didn't support Hezbollah that the Party of God had become unstoppable, and was on the cusp of forcing unwelcome change on the nation and the region. "You might be able to establish what's happening if you can sneak into Hezbollah's forbidden zone in the South," one politician told me in his lavish Beirut living room. The area to which the politician referred—the border zone—was more off-limits to him because of his sectarian affinity than it was to me. I found a dash of dark humor in these rumors and accusations that were theatrically fed to me by anonymous Hezbollah opponents. Their fear wasn't funny at all, nor was Hezbollah's increasingly apparent ability to call the shots. The joke was that almost all of the spy-movie claims were true, and for the most part they described initiatives that Hezbollah was taking completely in the open.

I regularly reported in the supposedly "forbidden" zone after getting the permission required of all foreigners from the Ministry of Defense. The roads Hezbollah was building with Iranian money were only the most visible project. The drive to Baalbek now took half as long on a divided highway, smoothly paved and graciously engineered, that bypassed all the congested village centers and swooped through the Beqaa to Hezbollah's founding city. An extension of the Beqaa road now stretched all the way to the south, to Khiam and onwards. In addition to the patchwork of tiny one-lane roads, a web of modern carriageways connected the two flanks of Shia Lebanon. New routes were carved out south and north of the Litani, speeding the way to villages like Srifa and Bourj Qalaouay, and creating redundant routes in the event of future wars. Next time Israel wanted to shut down transportation links to the South and the Beqaa, it would have to bomb many more bridges and roads than in 2006. USAID was afraid to mention in public the reconstruction projects it had funded, but Iran and Hezbollah weren't so demure. Alongside all the new roads their sponsors had unabashedly unfurled banners: "The Iranian Contributory Organization for Reconstructing Lebanon." Billboards and banners declared: "Thanks to the Iranian Council! Rebuilding Our Nation. Lebanon Forever!"

Christian and Druze landowners, bowing to demography and the shrinking of their communities, *were* in fact selling major parcels of land to the highest bidders, who happened to be Shia. Both sects were witnessing the tail end of a long decline. Their populations had shrunk, their wealthiest and most dynamic citizens tended to move abroad, and over the decades many of their most emblematic villages had been depopulated, springing to life only when tourists visited in the summers. Their coreligionists didn't want to buy, and landlords increasingly found themselves making the pragmatic decision to sell, even if it meant their villages were in the process of becoming Shia areas.

Hezbollah already had its own phone and communications network, and its own surveillance system. Telecommunications Minister Marwan Hamadeh had begun leaking information about Hezbollah's network, describing it as an Iranian-built parallel fiber-optic system with no connections to the national grid. Hamadeh was a member of Jumblatt's party, a tough and articulate man who had survived an assassination attempt in 2004. It became clear during the 2006 war that Hezbollah had its own command-and-control systems, which survived extensive bomb damage to the national infrastructure. Somehow Hezbollah was able to monitor other people's communications—inside Lebanon and apparently in northern Israel as well—while continuing to send orders to its own front-line troops. That kind of resilient communications system was considered essential to modern warfare, but it also sent a message to the people of Lebanon and to the admiring audience in the Arab world: Hezbollah answered to no force but itself, and operated beyond the ken of a government or a state. It made war and governed its subjects on its own terms. Unlike the other militant movements that had come and gone, Hezbollah didn't limit its innovations to making war; the Party of God didn't plan to prevail on the killing fields alone, but by taking control of its sphere of influence and replacing the nation-state. Hezbollah provided the ideology, identity, and military security that usually defines a state; and as its wherewithal grew, it would provide roads, housing, and maybe even phone service as well. Hezbollah didn't bother to deny the slightly exaggerated details since the underlying claims about their para-state were true—and the fear with which the rumors of Hezbollah's prowess were repeated only strengthened the party's bargaining position.

The recipe now required riling the base. The ideological ground was well groomed and the seeds sown. I wanted to see up close the two institutions where the young were most concertedly inculcated into Hezbollah's view of the world, the schools and the scouts. Hezbollah carefully protected its private school network, the Mahdi Schools, and the other hard-line Shia school networks affiliated with Hezbollah politely refused my requests to visit over many years. Public primary education throughout the Arab world languished, and traditionally the only appealing alternatives were clerical, run by missionaries or religious orders. Centuries earlier, missionaries and monastic orders had founded well-regarded academies which educated generations of the Arab elite. Over time, Muslim activists founded their own institutions to compete with the boarding and day schools run by Christian nuns and monks. With rare exceptions, the only quality schools in the entire Middle East were private, and the overwhelming majority of them were linked to a religious sect. The Shia had come late to the game, but the influx of Iranian money and of alms from the Shia disapora had spawned a half-dozen private school networks. Some, like the Mahdi and Mustafa Schools, were considered feeder institutions for Hezbollah. Other Shia schools were simply religious-themed private schools with some sympathy for Hezbollah or Amal but no organizational ties.

The Mahdi Scouts, on the other hand, were a pure and simple recruiting tool for Hezbollah. Every movement in the Middle East had a youth scouting movement, and they all smacked of militarism and indoctrination. As far as I could tell, the point of youth scouts was to inculcate children to loyally obey authority; spread religion; and impart survival (read: early military) skills. Hezbollah's scouts were a well organized lot. A successful scout would grow up to be a productive soldier or movement activist. And a mediocre scout would still absorb the values and ideology of the movement. Hezbollah cared about the services it offered, but treasured above all its ideology. And the Mahdi Scouts provided a direct channel through which to spread its beliefs. In school, Hezbollah had to teach many subjects. In the scouts, it could focus on one: the essence of solid citizenship in the nation of the Islamic Resistance.

The Mahdi Scouts, named for the Awaited Imam, operated on a slightly modified version of the international scout movement's promise and law. The international template asks the scout, to swear "on my duty to God . . . to obey the Scout Law." Among other things, that law requires the scout to behave with "honor" and "loyalty," "to be useful and help others," and "to obey orders . . . without question."[73] Hezbollah's oath also mentioned obedience to God, the Mahdi, and the *faqih,* or supreme Islamic jurist. All Hezbollah loyalists enrolled their kids in the Mahdi Scouts, which kept them busy every weekend throughout the year and for extended periods during the summer. Parents who wished their children to grow up to be party members or fighters knew the surest route was through the scouts. In the scouts Hezbollah presented its unvarnished ideology, beginning with *wilayat al faqih,* the concept of absolute clerical rule first implemented by Ayatollah Khomeini. This principle preceded all others for Hezbollah. The *faqih,* or jurist, was the custodian of God's will on earth until the return of the Awaited Imam, the Mahdi. He was infallible and had final say over all affairs; he was as close to God as a mortal man can be. The first jurist was Khomeini; after his death, authority passed to his successor as Supreme Leader, Ayatollah Ali Khamenei. National identity took a backseat to religion for followers of this doctrine; you could swear fealty to the faqih whether you happened to be Iranian, Iraqi, Lebanese, Afghani, Pakistani, or so on. Your loyalty lay with God's regent, and not with any nation or government or political party. Hezbollah derived its religious authority from this principle, which accounted for its legitimacy (Nasrallah had a direct link to God in the chain of command) and its means (its final arbiter was a religious authority who *happened* to have the formidable tools of the Iranian state at his disposal).

Thus the young scouts were steeped first in Khomeini's model of Islam, which quite succinctly resolved a lot of normally more complicated questions children pose about the roots of power and justice in the world. Beginning at age six the scouts, boys and girls alike, absorbed this very particular view of authority. In their country, they were taught, Hezbollah executes God's will and can address any concern, from security and well-being to issues of sexuality and hygiene. I had heard of the spectacle of young scouts in fatigues marching through the Dahieh on Jerusalem Day in fatigues with plastic guns, and I had also been told that in the Scouts I could get a close look at the core beliefs beneath Hezbollah's politics—what kind of world they really wanted to create, what they really thought of Jews and other religions, how they rationalized violence and made it instrumental. After months of foot-dragging and many rebuffs, in late November 2007 officials in the party relented and decided to grant me access to the Mahdi Scouts. They were reluctant because the scouts had been portrayed in some news accounts as a terrorist youth group and a wing of Hezbollah's militia.[74] I don't think they saw a percentage in granting foreign reporters entry to scout activities, because they knew that Westerners would perceive those activities as a process of indoctrination to fanaticism. They relented in the end because of my persistence and because, when it came down to it, they were a tad vain and proud of what they had achieved, and wanted to show off.

The chief of Hezbollah's scouts, Bilal Naim, met me in an unmarked apartment in the Dahieh that housed the Mahdi Scouts national head-quarters. It was beside a deep bomb crater from the recent war, filled with swampy sludge, garbage, and rainwater. Metal plates blocked any light from entering the windows of the Scout office. Bilal Naim was a short, chubby, unassuming man, direct and to the point. He was a physician, and had a doctor's friendly but business-like affect. Usually Hezbollah officials quizzed me about international affairs and Israel at the outset of an interview to gauge my politics and adjust their rhetoric accordingly. His subordinates already had vetted me so Naim didn't waste his time duplicating their work.

The entire purpose of the scouts, Naim said, was to steep children in Hezbollah's vision of Islam, or as he put it, "The Mahdi Scouts is charged with building the interior of kids." Full-time psychologists and social workers supervised the scout programming, all of it oriented toward two aims. First, Naim said, scouting should make children commit to an Islamic way of life. Secondly, it should convince children to join Hezbollah's bureaucracy or militia after they turned sixteen. Very deliberately, the Mahdi Scouts strived to shift community norms; once the scouts taught children how to behave, pray, and talk, Hezbollah used them as leverage to change the values of their families. Examples abounded of families like the Haidars in Srifa, where the children first adopted strict Islamic mores and Hezbollah's political line, and gradually convinced their parents to follow them into a more religious lifestyle and more extreme politics. In the process, the scouts reinforced Hezbollah's central role in the Shia community. Every time the scouts painted a playground, planted a tree, or brought food to a homebound widow, they reminded people that Hezbollah—and not the state—was taking care of them. "The Mahdi Scouts have direct influence through our activities in the community. We have indirect influence through the way children change their behavior, become more aware, and affect their families," Naim said. "You can see our activities any Sunday."

In the year since the war, the Mahdi Scouts had nearly doubled its national enrollment to 60,000. They had run out of capacity to admit more, he said, but they were expanding as fast as they could. Hezbollah policed its community tightly, but not without concern for its mental well-being. Constant warfare (or mobilization for such) took its toll, especially on children and on the families of martyrs. One goal of the scouts was to comfort the afflicted. The scouts tried to maintain a state of normalcy—at least as Hezbollah defined it—for its most vulnerable members. If left to their own devices, Bilal Naim said, the children of martyrs would isolate themselves and develop emotional problems. "We try to raise the children in the community and find new husbands for the widows," he said. "Otherwise the children become complicated, and develop unhealthy behaviors like aggression."

On a rainy Sunday in December, we drove to Khiam to visit the scouts in action. We were an hour late because we had trouble with military intelligence when we tried to enter the border region. The former Israeli occupation zone of South Lebanon remains officially off limits to foreigners. Anyone wishing to visit the area—including foreign passport holders of Lebanese descent who have family homes in the South—must get special permission from Lebanese military intelligence. Mine had expired the day before, and we had to call in a favor from a sympathetic officer who let us through the checkpoint at the Litani River. Mohammed Dawi, the sweaty and plump scout leader, met us at the entrance to Khiam town. He was a redhead with freckles, and looked more Irish than Lebanese. The younger scouts were waiting in the basement of a high school a mile or so from the prison. The troop leader led them in a chant of welcome. Most of them wore blue shirts with epaulets, white scarves, and oversized badges featuring a photograph of a scowling Ayatollah Khomeini. Two boys who looked about ten wore full military fatigues. It seemed the day's activities had been planned with my visit in mind. The children marched downstairs single file and broke up by age group. The "buds," six or seven years old, assembled for a puppet show, emceed by a man in a worn panda suit who sang lines from Nasrallah's speeches. The "sprouts," eight to ten years old, sat around tables at the rear of the room drawing pictures, their ideas inspired by a chubby and soft-spoken young woman named Malak Sweid. She was a graphic design student and zealous party apparatchik.

In "guided drawing," the kids drew pictures of Israelis weeping in defeat, denoted by Stars of David on their helmets, or of Israelis stepping on Lebanese. Other children, with evident direction by Malak, depicted crosses and crescents, symbolizing the Lebanese Christians and Muslims, chained by vicious Stars of David. Other pictures spoke less to the conflict with the Jews than to Islamic values. One child's picture showed women in low-cut gowns holding martini glasses and cigarettes in old-fashioned holders. "Smoking Harms Your Health" was the title. At the front of the room children jostled with the man in the bear suit and another man in a mouse suit. One child struck the bear-man in the head. A six-year-old boy with a thin high-pitched voice recited from memory a speech of Nasrallah's. "The Israelis target the innocent! We will destroy the Israelis!" intoned the child in his choirboy's treble.

The scoutmaster hovered over the children, sweating and incessantly eating bits of candy he had secreted into every one of his pockets. The library of scout manuals showcased better than any single document the essential ideology of Hezbollah. A quick scan of the selections on the shelf showed the party's priorities:

How to Learn the Koran
A Day in the Mosque
Praying
I Love My Country
How to Manage a Household
How to Read

Summer Camping
I Obey My Leader

Dawi gave me a handful of scout manuals, which helpfully encouraged children through cartoons to brush their teeth thoroughly and help the elderly across the street. Fun puzzles at the end of every lesson featured standard children's fare like mazes, but with Hezbollah themes—a bearded Hezbollah fighter at the start of the maze, with an Israeli bunker at the far end. The occasional illustration featured bearded fighters charging Israeli soldiers cowering behind sandbags. But the overwhelming substance of the scout manuals, like the programming itself, wasn't about spreading hatred of Israel—that was already taken care of out in the community. It was geared toward constructing an identity in which a child's entire moral sense flowed from a strict interpretation of Islam administered by the jurist, Iran's Supreme Leader Ali Khamenei, and his conduit, Hezbollah. Many illustrations depicted a small Satan hovering over a little boy's shoulder, egging him on to steal, litter, or misbehave. In the Mahdi Scouts, the little boy learned to resist devilish urges. Success in the Scouts led to an invitation to join Hezbollah as a probationary member. The most promising boys were recruited to join the ranks of the fighters. During the summer, scouts spent weeks at camps in the South and the Beqaa, where they practiced fitness and learned survival skills along with serious religion courses that imparted both the doctrine and vernacular that made so many of Hezbollah's activists sound identical when they explained their convictions.

After the show in the school basement, Dawi drove us around Khiam to see what the older scouts were doing. We stopped at one house where two teenage girl scouts were cleaning and shopping for a housebound war widow. Dawi picked two apples from the grocery bag they had brought the old lady and devoured them in a minute. At a new playground in the lee of the prison, another group was planting trees. Dawi looked on with satisfaction, joked with the teenage boys, and shoved an entire Kit-Kat bar into his mouth in a single bite. Malak, the nineteen-year-old assistant troop leader, explained to me that while the activities were fun, the most formative part of her scouting experience had been the religious education. Each week in the Scouts during her childhood she and her peers would study a single word or passage from the Koran, under the guidance of a Hezbollah member. Gradually, she said, she absorbed the party's faith—a more stringent practice of Islam than her parents'—and from that flowed all the rest: the politics, the lifestyle, the community, and eventually, her entry into Hezbollah's ranks. Malak was a product of the new Hezbollah age. When she talked to me about personal matters, she sounded like any college freshman. She aspired to a top-flight graphic design job at a satellite television network; she hugged her little sister Jana sweetly as she admired her drawings; and she asked me with a lot of concern how much I thought her education would disadvantage her on the job market—she was studying at a private school in Nabatieh with an American curriculum but second-rate professors. Whenever conversation turned to matters of politics or religion, though, she was like an automaton. I'm sure she believed everything she said, but it was eerie how her language almost word for word repeated the speeches of Hezbollah leaders. She mouthed the same jokes about Condi Rice's "New Middle East" and the perfidy of the Jewish children who sent missiles to Lebanon, and enumerated the same justification for Hezbollah's militancy and the same mock-sad resignation: "All we want is peace. Unfortunately a neighbor like Israel will never allow it." The Scouts implanted from a young age the idea that everyone in the homeland was an individual with aspirations and temptations, while everyone in the land of the enemy robotically contributed to a war machine. They humanized the Islamic fighters for imbuing their military struggle into every aspect of life, and demonized Israelis who did the same thing.

Mohammed Dawi, almost twice Malak's age (he was born in 1971), came from a different Hezbollah generation. The young scouts, and the recently-minted adults like Malak Sweid, never knew an alternative reality; in their universe, Hezbollah had always been omnipotent in the community and under threat from Israel. The Party of God always had been their patron and teacher, and the Jews always had been their enemies. Mohammed Dawi was more hard-bitten, and hadn't grown up with the same kind of certainty. The younger Hezbollah members often projected the calm inner focus of the religious acolyte. They lived and breathed Hezbollah's credos, like Rani Bazzi's children who took their father's word that Islamic purity applied to lunch and exercise in addition to jihad against Israel. In contrast, Mohammed Dawi appeared focused yet impatient, without the Zen forbearance of the elite Hezbollah members I had met. Earlier he had leaned against the wall in the school basement smoking directly in front of the children's drawings warning against the perils of cigarettes. Although he seemed to genuinely like all the kids and know them by name, he seemed bored by the sedentary indoor indoctrination activities. Drawing pictures about Israeli evil was clearly an important step in acculturating young children to the perpetual war, but Mohammed Dawi much preferred the spontaneity of getting outdoors or visiting Hezbollah families in their home where he could lead unscripted conversations about war and Islamic justice. He seemed like he'd be more in his element at a picnic or on a camping trip.

He took us to the home of his predecessor as Khiam's Mahdi Scout leader, the martyr Ahmed Sheikh Ali, killed in the 2006 war. Mohammed Dawi and Ahmed Sheikh Ali had spent several years together in the Khiam prison. Their children were friends and the redheaded scoutmaster clearly felt at ease with the Sheikh Ali children. The eldest son, Mahdi, was ten. He leaned against Dawi and smiled. The scoutmaster wrapped one arm tightly around the boy, and with the other shoveled candy from the coffee table into his prodigious mouth. Four teenage girl scouts delivered gifts to the four children of the martyr, and stayed for a long visit. Each scout focused on one of the children, and discreetly but persistently encouraged them to stick with their old activities and turn to the Hezbollah community whenever depression nipped at them. Young Mahdi seemed to enjoy the visit and the attention from this friend of his father's. He was an active scout, Dawi said, one of the best in the troop; he was destined, God willing, to follow his father's footsteps. "This is our role in the Mahdi Scouts: to transfer our ideas," Dawi said. "We want to live, but we don't want anyone to forget the enemy. Mahdi here is a child. His father died. Will he forget the enemy? No. The idea will be in his mind forever. It's something he will hold close."

Mahdi giggled. "I want to be like my father when I grow up," he said. It seemed as if he was about to speak of his dreams of being a soldier, to which his mother already had alluded, but Dawi cut him off. He didn't want the boy talking about death to me; he was trying to put forward a sanitized version of Hezbollah, and his theme all day had been about loving life.

"You'll be a doctor of the resistance," Dawi said.

Mahdi didn't miss the cue. "I'll be a doctor!" he repeated unconvincingly, not fully aware why he was supposed to say so, but happy to oblige Uncle Mohammed.

Back at the school about a hundred younger kids waited for their parents to pick them up. They were jubilant.

"What have you learned in the scouts?" I asked one of the boys.

"I've learned singing, camping, drawing," he said, the words tumbling out. "I've made houses out of paper. I've learned to make weapons out of paper. I ask the Mahdi Scouts to let me prepare to become a real fighter. I want to sing you a song!" Several of his friends joined in with their sweet young voices.

> *We are men. We are flowers.*
> *It's my flag, it's my nation.*
> *We sacrifice our blood.*

The ten-year-old, his name Ahmed, felt even rowdier after the song. He switched from Arabic to halting English. "I want to fuck Israel!" he said. "America, America, Fallujah, Fallujah!" He collapsed in convulsions of laughter.

A mass ideology like Hezbollah's could only appeal to millions of people if it translated into action. Hezbollah could preach its all-encompassing and austere brand of Islam, and exhort its followers to pledge eternal enmity toward Israel with little effect if it had no capacity for mobilization and warfare. Many frothing but fringe movements do little more than rave. Hezbollah's popularity depends on its effectiveness, and its effectiveness in turn depends on the resources furnished by Iran and Syria. Politicians and counterterrorism and military officials in Israel and the United States often overstate the operational links between Iran, Syria, and Hezbollah because it simplifies matters, even if their overblown claims obscure the truth and confuse the question of Hezbollah's motives and capacity.[75] Hezbollah's own claims about its relationship with Iran and Syria dovetail with the more levelheaded assessments of Israeli and Western intelligence agencies. Without these state sponsors, Hezbollah would lose the military capability that has made it such a formidable force in global extremism. Without external support, Hezbollah would still command enough resources to pose a serious threat to Israel, and to play a central role in Shia militancy—but the Party of God would likely suffer a major collapse in power and influence.

Nobody outside Hezbollah actually knows the group's operating budget. Leaked intelligence estimates of Iran's annual funding to Hezbollah range from $25 million to more than $200 million.[76] Other analysts I spoke to in Lebanon and the United States, including retired Lebanese military officers and high-ranking American officials, thought the amount far greater, especially if Iran's military and reconstruction aid was factored in along with direct cash payments and funds disbursed through charities. Several of them agreed that Iran had spent nearly $1 billion a year in the four years following the 2006 war. (As a point of comparison, Lebanon's relatively ineffectual government has an annual budget of about $10 billion, and is still incapable of providing simple services, like round-the-clock electricity. Lebanon has one of the highest levels of public debt in the world, surpassed only by Japan and Zimbabwe.)[77] Hezbollah itself has said it receives a great deal of its budget from Iran but has never specified how much—and ever since the September 11 attacks, the Party of God has intensified its fundraising efforts and investment strategy to diversify revenue streams.[78] Senior Hezbollah officials told me they wanted the party to achieve financial autonomy, but they admitted they haven't approached that goal yet. A close look at Hezbollah's core functions suggests that the precise amount matters less than the level of codependence between Hezbollah, Iran, and Syria, especially when it comes to the functions that can best be performed with state sponsorship, like spying and making war. Hezbollah's military operations—the capacity for force that has made the party so important—depend almost entirely on Iran and Syria, not just financially but logistically. Few militant movements have unfettered access to weapons and training from a sophisticated military power like Iran, which is willing to offer elite training to its allies in Hezbollah. Other equally ambitious militant movements are constrained by geography or the unwillingness of their patrons to share expertise. For example, even if Iran wanted to send the same aid to Hamas in Gaza as it sends to Hezbollah in Lebanon, it would simply have no means of moving major quantities of materiel and soldiers into the territory; nor would it have the ability to easily take people to Iran for training. In other areas where Iran supplies and trains proxies and allies, such as Iraq, the Revolutionary Guard appears to have limited its assistance because it knows in the future those militias could compete with or pose a threat to Iran.

No such constraints hamper Hezbollah's ties to Iran. Nasrallah's movement has proved its loyalty to the ayatollahs in Tehran; it is ideologically trusted. An Iranian government willing to provide its best military resources to Hezbollah encounters no logistical impediment to doing so. Trainers can fly from Tehran to Damascus unfettered, and bring cargo planes full of heavy weaponry. With the full cooperation of Syria's government and Lebanon's border police, soldiers and weapons can freely cross the frontier. There is no need for secret smuggling; Iran can send small arms or large rockets. Logistically it is as easy for Iran and Hezbollah to share equipment and expertise as it is for the United States military and the Israel Defense Forces. Hezbollah fighters often fill the direct flights from Damascus to Tehran (and Damascus is only a couple hours' drive from Beirut). If Iran ceased military support for Hezbollah, the party would depend on the much more limited aid it could expect from Syria, and what little it might acquire on the international arms market and smuggle in through Syria or the sea. If Syria cut its ties, Iran would find it very difficult to maintain the smooth flow between the Revolutionary Guard and Hezbollah's militia. Israeli officials regularly describe Hezbollah as a "division" of the Revolutionary Guards. In truth, Hezbollah would still exist and recruit fighters to attack Israel even without Iran's support; but its militia would pose a far less significant threat. It's difficult to imagine the Party of God as the Middle East's resident giant slayers without Iran. Without the Revolutionary Guard's support Hezbollah would do far less damage to Israel, and as its military capacity shrank, its recruitment effort and ideological momentum would falter.

More important in terms of Hezbollah's doctrine and actions is the question of who calls the shots. Many Middle Eastern critics of Hezbollah told me they consider Hezbollah a subservient stooge of Iran. The ayatollahs in Iran made all the major decisions, they said. According to this theory, Syria and Hezbollah had wider latitude when it came to tactics, but limited input on grand strategy. Israeli and American officials often paint Hezbollah that way as well—as a finger puppet on the hand of

Iran. As evidence they cite Nasrallah's frequent meetings with Iranian and Syrian leaders, and the incontrovertible military links. Hezbollah's public posture in Lebanon suggests a more complex reality. During the first decade of the century, Hezbollah alternated between pacific and belligerent phases, not always in tandem with Iran. Hezbollah, it seems, could chart the agenda that best served its own needs, and Tehran would concur so long as Hezbollah's independent strategic course didn't undermine any Iranian interest. On a tactical level, the party's militia acted quickly and continuously, especially during periods of tension or fighting on the Israeli border. The speed with which Hezbollah attacked, counterattacked, and improvised during clashes with Israel made clear that the local command in Lebanon made its own decisions. Statements from Nasrallah, his deputy Naim Qassem, and Nabil Kawuok, the Hezbollah chief in the South, portrayed a relationship in which Hezbollah had the role of a special operations team or a special envoy, and Iran that of the central command or state secretary. Major missions were made or approved at headquarters, and then the autonomous agents had complete freedom to choose how to execute the mission—and freedom as well to pursue any goals of their own that didn't contradict the central task. There was much debate in Israeli policy circles after the 2006 war, for instance, about whether the kidnap operation had angered Iran because of the unexpected backlash it provoked. The argument seemed silly. Israel had thwarted many Hezbollah kidnap attempts over the years. The strategy wasn't new; only its success was. Neither Hezbollah nor their Iranian quartermasters expected Israel to respond with all-out war. Hezbollah suffered an embarrassing intelligence failure, prompting Nasrallah's unusual apology and a renewed effort by Iran—and presumably the allied Syrian and Iranian intelligence services—to run counterintelligence operations against Israel and improve their own surveillance and analysis.

Speculation has also flourished about what Hezbollah would do if Iran's nuclear program were attacked. Some people who work with Israeli and American policymakers held the view that Hezbollah would do Iran's bidding at any cost, especially in the event of a serious crisis for Tehran. These people, who had access to classified intelligence reports, told me that Hezbollah had sleeper cells across the world that might strike Israeli or even American targets in retaliation for an attack on Iran's nuclear program.

These analysts also believed that Hezbollah would initiate a war on Israel's northern front, turning a bombing of Iran into a regional conflagration. In the fall of 2010, during another period of tension over Iran's nuclear efforts, I put the question to Mahmoud Komati, a Hezbollah founder and key member of its Politburo (one of his recent tasks had been overseeing the Hezbollah charter revision released the previous year). What, I asked him, was Hezbollah willing to do to help Iran? "There are people who would pay a lot of money for the answer to that question, Komati said with a belly laugh. He went on to say that Hezbollah embraced a policy of "strategic ambiguity," an intentional invocation of the term Israel uses to describe its policy of not declaring its nuclear weapons program. Komati implied that Hezbollah might attack on Iran's behalf or it might show restraint; uncertainty about the party's views would keep Israel and the United States off balance. On the border between Israel and Lebanon, Komati said, Hezbollah had developed its own deterrent power in tandem with Israel's. "Today we are living the balance of fear," he said. "This balance blocks war." It seemed clear to me that Hezbollah could not afford the appearance before its own public of fighting a war on some other nation's behalf. If Hezbollah wanted to get involved in a conflict sparked by a squabble between Israel and Iran, Hezbollah would need to preserve at least the appearance that some core Lebanese interest was at stake. The Party of God also would want to argue that war had been provoked by Israel, even if to outsiders the provocation would appear to have been wholly engineered by Hezbollah.

The destabilizing unknowns surrounding Iran's nuclear program highlighted the strategic importance of understanding Iran's relationship to Hezbollah.

Hezbollah's own description of the relationship with Iran seems to fit the facts. In its infancy, Hezbollah grew in the tight embrace of the Iranian Revolutionary Guards who organized its founding. But in its maturity, Hezbollah is no mere proxy, and seems to enjoy something closer to the status of a junior partner or favored ally with Tehran. Hezbollah has its own independent sources of strength, which give it legitimacy. No ideological gap separates it from Iran's Revolutionary leadership. Lebanon's Party of God considers Iran's Supreme Leader its faqih, and submits willingly to Iran's top cleric. On matters of strategic import it acts in concert with Iran.

On domestic matters it appears to act independently. Officials from Nas-rallah downward have said in speeches and interviews to non-Hezbollah audiences that all their policies have the approval of the faqih in Tehran. Ayatollah Khamenei, then, must have approved Hezbollah's proposal to capture Israeli soldiers in an attempt to gain leverage. It was up to Hezbol-lah to plan the timing and other specifics of the actual raid. Similarly, Iran had approved Hezbollah's links to Palestinian, Egyptian, and other par-ties, deputizing Hezbollah to spread militancy and leave plausible deniabil-ity for the Revolutionary Guards. But Hezbollah had its own reasons for pursuing the regional relationships, not the least of which was the Party's increasing prominence in global militant circles. Iran is an enormous state with all the headaches and factionalism of a massive and unwieldy govern-ment bureaucracy. Hezbollah, by comparison, is tiny and nimble, and has so far succeeded at maintaining internal unity. It has a simpler mission and more incentives to openly export radical militancy, with less to lose than a sovereign state actor like Iran. Paradoxically, while its material strength is insignificant compared to Iran's, its moral influence over militants has grown stronger precisely because it appears so purely wedded to its ideo-logical mission. It also helps that Hezbollah is an Arab group helping other Arabs, unhindered by the ethnic divide separating Farsi-speaking Persians from their Arab neighbors.

Hezbollah, with its unparalleled influence and string of military suc-cesses against Israel, boasts far more popularity with publics across the Islamic and Arab worlds than either of its state sponsors. Hezbollah has achieved partner status with those regimes, acting almost as a co-equal rather than a tool. Hezbollah's energy and expertise have shifted the dy-namic with Iran more in Hezbollah's favor. The Iranian government spends much of its energy policing internal dissent and holding together by force a massive polity challenged by millions of skeptics. Its military hasn't directly engaged in any sustained warfare since the conflict between Iran and Iraq ended in 1988. For nearly two decades its soldiers' only battlefield experi-ence has come as trainers or observers with militants in Iraq, Lebanon, and elsewhere. Hezbollah on the other hand has been on full, constant alert since 1982. It has refined the tools of asymmetric warfare, from the tools of the weak, like kidnapping and suicide bombing, to guerilla insurgent tactics like roadside bombs, hit-and-run ambushes, and cross-border raids.

Hezbollah has pioneered the use of satellite television as an international propaganda tool, recruiting millions of donors and tens of millions of soft supporters around the world using Al-Manar and the internet. Many of the most destructive tactics used by Palestinian militants against Israel and by Iraqi insurgents and Al Qaeda in Iraq were first developed by Hezbollah. That body of knowledge suggests that in the training camps of the Beqaa and Iran, the Revolutionary Guard has at least as much to learn from Hezbollah as the other way around. When Iran wanted to promote rocket firing, kidnapping, and suicide bombing by Palestinian groups like Hamas and Islamic Jihad, it could count on Hezbollah to teach, train, and arm the other militants. The two entities had a symbiotic rather than dependent relationship. Without Iran, for instance, Hezbollah would have been hard pressed to pull off attacks like the bombings of Jewish targets in Buenos Aires. In 1992, a suicide bomber struck the Israeli embassy there, killing 29 and injuring more than 200. In 1994, a truck bomb destroyed the Jewish Community Center, killing 85 and injuring at least 150.[79] Argentine prosecutors charged Iran with ordering the attacks and Hezbollah with carrying them out. An attack so far from Hezbollah's base in Lebanon would require the kind of logistics that only a government could provide, with its international network of embassies and communications. In fact, the evidence publicly presented builds a case that the attacks in Argentina were an Iranian operation that used some Hezbollah operatives, as opposed to a Hezbollah operation. At any rate, without Hezbollah, Iran would lose much of its ability to project power, pose an active threat to Israel, and perhaps most important, influence Arab politics. American and Israeli policy makers speculate about how Hezbollah would respond to an attack against its Iranian patrons. Hezbollah's domestic credibility depends largely on its reputation for acting in consultation with Iran rather than under Iran's orders. And Iran seems content with its investment in Hezbollah, an increasingly influential regional actor that serves Iran's interests while possessing heft and authority of its own.

There are two fundamental questions for those who oppose Hezbollah as well as those who march beneath its banner. What does Hezbollah really want? And how can its military reach be constrained? Those questions inform and transcend the speculation over Hezbollah's relationship to Iran and Syria, its balancing act between terrorist techniques and guerilla warfare, and its Islamist doctrine. The simplest guide to answering these questions lies in Hezbollah's own words and actions. What does the party tell its followers and recruits? How does it behave toward its Arab rivals and Israel?

Hezbollah's political ideology demands that its constituents *do* something instead of merely react to the world. The Party asks its followers to adopt an active form of Islam, questioning their own ways and drastically making over their lives where they fall short of Islamic dictates. Politically, Hezbollah wants its followers to see themselves as actors, not objects, on the global stage, as well as in Lebanon. It tells its followers they are always just, honorable, and right; even when they exhort the people to violence, the party frames it as a reluctant use of force in self-defense. Even when Hezbollah substantially outguns its rivals, it tells its followers they are fighting from a vulnerable position of weakness.

Above all, Hezbollah seeks to enshrine and extend its society of Islamic Resistance. This goal overlies and explains everything the party does. The culture of resistance dictates an all-inclusive view of Islamic life, which in turn demands a set of militant politics that mobilize the faithful to a state of perpetual alertness against enemies of the Godly. Like other compelling movement ideologies—Manifest Destiny in nineteenth century America, or early twentieth century Zionism—Hezbollah teaches self-reliance, empowerment, and a fearless confidence nourished by bracing and regular bouts of warfare. Hezbollah's ideology appeals to the self first and foremost. Men and women who support Hezbollah make themselves immortal by shedding their fear of death, and make themselves powerful by joining a worldwide militant movement that exerts disproportionate influence over global affairs. The Islamic Resistance keeps its people galvanized with projects at two levels. The first revolves around Islamic identity, and could take the form of constructive projects like religious classes or volunteer work at Hezbollah charities like the Mahdi Scouts, the Martyrs Foundation, the Shia schools, or any of the smaller but vital institutions that link Hezbollah to its community. The second level is more high-pitched and destructive: the state of perpetual war. Hezbollah is engaged in a great range of conflicts, and can cleverly incite a frenzy at any point by invoking one enemy or another, even adroitly switching enemies in an instant if tactical or strategic concerns require. In the early 1980s, Hezbollah trained its sights on the international peacekeeping force that included troops from the United States, France, Italy, and the United Kingdom, and later against Western cultural influence. Then it shifted its focus to Israel's occupation of South Lebanon. After Israel's withdrawal, Hezbollah has alternated between periods of calm, when it has suggested it could imagine a long-term truce with Israel, and bouts of frenzied hatred, when it vows to fight until the Jews are driven from Israel. During the winter of 2007 and the spring of 2008, when it wasn't Israel but moderate Arabs who posed a serious existential threat to Hezbollah, the party poured its vitriol on the parties it decried as morally bankrupt stooges, like Egypt's president.

To put it simply, Hezbollah wants its followers always in a personal state of exultation and self-improvement—and perpetually angry at some greater power out to destroy them or tarnish their claim to justice. The first requires a minimal amount of resources to maintain the party's religious, education, and propaganda functions. The second requires an enemy sufficiently compelling to unify Hezbollah's followers. Israel and the Jews are the easiest for Hezbollah to draft into that role. Israel is engaged in a very tangible conflict with the Lebanese Shia and with their neighboring Palestinians. If circumstances changed, if for example Syria made a peace deal with Israel, Hezbollah could keep its anti-Israeli stance at a low simmer and raise the fire against other targets near and far—American interests, Egypt's dictatorial secular president, the slippery Jordanians, or various factions within Lebanon and Syria that it could target at relatively little cost. In other words, Hezbollah's ideology allows for great opportunism. It will wage unyielding war against Israel as long as that approach expands its power base. If war with Israel were to become more costly, or if by some change in circumstance it endangered Iranian support, Hezbollah could shift its focus to other enemies. The truly crippling conundrum for Hezbollah would be if it ran out of enemies sufficiently compelling to its clientele. But given the failure of peace talks, Israel's shift to the right, the deep hatred of Israel among many Lebanese, and the current of anti-Semitism with which it is interwined, the prospects for a durable peace between Israel and its many enemies in the Middle East remain dim. It is unlikely that Hezbollah will need to replace Israel as its central villain any time soon.

In its quest for power, however, Hezbollah had immediate obstacles to ford, first and foremost the matter of presidential succession with Syria gone and the resistance-friendly President Lahoud's term expiring. Hezbollah had to find a new way to secure its place in Lebanese politics. November 23, 2007 came and went. President Lahoud gave a dark speech and left the palace in Baabda. A few hair-trigger reports sprouted on the internet claiming that Hezbollah had engineered a coup, but they proved unfounded. Lebanon limped on without a head of state. It didn't seem to matter. The prime minister and his cabinet would rule the country as a caretaker government with limited authority until a new president was chosen. The government had been paralyzed and ineffectual for more than a year, a sad reality unchanged by Lahoud's departure. The moment of truth had come and gone, with nothing revealed. Hezbollah had nothing to fear from a vacuum; its authority did not depend on a functioning state. The Party of God did best when the state did the least. It was the forces of moderation that needed a functioning government, a unifying and forceful state that could oppose Hezbollah's extremist adventurism. Hezbollah had let the deadline lapse, and hadn't ratcheted down its threatening posture one iota. Hezbollah wouldn't accept any of the March 14 presidential candidates, even the mild compromise choices that had been put forth, because all of them believed that Lebanese sovereignty required a state monopoly of force and foreign policy, which meant ultimately disbanding Hezbollah's militia and independent channels of statecraft. The hour for compromise had passed. Now the March 14 forces dared Hezbollah to impose its will on Lebanon. With the fruitless negotiations over, the Arab world would face a binary choice: the triumph of Western-oriented secularists, by perseverance and will—or domination by the ultra-religious Axis of Resistance, who would be exposed as brutal power grubbers, just as willing to use force against their Arab brothers as against their Jewish foes.

Hezbollah made its best effort in the court of public opinion to frame the issue another way, as a struggle between dignity and surrender. Nawaf

Mousawi, the party's chief of international relations, served as Hezbollah's de facto foreign minister. He met with Beirut-based diplomats, including lots of Europeans, and he was the official charged with back-channel communications to hostile or semi-hostile governments. I interviewed him in early December 2007, as Hezbollah's public relations offensive was in full swing. Mousawi over the years had earned a reputation as a smart strategist and suave diplomat. Since the war he'd become a bit unhinged, however, railing with bitter invective rather than the usual Hezbollah polished spin, and storming off the set of a popular Lebanese television show. A party member told me that during the war Mousawi had narrowly escaped death when an Israeli missile struck the SUV in which he was traveling; he jumped into a ditch just before the car exploded. Perhaps he had failed to heed Hezbollah's own advice, and was taking the war personally. When I met him at the international relations office, he was fiesty, less tactful than other senior Hezbollah officials. He mockingly referred to the March 14 coalition as "February 14," a reference to the date of Hariri's assassination. He derided the U.S. ambassador to Beirut for "meddling" in Lebanese politics, a charge that always struck me as disingenuous since every foreign power appeared to meddle as much as it could. "America has failed in its project to destroy Hezbollah," he said. "Now, the people who are betting with America think they can defeat us. They are misguided. Only a sick mind imagines that we can be sidelined."

Despite a few impolitic detours, the diplomat talked as diplomats do about Hezbollah's long-term interests, and it was fascinating to hear him speak with the confidence and vision of any Middle Eastern foreign minister, but with greater directness and a better grasp of his rivals' interests. Mousawi quickly catalogued the goals of Hezbollah's enemies: they wanted to destroy Hezbollah and its sister movement in the Palestinian territories, Hamas; they wanted to crush armed Palestinian factions and assure Israel's dominion; they wanted a weak, pro-American government in Iraq; they wanted an off-balance regime in Iran, weakened by the prospect, however dim, of an American strike; and they wanted to protect the Middle Eastern leaders who accommodated American or Israeli interests in the region. The enemy also had second-order priorities, he said, including the maintenance of a peace process that would engage Palestinian factions and Arab states without requiring any serious concessions from Israel.

All told, Mousawi's assessment of American and Israeli interests sounded quite on target. He proceeded to outline Hezbollah's response, in coordination with its allies in Tehran and Damascus. Hezbollah wanted a position in the Lebanese government that would force America and Israel to recognize that a group they legally had defined as terrorist now held elected and executive office in a supposedly moderate Arab country. The Party of God wanted to maintain tension and a viable military threat along Israel's northern border, and it wanted to increase Palestinian militants' capacity for war, governance, and mobilization. Regionally Hezbollah wanted to support its allies in Syria and Iran, in part by doing whatever it could to weaken the Accommodation leaders in Egypt, Saudi Arabia, Jordan, and the Palestinian Authority. Hezbollah could undermine those regimes through region-wide propaganda and by direct support to militant movements that opposed the pro-American Arab rulers. He referred to the double-edged sword of Hezbollah's dogma and pragma. "This project to destroy us has failed because of our capacity to stand and fight," he said. "Of course we owe everything to God, but that doesn't mean a lot to foreign leaders. Jesus Christ talked to George Bush and asked him to invade Iraq." In late 2007, an American or Israeli strike against Iran seemed imminent, and Hezbollah wanted it known that it might take part in a response—or as Mousawi put it, "the whole region will be engulfed in war. We won't have the choice. It will be one war." How, I asked, did Hezbollah plan to square its distinctly Shia religious pedigree with its desire to lead a regional movement against Israel? Mousawi thought Hezbollah could manage it through sheer fluidity. Hezbollah was a religious movement, a Shia one at that, and at the same time a resistance movement, rooted in Lebanese nationalism but defined more by its opposition to Israel than by fealty to any single Arab nation. "You can have your personal identity and your communal identity," Mousawi said. "One is private, the other national." So a Maronite Christian could serve as president of Lebanon but unequivocally support an opposition led by the Islamic Resistance. Mousawi saw no contradiction. "There have been nonsectarian parties in the Middle East before—the Communist Party, the Syrian Social Nationalist Party," he said. Hezbollah intended to follow in their tradition.

At the end of 2007, Hezbollah was confident it could win a showdown against the West and its proxies, convinced that the party's ideological support had reached at an all-time high. It was ready to redeem two decades of grassroots work indoctrinating and mobilizing constituents. The party's credo, at once pragmatic and blinding, had seeped into every corner of its community's life. Young loyalists believed Hezbollah was fighting a battle far more important than a dispute over land with the Jewish State. They were convinced that the Party of God was finishing the work begun thirteen centuries earlier by the Prophet Mohammed, fulfilling an apocalyptic Shia vision of Armageddon. Hezbollah had done much to popularize these cultish prophecies of doom, which turned out to carry great currency with the young. The end of history would come early in the twenty-first century, according to the Mahdists, and Hezbollah would lead the first wave of the final battle.

I had understood from the start that Hezbollah permeated every aspect of life in the areas under its control, but the more time I spent in that community the more impressive I found the party's attention to detail. On another visit to the Haidar family in Srifa, the father had invited me along to a ceremony at the town's main Husainiya, a Shia place of worship doubling as a community center. Hezbollah had invited all forty-seven students from Srifa who had passed the *brevet* or *baccalauréat* exams. The celebration lasted half an hour. Males sat on one side of the room, females on the other. All but two of the hundred-odd girls and women in the room wore headscarves, even the ones younger than eleven, the accepted age of *takleef,* the taking of the veil by pious girls. "God elevates those who educate themselves," the local Hezbollah head said. He quoted from what he said was an article published in the Israeli newspaper *Haaretz* in 1961; according to the passage quoted, better-educated Arabs would pose a greater military threat to Israel. "Resistance is not only through weapons, but also through education and thoughts," he said. Juice and cakes were distributed. At the close of his brief remarks, everyone went home. Hussein Haidar, the deputy high school principal and father of my friend Inaya, observed that in other countries the schools might organize an awards assembly to honor high-achieving students, but the Lebanese public system took little interest. Hezbollah, once again, filled a gap on such a mundane level, congratulating the students and putting forth its message at the same time. "In one hand, each student will hold a pen, and in the other hand, a rifle for the resistance," Hussein Haidar said.

The "Society of Resistance" soundtrack on the surface sounded two notes, the first about defending land from the Jews, the second about being a conscientious Muslim. But as I listened more carefully I began to hear undertones, a mystical bassline that drove a younger and more aggressive generation in Hezbollah. Back at Hussein's house on the edge of Srifa his daughter Aya—the one most dedicated to Hezbollah, and of all the people I met the one most eager to talk about the upcoming End of Days—wanted to tell me about the Mahdi.

"You know, when the Mahdi comes, his soldiers will be Christians," she said, almost babbling with excitement, her face flushed. "It is written that the Christians will be the first to recognize him."

The subject of the Mahdi got Aya more excited than anything else. When she talked about the Mahdi ("Do you know him?" she said with a serene smile) it reminded me of the born-again Christians around whom I grew up in the American South. Sometimes those teenage classmates of mine in North Carolina tried to proselytize, other times they were simply bursting with the Good News and had to share it; they would tell me about Jesus and the Rapture, how He was coming to save the world and how much they loved talking to Him. Aya, once she got going about the Mahdi, could stop only with great difficulty. Mahdi-talk also stripped away a lot of the finesse that informed Hezbollah political discourse. When the subject was regional politics, Aya, like most Hezbollah activists, carefully distinguished between the Israeli enemy and the Jews, a respected people of the book. When she rhapsodized about the advent of the Mahdi, though, she set aside such niceties, and made clear whose side the Jews were on: that of Dajjal, the false prophet who would battle the Mahdi upon his return.

"Israel already is funding an army in a secret place in the middle of Africa for Dajjal, the false Mahdi," she told me with perfect seriousness. "They are starting the army of the liar." She also mentioned a book hidden in a library in Germany full of revelations so shocking that "if the Jewish people learn them, they will kill themselves."

I had met many Middle Easterners who described contemporary conflicts as continuations of wars from the beginning of their religious history. Orthodox Jewish settlers often framed their disputes with the government of Israel in Old Testament terms, and secular Jewish politicians frequently did the same when discussing Palestinian or Iranian threats. Sunni Muslims in the Gulf and Iraq spoke of the heresy of Hussein as if it had happened yesterday, while the Shia locked in war with Sunni extremists in Iraq called their enemies "Yazids," after the seventh century caliph. So it wasn't unusual that the Shia in Lebanon viewed their recent history as an extension of Karbala and Qadisiyyah, one of the great early battles of Islam in the time of the Prophet. What was unusual was the bracing messianic, millenarian theology; they really thought the end of the world was nigh. Many of the younger Shia—bold, confident, unencumbered by the past compromises of their poorer parents—had embraced a form of Mahdism that expected the last imam to return to earth at any moment. Therefore preparations for the end of time for them took on special urgency—not the abstract imperative for self-improvement that judgment day imposes on all the religious, but a countdown clock ticking to zero in this generation. Aya and her peers, she believed, those who were serious about God, must prepare for the Shia version of Armageddon. Their belief reinforced the martyrdom cult of Hezbollah, as well as the Party of God's new, growing ambitions as it headed into 2008: confident it would force Israel to release prisoners, and that it would overwhelm the Jewish State next door and the secular forces in the Arab world. She was not alone. Messianic Mahdism flourished in Iran, Iraq, and all over Lebanon.

Aya had bought and studied an encyclopedia of Shia apocrypha.

"You Christians will be the first to accept the Mahdi, and you will fight in the first ring around him!" she said with delight, as if she breaking some happy news to me. "You could be with him!"

She had memorized the prophecies about the Mahdi's imminent return. He would come in 2020, during the month of Ramadan, she said. He would be thirty-three years old. The Angel Gabriel would announce the Mahdi's arrival. The leaders of his army would be waiting for him in an open camp, sleeping beneath the stars. There would be 313 lieutenants waiting to serve the Mahdi, 90 of them women. "I will be one of them," Aya said solemnly. Jesus Christ and others returned from the dead would fight at the Mahdi's side.

Most Muslims believe in the notion of an awaited prophet returning to earth at the indeterminate end of time. For the majority of Shia Muslims, that belief does not play a central role in their daily practice of their faith. The story of the Mahdi spoke to the profound yearning for justice and counseled patience and steady endeavor in the hope of improving the world. Those who espoused apocalyptic Mahdism found an entirely different set of imperatives in the narrative of the Mahdi's return. Prophecies that Aya had read convinced her that Israel would vanish by 2030 at the latest. She already was an extremely devout Muslim before she adopted Mahdism, and had studied the Koran since she first learned to read. When she turned eighteen and met her fiancé Selim, she embarked on another phase of her Islamic journey, and dived into Mahdist thought.

"To become a soldier in the Mahdi's Revolution you must have the morals of a modest and poor slave," she said. "The Mahdi needs soldiers, good ones, who really care about him, and always look for his news, and purely love him, and do their best to be in touch with him."

Aya prayed and communicated with the Mahdi, and attributed to his intervention happy developments in her life like her relationship with Selim, her fiancé. She also watched for divine signs of his return. One already had occurred, she told me: the discovery of the twelfth planet in our solar system, Nuberu. (The "last planet" appears all over the internet in doomsday scenarios of many religions, but has been debunked by astronomers.) Other signs were still pending, like the foretold death of a sixteen-year-old messenger of the Mahdi at the Kaaba in Mecca. When the planets aligned, she said, the sun would rise from the west and set in the east. "This is a big sign about the big day," she said. "Only God knows the exact date. Some people are not ready yet for the Mahdi, they are not pure."

In the tradition of Hezbollah, she was able to hedge even her most extreme views. Based on the signs, she rated a 70 percent chance that the Mahdi would appear in her lifetime. She accepted most of the prophecies as fact, but left wiggle room about the exact date, so she would be spared disappointment if 2020 passed without the Mahdi's return. She also didn't count on being around when the time came. She wanted to raise children who could recite the Koran, but she also said she'd like to be a martyr. "I have a lot of nervous energy," she said. "I am not a patient person."

In most ways, Aya came across like any gifted, vivacious, and ambitious woman in her early twenties. She took her work as a schoolteacher quite seriously, spinning creative ways to engage her elementary school students in lessons they disliked, such as math. Personally she was charming as well. She gleefully posted photos of the newly-crowned Miss USA Rima Fakih, who was born in Srifa. "Smart, cute, and definitely Lebanese!" Aya wrote on Facebook. She loved to paint, Hallmark pictures of trees whose leaves were changing colors, or veiled women in a harem. She listened to J. Lo, Shaggy, and Shakira. She made sappy computer slideshows of Selim and herself holding hands by the sea, set to romantic music. She was a Mahdist, a Hezbollah cadre, a schoolteacher fresh out of college, and a young girl in love, rolled into one bristling ball of energy.

Scholars have thoroughly documented the latest wave of Mahdism, a religious current that has ebbed and flowed for more than a millennium. Doomsday cults in Iraq and Iran have taken up arms in the last decade against their own Shiite clerics. Iran's President Mahmoud Ahmadinejad has made the Mahdi's return a motif in his speeches. Polemicists frequently evoke the Mahdist convictions of Ahmadinejad and of Hezbollah to argue that neither party can behave as a rational actor on the global stage. If Iran and the Lebanese Party of God were planning for the apocalypse, some argued, they might be willing to use nuclear weapons or otherwise fail to factor survival into their cost-benefit analysis.[80] I wasn't so sure. The Mahdists views of the end of the world certainly informed their approach to geopolitics, but I thought the connection wasn't so easy to parse; even a fanatically messianic Shia leader like Ahmadinejad responded to more than one factor when he decided whether, for example, to move ahead with nuclear weapon production or order an attack against Israel or the United states. Hezbollah represented a different school of thought than the suicidal cultists who attacked mainline Iraqi Shiites in 2007 and 2008.[81] They wanted to grow, expand, lead the entire Islamic world, and mold the militant world beyond Islam. They had a plethora of self-interests in addition to their imperative to pave the way for the Mahdi. Hezbollah's Mahdists, like Iran's, seemed comfortable planning for the future and for the end of the world at the same time, as if to say "You can't be too careful." In case the Mahdi was late, they said by their actions, there was no reason to burn one's possessions.

They also made a clever link between the here and now and the hereafter. The Mahdi needed a strong fighting force for his last stand, so the pious needed to amass martial skill and weapons. The Hidden Imam wouldn't solve all problems when he returned. His people would have to help him. On an individual psychological level, impassioned people like Aya, or many others I met who aspired to martyrdom (for themselves or their children), seemed capable of simultaneously embracing self-preservation and dooms-day prophecies. Aya wanted to fight at the front of the Mahdi's Army; she wanted another war with Israel sooner rather than later (why dread the inevitable, she argued); and found the idea of heroic martyrdom attractive. At the same time, she worked as a schoolteacher and was applying for ad-vanced degree programs, planning a career, and already strategizing about how she wanted to raise her kids. She and her fiancé were shopping for an apartment in the Dahieh. She was ready to die now, and ready to live a long life. Mahdism explained a lot, but not everything.

Out on the porch after sunset, the entire family assembled, savoring the breeze and the last view of the olive-studded hills before darkness fell. Conversation drifted from topic to topic. Aya's father thought the Mahdi would come in the distant future to redeem us all, not just the Muslims. Aya told me that Jews were conspiring to call Christmas "Xmas" in order to deny the existence of Christ. I told her that Xmas was just shorthand. "You think so, but you're wrong," she chortled. Saddam Hussein, every-one in the family agreed, had been an American pawn, created to advance Washington's interests in the Middle East and discarded when he no longer served them. Bin Laden, the father said, could have been captured by now, except the United States wanted to leave him at large to retain an excuse for the war on terror. Everything kept circling back to Israel and the Islamic world's war against it.

"Jerusalem should be for the Palestinians," Inaya said.

Her father corrected her: "Jerusalem should be for everybody. For all the world."

At the annual Jerusalem Day rally in October 2007 a capacity crowd filled the Princes of the Martyrs Complex in Dahieh. Rowdy young men who couldn't get in to watch Nasrallah's speech on the monitor packed the street outside and listened over loudspeakers. Some of the teenagers I met there were secular Shia, and some were Christian supporters of the Islamic Re-sistance. Many smelled like they'd been drinking beer. "Israel must go! We must wipe out Israel! Not the Jews, mind you, just Israel," one of them told me. I asked another man, a nineteen-year-old college student named Tarek Ibrahim, whose mother was Christian and father Shia, why the Lebanese should stake their lives on the Palestinian struggle. "Everyone must fight Israel. Jerusalem is not only for the Jews. It is for all religions," he said. "If we don't liberate Al Quds, who will?"

The confrontational tone found its echo across town among young pro-government Christians, who sounded awfully similar to Hezbollah except that their movements were too weak to make good on their threats of violence. Activists from the Christian Phalange party mourned their recently slain leader Antoine Ghanem at a rally at Saint Joseph University in Ashrafieh. Recent Christian rallies had turned into riots, so the army was out in full force. "The martyrs are with us!" thundered Zyad Raheb, a twenty-two-year-old student leader. "The Christians of Lebanon have been here for thousands of years. We won't disappear from this earth today." Zyad and his fellow Phalange members had been handing out Xeroxed fliers to their fellow students, including a sizable contingent of Aounists who supported Hezbollah. "Don't bet on us to stay calm," the bold print announced. "This is the age of confrontation, and we are ready." Hezbollah presented the current historical moment to its followers as a do-or-die turning point for the Islamic Resistance; using the same rhetoric about martyrdom and war, its rivals claimed a similar historical wave was poised to wipe Christendom from the Middle East. This overheated and cataclysmic framing only illustrated the weakness of the Christians. The regional axis led by Hezbollah, Iran, and Syria had no intention of wiping out the already marginalized and submissive Christian minority—but the zealous rhetoric of the anti-Hezbollah forces helped mobilize Hezbollah's base. It also allowed Hezbollah to justify its relatively new willingness to entertain the use of force against fellow Arabs.

Apparently Nasrallah's metaphor for annihilating Israel by sheer numbers and persistence—his aphorism that if every Arab marched to the border with a bucket of water and simply poured, they could wash Israel into the sea—had seized the popular imagination. Everywhere it was echoed: *What could Israel do if every Arab carried one stone to the border and threw it?* or *If a million Arabs gathered at the fence and started walking south, the Israelis couldn't kill them all.* To those not caught in the wave, it seemed incredibly delusional. Hezbollah was drinking its own Kool-Aid. As the Axis of Resistance saw it, Israel was hunkering down behind a barrier while the American occupiers in Iraq and Afghanistan were hiding behind blast walls. A European diplomat who had spent more than a decade working closely with Hezbollah and its constituents was aghast at the blossoming loss of touch with reality in its ranks. "The crazy thing, the dangerous thing, is that they really seem to have started believing their own rhetoric. They think they can defeat Israel!" he told me. "They're forgetting that if they attack Israel, they'll have reversed the roles. Israelis will defend their own homes with the same ferocity as Hezbollah, and with one of the most advanced armies in the world."

Why not? Hezbollah supporters kept asking me. *The world order has flipped time and again throughout history.* I replied that no one could predict what will follow over the next century, but the current power map was fairly clearly drawn. Old empires could collapse, new ones could rise up. The world could find alternate energy sources, quit oil and stop caring about the Middle East. America could collapse and Israel would have to make new strategic partnerships. However, none of those events appeared imminent or plausible, certainly not for generations to come, which meant that the Israeli-American alliance would remain the Goliath in the Middle East. Israel, a Jewish state, was unlikely under any scenario to commit demographic suicide by admitting the millions of Palestinian refugees and their descendants into its borders, even if its government agreed it was theoretically the right thing to do. Why choose, I asked them, a struggle sure to destabilize your world and unlikely to achieve a single one of your goals? The short answer was, they thought they could win sooner or later, by man's clock or by God's, and they were ready to extend the battle against their fellow Muslims and Arabs within Lebanon to protect the homeland of the resistance.

In response to the campaign of ideological mobilization some Hezbollah supporters were hardening without even realizing why. Ideas and phrases were diffusing into their subconscious, something much more profound and complex than simple propaganda regurgitation. Hezbollah had strung its ideological sound boards, and could soothe or agitate its followers without their having any sense they were being played by anyone at all. Some of the people I knew found themselves freshly angry, outraged at Israel and Amer-

ica and their stooges in the Arab world who would throw nails in the path of
the Islamic Resistance. Dergham—the one-time Atlanta drug dealer—was
the first big surprise. He had remarried, to a Lebanese woman, and his new
wife had given birth to a son, Ibrahim, at the beginning of 2007. The sex
club where his best friend worked had gone out of business and money
was tight. With less hell-raising on the agenda, Dergham spent his days
roaming the Dahieh, hanging out with "the boys," as he called anyone in
possession of street power. He had bought a motorcycle, but couldn't afford
furniture for his apartment beyond a couch and a bed. His wife still wore
her hair uncovered, a shiny mass of beautiful black ringlets, and Dergham
still drank, although not at home. He was still proud of his machine gun,
and showed it to me every time I visited. We went on reporting trips to the
Beqaa, where he was far more at ease with his old drug dealer friends than
with his relatives in Hezbollah to whom he introduced me. With the drug
dealers he lay back and joked about old times. With the Hezbollah fighters
he was stiff and unsmiling, like a job candidate at an office party. But he had
stopped identifying as an outsider and now spoke of Hezbollah's struggles as
his own. Around the neighborhood Dergham had taken to wearing martial
outfits—black pants, canvas shirts or Special Forces sweaters, little canvas
caps. In the twilight he looked like a paramilitary operative, which I guess
was the point. And he had stopped making jokes about religion.

"Hezbollah, that was a new thing for me. At first it made me mad the
way Hezbollah owned the neighborhood," he said, wistfully. "You're not
free to do whatever you want to. But then I got used to it. Now I'm a supporter. It took me a while to see what's going on."

What *was* going on, I asked? The answer was that Hezbollah had given
him a way to make sense of his divided life.

"I have a lot of hate today for the United States, not for the people, but
for the state and the government. I had a lot of time to think about what
happened. And I thought, how crazy an idea it is to divide a family." He
shook his head sadly. "Such a ruthless people, such ruthless laws to do such
a thing. That's what made me a supporter of Hezbollah today. I would not
go back to that society"—he meant America—"even if they let me go back."

I reminded Dergham that he had run afoul of American drug laws, not
its Middle East policy. His wife and son lived far away in Atlanta because
she had tried life in the Dahieh and couldn't stand it. He had chosen not to

try to go back home with her. Dergham had a new narrative though, and it was ideological and geopolitical. He found it less confusing and disappointing than his old story about personal choices.

"I realized how ruthless those people are," he repeated. "I didn't feel it so strongly before the war in 2006. Any party that can hurt the USA, I support. I never thought of it that way before. I was like the other Americans. I never thought the system is built to keep you from having time to think."

Dergham was his same old self, but he had a bit of the zeal of the newly pledged conspiracy nut: he had just learned the secret, and now everything made sense. He said that he had filled out a membership application to formally join Hezbollah, but hadn't submitted it because he wasn't quite ready to give up alcohol. But he was working out and keeping his shooting skills sharp.

"I want to fight the Israelis. I feel like fighting them next time. They're our strict enemy," he said, predicting another war in a matter of years. "It wouldn't be too nice for all the guys in the neighborhood to go down to fight the Israelis, while I'm sitting at home drinking tea like a coward."

I reminded Dergham of a trip we'd taken to the border a year earlier. Driving through the gilded valley between Khiam and Metullah, he had pointed at the Israeli settlement a few hundred yards away and laughed. "It's the same shit over there and the same shit over here, except that over there you can make more money," he had said back then. "If there wasn't an electric fence, everyone in Lebanon would be looking for jobs in Israel right now."

He remembered the drive, but not the thought he had expressed. That part of the loop had been recorded over. He had been warmly welcomed into Hezbollah's big tent, and the party acted like it needed him. They didn't care about his past. Being wanted by an entity as powerful and organized as Hezbollah eventually leveled any objection Dergham had to the Party of God, including a fundamental disconnect on the level of faith: Dergham didn't believe in God. He was coming to terms with that as well. I wouldn't be surprised to find him some years down the road praying and extolling the abstemious life.

"They're my friends. We fought together. They know who I am and what I did in America," he said. "They know I support them. So there's no problem."

* * *

I had written a story in December 2006 about Rani Bazzi and his family for *The Boston Globe* after learning of his death and meeting his widow. I always found it stressful to write with humanity about reviled characters. Rani and his family were more complex than the caricature of Hezbollah, but some of their beliefs were repugnant to me and most of my readers. I wanted to be truthful and accurate about his fanaticism and militancy, and at the same time to make sure that people far removed from the distorted realities of the Middle East would grasp Rani's duality—that he held kind as well as murderous views, that his psychology didn't come from a different planet. I wanted to show him as a complex human being. It was a tough balancing act no less with my editors than with the public. I'd already received hate mail for earlier articles ("During World War II would you have written about what the Nazis thought?"), because many readers thought that by explaining the motivations of a Hezbollah fighter I was endorsing his views. "In unguarded moments, Rani Ahmed Bazzi openly expressed his fear of death," I had written. "On a battlefield in southern Lebanon, in the middle of last summer's month long war between Hezbollah and Israel, he broke down weeping as he spoke with a pair of reporters: 'I'm afraid to die,' he sobbed." In my view, his words exposed the vulnerable side of a religious extremist.

Rani had wept while talking about the strain of a decade fighting the Israelis. From my scrawled notes and from memory I had reconstructed Rani's quote, typing it into a rough file on my computer. It didn't seem remarkable to me at the time, just another facet of the man's multilayered persona. Wouldn't it make sense for a man driven to martyrdom occasionally to know moments of apprehension? I'd spoken to other fighters who had allowed themselves glimpses of fear before combat; it didn't make them less courageous when they faced death. I had expected that Hezbollah would be pleased that I had written about a man they considered a hero, but I heard no immediate reaction from Lebanon. Readers in America responded with a mix of empathy and indignation. Most saw it as a portrait of a fanatic, perhaps illuminating in some respects, but more or less playing to type.

In October 2007, almost one year after the story was published, I tried to get back in touch with Farah. I wanted to learn more about Rani, so I also asked Hezbollah for permission to meet with the Martyrs Foundation. To my surprise, I found out that Hezbollah was furious at the story which had circulated from *The Boston Globe* to some Lebanese websites. "The Martyrs Foundation will never talk to him," a press official told my colleague and sometimes translator Hwaida. "There is too much anger about his story."

Fury was too mild a word to describe Farah Bazzi's reaction when Hwaida finally reached her. Farah wouldn't take her calls, so Hwaida finally used a borrowed phone so Farah wouldn't recognize the number.

"I don't want to hear about Thanassi. I don't want to see his face. I don't want to talk to him. Please understand, it's nothing personal against you," she told Hwaida. "He thinks he can make fun of us. He thinks we don't understand the words behind the words. He made fun of Rani. He made him look weak in his story. He doesn't understand what this martyrdom means for us."

Hwaida probed Hezbollah until they explained the problem: it was the "afraid to die" quote. Such doubts were anathema to Hezbollah's culture. At first I bristled; so what if Hezbollah didn't like what Rani had said? They were trying to blame me for something they didn't like about themselves, I believed. I wrote Farah a letter in which I explained that I had meant no disrespect to her husband, but only to make him and his cause comprehensible to my American audience. Hwaida tried to deliver the letter to Farah; she refused it. She tried to read it to her over the phone, but Farah cut her off. "If you want to be my friend, feel free to call me," she said to Hwaida. "But never again approach me as a journalist."

I didn't travel with my old notebooks, so I couldn't check the record. Long after I returned to New York—more than two years after the original story was published—I went back to my notes, and typed them out carefully, relying not on memory but on what was in my notebook. It turned out that in my haste and nervousness I had made a mistake—one that wouldn't matter to my American readers but infuriated Rani's family and Hezbollah. I had gotten it wrong. Rani had said that sometimes he felt afraid that he had angered God and would thus be denied martyrdom— exactly the opposite of what I'd reported. Rani Bazzi had been afraid of *not* getting killed. He hadn't been afraid of dying. "Sometimes I'm afraid I won't die," he had actually said. Slowly I grasped the unintended insult I had levied at Rani Bazzi. I hadn't yet understood him or Hezbollah's community when I wrote the story. If I had, the erroneous quote would have raised a flag for me. All of Rani's other idiosyncrasies were consistent with his life in Hezbollah. Talking about fearing death was not.

I was not going to learn how Farah Bazzi and her children had adapted to the new political order, and what choices they were making in their public lives as a martyr's family. Hezbollah wasn't interested in hearing my apology. Rani Bazzi already was public property, his death a thread in the party's martyrdom tapestry. Farah had been reabsorbed into the community and was surely more active than ever. For all I know, my *Globe* article had been folded into the mythology, a scurrilous attack by another foreigner eager to smear a Hezbollah hero.

Hezbollah's hardball, as far as the outside world was concerned, had veered into arrogance. Some Arab liberals had always considered Hezbollah a domineering totalitarian group, but by and large Hezbollah had succeeded in packaging itself to the Arab world as the small and plucky band of warriors standing up to Israel when no one else could. During the winter of 2007–2008, the March 14 parties were willing to negotiate. They wanted a president who would support prosecuting Rafik Hariri's killers, and who would steer Lebanon away from dependence on Tehran and Damascus. Their base believed that the Middle East suffered when its governments cast their lots with a single foreign patron, and that a comparatively independent republic that had relations with both West and East, Axis of Resistance and Axis of Accommodation, had a better chance at security and prosperity. Meanwhile, the Party of God was using all the tools in its arsenal to stoke the anger of its base. It had accused the elected officials in the March 14 coalition of insulting the honor of the Islamic Resistance, of doing the bidding of Israel and the United States, of stoking sectarian division instead of unity and pride. It had promised there would be no compromise.

The urbane Christians and Sunni Muslims hoped that once Hezbollah ordered its supporters in the streets to raise their fists against fellow Arabs, the support cables holding up the Society of Resistance would snap. They thought Hezbollah would lose the moral authority with which it had kept in line its millions of fans, from the willing like the Bazzis and the Haidars, to the ambivalent like Dergham and the mokhtar of Borj Qalaouay, to the skeptics. Hezbollah's partisans were true believers. The question was, when the time came to join battle in the streets against fellow Lebanese, how many Hezbollah sympathizers would be ashamed to fight for a party that claimed to champion the underdog but behaved more and more like a despot?

6

Hezbollah Rising

Two years of jockeying and tension finally exploded in a few days in May 2008. The standoff in downtown Beirut had proved little—only that Hezbollah was willing to use some force and that neither faction would back down quickly. In the boys-circling-each-other-on-the-playground phase, Hezbollah and March 14 had established they could act tough. They had clarified their core differences as well, to a point that the choice between them felt starker than ever, more replete with consequences beyond little Lebanon. The March 14 movement had come to represent a threatened breed of Middle Eastern moderation—deeply flawed but committed to the secular institutions of a national state, open to the West as well as to the Islamic world. They were by no means pro-Israeli or pro-American, but they advocated progressive pluralism and had mostly moved beyond armed militancy. They wanted good relations with Washington. They wanted to resolve the war with Israel that began in 1948 and officially never ended. They wanted to preserve a diverse Lebanon, which despite some appalling institutions had provided a lone beacon of coexistence and power sharing in the region. Lebanon's experience had been ambiguous, and during the civil war, bloody, but in the absence of more successful experiments Lebanon had been held up as a model in contexts as far afield as Iraq and Afghanistan. Lebanon's dysfunctional comity offered an alternative to the dozens of violent cleavages around the Middle East, a meek starting point to quiet the squabbling Israelis and Palestinians, Kurds and Arabs, Iraqi Shia and Sunni, and so many others. In contrast, Hezbollah had staked itself and the entire Arab and Muslim world on a narrative of redemption through conflict. The Middle East would regain its destiny and vitality only by defeating Israel in a direct and decisive war, which might take decades, but was the only acceptable path forward. In that narrative, malignant forces wanted to disarm Hezbollah, in merely one twist in a long war between the forces of global tyranny and the Islamic Resistance. Anyone who stood against Hezbollah or its militia was, in the words of Nasrallah, just another agent of the Jews and the Americans, of Tel Aviv and Washington. Self-consciously, Hezbollah linked its crusade with all the militants who preferred confrontation to negotiation; they were joined not only to the states of Iran and Syria, but to the suicide bombers in the Palestinian Islamic Jihad and the rocket launchers in Hamas, to the Iraqis who fought the Americans, and to a panoply of groups small and large that considered moderation and dialogue an abomination in international politics. With the lines so clearly drawn, there was little room for a negotiated settlement between Hezbollah and the moderates until the sides met in a test of strength and one of them failed. Only then would they back down from their irreconcilable claims.

Walid Jumblatt finally pushed the standoff to its climax. His telecommunications minister had been grumbling for long enough about Hezbollah's secret phone and fiber-optic system. Finally Jumblatt convinced the government to declare it illegal and shut it down. He also exposed one of the many ways that Hezbollah exerted its grip over Lebanon; the Party of God had its own spy network at the country's only airport, replete with runway cameras that allowed Hezbollah intelligence to watch all comings and goings. The brigadier general in charge of airport security was understood to be loyal to Hezbollah rather than to the national army (a common predicament in Lebanon, where the military was the most functional national institution but constantly threatened to split along political or sectarian lines). Jumblatt convinced the government to dismiss him. It was the first time that the March 14 alliance—which after all controlled the government and had won an electoral majority—was acting like it had real power. Finally the Lebanese government was taking action to curtail the Hezbollah behemoth. The party had presented itself for too long as a force of nature. After years of jawing around "tables of national dialogue," March 14 had found its oats.

Nasrallah made his calculations and decided what he was willing to give up: not his army's independence, but instead, Hezbollah's hitherto unsullied record on Arab unity. Until May 2008, Hezbollah had never taken up arms against Arab or Muslim rivals, only against the Israelis—at least that's how most Lebanese and Middle Easterners felt.[82] Now that a democratically elected, pluralistic government, backed by Washington and Saudi Arabia, had moved against Hezbollah's militia, the Party of God had only two options: relent, and begin to dismantle its machinery of war, or else turn its guns against its fellow Arabs. For Nasrallah it appeared to be an easy choice. Hezbollah would go to war against the moderates. Once it came down to a raw test of military power, Hezbollah would almost certainly win. Jumblatt hoped that Hezbollah would be loath to send its men into the streets against the government. To his surprise, Hezbollah proved him wrong.

On the back of an already scheduled national labor strike, Hezbollah ordered its fighters to deploy. Cleverly, the Party of God put allied militias at the front while its own better equipped and disciplined fighters supervised the assault from the margins. Unruly thugs from the Amal Movement and the Syrian Social Nationalist Party rampaged through West Beirut. They cut off the road to the airport. They shut down the television stations and newspapers of Hariri's Future Movement, and surrounded the palatial homes of Walid Jumblatt and Saad Hariri. At a press conference on May 8, Nasrallah insisted that Hezbollah was acting in self-defense; the government was doing the bidding of the Jews and the Americans, trying to compromise the command-and-control system of the Islamic Resistance. "We have entered a new stage," Nasrallah said. "If you insist on war, then our reactions will be unpredictable. Make your calculations as you wish. There is no problem." Supporters of the Axis of Accommodation believed justice was on their side, but they feared that when it came to a street fight, the moderates would fare poorly against a militant party that had founded itself and organized every activity for decades around mobilizing for war. For its part, Hezbollah was applying to its kinsmen the same rhetoric that for years it had reserved for its fight against "the other," Israel.

For two days, on May 8 and 9, Lebanon teetered on the precipice of massive bloodshed. The fighters stayed out of Christian areas. In the mixed Muslim neighborhoods families invoked the habits of the civil war, pulling mattresses into stairwells, shutting the windows, stocking up on canned food and bottled water. "The difference is, with the Israelis you know how they're going to behave in a war," Inaya said. "In this kind of war you don't know what might happen." Inaya wanted to be on duty when war broke out because she felt it her calling, just as she had during the 2006 war. She rushed to her post at the hospital. In a fratricidal war everyone was at risk. Those who had forgotten Lebanon's civil war had seen the more recent footage from Iraq's. Snipers shot civilians through their apartment windows for fun. If full-fledged war broke out, checkpoint commanders could execute a carful of passersby on a whim. Shells and rockets could easily go astray in the narrow city streets.

The brief but vitriolic days of fighting in May 2008 were more a probe than a full clash. Both sides wanted to test the ability and resolve of the other, without throttling up to the maximum. In Beirut only a few dozen people were killed, many of them bystanders and neighborhood boys caught in the crossfire rather than fighters. The calculus of force nonetheless quickly became apparent. Everywhere in the capital that Hezbollah's forces encountered resistance it was crushed within hours. They silenced the media of the pro-government parties, and ran roughshod over their amateurish militias—and pointedly, they did so without using their elite assets. The brutish and clumsy fighters from Amal and the SSNP had the reputation of street hooligans. They were the ones who trampled through West Beirut firing aimlessly into the air, defacing posters, and spray-painting the walls. Only after the low-rent thugs had pacified the pro-government areas did Hezbollah fighters in full battle dress make a show of marching through the subjugated areas: through and *out*. They didn't want a full civil war if it could be avoided, and they didn't want the headache of occupying hostile urban areas. They humiliated the pro-government forces, but they didn't stay in the routed neighborhoods. They left them for the national military to secure.

In the Chouf Mountains, however, Druze fighters momentarily set aside their political differences and lined up against Hezbollah, giving the party's militia its stiffest resistance. Druze fighters ambushed a Hezbollah convoy and fought through the night. A dozen or more on either side were killed. Druze fighters kidnapped and tortured a Hezbollah detail in retribution for the killing of one of their own. Jumblatt knew that his people couldn't withstand the full brunt of Hezbollah's force were the fight to spiral out of control, but for one day the Druze had shown they were able to compete with Hezbollah in the sweepstakes of brute violence, even if they couldn't tip the balance.

A few days of fighting and fewer than one hundred dead sufficed for the players in the great tournament to know the winner. Hezbollah had shown to everyone's satisfaction that it would win a contest of strength. Its fighters also had shown themselves ready to use force and escalate quickly. Everyone had been playing chess, but Hezbollah had come also prepared to box. Jumblatt and his allies in the government relented. They reinstated the pro-Hezbollah security chief at the airport, and they withdrew the order to shut down the communications system. They agreed to enter negotiations with Hezbollah and the rest of the opposition. In five days of talks in the Persian Gulf emirate of Qatar, they caved to all of Hezbollah's main demands. They would stop trying to disarm the Party of God. They would give Hezbollah veto power in a reconstituted cabinet. They would agree to a president acceptable to the Axis of Resistance: General Michel Suleiman, a career officer with a historic fondness for the Islamic Resistance, originally installed in his post in 1998 when Syria still directly controlled Lebanon. In exchange, Hezbollah would disband the tent camp in downtown Beirut. Hezbollah and March 14 agreed on some minor procedural changes to allow parliamentary elections in the summer of 2009. Hezbollah proposed a major democratic overhaul of Lebanon's electoral system: lower the voting age to eighteen, and award seats in Parliament based on proportional representation. The idea was roundly ignored, since everyone assumed that Hezbollah, with the greatest bloc by far of voters, would dominate a revamped system.

Dergham spent the days of the May fighting whizzing around the city on his motorbike. The action was hard to cover. In the few spots where there really was heavy fighting it was too dangerous to walk around and find the small units of men firing grenades and bullets at each other. Still, Dergham found the whole affair grounds for celebration. "The government is acting like traitors. The resistance needed to do this," he said. He added with a trace of disappointment that Hezbollah had restrained its fighters in the interest of making its point with minimal casualties. "Hezbollah didn't want any bloodshed. They ordered the boys to take it easy," he said. "Otherwise they would have killed five thousand people. Hezbollah could kill five thousand Sunni and Druze in one day. You cannot call what happened a real confrontation."

Walid Jumblatt went on television and asked his supporters to give up their doomed battle. At the start of the week he had blustered about crushing Hezbollah's paramilitary state once and for all. By the weekend he was scurrying to arrange a ceasefire in the mountains before more of his fighters were killed, and his emissaries told Hezbollah he was willing to negotiate everything. So what if Hariri announced on TV that "men like Saad Hariri and Walid Jumblatt don't negotiate at gunpoint"? Jumblatt had played the only card he had. It was a weak card, and the moderate axis had lost. Over a glass of vodka on the rocks at Mokhtara, after it was all over, he said things might have turned out differently if the United States had been willing to back the liberal forces as wholeheartedly as Iran backed Hezbollah. I asked him in January 2009 what he had been thinking when he went after the telecommunications network and the airport security chief. He threw his hands up in the air and rolled his eyes, as if I were asking him about someone else, some wacky and enigmatic character. His wife turned to him and repeated my question: "Yes Walid, I'm curious too. What *were* you thinking?" He mugged a bit, gave a goofy smile, and still didn't answer. "Did you think you might actually prevail against Hezbollah?" I pushed. "Or did you think that if you provoked them to use force, they would be exposed as power hungry and lose their public support?" "Maybe," he said. "I don't remember now what I was thinking." That was the closest I discovered to a March 14 strategy, the last best hope to stop the juggernaut of the Axis of Resistance from writing the lexicon of the New Middle East: a sort of damned-if-I-didn't-try resignation.

For the families of the dead, May 2008 was another civil war, small perhaps but tragic. For the rest of the country and the Arab world, it was a turning point. Of all the divisions that sundered the Middle East, Hezbollah had succeeded at polarizing the entire region around the most radical and ideological question: militancy versus moderation, or as the actors themselves framed it, resistance versus accommodation. This formulation was especially dangerous because it subsumed and advanced existing enmities (between Arabs and Jews, between religious and secular, between

Middle-East-firsters and pro-Western internationalists) while breeding a whole new set of animosities. The opportunistic and militant ideology of resistance allowed for a string of wars against a rotating cast of enemies. The "honorable resistance" could be as aggressive, totalitarian, and indifferent to the rule of law and the laws of war as it liked, all the while invoking the right of self-defense as it joined battle now against Israel, now against American interests, now against Lebanese democrats and now against Arab warlords, now against liberal modernizers and now against Jews.

Hezbollah had passed its teenage phase of rejectionist rebellion and entered a warrior adulthood. It was no longer a tiny clandestine terrorist group determined to win notoriety and awaken the Islamic masses to the cleansing power of violence. The party had outgrown the strident voice of its early manifestoes. Now it was a modern entity of its own, indistinguishable from a nation-state except for formal recognition, easily wealthier, stronger, and more viable than a dozen runt members of the United Nations. The negotiations at Doha featured a series of backroom deals reluctantly reached by Lebanese warlords in constant contact with their Iranian, Syrian, French, or Saudi patrons. But the image everyone would remember from May wasn't the press conference in Doha. It was the picture of uniformed Hezbollah commandos sweeping Hamra Street after the fighting, strutting past the Starbucks and Crowne Plaza with their shiny gear and machine guns. They were in their element if off their turf, completely relaxed; taking Beirut had been easier than fifteen minutes of a war with Israel. In a week, Hezbollah had dispensed with the fiction of the Lebanese government, and it had made clear once and for all the Middle East's new dynamic. The Axis of Resistance was on top.

Samir Quntar already had heard the news on Al Jazeera in July 2008 when his irritable jailers told him he was going home. The prisoner too evil to trade, the Druze fighter with the Tom Selleck mustache who had become the face of soulless Jew-hating child-killing terrorism, was being handed his freedom three decades after his waterborne invasion of Nahariya. Samir Quntar had grown plump and well-spoken in Israel's prisons. He'd obtained a bachelor's degree, married and divorced, mastered the ins and outs of Palestinian factionalism and the new order that had shaped up in the

Middle East after the cold war. He had shed the vocabulary of Marxism and picked up the lingo of Islamic Resistance. For years he had repeated to his captors that he would not grow old in prison, a bit of bravado that eventually came true.

To Israel's great distaste, the foe it had sought to eliminate in 2006 had by 2008 established its supremacy in the only bordering country still engaged in a hot war with the Jewish state. Syria was still technically at war with Israel, but had avoided any direct contact with Israeli forces since the 1973 Yom Kippur war. Other than the threat from Lebanon, in its immediate neighborhood Israel only faced concerted military harassment from Palestinian factions. Palestinian rockets distressed Israelis, and Israel's retaliatory attacks horrified much of the world, but neither tactic hurt Israel strategically. These were murderous nuisances, not existential threats. Israel had pushed for decades to secure its northern border through an amicable government in Beirut. Its interventions instead had midwifed the opposite outcome. Hezbollah had become the government. Before, Hezbollah had agitated outside the institutions of state, affecting but never controlling the levers of government. Two years after Israel had failed to destroy the party's infrastructure, Hezbollah had made a deal through which it gained control of one-third of Lebanon's ministries, and approved a president who believed in Hezbollah's right to bear arms. And so with great distress, Israel continued the back-channel negotiations to seek the return of its missing soldiers even though its adversary was growing bolder and more aggressive. In the end it made an unpalatable deal with Hezbollah, negotiated by German diplomats and the good offices of the United Nations. The soldiers, Ehud Goldwasser and Eldad Regev, would be returned to Israel. Hezbollah would also tell Israel whatever it knew about the fate of Ron Arad, a navigator who disappeared in 1986 when his plane was shot down over Lebanon. In return, Israel would release Samir Quntar and four other Hezbollah fighters, along with the remains of nearly two hundred others; it also promised to release Palestinian captives after the conclusion of the main deal. Israel valued the return of its captured soldiers enough to pay a ghastly price.

On a sweaty humid Wednesday morning, thousands thronged at the border to welcome Samir Quntar, where he would first cross onto Lebanese territory; even more people waited at the Beirut Airport, where he would fly by helicopter from the border, and at Hezbollah's rally grounds in the Da-hieh. In Israel he had come to symbolize the most heartless face of terrorism, so his release represented an all the more humiliating defeat for the Jewish State, and sent thrills through the supporters of the Axis of Resistance. Even many Lebanese who kept their distance from Hezbollah admired this "victory," and were willing to forgive many things, including the internecine violence of May, because of Quntar's release. Tellingly, they accepted Quntar's own version of events, that despite his conviction for murdering the two girls and their father, he had in fact been framed by the same Israelis whose crossfire had killed Danny and Einat Haran. Many Hezbollah supporters had no regard for the laws of war; they believed the party had been wise and disciplined to reduce attacks on civilian targets and to suspend suicide bombings. But these were only tactical decisions. As a matter of policy and ideology, supporters of Hezbollah described Israel as a "militarized state" in which everyone was a legitimate target. Even with that distorted worldview, Samir Quntar's acts appeared odious, so he could only achieve heroic status if his story was rewritten, and the burden of child killing placed on lying Israelis rather than on an amoral and fanatic militant.

On July 16, 2008 Hezbollah's victory in Operation Truthful Promise was finally at hand. The Party of God had smashed the moderate Arabs who wanted a tamer, more cooperative polity; now it had an opportunity to sucker-punch Israel. A banner in English hung at the border: "Pain in Israel, Joy in Lebanon." Like most of the day's proceedings, it was a carefully designed piece of stagecraft, directed at Israel and the West. Hezbollah wanted the world to know just how many people lauded Samir Quntar; they knew the headlines would read "Child killer gets hero's welcome," and they wanted their enemies to see the multitudes willing to fete Israel's terrorist as a freedom fighter. Hezbollah delivered the captured Israeli soldiers in a black SUV to the border crossing at Naqoura, on a high bluff overlooking the Mediterranean. Ehud Goldwasser and Eldad Regev were in coffins, long dead. Samir Quntar, meanwhile, changed into a military uniform and mounted a white horse, which he rode into the ululating crowd. The people of Lebanon were rapt. Here in one easy-to-grasp image was their victory: Hezbollah had forced Israel to do the unthinkable.

Inaya and her family in Srifa spread a massive feast. They had two reasons to celebrate: Quntar's release and the return on the same day of her brother Ali for a rare visit from the Ukraine. For the Haidar family, the prisoner release didn't signify the end of war with Israel, but it concluded a cycle that began in 2000. After the withdrawal of the Israelis from South Lebanon, the spirit and doctrine of the Islamic Resistance had been in flux. The Party of God had dallied in politics, dialogue, pragmatism, even the prospect of limiting its martial aims. Some people wondered how resistance could continue in the absence of an occupation. Finally, though, Hezbollah had opted to stay true to its core: all-or-nothing Islamist ideology, perpetual motion through perpetual war. The first round had taken nearly a decade and had involved almost every government and nonstate actor with a finger in the Middle East: Saudi Arabia, Syria, Iran, Israel, the United States, the United Kingdom, and France, among others. Hezbollah had provoked a war with Israel, and another with the Lebanese government. It had antagonized all its rivals, branded as traitors those who questioned its motives and methods. Through cunning and brute force it had staved off the attempts of powerful and organized states to corral its militancy. And that long round had concluded on one summer day with a carnival for Samir Quntar: a single day that distilled nothing about the man Quntar but everything about the movement that had adopted him and could now use him to bring its enemies' morale to heel. "The July War was finally over," Inaya said. "I felt proud and happy."

Dergham chanted slogans with the crowd at Naqoura when Quntar came through on the horse. The doughy convicted-murderer-turned-resistance-totem looked like an accidental hero—a stunned smile pasted on his face, his eyes bulging, cheeks bloated, and body popping out of the uniform into which it had been stuffed. The crowds went wild, but the man they were really cheering was Nasrallah, who had sworn to win the prisoners' release from Israel and had managed to keep his word. "This man was a hopeless case. He was never supposed to leave prison," Dergham said. "It seemed like God sent an angel to release this man." The angel, in his mind, was Nasrallah. The reception at the border crossing was designed to enrage Israel and the West. The next episode in the spectacle of Hezbollah's coronation, a welcome ceremony at the airport, was designed to humiliate the Arabs who had resisted Hezbollah's march to power. The entire Lebanese political class was obliged to show up. Samir Quntar's release was going to become a national holiday. No one dared express anything but admiration for the man and astonishment at the steadfastness that had sprung him from the Jewish jail. Walid Jumblatt, Saad Hariri, and members of their coalition who had spent much of their lives fighting the influence of Hezbollah's Syrian backers swallowed their pride and lined up behind their new president—another imposition from Hezbollah—to greet Samir Quntar at Beirut International Airport as if he were the most notable dignitary ever to set foot in Lebanon. Walid Jumblatt's hair wilted in the heat and sweat poured down his brow. He fidgeted and glanced everywhere but the rostrum; he'd probably have looked happier at his own funeral. "Your return is a new victory," the president declared, addressing Quntar and the other prisoners, while the dignitaries on stage squirmed miserably. "With you, the future will only be a bright path through which we will achieve the sovereignty of the land, the freedom of the people and the culture of peace."

The five prisoners moved on to the Dahieh. Tens of thousands of spectators had crammed into the open air field on the edge of Haret Hreik where Hezbollah staged its largest rallies. The five released prisoners burst onto the stage through a cardboard simulacrum of prison bars. "Samir! Samir!" the crowd chanted. The cries turned delirious when unexpectedly Nasrallah himself emerged onto the stage. One at a time he hugged the five men and kissed them ceremoniously. It was his first appearance in public since the victory rally at the end of the war in 2006. "I left Palestine only to return," Quntar said, promising to continue fighting Israel. Hezbollah's secretary-general draped an arm around Quntar. "I just came by to congratulate you on this victory," Nasrallah said. "As we have said in the year 2000, the time of defeat is long gone. And today is the time of victory."

Back in his undisclosed location, Nasrallah addressed the multitude over a closed-circuit monitor, which he pointed out was part of the Hezbollah communications system that the government had sought to dismantle. The secretary-general turned the remaining screws with a long speech imbued with Hezbollah's new triumphalism. The prisoner release closed the circle of the July War, the Hezbollah leader said, and enshrined Hezbollah's identity as catalyst of regional radicalism. The Party of God wasn't just a nationalist political party, he said; no, it aspired to lead a global resurgence of militancy on behalf of the Palestinians. Arab governments had given up on the Palestinian cause, he said, but Hezbollah would keep attacking. In the process it would not only advance the cause of uprooting the Jewish State, but it would seek to embarrass and destabilize all those leaders around the Middle East who had chosen the course of negotiations and alliances with the West. This was no cold war. It was a very hot business, in which Nasrallah promised to share more and more of Hezbollah's expertise with militants around the region arrayed not just against Israel but also against the pro-Western leaders in Egypt, Saudi Arabia, Jordan, and elsewhere. "The resistance flag does not fall, but it moves from the hand of one group to another, from one faction to another, from one party to another, and from one heading to another," he declared. The Lebanese Islamic Resistance had provided the template for others to imitate, he said, and it would pour its energy into spreading its model of mobilization and radical militancy as far afield as it could. "We will have the honor to have this example generalized," he said, "even if the generalization of this example leads to our being placed on the lists of departments of the terrorist states."

He mocked those who avoided the obligation for holy struggle. The state, he argued strenuously if disingenuously, had the obligation to defend the nation and the inherent right to the monopoly on the use of force. The state of Lebanon, like most Arab states, had abdicated that right, he argued, when it ceased fighting Israel. Hezbollah had its army only because no one else could do the job, he said, ignoring the fact that Lebanon's machinery of statecraft and war would never grow past infancy unless Hezbollah ceased opposing it with its militia and institutions. Hezbollah would cling to its fundamental agenda of eternal holy war: not until the war was won, since it was a war with moving goal posts, but until the day when the world around it had adopted the same level of militancy and Hezbollah's catalyzing function no longer would be necessary. God's War was Hezbollah's identity, and despite Nasrallah's political analysis, the bottom line—war without end—remained the same:

> Usually people escape from the fighting. Even the believers. Almighty God says: "Fighting is ordained for you, though you dislike it."[83] It is human nature to prefer to turn to politics, economic activity, cultural activity, and commercial activity, but people do not want to hear about fighting, staying up all night, captivity, wounds, sacrifices, hunger, staying in the valleys and plains. What is this thing which we are monopolizing and for which we are envied? Are we envied because our youth are in prisons, and that we are

getting them back? Or are we envied because hundreds of our young have lost the flower of their youth to defend this homeland, and we get back their dead bodies? We will ask everyone to contribute to protecting and defending this country, and whoever abandons this duty is the traitor.[84]

If any other group with a different political agenda, say the moderates or the secular reformists or the Axis of Accommodation, was willing to create a culture of warfare and lead the guerilla life, it might be able to compete with Hezbollah in the arena of power. So far, however, no one was willing, so the party was left unchallenged to gather what authority it wanted, until it unraveled of its own accord or until an outside power cut off its sources of nourishment or pulverized its institutions.

Samir Quntar milked his celebrity. Al Jazeera threw him a birthday party on air, and in response Israel threatened to expel the network's correspondents from its territory. Syria's dictator Bashar al-Assad awarded Quntar a presidential medal. From the Syrian side of the border Samir exhorted the Druze in the Israeli-occupied Golan Heights to rise up. He toured the Middle East, meeting dignitaries and heads of state and appearing on the most popular television shows. Iran's President Ahmadinejad gave him another prize. The convicted child-killer was a sought-after VIP. He converted to Shia Islam, officially joined Hezbollah, and began courting a reporter for an Iranian television network. Israeli officials announced that they would find a way to "neutralize" Quntar if he took up arms again.

His younger brother Bassam Quntar had indefatigably promoted Samir's cause during his imprisonment, although he'd been too young when Samir was jailed to have any personal memories of him. Bassam was a political activist and a journalist for *Al Akhbar,* an independent newspaper that supported Hezbollah. He told me that I could meet Samir Quntar, but that his brother wouldn't go over the details of the Nahariya raid again. "He has explained what happened, and how the Israelis manufactured the case against him," Bassam said. "He has no more to say on this subject." I agreed to this condition because I thought it would be useful to hear Samir Quntar explain his current view of Hezbollah. Bassam also said that his brother was a radical to begin with, but that prison had made him even more extreme. "In short," Bassam said, "he is getting even more radical." We went at lunchtime to the Fantasy World Café, a sprawling family restaurant at a Dahieh amusement park, wedged between a Ferris wheel and the airport highway. Bassam and I smoked a narghileh while awaiting his brother. Bassam was well read and liked politics, and was engaging me in a spirited discussion of Lebanese and Palestinian factionalism, and the prospects (which he considered dim) for serious change in Middle East policy once Obama took over from Bush.

Samir appeared suddenly, wearing ironed blue jeans and a denim jacket. The waiters swarmed him, kissing him and posing for cell phone snaps. He smiled and nodded and kissed everyone, and then sat down for a cup of instant coffee. He was polite but laconic. I couldn't tell whether he was a fighter of few words or whether he just didn't have that much to say. He cut a flat figure. This man represented great evil to much of the world. Millions of people had fought a war over him. He had become a symbol of villainy, of hope, of the moral mushiness of the Islamic Resistance cause, which embraced anyone who hurt Israel no matter how vile his actions. I expected something more than what I found: an inarticulate, matter-of-fact guy, vain enough to enjoy his fame but measured enough to know that his future depended on his willingness to follow Hezbollah's orders. "What do you want to do now?" I asked him. "I want to get married," he said. "Beyond that, I'll do whatever the party asks me to." It reminded me of the curt military officers who always said, "That's not in my lane" when asked their view of policy.

He smoked Marlboro Lights, sucking down a cigarette every ten minutes. I asked him about his transition from secular militant in the 1970s to Islamist three decades later. The question didn't really make sense to him, as if I'd asked him why guerillas were using guns now instead of bows and arrows. "Around the world and in the region the resistance has become an Islamic resistance," he said. "I feel at home in the resistance. I am adapting to this new situation because I too have changed. I have adopted an ideology closer to Hezbollah's. I am becoming more religious myself." Samir Quntar believed in militancy. He would shift his ideology to conform with the dominant group fielding soldiers. Simple enough. "The resistance did its job and stood by me," he added. "I have to treat them the same way they treated me." His responses were so clipped that I found it impossible to get any conversational rhythm going. He was in no hurry to end the interview, but all my questions led to cul-de-sacs. The only time he grew animated and spoke at length was in a sudden disquisition on Israeli politics. Without any vitriol, he launched into an analysis of the strains that internal factionalism was placing on the Israeli government—the demands of the ultra-Orthodox for free education and exemptions from military service, the growing numbers of poorer immigrants, the schism between hawks and doves. He believed these internal divisions were weakening the Israeli government and had profoundly distracted Israel's defense establishment. The rest of the time, his observations echoed published quotes of his I'd already read, or Hezbollah's official position on Middle Eastern politics, Israel, and the need for militancy.

Bassam was interested in his brother's ontological significance. "Samir will become a good example for your Western audience of how the resistance can absorb people from different backgrounds," Bassam said as we sat around the table smoking. He went on to complain that too many Arabs and Muslims worried how their views would come across to Westerners. "The West must accept us the way we are," Bassam said. "Until they do, we shouldn't care so much about what they think." Samir Quntar, I hazarded, represented to the West a disturbing propensity among its detractors to adopt as a cause célèbre anyone who stuck a finger, so to speak, in the eye of Israel or America, even if they did so in a morally reprehensible, illegal, or counterproductive manner. Bassam couldn't engage that proposition since he believed the accusations against his brother had all been fabricated.

Dergham, who already had posed for a picture with Samir Quntar and kissed him warmly three times, summed it up most directly. He didn't really care who Samir Quntar was or what he had done. He cared that Hezbollah had sprung him. Samir Quntar was just a foil for the persona of the resistance, a mammoth that could absorb followers of different stripes and stick by them for the long haul. "In combat, you need to have confidence," Dergham declared, one hand on Samir's shoulder. "You know that if something happens to you, or to your kids, you're coming back. That's the proof right here. It strengthens the resistance. This is one of the Lebanese heroes right here, Mr. Samir." His reasoning uncannily echoed the sentiment of Israelis I knew who struggled to explain why they felt it was worth releasing a convict like Samir Quntar, as well as hundreds of other prisoners, in exchange for dead bodies. When the news of the prisoner exchange broke, I turned to an Israeli friend for insight. My own point of reference was the approach of the American military in Iraq, which considered kidnapped soldiers just like other casualties. The Americans refused to treat a soldier taken hostage as a great secret or a public ordeal, just as another MIA, an approach that seemed difficult but reasonable. And the Americans had no tradition of valuing ransomed body parts as highly as living hostages. Why help an asymmetric enemy by granting excessive value to one of the more easily obtainable sources of leverage—a soldier's corpse or severed appendages? Israel, however, had consistently traded dozens, sometimes hundreds, of prisoners for information on captives, partial remains, and dead bodies. My Israeli friend had trouble explaining what she saw as a natural and commendable commitment by her government to bringing home its soldiers, dead or alive, in whole or in part. "It's a spiritual obligation," she told me. "We must never leave anyone behind. We must not abandon anyone. It is as important to bury them at home as it would be to bring them back if they were alive."

With Samir Quntar's release, Hezbollah's marketing gurus were able to claim victory in the July 2006 war, and to indelibly blend their cause with an entire current of pro-Palestinian, anti-Israeli, anti-Jewish, and anti-American sentiment. Hezbollah, with its profoundly militant and adaptable ideology, had become the dominant source of a bubbling river carving new terrain in the Middle East. The Party of God had pushed hard. In less than two years it had expanded its stakeholder's share of political power from that of the strident fringe to the heart of government. Regional war, civil war, political brinkmanship, and uncompromising ideology had served Hezbollah's interests.

What happened to the moderates? The chastened Axis of Accommodation went about the sad business of sorting through its wilted assets. Wide swaths of the public were losing hope: many of my friends and acquaintances considered themselves friends neither of Hezbollah's axis nor of America's. In comparison to Hezbollah the agenda of March 14 sounded liberal, but in truth, it could hardly be considered moderate, democratic, or reformist. Each of the parties in March 14 functioned as a hereditary fiefdom, and the leaders routinely mobilized support through baldly sectarian appeals and calls to violent militancy. Still, the sincere moderates had no more appealing alternative, and hoped March 14 would forge a third way. They had been disappointed. In the political culture that counted—the realm of militants and power brokers—the choices were binary. The hopes of regular citizens might be noble, but their leaders tended to represent the worst extremes of belligerence, corruption, or both. Hezbollah's chieftains were interested in advancing their hold over their community, keeping the war fires alight, and expanding their share of power. They had succeeded in these goals through crafty maneuvering and through a surprisingly effective web of alliances. They had retained the support of the megalomaniac Christian leader Michel Aoun, whose movement claimed to want to eliminate sectarianism, implement economic and political reform, and push the Arab world into the twenty-first century. More often, though, Aoun's party seemed engineered primarily to extend its leader's personal influence. The Shia Amal movement made a steady business of funneling jobs and money to underserved Shia communities, wildly enriching a small coterie of its bosses and providing an outlet for militants who wanted to play with guns but had no stomach for the level of practice and discipline demanded by Hezbollah. The Party of God had figured out a smart recipe, stoking fanatical commitment among its own followers but protecting its domain with freewheeling allies who behaved however they desired in their own spheres. As long as they let Hezbollah make the big decisions, the partners could stray as far off message as they liked in their own neighborhoods.

Leaders of the moderate or accommodation parties had many interests that conflicted with their rhetorical devotion to pluralistic democracy. First and foremost was their compulsion to keep a death grip on the power that most of them had inherited from their fathers. Not a single powerful political party in Lebanon, with the exception of Hezbollah, argued for a wholesale redesign of the political system because all of them knew that a more fair, just, or representative system would cast them from their perches. None of the movements allied with the moderates or with Hezbollah had anything resembling internal elections or party congresses. They were run like family mafias. Lebanon's most liberal overlords, in common with almost every leader in the Arab and Islamic Middle East, had no interest in civil liberties, economic liberalization, an independent judiciary, or transparency in government. They preferred to preserve small islands of power over which they could rule and from which they could steal with impunity. It came as little surprise that Saad Hariri might be distracted from Lebanon's endless political crisis by the operations of his family's billion-dollar real estate and telecommunications interests. Walid Jumblatt was making money too, and couldn't always focus on politics when he had to oversee his own investments.

Mohammed Kabbani, the earnest member of parliament from Hariri's Future Movement who had so presciently and sadly anticipated the erosion of his coalition's influence, still fantasized that the peaceful pragmatists could salvage something. But he seemed to understand that Hezbollah had the upper hand for now and he could only wait for time to change the equation. His apartment in Raouche overlooked the Pigeon Rocks, a dramatic formation springing from the sea just off the tip of Beirut. The last time I'd seen him, at the Phoenicia Hotel, Kabbani was frantically trying to negotiate the selection of Lebanon's next president. Now he sat by his apartment window fielding outraged calls from his constituents about parking. Beirut City Hall had installed meters and to their horror his voters were getting tickets. Could Kabbani get the parking meters removed, or make City Hall dismiss his supporters' tickets? "I'll see what I can do," he said wearily into the phone. He apologized to me for the interruption and then returned to the matter of the March 14 coalition's prospects after Hezbollah's victory. Hezbollah had "played the sectarian card" when it marched through West Beirut, he said, a Shia militant movement invading a Sunni bastion. The party had angered many Muslims who had previously viewed Hezbollah as an inclusive Islamist movement, welcoming to anyone who wanted to fight Israel and the West. Now, he thought, many Sunni Muslims and other moderate people of faith would start to mistrust Hezbollah. But it would take a long time for Hezbollah to weaken again, he feared, and until then Lebanon and the Middle East would be subject to its militaristic plans.

For most of Lebanon and the wider Middle East, Hezbollah's era was only just fully dawning. Down by the Israeli border in Qlaya, however, the Maronite Christian villagers already had taken a long draught of Hezbollah's brew. They had lived as minorities under Hezbollah's rule since 2000, when Israel pulled out of South Lebanon. The Maronites of Qlaya had wholeheartedly supported Israel beginning with Israel's first incursions into Lebanon in the early 1970s to strike Palestinian militants. These Maronite Christian Arabs considered themselves free, independent, indigenous, and under threat from a Muslim population expanding in numbers and power. They were geographically closer to Haifa than Beirut, and politically had more in common with the Israelis than with either the nascent Lebanese Islamists or the Palestinians. From 1982 to 2000, Maronite officers from a few key border villages formed the backbone of Israel's proxy South Lebanon Army, with Shia filling the enlisted ranks. Maronite collaborators also filled senior positions in Israel's administration of the occupied security zone. One of those villages was Qlaya, right next door to Khiam Prison, where nearly the entire population depended on Israel for their livelihoods. Some of them grew rich and many others made a decent living working with the Israelis. The illicit drug trade flourished, making fortunes on both sides of the border. When Israel withdrew from South Lebanon in May 2000, Hezbollah flowed in and took over. The Shia masses vastly outnumbered the Maronites, and the collaborators feared for their lives in a Hezbollah-controlled South. To their surprise, however, Nasrallah had ordered his followers to refrain from vigilante justice. Thousands of collaborators who initially fled to Israel, fearing execution, torture, and revenge attacks, chose within a few years to return to Lebanon, where most of them served a year or less in prison and were then allowed to return to their communities. They had intimate knowledge of life under Hezbollah's control as reluctantly tolerated outsiders, potential suspects but not outright enemies. They'd seen the Party of God operate when the klieg lights were on during big occasions, and they'd seen how things ran day to day, the unrehearsed moments. Their experience endorsed some fears and assuaged others. Hezbollah had distinct rules for members of its own community and for its sworn enemies. For the vast majority who fell in the blurry area between, the rules for survival and prosperity were murkier. Qlaya's experience taught that outsiders could survive if they acquiesced to Hezbollah and didn't resist the Islamic Resistance agenda.

Thousands of former collaborators never had returned. Unlike some men I met in South Lebanon, they hadn't gotten a favorable response from their contacts. If they came home, they could face a lot worse than a year in prison. Some had been advised never to return, and they'd moved on to new lives in Israel, Sweden, Europe, and America. Hezbollah's magnanimity had its limits. Under its rule, the South remained a poor and cut off region, as always. The only difference now was that the development that flowed to the region went to areas that supported Hezbollah. The Christian towns and collaborator hubs that had thrived under Israeli occupation were dreary now, decimated by emigration. Collaborators had been spared widespread vigilante justice, but they were largely shut out from most public sector jobs and juicy contracts. The few bright spots were anomalies—towns that got a bump in commerce from the UN peacekeepers deployed after the 2006 war. Hezbollah didn't appear corrupt, per se, but it countenanced endemic corruption by its coalition partners. Such was the spoils system that Hezbollah left Amal alone in the areas under its control. One Christian landowner I knew went to Hezbollah's security court for help after Amal confiscated a large tract of his property and built houses on it for its supporters. The answer came back: Sorry, there's nothing we can do. If it were our people we would resolve it, but we've agreed to leave our allies alone.

By the winter of 2008, with Hezbollah's fortune secured, the Party of God turned to counterintelligence. Israel's 2006 bombing campaign was accurate enough to convince Hezbollah that Israeli intelligence still had a vast network of informants on the ground in Lebanon. And after the war Israel had made a priority of collecting better intelligence about Hezbollah. In the fall of 2008, Hezbollah and Lebanese military intelligence began rolling up alleged Israeli spy cells, Lebanese who had performed surveillance and other tasks for the Israelis, some of them for decades. One Shia man in Nabatiyeh, a car dealer trusted by Hezbollah, was arrested and accused of providing senior Hezbollah officials with cars that had Israeli tracking devices inside. Several Christians were arrested, and a senior official at the airport disappeared on his way to work. Another suspected spy, a handicapped math teacher, made a cinematic border break through an orchard into Israel. Paranoia ran high and some government supporters said Hezbollah was fanning spy hysteria ahead of the 2009 parliamentary elections. But no one disputed the actual accusations, and sources with access to intelligence told me they found the allegations credible. The crackdown didn't change the generally gray shade of life under Hezbollah rule for the unfortunates who weren't part of the "Society of Resistance" but lived within its boundaries. Still, it made many of them nervous, and they expected heightened scrutiny for some time to come. Everyone who didn't actively support Hezbollah fell under tentative suspicion.

The poorer Sunnis, Christians, and Druze toiled in conditions that appeared premodern. The more successful sent their kids away for school, knowing they never would come back. Jean Salame had served as a foot soldier in the South Lebanon Army and had fled to Israel in 2000—in his case, because his wife had cancer and he believed Israeli health care held her only chance of survival. When she died, he came back to Qlaya. He was pardoned after a three-week investigation. He remarried and now had a sweet two-year-old daughter, whom he was saddened to be raising in a morbid and decaying village. On the western side of the main road in a little strip mall was Jean Salame's shop: "Tony 4 Men: All Men Need." And it more or less stocked everything a man needed in Qlaya: camouflage cargo pants, silk ties in bright orange or a Lebanese flag motif, hunting knives, survival knives, souvenir mugs with land mine warning signs in Hebrew, Arabic, and English ("Welcome to Lebanon!"), and miniature Baalbeck temples. In the back were dress shirts, slacks, winter coats, and his sister Lea at the sewing machine, ready to do alterations. Jean was forty-nine, thick-trunked and bovine-faced. He held his daughter gently in his lap, and she responded to his soft requests with surprising alacrity. Jean had dropped out of high school, and had made most of his life's decisions under duress. He hoped his children would live better lives, somewhere far from this benighted border.

Hezbollah, he said, had treated them decently; not well, but well enough. His brother had stayed in Israel to await Jean's report: Jean told him not to come back. The South was dying economically and culturally. The future held dread, the likelihood of more wars, and always the possibility that Hezbollah would get tougher. His wife had died in Israel, but Hezbollah let him bring her body to Lebanon. For that he was grateful. When he visited Qlaya the first time after his return in 2002, he was overwhelmed by all the signs of Islamic rule in the Shia villages of the former Israeli occupation zone: green Hezbollah flags, billboards of Hezbollah martyrs, party slogans on the walls and stickers on the electric poles. "I was scared of Hezbollah. Returning from Beirut, after my trial, I saw all these Hezbollah signs. It was like psychological war," Jean said. "I felt petrified, like I was coming to a different country. I was afraid they would hurt me, but thank God, they didn't, nothing happened." Not long ago, he'd been part of the privileged team, and regular people who opposed the Israeli occupation but were otherwise just like him had to cower or seethe when Jean and his comrades passed. "How the people here feel about Hezbollah now, Hezbollah once felt about us too," he said. Jean had fought for the SLA for seventeen years, and he had lived in Israel for two. For all that, he didn't seem to view any of it—the collaboration with Israel or the fear of the Islamists in Hezbollah—in emotional terms. "The Israelis are not our friends to love them. There was nothing but common interests between us," he said. Times had changed and now the Party of God ruled the South, in tandem with some government institutions. There was nothing to be sentimental about, only new masters to placate. "Now our interests lie with the Lebanese state, with Hezbollah," he said with a shrug.

On another day, a foggy December afternoon, I visited a friend of Jean Salame, a retired South Lebanon Army general named Suleiman Said who had fled for two years to Israel and then had spent a year in prison in Lebanon. He spoke Hebrew and had thrived during the decades of Israeli influence in South Lebanon, eventually sending two of his sons to university in Germany. From the vantage point of nearly a decade since the Israeli pullout, I asked him how life under Hezbollah had measured up. On earlier visits, he had received me in an enormous salon full of *objets d'art*, prize rifles, elephant tusks, and a marksmanship trophy the Israel Defense Forces had awarded him. This time we sat upstairs, in a cozy dining room with a low couch and a raised brick fireplace. Suleiman threw shovelfuls of dried, crushed olive pits onto the logs, filling the room with a warm smell like potatoes frying in a cast iron pan. Hezbollah, he said, had imposed its will on the South. Soon the rest of Lebanon would follow. "They have discipline," he said. "No element will deviate from its leader's decision. Even in a legitimate army, some soldiers will disobey orders. Not Hezbollah. They are truly disciplined." But, he said, the party was too insular because of its members' obsession with religion and the closed company they kept. "They concentrate on each other and their culture and history, and that makes them a little backwards," he said delicately. No one was likely to challenge Hezbollah for the time being, he said, because of their primacy of force. He cited an Arab proverb to explain the go-along-to-get-along vibe that had once benefited the Israelis and now benefited the Party of God: "The man who marries your mother, you call him uncle." He didn't admire Hezbollah's prowess overmuch. He thought they had organized their militia exceptionally well, and they had outlasted Israel. But he thought that time would unmask the Party of God as vainglorious and domineering. As Nasrallah and his followers fancied themselves regional or global leaders, they would stumble into the traps of all pretenders to hegemony. If their political aspirations expanded out of control, he said with no small hope, they would overreach and lose their military vitality. "Hezbollah and Israel think the same way," he said. "Hezbollah already has stopped fighting Israel. The only war they still wage is with their mouth."

The "new" Hezbollah faced its first big test in the waning days of the Bush administration. President-elect Obama was promising a less confrontational and more even-handed approach to the Middle East. European diplomats, led by the British, were trying to normalize relations with Hezbollah and Hamas on the grounds that these groups now governed critical chunks of the region. Hezbollah, however, had kept its distance, rebuffing the outreach effort with cool hostility. Britain said in March 2009 that it wanted relations with Hezbollah's "political wing," a convenient fiction when applied to a group that was militant through and through. Hezbollah could easily have accepted the device in order to re-open diplomatic relations with a major Western power. Instead, the party announced that all its officials had military responsibilities, and Hezbollah would only talk to powers that recognized its inherently military nature.

Flush with triumphalism and perhaps an outsized perception of its power and influence, Hezbollah felt itself a lion of a New Middle East. The Party of God expanded its relations with Hamas in Gaza. For years Hezbollah had sought to lead the Palestinian militants by example, teaching them tactics like suicide bombing and land-mine construction. Hamas had captured an Israeli soldier on the Gaza border in an intricate operation in 2006 that bore the hallmarks of Hezbollah: tunnels, meticulous planning, a staged diversion, and a speedy kidnapping. Hamas had ratcheted up its firing of rockets at civilian population centers near Gaza, framing the Qassam launches in the same terms that Hezbollah always described its shelling of northern Israel—as self-defense in response to Israeli aggression. The technique had played well for Hezbollah in the Arab world. Now Hamas was trying the same approach. Nasrallah, the most popular leader in the Arab world, had spent a decade describing Israel's military as an easily breakable "spider's web" despite its invincible reputation. He had bragged about Hezbollah's string of victories in South Lebanon. Adapting many of Hezbollah's techniques, Hamas had taken over Gaza and apparently believed the time ripe for it to confront Israel in the same style as Hezbollah—and with Hezbollah's direct assistance.[85]

Israel was determined to remind its Arab neighbors and Iran that its storied army could shatter anything its enemies could field. The Israeli military still possessed unmatched wells of deterrent power, especially when Israelis were defending their own homeland against outside aggression, as they were doing in the Negev against Hamas' rockets. The Axis of Resistance talked so often about Israeli occupation and aggression that it had stopped making important distinctions: When Israel was cast in the role of occupier, as it had been in South Lebanon and as it was in the West Bank, it behaved differently than when it fought to protect its own territory, as it was on the outskirts of Gaza and in northern Israel. On December 27, 2008, Israel launched "Operation Cast Lead," a pulverizing bombing campaign against Hamas that surpassed in its scope and fury anything witnessed in South Lebanon. In twenty-two days Israel destroyed virtually the entire infrastructure of the government in Gaza—barracks, jails, training facilities, police stations, administrative buildings. Nearly 1,400 Gazans were killed, more than half of them civilians.[86] Ostensibly, Israel wanted to incapacitate Hamas as a fighting force. Clearly, however, Israel wanted to accomplish something bigger: It wanted to remind the whole region of Israel's might and will to fight. Deterrence is psychological, rooted in reason (it will cost us X if we do Y) as well as emotion (our people fear our rival and thus will be less willing to fight). Israel wanted to demonstrate afresh that its army had not only the tools of destruction but the will to use them with abandon if the Jewish State deemed it necessary. Much of the outside world was aghast at the indiscriminate targeting of civilians in Gaza in blatant contravention to the norms and laws of war that Israel nominally embraced. But to its target audience, the fans of the Axis of Resistance, that was exactly the point: Enrage a tiger, Israel seemed to be saying, and pay the price. The rules of war sadly were viewed by players on all sides of the conflict as irrelevant niceties, only to be invoked for political gain. Hezbollah, its mentors, and the movements it hoped to spawn, cared only for tactics and strategy, not for humanitarian concerns or the rule of law. They targeted civilians with impunity when it served their agenda, and cynically decried their enemies who did the same. To Hezbollah's axis, Israel's strategy made sense; it's what they would do in the same position. Israelis used a Hebrew phrase that could translate as "The Boss Has Gone Crazy" to describe their approach in Gaza. It usually was applied to the kind of frenzied sale at a shop where the owner has dropped prices so low that his clerks claim he's insane, when in fact he's shrewdly moving his inventory at a profit.[87] Think of those frenetic television ads where a fast-talking car dealer babbles that he must sell every last car at prices so low they can't last. In the case of the Gaza War, it meant that Israel might appear to have gone mad but in actuality was acting quite intentionally; Israeli power could unleash unpredictable consequences, and should not be casually provoked.

Having riled up its audience for years about Israel's alleged weakness, Hezbollah found itself in a bind. If Israel was a paper tiger, a house of cards, a spider's web, shouldn't Hezbollah attack Israel from the north while Hamas was fighting on the southern flank? That's what some Hezbollah followers thought, having been told for a lifetime that the Jews and their state were the paramount enemy and that Israel was weaker than ever. At a rally in the Dahieh during the Gaza War, thousands of men chanted "We are at your service, Nasrallah!" and "Death to Israel!" Afterwards a parade of them wanted me to know they were positively *chafing* for an order to attack. Hussein Haidar in Srifa told me over after-dinner tea that he believed the Islamic Resistance had a religious obligation to attack Israel in support of Hamas. Throughout the South, school had been canceled and those who didn't support another war already had relocated to the safety of Beirut. Throughout the border zone, committed members of the Society of Resistance prayed for Hezbollah to strike. Hezbollah's supporters had gone onto war footing of their own accord, and the Party of God found itself in the uncharacteristic position of restraining them. It turned out that Hezbollah was growing too big to fail; it was afraid to risk all its newfound power. The Party of God also didn't want to be seen fighting the Palestinians' war for them. In another war with Israel, especially this "boss-has-lost-it" Israel that was rampaging through Gaza leaving a trail of dead noncombatants and ravaged infrastructure, Hezbollah stood to lose a lot. Many of Hezbollah's supporters in Lebanon hadn't yet rebuilt the homes destroyed in 2006. The broad new coalition forged after the Divine Victory hadn't been tested by fire: Hezbollah couldn't be sure that Aoun's Christian Party and Amal's less zealous Shia followers would stay for the ride if Hezbollah recklessly embarked on yet another war with Israel. And Israel had studiously avoided any action that could be seen as a provocation against Hezbollah. The border was quiet. If Hezbollah wanted war, it would have to start it. And they'd have difficulty painting Israel as the aggressor, even among their ideological loyalists.

"I'm one of the ones who says Hezbollah should attack now. Everyone should attack," Hussein said. We were sitting outside on the porch despite the biting cold, wearing layers of fleece and sweaters. Everyone in the family had a cold and I did too. A pile of crumpled Kleenex covered the coffee table. The night was so clear I could see the Milky Way. "But Hezbollah probably has its own reasons. There are many who suffered. And there are cowards who don't want to repeat 2006. The whole Arab world should attack. There's a Palestinian saying: If you refuse to kill him, at least break his neck."

"Maybe Hamas can achieve something on the ground," Inaya said. "Maybe they can put fear in the hearts of the Israelis."

"Israel is stronger, but the resistance is stronger too," her father added.

"Israel won't last another twenty years," Inaya said.

"That's what they say about you too," I said.

In Aita Shaab, the border village from which Hezbollah launched the 2006 kidnapping raid, people were also ready for a brawl, but they weren't in as much of a hurry. Almost as a taunt to Israel, Hezbollah had made it a policy to expand the town after the last war. While some areas in Lebanon had yet to be rebuilt, Aita Shaab was gleaming and nearly reconstructed, with several hundred more houses than it had before the 2006 war. Hezbollah didn't want its key border positions depopulated, so it had provided supporters lots of incentives to stay in the most perilous areas. I visited a neighborhood at the southernmost edge of town where I had been in August 2006. At that time not a single structure was standing. The blocks had been completely rebuilt and the homes were full once again with Hezbollah's finest. An off-duty soldier named Abbas Khalil, visiting his aunt in one house, told me that the minute Hezbollah ordered its fighters into action against Israel, he would shed his Lebanese Army uniform and join his comrades in the Islamic Resistance. Another aunt named Khadija Khalil, an unmarried woman of fifty-four with a riotous laugh, told me she had spent the last war in Aita Shaab baking bread for the fighters, moving from house to house as the structures were bombed. "We are stronger now! I'm ready to do it again," she said.

"Israel's fate is linked to the Islamic Resistance movements," Abbas said. "If Israel can finish them off, Israel can survive longer. If we can finish off Israel, we will remove the daily threat that we face."

They all agreed that Hezbollah would wait for Israel to attack first, and they expected another war within about three years. They predicted a continuing cycle of wars, about twice a decade, until Israel disappeared.

"Israel cannot kill the spirit of the resistance," Abbas said. "Even if they killed Hassan Nasrallah, they would not stop the resistance. Hezbollah is a popular movement, and you cannot kill all the people." The last war, Abbas added, was a "picnic" for Israel compared to what was in store. "The next war will not be on our land," he said. "The next war will be on their land. The resistance will enter their villages. There will be no limits, no restraints. We will to them what they are doing in Gaza."

Hezbollah officials admitted to me that the party was sending what weapons it could to Hamas and giving the Palestinian group advice. Hamas' public relations strategy after the Gaza War ended in January 2009 closely followed Hezbollah's approach in 2006. Hamas lost the war but focused on Israel's destruction of civilian infrastructure and large-scale killing of civilians. Israel's military crushed Hamas' fighters, but just as Hezbollah had done earlier, Hamas claimed a victory merely by surviving. A few months after the Gaza War, Egypt claimed to have uncovered a Hezbollah cell in the Sinai, which allegedly was plotting attacks against the Egyptian government. Hezbollah claimed that its operatives in Egypt were only providing logistical support to Hamas and had no designs against Egypt. Either way, Hezbollah unequivocally had expanded its zone of direct influence into Egypt and Gaza. Israel had to look with satisfaction on some of the developments. Hezbollah had crowed a lot, but at a moment of truth it hadn't fired a shot. Hamas had survived, but was vastly weakened. By some measures, Hezbollah was too; the Party of God seemed to recognize that despite the voices of its most committed followers, it could ill afford another clash with Israel like the 2006 war. Maybe a few years in the future, but not just yet.

Hezbollah felt more confident than ever in its ideology and regional leadership. The government of Egypt had engaged in a rhetorical pissing match with Hezbollah after uncovering the Sinai Cell, revealing the significance they accorded the Party of God. American intelligence had uncovered Hezbollah trainers in Iraq, teaching Shia militants how to organize ambushes and lay roadside bombs. During the last week of the Gaza War, Hezbollah organized an international conference for a who's-who of radical militants, entitled "Beirut International Forum for Resistance, Anti-Imperialism, Peoples' Solidarity, and Alternatives." Ali Fayyad, from Hezbollah's think tank, was one of the conference chairs, and he drew a range of left-wing and antiwar activists from Europe along with the established militant Islamist groups from the Middle East.

Hezbollah had convinced a generation of Middle Easterners that Israel and the West could be vanquished by force, not through diplomacy and reform. The Party of God's principal patron, Ahmadinejad's Iran, had turned more bellicose, fundamentalist, and authoritarian than ever. The success of Hezbollah's ideology drove a new surge in support of confrontation instead of realism. The self-styled Axis of Resistance thought it needn't accept the world order it found, in which Israel and America had the economic and military strength to have their way. This violent and idealistic cohort believed it could shape a new reality. Even as its adherents praised the example of Nasrallah and his anticorruption record, they proved happy to forgive their tyrannical and corrupt allies, from the election-stealing and demonstrator-beating mullahs in Iran to the nepotistic family-run dictatorship in Syria. Hezbollah and the movements that emulated it had endowed their sponsors with legitimacy. Not only were the front-line militants fighting Israel, but they were living the ideals of Islamic fundamentalism, austerity, and combat that their comfortable cronyistic state backers had long since discarded in practice if not in rhetoric.

Hezbollah had sold itself as the promise for a weakened Arab and Islamic world. Nasrallah had kept his word; in a region suffering from terminal bombast, he had displayed modesty, an economy of rhetoric. Now, he had moved into another dimension, claiming that previous wars were a "walk in the park" for Israel, a "picnic" compared to the coming conflicts. He had switched from talk of defending Lebanese land against foreign occupation to preaching an aggressive war to "liberate" Palestine and Jerusalem from its Jewish rulers. He promoted millennial conspiracies that connected modern politics to Koranic battles and blood libel. Nasrallah's position was all the more radical because he truly meant it, all but guaranteeing a wave of new wars. Hezbollah couldn't come down from its new and more extreme position. It would have to make good on its oath of confrontation. The Party of God could try to delay the inevitable wars to maximize its tactical advantages but ultimately, it could not retain its identity while skirting conflict. Eventually, Hezbollah would have to test its premise against reality with the only tool its ideology blessed: force of arms. And given the reality of the balance of power in the region, Hezbollah's people would pay a steep price for their agenda.

7

ETERNAL RESISTANCE

Hezbollah's alternate realities might begin with a delusion, but through force of will its imagined parameters become literal. Heading confidently into the century's second decade, Hezbollah's followers could contemplate a Lebanon redrawn with the palette of the Islamic Resistance. The Party of God believed that Arab revolutions would enhance the Axis of Resistance. Nasrallah spoke often of the 40,000 rockets that Hezbollah had acquired—ten times the number it had fired in 2006. The Party of God opened a theme park in the one-time garrison of Mleeta that uncannily echoed Israel's Masada. There Hezbollah showcased captured Israeli weapons and dramatized its fighting techniques from 2006. All around Lebanon, Hezbollah's areas gleamed with new construction and infrastructure. Iran built a victory park in Maroun al-Ras, overlooking the Israeli border. Bint Jbail's market was rebuilt in glitzy Gulf style, and wouldn't have looked out of place beside a Qatari shopping mall. United Nations peacekeepers were allowed to patrol south Lebanon, but Hezbollah supporters made clear through a few carefully choreographed clashes that they would not allow the United Nations to do anything that tangibly threatened the Islamic Resistance's ability to arm and train. Aita Shaab bustled with more business, more construction, and more people than at any time in recent history. Faris Jamil put the final touches on his reconstructed mansion before the cold weather, and he deemed his family ready to put it all on the line again for another war. We were sitting in the garden, with the Christian family that had sheltered Faris and his children in the neighboring village during the 2006 war. His friend, a schoolteacher, dreaded the inevitable consequences of Hezbollah's bellicose stance. "We don't want to die," he said. Faris, without any animus, disagreed. "Our destiny is to die," he said simply.

On the national front, Hezbollah was busy dealing with a significant existential threat, perhaps the most problematic since 2006: increasing evidence linking Hezbollah operatives to the Hariri assassination. A group of Hezbollah members, apparently, had been shadowing Hariri in the weeks before his assassination and was nearby when the bomb that killed him went off. The operatives were tracked by their prolific cell phone use, which ceased forever after the murder. For Hezbollah, this accusation carried an undeniable price. If Hezbollah members were proved to have been behind the killing of a popular Sunni Muslim nationalist leader, the Party of God's probity with its own constituents would be tarnished. Furthermore, Lebanese and Arab detractors of Hezbollah might finally be pushed to act decisively. So Hezbollah set to the task of defusing its critics and writing a new narrative. Beginning in the summer of 2010, Nasrallah began a series of speeches lambasting the International Special Tribunal investigating the Lebanon murders as an Israeli tool. He explained to his listeners that Israeli agents had cloned the cell phones of Hezbollah members and then falsely implicated them in Hariri's murder. He shared intelligence that showed Israeli had penetrated Lebanon's entire communications system (which appeared true), and he also revealed that Hezbollah had been able for a long time to intercept Israeli drone footage, in real time (a feat confirmed by Israel). Building on these facts, Nasrallah elaborated a case built on unverifiable innuendo, arguing that Israel had killed Hariri and all the other Lebanese figures murdered since 2005; now, he told his followers, the Jewish state was trying to frame Hezbollah for its crimes. Nasrallah warned the Lebanese government that if anyone tried to arrest a member of Hezbollah in connection with the Hariri investigation, Hezbollah would consider it an act of war. No one had forgotten the show of force in May 2008. Hezbollah's followers believed the narration Nasrallah was spinning. Hezbollah had even put on its payroll the teenage toughs on Dergham Dergham's street. The kids in skinny jeans rode ramshackle mopeds with pistols tucked in their belts. Until now, they had been mere wannabes, scorned by Hezbollah. These weren't commandos to deploy against Israel; as Dergham said, they were on hand for the "internal clashes." It didn't matter that the alternate history of the Hariri Tribunal was built on specious evidence; it only mattered that it gave Hezbollah's partisans reason to feel unjustly persecuted, and inspired to fight back. No setback or error seemed too great for Hezbollah's capacity to rebound.

Until now, no other group has mastered the formula for radical strength as Hezbollah has done. It has built a movement on two pillars: ideology and services. Other movements in the Middle East have won power for a time by excelling at either one or the other—inspiring cultish devotion through their ideas, or weaving together a community by providing the schools, electricity, and other public goods normally delivered by a functional government. Hezbollah, uniquely, has done both for nearly three decades. The Party of God's success makes no sense without taking both threads into account. More successfully than any Islamist movement, and more effectively than most Middle Eastern governments, it has provided for its community's needs efficiently and with a minimum of corruption. Hezbollah takes out the trash, pipes in drinking water, builds schools, clears traffic jams, and even provides college and job-hunting counseling for graduating high school students. Its bedrock, however, remains its ideology. Outsiders largely care about Hezbollah because of the security threat it poses to Israel and to Western interests, and so they focus on the most militant and violent elements of the Party of God's beliefs: jihadi ideology, anti-Semitism, and the culture of martyrdom. But the reason why Hezbollah poses a threat at all is because of its public support and ability to deliver on promises to execute war as well as to take care of its constituents.

Hezbollah has cultivated a core of believers whose loyalty to the party begins with its Islamist message of faith, probity, empowerment, and self-reliance. They're committed to a community of Islamic Resistance that transcends national borders and gives new vigor and meaning to Middle Eastern politics. Most of Hezbollah's supporters are committed to fighting Israel and many of them endeavor for its complete destruction. All of Hezbollah's supporters, the hard inner core and the soft sympathizers, trust the party because of its track record of governance and community services. Social welfare services have proved especially important in convincing the multitudes of casual Hezbollah enthusiasts in Lebanon and across the Arab world who lend Hezbollah support in small ways: a donation in the Friday prayer alms-box, a vote on election day, attendance at a street rally.

Hezbollah has established itself as the standard-bearer of Islamism because it has articulated a clear ideology, implemented a comprehensive system of providing services, and finally—and perhaps most important—because it has achieved military success against Israel. From 1948 through 1967, the Arab leaders who grandly promised to push Israel into the sea met defeat after defeat at the hands of the Jewish State's vaunted military. Hezbollah, in contrast, succeeded at the smaller aims it set forth, like expelling Israel from the territory it occupied in South Lebanon from 1982 to 2000, or securing the release of Lebanese prisoners held in Israeli prisons. It has bruised the reputation of the Israel Defense Forces, forcing a retreat from Israel's declared security goals along the Lebanese frontier and embarrassing the Israeli military establishment during the 2006 war. It has racked up measurable success in its guerilla war against Israel, worrying the Jewish State's security establishment far more than any Palestinian faction. In its most recent clashes with Israel, Hezbollah has framed the agenda in a way that makes it hard to lose: victory, Hezbollah has taught its followers, means staying fast and surviving. No matter what the outcome, on those terms Hezbollah can claim victory whenever it meets Israel on the battlefield, which if history is to be any guide will happen every decade and probably more frequently. Militancy gives Hezbollah its momentum. Without war it loses its purpose. Engaged in a crusade without foreseeable end, Hezbollah can maintain the fervor of its growing community of supporters, and it can use the openings created by destructive war to outmaneuver its moderate Arab political rivals, who would wish to steer Lebanon and the Arab world away from a pose of perpetual confrontation with Israel.

Hezbollah is not negotiating. It's expanding. It has won unparalleled popularity by challenging Israel militarily. Its future depends on further war. Hezbollah's model requires Islamic fervor, viable force, and popular supporters willing to withstand Israeli bombardment. Continuing confrontation, the party believes, will prove that its approach of endless assault reaps more than peace talks and diplomatic relations with Israel. The last two decades have taught Hezbollah that the more it gambles the more it gains. And a cycle of four full-fledged wars with Israel beginning in 1982, along with countless skirmishes, has taught Hezbollah that frontal conflict with Israel benefits the Islamic Resistance. Whatever the results on the field of battle, Hezbollah wins on the homefront. That formula guarantees future provocations and future wars; and the Israeli military, smarting from the blow to its deterrent power in 2006, appears eager to oblige Hezbollah with a rematch.

For those whose major concern is Israel's short-term security, Hezbollah poses a major threat because of its ability to make war. The greater cause for concern, however, comes from Hezbollah's ability to export its ideology of Islamic Resistance and teach imitators the Party of God's recipe for perpetual conflict. Since the 1990s, Hezbollah has schooled Palestinian and Iraqi militants in its military techniques, from suicide attacks to roadside bombings. In addition to its technical expertise, Hezbollah knows how to fire up ideologues with the belief that war is the answer, that they're fighting Israel and America, Jews and imperialists, not in a merely noble and quixotic contest but in a long battle that they actually can win. Hezbollah is the harbinger of wars to come because it has convinced legions throughout the Arab world that victory lies in the grasp of an Islamic Resistance that fights on many fronts and measures its campaigns in decades instead of days.

Over the course of three decades, Hezbollah has refined its new paradigm for confronting Israel and the West in the information age. Its approach is simple and durable, built on easy axioms. Convert your base to your ideology: true believers follow orders and fight better. Train hard, and manage expectations downward. Market survival as victory. Confront your foe by exhausting him. Never take your eye off the ideological war, waged on the information stage. Start with religion, and then build the widest alliances you can. Discredit or destroy those who oppose you; but make any compromise necessary to keep your friends. Copycats all over have borrowed the strategy. The most important are those with direct links to Hezbollah or indirect links through Iran: Hamas, Palestinian Islamic Jihad, the Iraqi

Sadrists. Many more organizations have carefully studied Hezbollah, including the region-wide Muslim Brotherhood, Iraqi Islamists like Dawa and the Islamic Supreme Council of Iraq, and even the most militarily important organization of all, Iran's Revolutionary Guard. American war planners wrote extensively about the lessons of the 2006 war between Israel and Hezbollah, changing United States Defense Department doctrine as a result. Taliban fighters in Afghanistan and Pakistan employ guerilla tactics that evoke Hezbollah's. Arab satellite channels exert influence with incendiary talk shows and dramatic news clips, borrowing the techniques of Al-Manar. There are even allegations that Hezbollah collaborates with Latin American guerilla movements. American and Israeli military officials often appear to exaggerate Hezbollah's operational reach, presenting without evidence claims that Hezbollah has cells all over the world or has trained fighters from Colombia to Ireland to Iraq. Some of those claims could prove true, but what is already known is that Hezbollah has become the exemplar for radical ideologues who hope to challenge Israel, America, or the West by force.

Today incontrovertibly in power, the party has to search for a way to square its irreconcilable aims. Hezbollah wants to Islamicize and control the Shia community, imposing a religious regime over the Shia and squashing any competing organization or ideology. It wants to advance Iran's aims. Increasingly, it has bound itself to a noxious trend of anti-Semitism. On occasion, it seems to suffer delusions about its military strength and the staying power of the Jewish State and its enemies. In Lebanon, Hezbollah wants to secure all its aims without toppling the sectarian political order, which provides what little stability Lebanon knows. In the region, Hezbollah wants to spread its message of Islamic zeal, militancy against Israel and the West, and responsible service and governance by Islamist parties. Hezbollah carries the mantle of pure revolution and simultaneously has to govern.

So far, Hezbollah has tried to pretend there is no problem squaring the circle, and successfully juggles the contradictory currents in its own membership. Some party loyalists fight to the death against Israel and Westoxication, the blanket term for contaminating Western secular ideas, popularized during Iran's Islamic Revolution of 1979. Other more pragmatic activists stand in elections, negotiate for government posts, and propose bureaucratic reforms. Some Hezbollah members trumpet their fealty to Iran's leader, whom they consider the supreme Islamic jurisprudent, and cite him as the authority for every major decision. Other less doctrinaire Hezbollah members invoke Lebanese nationalism and debate policy inside party organs. Some tout Hezbollah's war as a glorious, death-strewn path to power and enlightenment. Others locate in Hezbollah a utopian community of resistance. As a political party and a militia, Hezbollah depends on different communities for different kinds of support, and so far has held its popular coalition tight. For its stakeholders, however, the competing causes of loyalty cause strain. Many in the party's base wondered why Hezbollah did not attack Israel during the Gaza War in 2009. On the other hand, peripheral supporters questioned why Hezbollah had in May 2008 attacked its fellow Lebanese. How could the Party of God claim to transcend sectarianism while attacking Sunni Muslims and Druze? How could Hezbollah champion the underdog, ridicule autocrats in Egypt, Saudi Arabia, and the Palestinian Authority, and at the same time give full support to abusive dictators in Syria and Iran? What would Hezbollah be worth if it couldn't win battles? Its momentum only runs while the oily mix of fervor, money, and internal integrity flows; a bit of grit, or the loss of a single ingredient, would quickly gum up the motor.

For the time being, opposition to Hezbollah's arms has been neutralized in Lebanon. The Party might have to fight for specific cabinet positions, but no longer will any powerful faction question its state-like trappings. Its consolidation of power complete and its ideological apparatus vibrant, Hezbollah has turned its sights toward the future: further conflict with Israel, the struggle against Western influence, and the spread throughout the Arab heartland of Hezbollah's messianic ideology and saturation Islamism.

Hezbollah has lots of fellow travelers who like the party's tough rhetoric without considering where it will lead, and how illiberal it really is. They dismiss its violence and its intolerance of dissent as minor flaws, justifying their insouciance by citing the dictators in the region who behave far more repressively. Hezbollah is the best of a bad lot, the thinking goes. Many of these armchair radicals avoid the intellectual conundrum because they don't live under Hezbollah's control, only nearby. Over a glass of wine at a party in Beirut, they admire Hezbollah's principled resistance as long as it stays in other neighborhoods; beyond Lebanon, Syrian and Egyptian fans applaud the fight because they aren't expected to actually join it. This facile outer ring of support, however, amounts only to a monument to Hezbollah's influence, not the cornerstone of its power.

The gradual drift of many Lebanese into Hezbollah's fold has drawn a blueprint for groups as far removed from Hezbollah's Shia Levantine context as the Afghan Taliban and the Indonesian Jemaah Islamiya. The men and women I met who lived in Hezbollah's orbit were willing adherents of a movement they revered not as passive cultists but as empowered activists. The mission that lit them had no limit: defeat Israel and the Jews, liberate Muslims (politically and spiritually), kindle the faith. No real-world development will suffice to sate these radical and comprehensive demands. It will be war without end, unless Hezbollah loses its capacity to mobilize, propagandize, and fight. The ideology is designed to rebound and flourish under assault without altering its nature, like the Hydra. Hezbollah's belief system has triumphed in an internal struggle and will now fuel a series of nasty wars. It won't go away; as a mass movement and ideological force it is around for the duration. What is not clear is how long it can retain its material power and influence. The structural factors that have vaulted Hezbollah to the leadership of the Islamic Middle East could change, drastically altering its reach. A competing and constructive ideology that achieved power of its own could woo away supporters. A real defeat in battle or intelligence could cripple the legend of Hezbollah and dampen its core's appetite for confrontation. Hezbollah officials could fall prey to the lure of power and corruption. A coherent Lebanese state could emerge, with a strong government, legitimate army, and the ability to deliver basic services. And the most important structural factors contributing to Hezbollah's power (as opposed to its appeal) are also the ones most subject to abrupt change: the support of Iran and Syria. Both regimes unconditionally back Hezbollah. At present a radical realignment doesn't appear in the works. But it isn't inconceivable that sometime, in a few years or a few decades, Iran and the United States could normalize relations or Syria and Israel could sign a peace deal. Either of those scenarios in a historical instant would redraw Hezbollah's parameters. Hezbollah could easily preserve its ideological dynamism and tentacles of persuasion and control. Without the money, weapons, and logistical support bequeathed by its state godfathers, however, Hezbollah will lose the wherewithal to translate its popularity directly into power.

Short of such a major regional realignment, is there anything Israel or the West can do that would significantly change Hezbollah's behavior and abilities? The extent of the party's popular support militates against trying to unseat Hezbollah by force. Confronting Hezbollah with raw military power only enhances its prestige, does little to thwart its ideology, and ultimately begets only short-term tactical benefits. In terms of security, Israel and the West can expect the most consistent, if limited, results through politics and old-fashioned counterterrorism: intelligence, counterintelligence, raids, arrests. None of these tactics would eliminate Hezbollah as a mass political movement or a security threat, any more than nearly three decades of sporadic full-scale warfare have. None of the practical options provide easy or comprehensive solutions, but all of them offer avenues to influence Hezbollah's behavior in ways that might calm rather than inflame the region. Outside powers have met success in the Middle East when they work through proxies that have local power and legitimacy. The West could promote the Lebanese state as a counterweight to Hezbollah, but would face the Sisyphean task of turning the shambling government into something sleeker. It also has to navigate an ambiguous order in which Hezbollah holds the controlling share in the national government, although the government operates by a consensus of all sects and parties. So far the moderate forces willing to accept Western help have proved ineffectual at best and buffoonish or corrupt at worst. There is little hope that Saad Hariri, Walid Jumblatt, and the other warlords will scrap Lebanon's sectarian spoils system in favor of a unitary central government able to compete with Hezbollah. The most promising long shots for a radical realignment are deals with Syria or Iran that would seal off Hezbollah's deepest wellspring of support.

Other scenarios for a tamed Hezbollah appear less likely. Over time, Hezbollah might unravel of its own accord. The Party of God might so believe its own hype that it fatally overreaches. Its ideological vigor depends on being a small underdog. As it gets bigger and more powerful, Hezbollah risks the fate of the region's dinosaurs, once-ascendant leaders who have come to symbolize the Middle East's failure to innovate politically, like Syria's Bashar al-Assad, Iran's Ayatollah Khamenei, Egypt's ousted President Mubarak, and the brittle royal houses of Jordan and Saudi Arabia. Some of these obsolete leaders despise Hezbollah and others subsidize it, but all of them watch it carefully. Hezbollah will have to continue sparking wars and doing well on the battlefield if it is to avoid a decline into reaction and ideological ossification. It will also have to compete with the fresh ideas of a new wave of Arab revolutioners. Otherwise it will have trouble simultaneously waving the banner of the dispossessed, the encircled partisans of Karbala dying for the just cause, and also the billy club of the autocrat corralling his empire. Given the forces on Hezbollah's side, it's likely that for decades to come the party's stature and potential to wreak havoc will only grow. It claims in its corner political dynamism, religious fervor, and the military and financial support of two crucial states, Iran and Syria. The "Axis of Resistance" formulation has a proven mass appeal around the entire Middle East, drawing Palestinians, Arab Christians, Druze, Sunni and Shia, Persians, pan-Islamists, and secular nationalists. Hezbollah is marching at the front of the wave.

As Hussein Rumeiti, the mokhtar of the village of Borj Qalaouay, said, the project of the state had failed not just in Lebanon and Palestine, but everywhere in the Middle East. Something else had to take its place, and he believed that something was Hezbollah, the Party of God. People would believe in resistance, even Islamic Resistance, he said, if it gave them dignity; they would love a life of conflict if war became their creed. The project of resistance would thrive because it had Hezbollah as a model and Iran as a bankroller. We were sitting in his salon on a rainy winter's day. Neighbors came and went with papers to sign. He argued at length with a friend from the Ministry of Education who complained that Lebanon and the rest of the Arab world would amount to nothing until governments invested in public education. Hussein's two-year-old daughter Rawaa kept interrupting us, jumping into his lap and shouting at me "I'm going to break your face."

Hezbollah (and to some extent, American policy in the region) had succeeded at polarizing the choices so extremely that most people saw only two options, the mokhtar said: the resistance way and the path of the

Americans. "I want Hezbollah to take power," he said. "When this area was occupied, only the Islamic guys helped us." He felt this way even though he was not at all a man of faith. "We in this family are religiously committed, but not so religious," he said, explaining why he was ignoring the call to prayer bellowing from the mosque down the street. "I am committed, but not so much a believer." Here was a man in Hezbollah's heartland, a Shia community leader and Islamic Resistance stalwart who didn't necessarily believe in God. But he was on board because the Shia had grabbed their destiny and turned their once meek lot right-side-up. Now the resistance partisans were writing a new script for the Middle East, because they had the convictions and the power to make everyone else listen. "He who created Hezbollah here can create another one in Iraq," Rumeiti said, growing animated. "The Shia in Iraq will rise up. Imagine! Here, we are a small country. There in Iraq, the Shia are 70 percent of a population of 27 million. The Shia are many, and they are close to Iran. Hezbollah is the model. They have succeeded here, and they can succeed elsewhere."

Over a five-year span of war, internal strife, and regional turbulence, the people I met in Hezbollah's community all moved toward a harder view of their world. Their journey paralleled a polarization I saw everywhere in the Middle East, including among Israelis. On all sides ideologues were triumphing over incrementalists, as if everyone would rather go down fighting for an absolute victory than find a way to coexist. Even the gentler types I'd come to know were changing their hue, like chameleons, to match the Society of Islamic Resistance. Issam Moussa, the former soccer player who had worked as my translator in Tyre, had bought an encyclopedia of Hezbollah history, and displayed it prominently in his living room. He was earning a decent living working for the UN peacekeepers, and had moved his family into a larger apartment in a tower on Tyre's waterfront, with a nice view of the sea from the balcony. It made him nervous that Hezbollah had gotten angry about my Rani Bazzi article. "There's nothing to worry about," I told him. "They didn't like the story, they told me so. They understand that I'm a journalist, and they'll deny me access to certain stories to punish me for things I've written. That's all there is to it." But Issam was concerned. He thought maybe he'd be tarred with guilt by association. "You don't know these guys. They were really upset," he said, flinching a little.

In June 2009, the supposedly decisive parliamentary elections came with much hullabaloo. But the expectations surrounding them quickly dissipated. The March 14 parties campaigned with chauvinism and raw fearmongering. The Christian candidates in the governing coalition whipped up hysteria with claims that Hezbollah was trying to expel Christians from the Middle East. With their Sunni partners they raised the alarm that Hezbollah wanted to transform Lebanon into another Iran. Western diplomats painted the election as a key struggle in a new cold war between Iran and the United States. Hezbollah, meanwhile, ran an understated campaign that it assumed would bring it victory. It was evident from previous elections that supporters of Hezbollah's coalition significantly outnumbered those backing the government; and districts had been redrawn in a manner the Party of God considered to its benefit. But because Lebanon's distorted electoral system gave disproportionate weight to Christian districts over Muslim ones, the outcome hung in doubt.

On June 6, 2009, the day before the elections, I visited the Hezbollah think tank chief Ali Fayyad at his home in the border village of Taibe, very near the spot where Rani Bazzi had been killed. Ali was preparing for a career shift. He had been named to Hezbollah's candidate list, and Lebanon's district system guaranteed that he'd enter parliament. After decades as a policy strategist, he'd get to be a politician. He had engineered Hezbollah's way forward through the thicket of its hard-to-reconcile principles. He had supervised the creation of a body of policy analysis that made Hezbollah a serious contender to govern and at the same time, as a militant political theorist, he had refined Hezbollah's ideology of extreme and total war against Israel. On his home turf at the family summer house in Taibe he was even more approachable than in Beirut. He was forty-six years old and the eldest of eight children. His father, an illiterate porter in Beirut harbor, had asked Ali to take over as head of the family when he was fourteen. His parents and siblings revered him. His mother told me that Ali had weighed ten pounds at birth and she had known immediately that he was destined for greatness. His sisters and brothers, half of whom were academics, bantered with each other in French and English to sharpen their foreign language skills. A flamboyant younger brother who worked in fashion in Switzerland was visiting for the elections. "I love Mykonos!" the brother told me meaningfully. Some of the women prepared a chicken feast inside.

Ali's younger son returned from a jog and asked me what action movies I liked. His latest favorite was *Kingdom of Heaven*.

For the last day of campaigning Ali Fayyad had set out sweets and water pipes on the rear terrace of his house and was welcoming visitors. When I got there emissaries from former President Jimmy Carter—his son Chip and his chief of staff Bob Pastor—were telling Ali that Carter would be willing to meet with him and any other Hezbollah officials, to engage in back-channel diplomacy as the former president already did by meeting with Hamas leaders in Damascus. After the Carter team left, we sat and smoked together (although Ali didn't want to be photographed holding the pipe) while he told me about the steady future he expected for Hezbollah. The way he saw it, the cataclysmic turning points were over. If Hezbollah won the elections, as he expected, it would form a national unity cabinet with March 14. If Hezbollah lost, it expected March 14 to do the same. Hezbollah already had established that it wouldn't let any coalition rule the country without giving the Party of God veto power. It had the street power to back its demand. Ali was confident Iran would keep the taps of financial and military aid open to the Islamic Resistance in Lebanon no matter how it resolved its own political disputes.

Most interesting to me was his read on Hezbollah's new agenda. "We live in a world that respects only power and the strong player," he said, but while Hezbollah would never back down from its fight with Israel, the party was willing to negotiate most other issues. The party had to work now, he said, to repair the damage of its three-year march to power; Hezbollah could not take support for granted. "We cannot overestimate public opinion. Hezbollah has taken a decision to improve its foreign relationships and foreign ties. We need to explain how we are moderate with our internal Lebanese issues. We have a constant position to resistance, but on other issues we are reacting to make compromises. You see how European and Western propaganda makes problems for our image. We need to do a lot of things and focus about our image, to clarify our reality." The political playing field was far less fraught for Hezbollah now that everyone had agreed to end any discussion of disarming the Islamic Resistance militia. Other political disputes ran a distant second for Hezbollah. As Ali Fayyad presented it, Hezbollah's agenda for the near term involved retrenchment and consolidation. That meant that the Party of God was reasonable enough to recognize its limits, and it also revealed the party's sense of its own weaknesses. Hezbollah had recognized that another war with Israel in early 2009 would probably hurt the party, unlike the 2006 war which had fueled its ideological ascendance. It would take some time, perhaps a few more years, before Hezbollah would regard another war as an invigorating infusion. It wanted some influence over the next war's timing and scope. Ali Fayyad understood that Hezbollah would have to tread carefully if it wanted to retain the power it had amassed.

Hezbollah had to keep its own house in order too. Some of the people closest to the fight against Israel had started to resent the privileges granted to party members. On election day I visited Srifa, where the town was turning out en masse to almost unanimously elect a Hezbollah MP. Party members milled all over the high school chatting with voters at the polling sites. A few token votes went to the tiny independent Shia party of Ahmed al-Assad, son of an infamous landowner and once-powerful zaim. His supporters were marginalized but tolerated in the village, like harmless but disliked lechers. Inaya and her sisters had all voted for Hezbollah. Mohammed Nazzal, their friend the English teacher, shocked them when he dropped by the Haidar house and announced that he hadn't been able to bring himself to vote for the Party of God. At first he wouldn't answer when asked whom he had chosen instead.

"We must vote for the people who protect us!" yelled Samar, the eldest sister, the one married to the Hezbollah member.

"Why does Hezbollah pay the wedding costs of its members, but not of the other men in the village?" Mohammed said.

"If you are from this village, you must be with the resistance," Samar said. They were both shouting with real anger. Muna, the youngest, was giggling, enjoying the fight as a spectacle. Whenever the argument grew too heated, Muna would sound a yellow air horn distributed by Aoun's campaign which made three short toots and two long ones, ta-ta-ta, TAA TAA!

"The party must give something to me," Mohammed said.

"You voted for Hezbollah before," Samar replied. "Those who vote against Hezbollah, who are not with us, are traitors."

"Traitors?" Mohammed said, smashing his fist on the Formica dining room table.

"Traitors! If you voted for Ahmed al-Assad, you might as well vote for Israel," Samar shouted.

"This is the problem," Mohammed said, suddenly quieted. "Those people who don't support Hezbollah have a point of view, and we must respect it, even though we have our own point of view."

Samar calmed down too, mollified that Mohammed had identified himself as being on her side. "Now tell us, who did you vote for?" she asked.

"I took a blank sheet of paper and wrote 'resistance' on it," Mohammed said. "That was my ballot."

Samar was satisfied, but Mohammed's choice seemed cause for Hezbollah to worry. There was discontent in its heartland.

Hezbollah ended up losing the elections it expected to win, but it wasn't much of a defeat. March 14 hung on to a slim majority in parliament, and its coalition collapsed when Jumblatt defected. Hezbollah and its allies, meanwhile, decisively triumphed in the popular vote, denying Saad Hariri and his backers an opportunity to trumpet the election as a great victory for the moderate axis. Hariri and his March 14 coalition could only wield power at the pleasure of Hezbollah. Of the roughly 1.5 million people who voted, 54 percent voted for Hezbollah, and 46 for the governing coalition. There was nearly a 130,000-vote gap between the two groups.[88] Hezbollah could claim a popular mandate even while breathing a sigh of relief. It had lost the contest for parliament, but it also had escaped responsibility for having to form and lead a government. It would be much easier to criticize from the ranks of the opposition. (And later, when it saw fit to do so early in 2011, Hezbollah was able to topple the government and install an allied prime minister of its choosing.)

Ali Fayyad was chastened when I saw him again in Beirut the week after the vote. "We thought we would win. We were surprised. The whole world was surprised," he said. "We have to make a deep revision." He didn't think the loss made a significant difference, but he considered it an embarrassment. Hezbollah didn't like to brag, and had predicted a victory based on careful analysis; the party had been mistaken. "By winning, March 14 has taken away the responsibility of Hezbollah for running and controlling the country. The role of opposition is easier than the role of running the country," Ali Fayyad said. "We can see all this, but we must also say that we have done our best to win a majority and we failed."

*   *   *

His stark admission of error hearkened back to Hezbollah's root strength. Its followers trusted the party to do right because they saw the party address its mistakes. On the decisive issues they agreed. Its constituents hoped Hezbollah would avoid the avoidable wars, take heed of their needs, and help them recover after a bombing. In exchange they would go to the trenches when summoned and to the mosque when called. Their loyalty only could be understood as a leap of faith. They were like penitents at Lourdes, or holy warriors from another time, an era of devotion and crusades. They lived in the modern world and had mastered many of its ways; but they were not completely *of* it.

Bint Jbail was the beating heart of Hezbollah, the capital of the resistance—the pilgrimage point for the ideology that had kindled a fresh thirst for conflict across the Middle East. There in Bint Jbail, Hezbollah's dichotomy of faith and works, fanaticism and pragmatism, was most clearly revealed. There I could best understand why Hezbollah mattered, why it wasn't going away, why it was to be feared. On the first anniversary of the July War, Hezbollah commissioned a local woodworker known as Abu Mohammed to make a memorial to the martyrs of Bint Jbail. He was an old craftsman in his sixties who specialized in a slightly tacky form of vernacular folk art, painting Koranic inscriptions on gnarled and artificially aged slices of wood: Islamic bric-a-brac. For the Bint Jbail memorial Abu Mohammed selected a hefty poplar he had cut down a year earlier. It had many branches, and the way they twisted reminded him of the characters that spelled Allah, God. He varnished it, stuck it on a base, and nailed 43 wooden placards to its branches, each inscribed with the name of one of Bint Jbail's fallen. He delivered it to the Bint Jbail community center, his work done. As the anniversary neared, some Hezbollah workers telephoned Abu Mohammed: Why, they asked, were green shoots growing from the shellacked trunk? "We had nothing short of a miracle on our hands," Abu Mohammed said. The dead tree had sprung to life, eventually sprouting 43 new leaves, one for each martyr. Thousands made the pilgrimage to Bint Jbail to touch the tree and pose for a photograph beneath its miracle leaves. A lucky few drank its sap, a sort of holy manna they described as possessing a lingering sweetness. Experts on Al-Manar debated and discarded all scientific explanations for the Martyr Tree. It could be nothing but a sign of God's favor. Engineers and doctors and civil servants paid homage to the tree; none doubted its authenticity.

With this kind of belief stoking its boiler, Hezbollah had a lot of mileage in it yet. Abu Mohammed had carved thousands of trees in his career, and I suspected he knew a thing or two about making miracles. He swore a divine hand made the Martyr Tree, and who knows? Maybe he had nothing to do with the fresh growth that elevated his kitsch into a war-sanctifying blessing from God. But he knew his role, and he spent weeks beside that tree, telling the story of its divine provenance over and over in that folksy voice to anyone who stopped by. One day the exhibition ended, Abu Mohammed returned to his workshop, and the wonder Martyr Tree vanished. I had no doubt it could reappear again when Hezbollah needed it.

Three years after the July War, I visited Rani Bazzi's grave again. His voice lived on in the martyr's will that thousands viewed on YouTube and the private testaments, written and videotaped, he had bequeathed his friends and family. His family no longer would speak to me. I had merged in their minds with the faceless enemy. When I first met them—Rani, Farah, his cousins and friends—they were individuals, combustible and comfortable, men and women with whom I had something in common that helped me understand the part of them that I found brutal and incomprehensible. They had closed ranks, however, and to some extent closed their minds to me; more than individuals, they now presented themselves to me only as ions in the vapor cloud of Islamic Resistance.

Hezbollah had constructed a park over Rani Bazzi's gravesite. A ceramic-shingled canopy shaded the two long rows of martyr graves, flanked by marble benches. Grandiose statues to the martyrs, with plaques and stone carvings of their faces, gave the whole hilltop the air of a theme park. The revolution had been institutionalized. Hezbollah, I thought, could not be erased. Forever it would be part of the landscape. It would expand and bring on more wars, with the momentum and confidence it acquired during its exponential jump from militant fringe to the Arab world's ideological center. Somehow, Hezbollah had pulled off an artful feat: it had preserved its dynamism and radical pedigree while making itself into an establishment. Hezbollah's followers trusted the party, even adored it. That love gave Hezbollah its unique power. It enabled the party to strike a pose of eternal confrontation, knowing that any war it sparked would only strengthen Hezbollah's hand with its followers.

When first I'd visited the Bint Jbail cemetery immediately after the 2006 war, the fighters' graves lined the edge of a barren gravel lot. Now, years later, through the riot of monuments and plastic flowers, the faces of the individual martyrs still held pride of place. This, I realized, was what distinguished Hezbollah from its less successful peers in the world of Middle Eastern militancy. In other Arab countries, the visage of a single leader would dominate the landscape; some of the more extreme and less influential Islamist movements would avoid any imagery of the human face altogether as sacrilegious. Hezbollah, however, lionized both the movement and the masses, the ideology and the individual. Here on the hilltop in Bint Jbail, I wandered among statuary, graves, and dioramas that appealed directly to the aesthetic of heroic kitsch that seemed to most resonate with the Middle Eastern public. The faces depicted, however, were not likenesses of Hezbollah's supreme leader. The visitor to Bint Jbail cemetery instead beheld a wall of bas-relief statues and photographs of the footsoldiers, Rani Bazzi and his comrades. Hezbollah had built a shrine to the men of the neighborhood. The Party of God was still a party of men. To me, to the outside world, Hezbollah members might show only a party-sanctioned monolithic persona. Internally, however, the party left open a space for its recruits and followers to live, die, strive, and teach, as individuals.

The whole of Bint Jbail was a monument to a triumphal movement: not just the cemetery, but the residential quarters rebuilt with foreknowledge that they would soon be destroyed again in the next war with Israel. Hezbollah meant its ideology to be greater than any single one of its adherents or leaders, but it was not an ideology that erased their individual lives. It was meant to unify and enhance them into an ummah, a community in which each individual mattered all the more because he or she was willing to sacrifice a meaningful life for an even more meaningful higher cause. Over the years I had come to know many of these partisans, some of them like Rani's family fully transported by Hezbollah's wave and others, like Inaya and the mokhtar of Borj Qalaouay, capable of some distance. The more I encountered the human side of some of these supporters, however, the more I came to shudder at the movement. Hezbollah accomplished plenty of good, but ultimately it used its power to shape human hearts in service of something destructive. With the force of its enchantment and its fury, Hezbollah was sculpting the trajectory of an entire region, propelling it onto a fiery footing of eternal war. Its ideology, too, left no room for doubt, and erased the space for dissent and discourse. Hezbollah had found the secret to harness individual potential, empowering its constituents to more active, productive lives; sadly, however, its formula for inspiration relied on mobilizing people for an endless cycle of war, destruction, rearmament, reconstruction, and war again.

Rani, I imagined, would not soon be forgotten in Bint Jbail. Over the years others would take their place beside him in the martyrs' pantheon. Perhaps in another decade there would be a matching statue of his young son Shaheed Bazzi, a boy raised in such a ubiquitous Hezbollah culture that he'd scarcely be able to imagine another way of thinking. Hezbollah's identity clearly identified God and the individual with a holy struggle for a better life at home and a total military victory against Israel. The simple formula had potent lasting power: it appealed to a constructive embrace of faith and community in the modern world, and then unleashed that positive energy in the service of expansive and destructive militancy. Sayyed Hassan Nasrallah had dubbed Bint Jbail "The Capital of the Islamic Resistance," and to it had flocked not desperate men bereft of opportunity but comfortable and educated middle-class Lebanese like Rani Bazzi. The fresh generation of Islamic Resistance, the children who could only remember a time when in their eyes Hezbollah was triumphing over its enemies, rode a wave of belief and almost arrogant hubris that perpetual war would eventually reap conclusive victory. Frighteningly, that view left no room for the gray workaday road to peace, marked by negotiations, compromise, and uneasy but nonviolent coexistence. A new generation had internalized Hezbollah's lesson: war, indeed, was their answer. For the foreseeable future, it looked like the Party of God would shepherd its society of Islamic Resistance headlong into conflict, where its stakeholders could prove themselves over and over again in the crucible of war. Hezbollah's clarion call was overpowering all other drumbeats, marching the Middle East deeper into a war without end.

ACKNOWLEDGMENTS

I would never have been able to report and write this book without the generous help of two talented Lebanese journalists, Hwaida Saad and Leena Saidi. They gave freely of their time and insight to bring me closer to the individuals I wanted to write about and open up to me the culture of Lebanon and Hezbollah's community. During years of reporting trips Hwaida, Leena, and their families offered me a home away from home, and made my reporting not only possible but enjoyable. Many other friends and colleagues in Lebanon selflessly and warmly aided me. Borzou Daragahi and Delphine Minoui opened their home to me for months at a time. Farnaz Fassihi, Oliver August, and Andrew Lee Butters warmly hosted me. Inaya Haidar and Dergham Dergham welcomed me into their homes and trusted me enough to share their intimate thoughts and family lives. Issam Moussa enabled me to do my job at a critical and dangerous time in the 2006 war. Many of the people who appear in the book and at least a dozen others who don't sacrificed countless hours to explain to me their feelings about Hezbollah, despite the party's conviction that talking to an American reporter would not serve its interests. Anthony Shadid encouraged me from the inception of the project and provided invaluable guidance at every stage. Along the way I benefited from the companionship of fellow journalists: Babak Dehghanpisheh, Charles Levinson, Anthony, Borzou, and too many others to name.

The foreign editors of *The Boston Globe* and *The New York Times* sent me on the assignments that gave rise to this book at a time when most newspapers were slashing their budgets for international coverage. Princeton University's Humanities Council supported me as a Ferris Professor during some of the time I spent working on the manuscript. My agent Wendy Strothman was instrumental in keeping my spirits up when publication seemed a distant prospect, and my commissioning editor Martin Beiser saw the book's potential and shaped it critically and crucially. Hilary Redmon and the rest of the team at Free Press kept the editing process smooth.

Bryan Denton, Tanya Habjouqa, and Michael Robinson Chavez kindly shared their photographs. Brian Katulis organized an invaluable review panel. Eamon Kircher-Allen helped with research and an early edit. Michael Hanna, Elias Muhanna, Jon Alterman, Brian, and Anthony all offered thoughtful feedback.

My family made this book possible. My mother Miranda and my brother Alexis have encouraged me all along. Anne Barnard has been a steadfast and inspiring wife, partner, editor, and friend. We've been blessed to live a great adventure during the many years over which this book took shape, and were joined along the way by our son Odysseas and our daughter Athina. All of them exhibited great patience and forbearance during my many long trips away from home.

Credit goes to all these people and the many more whom I don't have the space to name. Naturally, the mistakes and shortcoming are all mine.

NOTES

1. The Anwar Sadat Chair for Peace and Development at the University of Maryland has conducted Arab public opinion surveys since 2003 with Zogby International. The results can be accessed at http://sadat.umd .edu/surveys/index.htm. Nasrallah has consistently scored as one of the most popular figures, with minor fluctuations; he appears to tap into a public desire for bold rejectionist leaders perceived to stand up to America. His standing appears to fall when Hezbollah comes across as a sectarian rather than unifying figure. In the 2009 poll, for example, when the Egyptian government claimed that Hezbollah was working with militants in Egypt, the Hezbollah leader's popularity dipped there; he was supplanted in the public opinion poll by Venezuelan president Hugo Chavez. Opinion polls in the Arab world are notoriously unreliable because of the constraints on sampling, and the Zogby polls should not be taken as accurate representations of the countries in question as a whole.

2. Nasrallah refers here to the former Israeli Defense Minister Ehud Barak, Israel Defense Forces Chief of Staff Gabi Ashkenazi, Israeli Prime Minister Benjamin Netanyahu, and United States President Barack Obama.

3. Hezbollah denies responsibility for the simultaneous bombings of the U.S. Marines and French barracks on October 23, 1983, on a technicality. At the time Hezbollah was coming together through the union of several Islamist militant groups that had ideological affinity and com-

mon ties to Iran's Revolutionary Guard. One of those groups, Islamic Jihad (distinct from the Palestinian group of the same name), claimed the barracks attack and was later absorbed into Hezbollah. Hezbollah has distanced itself from the attacks, which killed 241 Americans and 58 French. The Party of God and important allies like the Ayatollah Muhammed Hussein Fadlallah have remained on Western terror lists; and Hezbollah has also made clear that it supported the attacks and considered them an effective act of Islamic resistance. Scholars and the intelligence analysts they quote have built a compelling case that an overlapping constellation of operatives, including Imad Mughniyeh, formed Hezbollah and also conducted the major suicide attacks of 1983.

4. Judith Harik, "Hizballah's Public and Social Services and Iran," in H. E. Chehabi, ed., *Distant Relations: Iran and Lebanon in the Last 500 Years* (London and New York: I.B. Tauris, 2006).

5. Amos Harel and Avi Issacharoff in *34 Days: Israel, Hezbollah and the War in Lebanon* (New York: Palgrave Macmillan, 2008) recount the Israeli military command's clumsy decision-making that led unprepared units to engage Hezbollah first in Maroun al-Ras and then in Bint Jbail. According to the Israeli journalists, Israeli military commanders named the July operation in Bint Jbail "Web of Steel" because they were irritated that Nasrallah had long mocked Israel's supposedly invincible military as a "spider's web."

6. See reports on Khiam Prison by Human Rights Watch, available at www.hrw.org/en/news/1999/10/27/torture-khiam-prison-responsibility-and-accountability, and Amnesty International, available at www.amnesty.org/en/library/info/MDE15/021/2000.

7. Zeina Karam, "Hezbollah and its backers appear in control of Lebanon's fate," The Associated Press, July 17, 2006.

8. The British government estimate of the Lebanese diaspora conforms with the generally cited figure in Lebanon of 14 million. See www.fco.gov.uk/en/about-the-fco/country-profiles/middle-east-north-africa/lebanon, accessed August 2009.

9. An international tribunal has been charged with investigating the crime, but five years after the killing had yet to issue any indictments.

10. March 14 had trouble coming up with an alternate name that suggested a unifying idea, resorting to unsatisfactory terms like "the Majority"

and "the Government." Hezbollah's March 8 coalition—with smaller numbers but arguably a more dedicated group of activists—called its parliamentary delegation the Loyalty to the Resistance Bloc, and usually described its wider coalition as the "opposition."

11. Harel and Issacharoff tell the story of the war's opening day in great detail from an Israeli perspective in *34 Days: Israel, Hezbollah and the War in Lebanon*.

12. The United States military had embraced a similar doctrine under the general category of effects-based operations, or EBO, and experimented with the approach in Afghanistan and Iraq. By 2008 the Pentagon discarded the concept as "vain" and "confusing," in large part after studying Israel's war with Hezbollah. General James N. Mattis, commander of the U.S. Joint Forces Command, announced the decision to abandon the concept of effects-based operations and expunge its entire vocabulary from military parlance in a commander's guidance distributed in August 2008 and published in the *Joint Force Quarterly* (JFQ), 51 (4th Quarter 2008). Discussions of Israel's application of effects-based warfare can be found in Matt M. Matthews, "We Were Caught Unprepared: The 2006 Hezbollah-Israeli War," The Long War Series Occasional Paper 26 (Fort Leavenworth, KS: Combat Studies Institute Press, 2008); and Harel and Issacharoff, *34 Days: Israel, Hezbollah, and the War in Lebanon*.

13. Javed Iqbal was sentenced in April 2009 to 69 months in prison for providing material support to a terrorist group in Federal District Court in Manhattan.

14. Interview with Abdallah Kassir at Al-Manar headquarters, December 12, 2008.

15. I first met Inaya Haidar at the Najem Hospital in Tyre in July 2006. We stayed in touch, and met again in Srifa on many occasions in 2008 and 2009. She and her immediate family offered extensive recollections in interviews in November and December 2008 and January and June 2009.

16. United Nations, "Letter Dated 7 May 1996 From the Secretary-General Addressed to the President of the Security Council." Accessed August 18, 2009, at http://domino.un.org/UNISPAL.NSF/0/62d5aa740c1429 3b85256324005179be?OpenDocument.

17. There were a few notable exceptions like the Sunni village of Shebaa, which was destroyed by Israeli retaliatory fire after Hezbollah used it as a staging ground, even though none of the locals appeared to support the Islamic Resistance.

18. Interview with Amina Aydibi, on Tuesday, July 26, 2006.

19. A media brouhaha erupted over the death toll, with Israeli officials disputing the Lebanese account of the bombing. Lebanese Red Crescent officials initially announced 54 dead, but by the end of the day on Sunday had revised the confirmed death toll to 28. See Human Rights Watch, "Qana Death Toll at 28," http://www.hrw.org/en/news/2006/08/01/israellebanon-qana-death-toll-28.

20. The Israeli government has published many of the fliers it dropped at www.mfa.gov.il/MFA/Terrorism-+Obstacle+to+Peace/Terrorism+from+Lebanon-+Hizbullah/IDF+warns+Lebanese+civilians+to+leave+danger+zones+3-Aug-2006.htm on the Foreign Ministry website. The first leaflet quoted was dropped frequently after July 25. The second was dropped on August 7.

21. Ahmad Nizar Hamzeh has produced a comprehensive and insightful study of Hezbollah's party structure that goes into great detail about the party's administration and membership. It's an invaluable tool for understanding Hezbollah's hierarchy. Ahmad Nizar Hamzeh, *In the Path of Hezbollah* (Syracuse University Press, 2004).

22. The clerics of Jabal Amel in the fifteenth century were the main repository of Shia jurisprudence, summoned to teach the faith in Persia when the Shah converted his entire empire in the sixteenth century. After that apogee, the South withered into agrarian poverty, its Shia in agrarian servitude to the *zaims,* a term for the landlords who possessed the power of feudal lords. See Albert Hourani, "From Jabal 'Amil to Persia," and Rula Jurdi Abisaab, "History and Self-Image: The 'Amili Ulema in Syria and Iran (Fourteenth to Sixteenth Centuries)," in H. E. Chehabi, ed., *Distant Relations.*

23. Fouad Ajami provides a layered and lively account of the Shia awakening in Lebanon in *The Vanished Imam: Musa Al Sadr and the Shia of Lebanon* (London: I.B. Tauris, 1986).

24. For readable but well-sourced narrative scholarship about Shia history, see Yitzhak Nakash, *The Shi'is of Iraq* (Princeton University Press,

2003); Juan Cole, *Sacred Space and Holy War: The Politics, Culture and History of Shi'ite Islam* (New York: I.B. Tauris, 2002); Vali Nasr, *The Shia Revival: How Conflicts Within Islam Will Shape the Future* (New York: W.W. Norton, 2006); and Reza Aslan, *No God But God: The Origins, Evolution and Future of Islam* (New York: Random House, 2005).

25. Ali Hamdan, director of international relations for the Amal Movement, interview with author, December 2008.

26. Many of Fadlallah's writings and sermons are translated into English on his website, http://english.bayynat.org.lb/.

27. Nida al Watan interview with Hassan Nasrallah, August 31, 1993, in *Voice of Hezbollah: The Statements of Sayyed Hassan Nasrallah*, edited by Nicholas Noe (New York: Verso, 2007).

28. A translation of this key document into English as well as thorough disquisition on its significance can be found in Augustus Richard Norton, *Amal and Shia: Struggle for the Soul of Lebanon* (Austin: University of Texas Press, 1987).

29. Several authors discuss this period in great detail and with useful insight into the relationship between Tehran, Damascus, Hezbollah, Mughniyeh, and other "special group" operatives during the 1980s. Overall, their reporting and analysis suggest that much (but not all) of the militia activity, anti-Western attacks, and "martyrdom operations" were coordinated by Iran and that leaders in Iran and Hezbollah shared a common agenda and ideology (and on occasions, as with Mughniyeh, organizational affiliation) with the perpetrators of the attacks. Iran has used all kinds of organizations to project power in the Middle East, including direct proxies, front groups, semi-autonomous groups like Hezbollah, direct action by Iranian personnel, and use of free agents to conduct violent attacks. Some officials in Washington and Tel Aviv have spent a considerable amount of time trying to sort through the official chain of command connecting the hostage takers, the barracks bombers, Hezbollah, and the ayatollahs in Iran. None of the parties involved, however, deny their logistical overlap and shared ideology. Ayatollah Fadlallah and Hezbollah publicly approved of the attacks even while denying direct responsibility. Their claims may well be true, technically, but also irrelevant; their statements suggest that they didn't order or conduct the attacks but would have been proud if they had.

Hezbollah took public credit for other suicide attacks like the car bomb at Israel's headquarters in Tyre on November 11, 1982, which killed at least 75 Israelis and 14 Lebanese. Hezbollah flaunted Mughniyeh's role as a military planner for the group after his assassination in 2008. For further discussion see Hala Jaber, *Hezbollah: Born with a Vengeance* (New York: Columbia University Press, 1997); Judith Palmer Harik, *Hezbollah: The Changing Face of Terrorism* (London: I.B. Tauris, 2005); and Magnus Ranstorp, *Hizb'allah in Lebanon: The Politics of the Western Hostage Crisis* (London: Macmillan Press, 1997).

30. After his assassination in 2008, Hezbollah lauded Imad Mughniyeh as the group's longtime security chief, making their relationship public but still leaving the details murky.

31. See Jaber, *Hezbollah*, 29–30.

32. Hezbollah suffered many casualties and for a time lost access to southern Lebanon during the internecine war with the Amal Movement that flared in 1988. Hezbollah had refused to follow Syria's dictate to share power with Amal on terms established by Damascus. Syria proved its superior firepower and ability to curtail Hezbollah, and orchestrated a settlement. Hezbollah learned not to cross its quartermasters.

33. It's important to keep in mind that there's no single document that details Hezbollah's ideology. The scholar Ahmad Nizar Hamzeh points out that the Open Letter is a "programmatic document," not a complete explanation of Hezbollah's ideology at the time (Hamzeh, *In the Path of Hezbollah*, 27). A full examination of speeches, party publications, and official documents allows a fuller, but still incomplete, picture. One excellent collection of party documents translated into English is Joseph Alagha, *The Shifts in Hizbullah's Ideology: Religious Ideology, Political Ideology, and Political Program* (Amsterdam University Press, 2006). A useful exploration of the party's ideology is Amal Saad-Ghorayeb, *Hizbu'llah: Politics, Religion* (London: Pluto Press, 2002).

34. "Lebanese Hezbollah leader says time not right to disarm 'resistance,'" Nasrallah speech broadcast August 14, 2006, on Al-Manar, transcript by BBC Monitoring Middle East—Political, supplied by BBC Worldwide Monitoring, August 15, 2006.

35. Even the release of the Winograd Commission's Inquiry into the Lebanon War on January 30, 2008, lagged behind Israeli public opin-

ion. The commission carefully examined the responsibility of various politicians and military officials in the conduct of the war, while avoiding the wholesale blame that a large portion of the Israeli public already had assigned to the upper echelons of the government and military.

36. By 2009, Israeli public opinion seemed to have shifted again, with widespread calls for a tougher stance against Hezbollah and a widely stated conviction that Israel's best bet with militants was to engage them with the full brunt of the Israel Defense Forces.

37. Official death toll published by Israeli Ministry of Foreign Affairs. Accessed July 17, 2009 at www.mfa.gov.il/MFA/Terrorism-+Obstacle+ to+Peace/Terrorism+from+Lebanon-+Hizbullah/Israel-Hizbullah+ conflict-+Victims+of+rocket+attacks+and+IDF+casualties+July-Aug+ 2006.htm.

38. Damage figures compiled by Israeli Ministry of Foreign Affairs. Accessed July 17, 2009, at www.mfa.gov.il/MFA/Terrorism-+Obstacle+to+Peace/ Terrorism+from+Lebanon-+Hizbullah/Hizbullah+attack+in+northern +Israel+and+Israels+response+12-Jul-2006.htm.

39. Official Lebanese Government reconstruction authority website accessed July 17, 2009, at www.rebuildlebanon.gov.lb/english/f/page.asp? PageID=1000007.

40. Damage estimates collected and published by the United Nations Development Program in a one-year retrospective of the war, "UNDP's Participation in Lebanon's Recovery in the Aftermath of the July 2006 War."

41. Impact of the July Offensive on the Public Finances in 2006: Brief Preliminary Report, August 30, 2006, Ministry of Finance, Republic of Lebanon. Accessed July 17, 2009, at www.rebuildlebanon.gov.lb/ documents/ImpactonfinanceReport-Englishversion-06.pdf.

42. Hezbollah politburo member Mahmoud Komati gave the figure of 250 in an interview with The Associated Press published on December 15, 2006. Israeli officials claimed that 600 Hezbollah fighters were killed in Lebanon. One explanation for the discrepancy could stem from the fluid status of many fighters as well as many of the civilians who remained in the war zone. Many fighters were not officially members of Hezbollah, for example, and could thus be defined by

Hezbollah as not technically being fighters. Others killed might have been Hezbollah members or sympathizers not acting in a military or official capacity at the time of their death.

43. Quoted in multiple news accounts. See for example www.cnn.com/2006/ WORLD/meast/07/21/mideast.diplomacy. Accessed August 2009.

44. Their view echoed the Bush administration's paradigm about the reality-based community, which passively accepted the realities of the world, in contrast to visionaries and empires, which could shape new strategic realities.

45. Michel Aoun's Free Patriotic Movement, at the time the largest single Christian party, afforded crucial political cover to Hezbollah during the war. Aoun and Nasrallah had formed an alliance announced with a detailed Memorandum of Understanding signed in February 2006, and many observers in Lebanon speculated that the alliance would fray or collapse under the pressure of a war so unpopular among the Christian rank-and-file. At considerable political cost among Christians, Aoun stuck with his alliance and was amply rewarded with an outsized share of political spoils that Hezbollah won down the road.

46. "Lebanese Druze leader on Hezbollah policy after war, army, Syria's role," Transcript of August 17, 2006, news conference aired on Al Arabiya, BBC Monitoring Middle East—Political, supplied by BBC Worldwide Monitoring, August 18, 2006.

47. Interview in Taibe cemetery, Monday, August 21, 2006.

48. Ali Ibrahim Sirhan, interviewed in Kfar Kila, Monday, August 21, 2006.

49. Mustafa Muhanna Hussein, forty-five years old, interviewed in Dahieh, Sunday, August 13, 2006.

50. This account is pieced together from author interviews with Samir Quntar and his brother Bassam Quntar in Beirut in 2008 and 2009, and from numerous interviews given by Smadar Haran and Samir Quntar. Much of Samir Quntar's recollection of the raid comes from an interview broadcast by Al-Manar Television on July 17, 2008, and Chen Kotes-Bar, " 'The girl screamed. I don't remember anything else.' A consolidation of four years of interviews with Quntar between 2004–2008," *The Guardian*, July 19, 2008. Available at www.guardian.co.uk/ world/2008/jul/19/lebanon.israelandthepalestinians.

51. *Newsweek*, U.S. edition, "At War With the PLO," May 7, 1979, and

William Claiborne, "Begin Seeks Death For Extreme Acts of Terror in Israel," Washington Post Foreign Service, April 25, 1979.

52. Smadar Haran Kaiser, "The World Should Know What He Did to My Family," *The Washington Post*, Sunday, May 18, 2003. Accessed August 23, 2009, at www.washingtonpost.com/ac2/wp-dyn/A2740-2003 May17?language=printer.

53. According to Kassir, Hezbollah owns 55 percent of the holding company that owns Al-Manar, and can appoint the general manager, but the station operates with complete independence: "I am the boss here," he told me.

54. Author interview with Ibrahim Mousawi, Safir Hotel, Beirut, August 23, 2006.

55. The day before the rally, the Israeli daily *Maariv* published irritable comments from Prime Minister Ehud Olmert about the planned victory rally. The newspaper asked Olmert whether Nasrallah was still being targeted for assassination by Israel, as he had been during the war. "There is no reason for me to notify Nasrallah through the media how we will act. We will not give him advance notice. He is holding a victory march because he has lost," Olmert replied. *Maariv*, September 21, 2006.

56. The completeness of the destruction reminded me of another disaster whose aftermath I had witnessed. A few months after the 2004 tsunami my wife and I visited Sri Lanka where at least 35,000 people were killed and half a million displaced. We rode along the southern coast through a gorgeous nature preserve, an Eden of mangroves, wild grasses, and birds. The taxi driver grew increasingly morose. "There used to be an entire village here," he explained, gesturing hopelessly at the seaside plain we were passing.

57. In her narrative book about Hezbollah in the 1990s the journalist Hala Jaber describes how Salah Ghandour persuaded his Hezbollah commanders to let him conduct a suicide operation even though he had a family; if Hezbollah prohibited married men from martyrdom operations, it would in effect discourage fighters from obeying the Islamic dictate to have families (Jaber, *Hezbollah*, 4). Hezbollah's Deputy Secretary-General Naim Qassem writes that Islamic law distinguishes between suicide, which is forbidden, and martyrdom, which is a sanctified weapon, "one that has proven its effectiveness and that prompts the

enemy to reconsider its objectives." Naim Qassem, *Hizbullah: The Story from Within* (London: Saqi Books, 2005), 47–49.

58. Author interview, Wednesday, August 16, 2006, Abassiya.

59. Nasrallah interview with New Television, August 27, 2006, in *Voice of Hezbollah*, edited by Nicholas Noe.

60. The best nugget of biographical data about Nasrallah comes from an interview he gave to the Lebanese paper Nida al-Watan published on August 31, 1993. It is available in translation in Noe's *Voice of Hezbollah*. Hezbollah seems to borrow heavily from that interview for the official biography it has published on the party's English-language website, english.moqawama.org.

61. He told one interviewer that as a child he would wrap a long scarf belonging to his grandmother around his head and tell people he was a cleric. Robin Wright, *Dreams and Shadows: The Future of the Middle East* (New York: Penguin, 2008), 162.

62. See Hamzeh, *In the Path of Hezbollah*.

63. Nasrallah had four more children: Jawad, Zeinab, Ali, and Mahdi.

64. Harik, *Hezbollah: The Changing Face of Terrorism*, 59.

65. In contrast to Palestinian factions like Hamas and Islamic Jihad, which routinely targeted random civilians in suicide bombing attacks, almost all of Hezbollah's attacks came against military sites, like the U.S. and French barracks in Beirut, or specific political targets like the U.S. Embassy in Beirut or Israeli intelligence headquarters in Tyre. Hezbollah's suicide operators in South Lebanon targeted the Israeli military. Only the attacks against the Jewish targets in Buenos Aires in 1992 and 1994 struck completely uninvolved civilians. This discrimination doesn't suggest any legal, philosophical, or moral distinction between Hezbollah and the other militants, only that Hezbollah made a substantially different calculation in deciding what kind of targets to attack.

66. August Richard Norton, *Hezbollah: A Short History* (Princeton University Press, 2008), 83–88.

67. Augustus Richard Norton, "Hizballah and the Israeli Withdrawal from Southern Lebanon," *Journal of Palestine Studies*, Vol. 30, No. 1 (Autumn, 2000), 30.

68. Qassem, 119–121.

69. Hezbollah is quite sensitive to international public opinion and carefully

constructs the case for the legitimacy of its actions. The group also has been careful in recent years to behave in a manner that would strip it of the "terrorist" label. Hence, since the 1980s, Hezbollah has focused its acknowledged attacks on Israeli military targets, and has fired rockets into Israel almost exclusively in response to Israeli attacks on civilian targets in Lebanon. It has denied any connection (despite being held responsible by Western intelligence) to the bombings in Buenos Aires of the Israeli Embassy in 1992 and the Jewish Community Center in 1994, which hearkened back to the hostage takings and bombings of the 1980s that branded Hezbollah a terrorist group in the first place. Party leaders take care in communications with Westerners to emphasize the party's just struggle against Israeli occupation. On their English language website alwa3ad.com in 2009, Hezbollah posted a banner that read "We do not want to kill anyone. We do not want to throw anyone in the sea. Give the houses back to their owners, the fields back to their landlords, and the homes back to their people. Release the prisoners, and leave us to live in this region in security, peace and dignity." This rhetoric, designed for the English-speaking outside world, contradicts a copious record of inciting and racist speech. Leaders from Nasrallah on down have cited the perfidy of Jews as a motivation for the struggle. In a frequently quoted 2002 interview with Jeffrey Goldberg, a Hezbollah spokesman named Hassan Ezzedin said, "Our goal is to liberate the 1948 borders of Palestine. . . . The Jews who survive this war of liberation can go back to Germany or wherever they came from. However, the Jews who lived in Palestine before 1948 will be allowed to live as a minority and they will be cared for by the Muslim majority." Jeffrey Goldberg, "Inside the Party of God," *The New Yorker*, October 14, 2002.

70. Accessed August 12, 2009, at http://english.wa3ad.org/index.php?show=news&action=article&id=1808.

71. The four men were detained without charge in September 2005 on the orders of the international tribunal, based in the Hague, that investigated Hariri's death. A tribunal judge ordered their release in April 2009, saying there wasn't enough evidence to indict them. The four officers were former head of General Security Major General Jamil al-Sayyad, former chief of police Major General Ali Hajj, former military intelligence chief Brigadier General Raymond Azar, and Republican Guard commander

Mustafa Hamdan. See Robert F. Worth, "Suspects in Hariri's Death Released," *The New York Times*, April 29, 2009, accessed at http://www.nytimes.com/2009/04/30/world/middleeast/30lebanon.html and Menassat, "Hariri Tribunal Orders Release of Detained Four Generals," April 29, 2009, accessed at www.menassat.com/?q=alerts/6459 -hariri-tribunal-orders-release-detained-four-generals.

72. http://english.aljazeera.net/focus/lebanon2009/2009/06/2009611 45224882101.html.

73. The "Scout Promise and Law" template of the World Organization of the Scout Movement was accessed in September 2009 at www.scout .org/index.php/en/about_scouting/promise_and_law.

74. Israel's Intelligence and Terrorism Information Center released a widely circulated dossier on the Mahdi Scouts on September 11, 2006, which contained a thorough and rather measured analysis of the Mahdi Scouts (available at www.terrorism-info.org.il). Although that report contained mostly substantiated and well-documented claims, it was cited in a proliferation of breathless media and blog reports that described the Mahdi Scouts as "Hitler Youth" and "terrorist training." Hezbollah public relations officials cut off all press access to the scouts for some time as a result.

75. For example, Israeli officials routinely describe Hezbollah fighters and installations in Lebanon as divisions of the Iranian Revolutionary Guard, holding Tehran directly responsible for military actions taken by Hezbollah.

76. GlobalSecurity.org analysts believe that the actual funding is $25 to $50 million, and that the higher estimates are exaggerated. Because Hezbollah's active fighting force numbers around 1,000 and uses the light weaponry of guerilla warfare, it doesn't require an expensive investment from Iran. See www.globalsecurity.org/military/world/para/hizballah .htm.

77. CIA World Factbook, 2009.

78. Hala Jaber reported in the *Times* of London in August 2006 that President Ahmedinejad had made $1 billion available to Hezbollah after its war with Israel, although little evidence emerged in the years that followed to suggest Hezbollah had actually acquired and spent such a large amount of funds. When Hezbollah distributed cash payments to fami-

lies the week after the 2006 war, the party thanked Iran; those initial payments totaled only $2 to $3 million, a fraction of the group's budget. Other aid comes directly from Iran without the pretense of money changing hands—for instance the 40,000 rockets Nasrallah claims are in Hezbollah's arsenal. Al Waad, the new corporation established in 2006 to redevelop bombed parts of the Dahieh, announced an initial budget of $370 million. It was supposed to complete its work within three years, but Al-Manar reported on August 14, 2008. that the project was running over budget because of unexpectedly high costs of construction materials, and because the Lebanese government was lagging in its share of payments to the displaced families, who had pledged to donate their compensation to Al Waad.

79. Nick Calstor, "Pressure on Iran Over Argentina Blasts," The BBC, May 2, 2007. http://news.bbc.co.uk/2/hi/americas/6612951.stm.

80. See Timothy R. Furnish, "The Importance of Being Mahdist: Among Iran's Twelvers," *The Weekly Standard,* September 8, 2008; and Tel Aviv University's Center for Iran Studies *Iran Pulse,* numbers 1, 13, 28, and 33, available at www.tau.ac.il/humanities/iranian_studies/pulse_index_page.eng.html.

81. A messianic Mahdist group called Heaven's Army attacked Shia security forces in Najaf in January 2007. Hundreds were killed in the clashes. Iraqi police fought a similar group called Supporters of the Mahdi in January 2008 in Basra and and Nasiriya; nearly a hundred people were killed. Saad Fakhrildeen and Kimi Yoshino, "Radical Shiite cults draw concern in southern Iraq," *The Los Angeles Times,* January 26, 2008, accessed September 2009 at http://articles.latimes.com/2008/jan/26/world/fg-iraqcult26.

82. During the "War of the Camps" in the late 1980s Hezbollah and Amal fought each other, but since both groups were Shia and later reconciled, the conflict didn't register in the Middle East as much as the other cleavages of the Lebanese civil war.

83. Koran, The Cow: 2: 216.

84. Speech broadcast on Al-Manar, July 16, 2008. Translation by BBC Monitoring.

85. Ahmed Yousef, the Hamas deputy foreign minister in Gaza, said in an interview with the author in January 2010 that Hamas had much to

learn from Hezbollah's record and from Nasrallah's style. Yousef said that he had met Nasrallah twice in the previous decade. In 2005, Yousef said that he had proposed forming an "international Islamist round-table" so that Shia and Sunni movements could "present a united front against America's War on Terror." Hezbollah and Hamas never followed up on the idea, he said. Hezbollah's international media strategy also made a striking impression on Yousef. "I wanted to copy Hezbollah's approach," Yousef said. "They had two attractive women with headscarves who spoke perfect English on television. It is very effective, very nice. I suggested that we do the same here, but no one wanted to."

86. The Israeli government claimed 1,166 Gazans perished in the conflict, while the Israeli human rights group B'Tselem put the toll at 1,385. The Palestinian Centre for Human Rights counted 1,417 deaths. According to a B'Tselem study published one year after the Gaza War, Operation Cast Lead killed 762 civilians 623 Combatants, and wounded 5,300 Palestinians. December 27, 2009.

87. See Ethan Bronner, "Parsing Gains of Gaza War," *The New York Times,* January 18, 2009.

88. The entire outcome hinged on a single district where Aoun's Christians lost to the March 14 Christians. Lebanon's gerrymandered electoral system meant that the results in most districts were a foregone conclusion. The Shia districts went to Hezbollah, the Sunni districts to the Future Movement, the Druze districts for the most part to Jumblatt. There were only a few districts where the outcome wasn't known in advance. The pro-Western March 14 coalition won 71 seats in the 128-seat parliament; Hezbollah and its allies won the remaining 57 seats. Matters were further complicated when Walid Jumblatt quit the March 14 group in August, taking his 11 seats with him and effectively leveling the playing field in parliament. Elias Muhanna explains the methodology for calculating vote totals in "Deconstructing the Popular Vote in Lebanon's Election," *Mideast Monitor,* July–August 2009, Vol. 4, No. 1. Accessed at mideastmonitor.org/issues/0907/0907_3.htm.

INDEX

Abassiya, Lebanon, 169, 183
Abdullah, King of Jordan, 181
Abdullah, King of Saudi Arabia, 190
Abou Deeb, Lebanon, 41, 69
Abu Hadi, 92
Afghanistan, 38, 260, 278
Ahmadinejad, Mahmoud, 181, 234,
        256
Aita Shaab, Lebanon, 5–7, 63, 83, 87,
        90, 269–270, 273
AK-47s, 31
Al Akhbar, 256
al-Assad, Ahmed, 286
al-Assad, Bashar, 181, 256
al-Assad, Hafez, 50, 187
Al-Manar (The Beacon) television
        station, 31, 51, 65–70, 78, 87,
        129–132, 138, 142, 150, 163,
        166, 195, 224, 278
Al Qaeda, 14, 15, 64, 108, 224
Al-Sadr, Mohammed Baqir, 101

Al Waad (the Promise), 139, 146
Ali, 28, 101, 189
Ali, Ahmed Sheikh, 217
Amal Movement, 9, 15, 31, 43, 54,
        57, 61, 72, 78, 99, 102, 103,
        105–108, 110, 112, 144, 171,
        173, 180, 182, 183, 189, 199,
        204, 210, 246, 247, 260, 263,
        269
Anti-Semitism, 11, 103, 188, 196,
        226, 275
Aoun, Michel, 140, 199, 260, 269
Arad, Ron, 251
Ashura, 186
Ayan, Abdullah, 95
Ayan, Mustafa, 95
Aydibi, Amina, 77
Aydibi, Mohammed, 77

Baalbek, Lebanon, 103–105, 182, 208
Ba'ath Parties, 36, 48, 182

Baqleen, Lebanon, 77

Bass Refugee Camp, Lebanon, 90, 92

Bazzi, Amir, 159–162, 166, 167, 216

Bazzi, Farah, 153, 156, 158–162,
    164–167, 188, 189, 240–242,
    289

Bazzi, Rani Ahmed, 20, 21, 27–36,
    100, 105, 151–162, 164–167,
    189, 216, 240–242, 283, 284,
    289–291

Bazzi, Shaheed, 159–162, 166, 167,
    216, 291

Beaufort castle, Lebanon, 85

Begin, Menachem, 127

Beirut, Lebanon, 4, 14, 40, 41, 43,
    44, 46–48, 51, 55–57, 59, 62,
    63, 90, 97, 104, 105, 115,
    197–200, 208, 246–249

Beqaa Valley, Lebanon, 38, 86, 97–99,
    104, 115, 120, 135, 143, 170,
    194, 207, 215, 224

Berri, Nabih, 54, 183, 204

Bin Laden, Osama, 235

Bint Jbail, Lebanon, 20–28, 30, 32,
    33, 80, 87, 90, 151–156, 159,
    162, 164, 273, 288–291

Blair, Tony, 35

Borj Qalaouay, Lebanon, 95, 99, 119,
    122, 208

Bush, George H. W., 35

Bush, George W., 35, 60, 84, 118,
    148, 197, 198, 229, 257, 266

C-802 antiship missile, 63

Carter, Chip, 284

Carter, Jimmy, 284–285

Cedar Revolution, 60, 148

Chemical weapons, 108

Chidiac, May, 203

Chouf Mountains, 40, 48, 77, 247

Christians, 15, 29, 36, 37, 42–44,
    46–50, 54, 55, 57, 72, 77, 83,
    91, 102, 107, 109, 117, 119,
    139, 140, 143, 167, 170, 209,
    236, 242–243, 247, 260–264,
    284

CIA (Central Intelligence Agency), 107

CNN (Cable News Network), 68

Cold war, 108, 110

Communist Party, 107, 171, 182, 229

Consultative Center for Studies and
    Documentation, 137–138

Dahieh, Lebanon, 37, 41, 43, 51, 52,
    59, 67, 88, 97–99, 110, 115,
    119, 121, 135, 170, 180, 194,
    212, 238, 252, 254

Dajjal, the false Mahdi, 231

Dawa Party, Iraq, 103, 104, 277

Dawi, Mohammed, 213–218

Dergham, Chloe, 144–145

Dergham, Dergham, 105–106,
    140–145, 149, 150, 167, 177,
    238–239, 248–249, 253, 258,
    275

Dergham, Ibrahim, 238

Dergham, Jackie, 144–145, 238–239

Dhaira, Lebanon, 93–94

Disarmament issue, 61, 136, 198,
    204, 245, 248, 285

Doomsday cults, 234

Druze, 41, 42, 46, 48–50, 57, 102,

107, 117, 119–120, 170, 209,
247–249, 256, 279
Education, 193, 210–211, 215–216,
230–231
Egypt, 11, 14, 36, 38, 80, 112,
118–120, 190, 204, 226, 229,
255, 270–271, 279
Eido, Walid, 203

Fadlallah, Ayatollah Muhammed
Hussein, 101, 103, 109, 149,
182, 183
Fayyad, Ali, 15, 136, 138, 271,
284–285, 287
Free Patriotic Movement, 15, 140,
199, 260
Future Movement, 246, 261

Gaza, 5, 11, 14, 17, 38, 62, 162, 219,
266–269, 270, 271
Gemayel, Pierre, 203
Ghajar, 62
Ghandouriye, Lebanon, 157
Ghanem, Antoine, 203, 236
Golan Heights, 256
Goldwasser, Ehud, 251, 252

Haidar, Ali, 171, 253
Haidar, Aya, 172–176, 231–235
Haidar, Hussein, 100, 106, 171–172,
176, 188, 230–231, 235, 268,
269
Haidar, Inaya, 69–71, 75, 106,
171–176, 178, 230, 235, 247,
252, 253, 269, 286
Haidar, Muna, 172, 173, 286

Haidar, Samar, 172, 286–287
Haidar, Samira, 170, 172
Haidar family, 213
Haifa, Israel, 34
Hamadeh, Marwan, 209
Hamas, 5, 14, 17, 118, 128, 179, 219,
224, 228, 245, 266–269, 277,
285
Hamid, 25, 30–32, 34
Haran, Danny, 126–127, 252
Haran, Einat, 126–127, 252
Haran, Smadar, 126–127
Haran, Yael, 126–127
Harb, Assem, 40–42, 44–46
Harb, Ragheb, 103, 186
Haret Hreik, Lebanon, 143, 144, 254
Hariri, Rafik, 55, 58
assassination of, 59, 64, 202–203,
205, 228, 242, 274–275
Hariri, Saad, 59, 120, 203–206, 246,
249, 254, 281, 287
Hashem family, 78
Hawi, George, 203
Headscarves, women and, 110, 172,
230
Hersh, Seymour, 192
Hezbollah (the Party of God). See also
Lebanon
Al-Manar (The Beacon) television
station and, 31, 51, 65–70, 78,
87, 129–132, 138, 142, 150,
163, 166, 195, 224
Amal and ("The War of the
Camps"), 179–180
capture of Israeli soldiers by, 3,
62–63, 116, 223

Hezbollah (the Party of God), *cont.*
   children and, 32, 35, 71, 164, 193,
      210–218, 225
   collaborators and, 8, 262–265
   constituency of, 9, 13, 15, 18, 167
   disarmament issue and, 61, 136,
      198, 204, 245, 248, 285
   distinguished from other Islamist
      movements, 13
   Druze leader Jumblatt and, 49–51,
      119–120, 170, 205–206, 245,
      246, 249
   export of model of, 34, 277–278,
      280
   founding of, 14, 103–104, 107,
      183, 221
   Gaza War and, 268–271, 279
   Hamas and, 17, 266, 267, 270–271
   Hariri assassination and, 202,
      274–275
   headquarters of, 97
   ideology and theology of, 3, 4–5, 7,
      9–10, 12–14, 15–16, 18–19,
      26, 34–35, 109–113, 152,
      190–194, 205, 209–211, 214–
      215, 218, 225–226, 237–238,
      249–250, 253–256, 259, 271,
      275–280, 284, 288–291
   intelligence and, 202, 207–209,
      221, 245, 263
   Islamicization of society and, 110,
      111, 145
   kidnappings and hostage takings
      and, 14, 104, 180, 184, 221
   leader of. *See* Nasrallah, Sayyed
      Hassan

   Mahdi Scouts and, 71, 164,
      210–218, 225
   March 14 alliance and, 148, 201,
      204, 206, 227, 228, 242,
      244–246, 248
   martyrdom, culture of, 28, 151–
      152, 154, 161–167, 173, 174,
      176, 185–190, 232, 241–242,
      275, 288–290
   May 2008 and, 246–249
   official manifesto of November 2 of,
      11, 12
   Open Letter of 1985 of, 11, 104,
      111, 112, 183, 191
   organizational methods of, 88–89
   platform of, 4, 13, 104, 111, 112,
      190, 191
   presidential succession issue and,
      227, 242, 248, 261
   prisoner releases and, 250–254, 256,
      258–259, 276
   protest against government and,
      197–200
   Quntar and, 114, 124, 128–129
   reconstruction and, 4–6, 115–
      124, 135, 139, 140, 145–
      146, 150, 168–170, 175,
      207–209, 273
   recruitment and, 104, 154, 155,
      210–218
   refugees and, 40–45
   relations with Egypt, 270–271
   relations with Iran, 14, 39, 49, 50,
      103, 104, 107, 112, 117, 119,
      135, 148, 168, 169, 180–183,
      191, 201, 207–209, 211,

218–225, 229, 245, 249, 271,
278–282
relations with Syria, 14, 39, 49, 50,
103, 104, 107, 110, 112, 117,
119, 135, 148, 180, 181, 191,
201, 207, 218–221, 225, 229,
245, 279–281
secrecy of military operations of,
24
social services and, 10, 13, 15, 16,
110, 275–276
suicide bombings and, 15, 17,
162–164, 184–185
think tank of, 137–138, 271
training camps of, 97, 103, 104, 224
2   elections and, 283–287
U.S. Marine barracks bombing and,
14, 104, 105
war with Israel (1996), 42, 76
war with Israel (2006), 3–5, 17,
20–27, 29–34, 38–53, 62–69,
75–96, 113–117, 119, 121,
135, 137, 153, 154, 157, 168,
181, 190, 269–270, 276, 277
weapons of, 30, 63, 77, 86, 96, 97,
116, 119, 196, 219, 220, 273
Hizbullah: The Story From Within
(Qassem), 197
Hoteit, Wafa, 140
Hussein, 27–28, 101, 157, 166, 185,
186, 190, 232
Hussein, Saddam, 103, 110, 182, 189,
196, 235

Ibrahim, Tarek, 236
Indonesia, 280

Intelligence, 90, 91, 99, 177, 178,
202, 207–209, 218, 219, 245,
263
International Special Tribunal, 274
Iran, 53, 59, 64, 118–119
doomsday cults in, 234
Islamic Revolution in, 14, 36, 98,
102, 103, 278
nuclear program of, 221–222
relations with Hezbollah, 14, 39,
49, 50, 103, 104, 107, 112,
117, 119, 135, 148, 168, 169,
180–183, 191, 201, 207–209,
211, 218–225, 229, 245, 249,
271, 278–282
Iran-Iraq war, 108, 110, 223
Iraq, 60, 119
Ba'ath Party in, 36
civil war in (2004–2007), 38
doomsday cults in, 234
Mahdi Army in, 14
U.S. invasion and occupation of,
25, 38, 64, 118, 229
Irish Republican Army, 193
Islamic Amal, 103
Islamic Jihad Organization, 104, 128,
179, 224, 245, 277
Islamic Resistance, ideology of, 7,
9–10, 13, 16, 47, 58, 60–61,
128, 225. See also Hezbollah
(the Party of God)
Islamic Revolution, in Iran, 14, 36,
99, 102, 103, 278
Islamic Supreme Council of Iraq,
277
Ismail, Mohammed, 80

Israel
  Al-Manar (The Beacon) television
    station and, 66, 129–132
  collaborators and, 8, 262–263,
    265
  Gaza War (2   ) and, 5, 17, 267–
    268, 270, 271
  Hariri assassination and, 274
  Hezbollah's capture of Israeli
    soldiers and, 62–63, 116, 223
  occupation of Lebanon (1982–
    2000) by, 31, 32, 55, 57, 58,
    61, 71, 73, 123, 196, 226,
    264, 265, 276
  Operation Grapes of Wrath and,
    42, 76, 86
  policies in Gaza and the West Bank,
    11, 38, 62, 64
  prisoner releases and, 250–252, 259
  Six Day War (1967) and, 36, 80,
    121
  war with Hezbollah (1996), 42, 76
  war with Hezbollah (2006), 3–5,
    17, 20–27, 29–34, 38–53,
    62–69, 75–96, 113–117, 119,
    121, 135, 137, 153, 154, 157,
    168
  Yom Kippur War (1973) and, 251
Israeli Air Force, 21, 64
Israeli military headquarters at Tyre,
    bombing of (1982), 106

Jabal Amel Hospital, Tyre, 70, 78
Jabal Sheikh, 61
Jamil, Faris, 5–7, 273–274

Jemaah Islamiya, 280
Jerusalem (Al Quds), 235, 236
Jerusalem Day, 186, 212, 235–236
Jibbain, Lebanon, 83
Jihad for Building Reconstruction,
    145–146
Jordan, 11, 14, 38, 100, 112, 118,
    120, 190, 226, 229, 255
Jounieh, Lebanon, 57
Jumblatt, Walid, 49–51, 119–120,
    170, 199, 205–206, 245, 246,
    248, 249, 254, 281, 287

Kabbani, Mohammed, 206–207, 261
Kalashnikovs, 26
Karbala, 28, 29, 101, 185, 190, 232
Kassir, Abdallah, 67–69, 106, 129–
    132, 163
Kassir, Ahmed, 106, 163
Kassir, Samir, 203
Katyusha rockets, 30, 63, 77, 86, 116,
    119
Kawook, Sheikh Nabil, 168–169
Kfar Kila, Lebanon, 1, 121
Khadija, 79
Khaibar rockets, 96
Khalil, Abbas, 270
Khalil, Khadija, 270
Khamenei, Ayatollah Ali, 180, 190,
    211, 215, 223
Khiam Prison, 32, 34, 85–87, 153,
    156, 159, 160, 188, 217
Khomeini, Ayatollah Ruhollah, 35,
    36, 101–103, 110, 118, 158,
    186, 211, 214

Komati, Mahmoud, 222
Kufa, Iraq, 28

Lahoud, Emile, 204, 227
Lakkis, Jihad, 43–45
Lebanon. *See also* Hezbollah (the Party
    of God); specific towns and
    cities
    civil war (1975–1990) in, 37, 49,
        52–55, 58, 110, 144, 182,
        183, 244, 247
    emigration from, 27
    Hariri assassination and, 59, 64,
        202–203, 205, 228, 242,
        274–275
    Israeli occupation of (1982–2000),
        31, 32, 55, 57, 58, 61, 71, 73,
        123, 196, 226, 264, 265, 276
    relations with Syria, 38, 55, 58–60,
        202, 203, 204
    relations with U.S., 117, 148–149,
        201, 206–207, 228, 244, 249
    sectarianism in, 46, 54–56, 64
Line-of-fire villages, 90
Litani River, 40, 41, 69, 82, 85, 87,
    95, 157, 213

M-4s, 31
M-16s, 31
Mahdi, 16, 26, 28, 192, 211, 231–235
Mahdi Army, 118, 179
Mahdi Schools, 193, 210
Mahdi Scouts, 71, 164, 210–218, 225
Manifest Destiny, 225
March 14 alliance, 147–148, 198,

        201–206, 227, 228, 242,
        244–246, 248, 259–261,
        283–284, 287
Marjayoun, Lebanon, 41
Maronite Christians, 36, 261–263
Maroun al-Ras, Lebanon, 21, 273
Martyr Tree, Bint Jbail, 288–289
Martyrdom, culture of, 28, 151–152,
        154, 161–167, 173, 174, 176,
        185–190, 232, 241–242, 275,
        288–290
Martyrs' Association, 154, 164
Martyrs' Foundation, 193, 225, 241
Middle East Airlines, 62
Mohammed, Abu, 288–289
Mohammed, Prophet, 8, 27, 96, 188,
        189, 192, 230, 232
Mokhtara, Lebanon, 48, 49
Mokhtars, 88, 90
Mount Hermon, 61
Mount Lebanon, 64
Mousawi, Ibrahim, 138–139
Mousawi, Nawaf, 227–229
Moussa, Issam, 22, 31, 73–75, 84,
        91, 93, 94, 100, 151, 152,
        283
Mubarak, Hosni, 181, 190, 226
Mughniyeh, Imad, 104, 105, 183
Murr, Elias, 203
Musawi, Hussein, 103
Musawi, Sayyed Abbas, 103, 111, 179,
        180, 182, 184, 186
Muslim Brotherhood, 14, 112, 118,
        179, 277
Mustafa Schools, 210

Nabaa, Lebanon, 183
Nabatieh, Lebanon, 41, 42, 85, 87,
    90, 216
Nahariya, Israel, 125, 250, 256
Naim, Bilal, 212, 213
Najaf seminary, Iraq, 101, 103, 182
Najem Hospital, Tyre, 69–70, 172,
    173
Naquora, Lebanon, 93
Nasrallah, Hadi, 183, 185–189, 194
Nasrallah, Sayyed Hassan, 17, 25, 26,
    29, 35, 36, 46–48, 59, 61,
    71–73, 84, 103, 128, 137,
    146, 158, 169, 173, 193, 207,
    214, 235, 236, 266, 271, 273.
    See also Hezbollah (the Party
    of God)
  anti-Semitism of, 11, 103, 196
  apologies by, 181, 221
  background of, 181–182
  birth of, 181
  change in position of, 272
  collaborators and, 262
  credibility of, 192, 196–197
  cult of personality and, 192,
    194–195
  death of son and, 185–189, 194
  early days of Hezbollah and, 104
  elected secretary-general (1991),
    111, 184
  Hariri assassination and, 274
  interviews and press conferences of,
    191, 192
  Iranian and Syrian connection and,
    180–181, 221
  July 2008 speech by, 254–256
  Jumblatt's criticism of, 49
  marriage of, 183
  Martyrs Day speech by (November
    2), 4, 10–11
  Martyrs of September 13 speech by
    (1997), 186–187
  May 2008 and, 246
  personal meetings with
    probationary party members,
    176–178
  physical appearance of, 8, 178
  political agenda of, 139
  popularity and charisma of, 4,
    44–46, 111, 118, 178–179,
    190, 194
  prisoner releases and, 17, 114, 129,
    253, 254
  protest against government and,
    197–200
  reconstruction and, 120, 123, 124
  religious studies of, 182, 184
  sense of humor of, 178, 179, 194
  television appearances by, 63,
    65–66, 69, 114–115, 200
  victory speech by (September
    2006), 146–147
  war with Israel (2006) and, 17, 38,
    51, 52, 62, 63, 65–66, 69, 81,
    114–115, 181, 190
Nasser, Gamal Abdel, 118
Nasserist movement, 182
Nazzal, Mohammad, 173, 286–287
Netanyahu, Benjamin, 187, 197
New Television, 181

Nuclear weapons, 221–222, 234

Obama, Barack, 257, 266
Olmert, Ehud, 118, 146, 196
Open Letter of 1985, 11, 104, 111,
    112, 183, 191
Operation Cast Lead, 267–268
Operation Grapes of Wrath, 42, 76,
    86
Operation Truthful Promise, 3–4, 17,
    20–27, 29–34, 38–53, 62–69,
    75–96, 113–117, 119, 121,
    135, 137, 153, 154, 157, 168,
    181, 190, 269–270, 276, 277
Oslo Accords, 11, 64, 186

Pakistan, 278
Palestine Liberation Organization
    (PLO), 110, 118, 125, 128,
    143, 182
Palestinian Authority, 11, 229, 279
Palestinian Liberation Front (PLF),
    125, 182
Palestinians, 8, 14, 17, 37, 56, 90, 91,
    102, 125, 196, 202, 226, 228,
    237, 251, 262, 277
Party of God. See Hezbollah (the Party
    of God)
Pastor, Bob, 284
Phalange Party, 236
Phoenicians, 71–72
Prisoner releases, 17, 129, 133,
    250–254, 256, 258–259, 276
"Protocols of the Elders of Zion,"
    193

Qadisiyyah, 232
Qalaouay, Lebanon, 94–95
Qana, Lebanon, 75
    1996 shelling of UN compound in,
        42, 76, 86
    2006 bombing of, 23, 77–83, 92
Qassem, Naim, 186, 192, 197
Qlaya, Lebanon, 261–262, 264
Qom seminary, Iran, 101, 183
Quietism, dogma of, 101
Quntar, Bassam, 256–258
Quntar, Samir, 17, 114, 124–129
    release from Israeli prison, 250–
        254, 256–259

Ramadan, 146, 153, 155, 205, 232
Reagan, Ronald, 109
Red Crescent volunteers, 20–22
Red Cross, 83
Refugees, 40–45, 51, 56
Regev, Eldad, 251, 252
Revolutionary Guards, 103, 104, 182,
    220, 222, 223, 224
Rice, Condoleezza, 117–118, 216
Rmeish, Lebanon, 83
Rumeiti, Hussein, 95–96, 99, 100,
    105, 122–124, 189, 194,
    282–283

Saad, Hwaida, 151, 158, 241
Sadr, Imam Musa, 35, 97, 98, 101,
    102
Safieddine, Hisham, 190
Said, Suleiman, 265–266
Salafi extremists, 14, 15

Salame, Jean, 264–265
Samarra, Iraq, 28
Saudi Arabia, 11, 35, 38, 53, 55, 58,
    80, 100, 107, 118, 120, 190,
    201, 204, 229, 255, 279
Save the Children, 173
Sea of Galilee, 64
Shabi, Adnan, 83
Shachar, Eliyahu, 125
Shadid, Anthony, 93, 94
Shalhoub, Fatima, 79
Shalhoub, Hala Ahmed, 78–79
Shalhoub, Rokaya, 79
Shalhoub, Zaynab, 78, 79
Shalit, Gilad, 62
Sharafedeen, Samira, 1, 121
Sharon, Ariel, 197
Shebaa Farms, Lebanon, 61, 114, 121,
    170
Shia Muslims, 9, 14, 15, 16, 18, 21,
    25–29, 35, 37, 39, 40–43,
    46–55, 57, 58, 73, 77–79, 88,
    90, 91, 94, 96–108, 111, 115,
    120–122, 124, 136, 140, 141,
    143–145, 150, 158, 167, 168,
    170, 171, 174, 176, 177, 180,
    182, 183, 185, 186, 188, 189,
    192, 193, 208, 210, 225, 226,
    229–236, 262, 278, 282–283.
    See also Hezbollah (the Party
    of God)
Sidon, Lebanon, 41
Sinai Cell, 270, 271
Siniora, Fouad, 64, 198, 199
Sinn Fein, 193
Sirhan, Ali, 1, 121

Sistani, Ayatollah Ali, 101
Six Day War (1967), 36, 80, 121
South Lebanon Army, 57, 111, 184,
    185, 262, 264, 265
Srifa, Lebanon, 171, 208, 213, 230,
    286
Srour, Amin, 83–85
Srour family, 70
Suicide bombings, 15, 17, 103, 107,
    162–164, 184–185, 224
Suleiman, Michel, 248
Sunni Muslims, 15, 28–29, 38,
    46–49, 53, 54, 57, 77, 91,
    100, 102, 117, 119, 143, 176,
    232, 242, 261, 279
Sweid, Jana, 216
Sweid, Malak, 216
Syria, 53, 118–120, 190, 227, 271
    Ba'ath Party in, 36
    Hariri assassination and, 202
    relations with Hezbollah, 14, 39,
        49, 50, 103, 104, 107, 110,
        112, 117, 119, 135, 148, 180,
        181, 191, 201, 207, 218–221,
        225, 229, 245, 279–281
    relations with Lebanon, 38, 55,
        58–60, 202, 203, 204
Syrian Social Nationalist Party
    (SSNP), 107, 182, 229, 246,
    247

Taibe, Lebanon, 94, 284
Taif Accords of 1989, 37, 53, 54, 112
Tair Harfa, Lebanon, 83, 94
Taliban, 278, 280
Tel Masoud, Lebanon, 24, 30–31

Tent City, Beirut, 199–201, 248
Tiberias, Israel, 64
Tourism, 55, 62
Tueni, Gibran, 203
Tufayli, Sheikh Sobhi, 103, 104–105,
    111, 183
Tyre, Lebanon, 41, 69–75, 78, 83, 86,
    90–92, 163

United Nations, 42, 76, 82, 86,
    90, 149, 196, 207, 251, 263,
    273
U.S. Embassy bombing, Beirut, 104,
    105
U.S. Marine barracks bombing,
    Beirut, 14, 104, 105

USAID, 148, 208

Wahhabism, 64
West Bank, 11, 38, 162

Yassin, Bassam, 52
Yassin, Fouad, 52
Yassin, Hawra, 52
Yassin, Jumana, 51–53
Yassin, Mohammed, 52
Yom Kippur War (1973), 251

Zaydan, Muhammad (Abu Abbas),
    125, 127
Zionism, 225

About the Author

Thanassis Cambanis has written about the Middle East since 2003 for *The Boston Globe, The New York Times*, and other publications. As the *Globe*'s Middle East bureau chief, Thanassis lived in Baghdad until 2005, and then reported on the Islamist revival in the Palestinian territories, Egypt, Jordan, and the Levant. He studied international affairs for a master's degree at Princeton University's Woodrow Wilson School. He teaches at Columbia University's School of International and Public Affairs. Thanassis lives in New York City with his wife Anne Barnard, a reporter for *The New York Times,* and his children. This is his first book.